D0924378

O'AHU

KEVIN WHITTON

CALGARY PUBLIC LIBRARY
NOVEMBER 2013

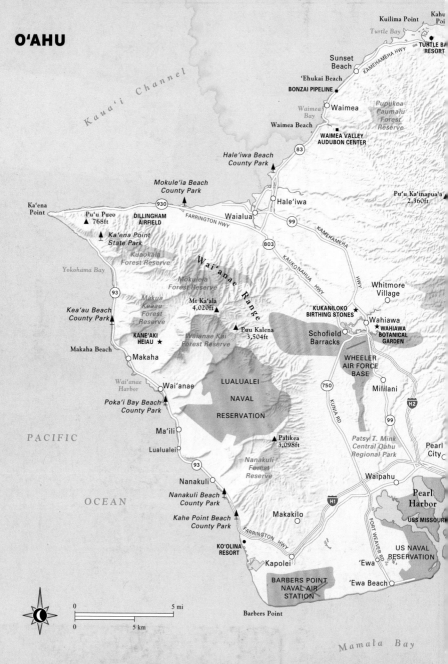

O'AHU

Kuilima Point

Kahu
Poi

Turtle Bay

TURTLE BAY
RESORT

KAMEHAMEHA HWY

Sunset
Beach

'Ehukai Beach

BONZAI PIPELINE

Waimea
Bay

Waimea

Pupukea-
Paumalu
Forest
Reserve

Waimea Beach

**WAIMEA VALLEY
AUDUBON CENTER**

83

Hale'iwa Beach
County Park

Pu'u Ka'inapua'a
2,360ft

Mokule'ia Beach
County Park

Hale'iwa

Ka'ena
Point

930

Waialua

99

DILLINGHAM
AIRFIELD

Pu'u Pueo
768ft

FARRINGTON HWY

803

Ka'ena Point
State Park

Kuaokala
Forest Reserve

KAUKONAHUA

KAMEHAMEHA

Yokohama Bay

Wai'anae Range

Mokuleia
Forest Reserve

HWY

Whitmore
Village

Makua
Keaau
Forest
Reserve

Mt Ka'ala
4,020ft

**KUKANILOKO
BIRTHING STONES**

Kea'au Beach
County Park

Puu Kalena
3,504ft

Wahiawa

**KANE'AKI
HEIAU** ★

Waianae Kai
Forest Reserve

Schofield
Barracks

★ **WAHIAWA
BOTANICAL
GARDEN**

Makaha Beach

Makaha

WHEELER
AIR FORCE
BASE

Wai'anae
Harbor

Wai'anae

LUALUALEI

NAVAL

RESERVATION

750

KUNIA RD

Mililani

H2

Poka'i Bay Beach
County Park

Ma'ili

99

Palikea
3,098ft

Patsy T. Mink
Central Oahu
Regional Park

Pearl
City

PACIFIC

Lualualei

93

Nanakuli
Forest
Reserve

Waipahu

Nanakuli

Pearl
Harbor

Nanakuli Beach
County Park

Makakilo

USS MISSOURI

Kahe Point Beach
County Park

OCEAN

FORT WEAVER RD

**KO'OLINA
RESORT**

FARRINGTON HWY

H1

'Ewa

US NAVAL
RESERVATION

Kapolei

'Ewa Beach

**BARBERS POINT
NAVAL AIR
STATION**

Barbers Point

0   5 mi

0   5 km

Mamala Bay

© AVALON TRAVEL

Kaua'i Channel

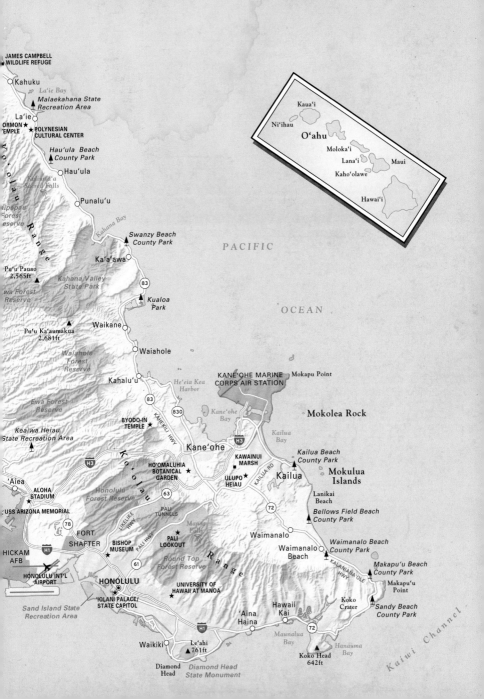

JAMES CAMPBELL
WILDLIFE REFUGE

○ Kahuku
La'ie Bay

*Malaekahana State
Recreation Area*

La'ie
★ ORMON
TEMPLE ★ POLYNESIAN
CULTURAL CENTER

▲ *Hau'ula Beach
County Park*

○ Hau'ula

*Kaliuwa'a
Sacred Falls*

○ Punalu'u

*Iipepau
Forest
Reserve*

Kahana Bay

▲ *Swanzy Beach
County Park*

Ka'a'awa ○

Pu'u Pauao
2,565ft ▲

*Kahana Valley
State Park*

*wa Forest
Reserve*

83

▲ *Kualoa
Park*

Pu'u Ka'aumakua
2,681ft ▲

Waikane ○

*Waiahole
Forest
Reserve*

Waiahole ○

Kahalu'u ○

KANE'OHE MARINE
CORPS AIR STATION

Mokapu Point

*He'eia Kea
Harbor*

*Ewa Forest
Reserve*

83

*Kane'ohe
Bay*

● Mokolea Rock

830

BYODO-IN
TEMPLE ★

KANE'OHE

H3

*Kailua
Bay*

Kailua Beach
County Park

Keaiwa Heiau
State Recreation Area

H3

HO'OMALUHIA
BOTANICAL
GARDEN ★

KAWAINUI
MARSH

Kailua

Mokulua
Islands

'Aiea ○

ALOHA
STADIUM ■

ULUPO
HEIAU ■

63

*Lanikai
Beach*

72

▲ Bellows Field Beach
County Park

USS ARIZONA MEMORIAL

*Honolulu
Forest Reserve*

78

FORT
SHAFTER

PALI
TUNNELS

*Mano
Falls*

Waimanalo ○

Waimanalo
Beach

Waimanalo Beach
County Park

HICKAM
AFB

H1

BISHOP
MUSEUM ■

PALI
LOOKOUT ★

61

*Round Top
Forest Reserve*

Range

✈ HONOLULU INT'L
AIRPORT

Makapu'u Beach
County Park

Koko
Crater

Makapu'u
Point

*Sand Island State
Recreation Area*

HONOLULU ⊙

UNIVERSITY
OF
HAWAII AT MANOA ★

'IOLANI PALACE/
STATE CAPITOL ★

Hawaii
Kai

Sandy Beach
County Park

'Aina
Haina

72

Waikiki ○

Le'ahi
▲ 761ft

H1

Koko Head
642ft ▲

*Maunalua
Bay*

*Hanauma
Bay*

Diamond
Head

*Diamond Head
State Monument*

Kaiwi Channel

PACIFIC

OCEAN

Kaua'i

Ni'ihau

O'ahu

Moloka'i

Lana'i   Maui

Kaho'olawe

Hawai'i

Contents

O'ahu

Aptly named the Gathering Place, O'ahu is the heartbeat of the Hawaiian Islands. The island is home to almost one million residents, about 70 percent of the state's total population, and is, by far, the most culturally and socially diverse of the eight main Hawaiian Islands. It is a unique destination where you can experience the comforts and convenience of city life with the natural beauty of verdant mountains and sparkling blue ocean within reach.

Home to Honolulu, the state's economic and political center, O'ahu initially comes across as a big city, where rush hour traffic, skyscrapers, and a pulsing nightlife capture your immediate attention. With no ethnic majority, O'ahu best exemplifies its east-meets-west melting pot culture through its exceptional regional cuisine. In Honolulu, historic buildings and art museums pepper the city's historic district, while Chinatown is the epicenter of O'ahu's local urban and fine art scene.

Pull back the curtain of O'ahu's urban landscape and there is a natural backdrop that makes up the ebb and flow of island style and tropical living. Thanks to its 112 miles of coastline, beaches and ocean activities are the cornerstone of daily life here. For pastimes from fishing and diving to surfing and kayaking, there are myriad beaches and locales that are just

right. The powerful waves of the North Shore draw the world's best surfers. The ledges off the leeward coast attract big game fish. Waikiki's calm water is the ultimate playground for the outrigger canoe. Kailua's fine, white sand rivals the most beautiful beaches in the world. And with two mountain ranges that span the island from north to south, valleys, ridges, and cliffs offer ample hiking and lush open space.

From the Polynesian roots of its first settlers and the gifts of surfing and the spirit of aloha to O'ahu's strategic role for the United States during World War II and its importance as an international agricultural hub, the breadth of the island's history and evolution is tangible from the leeward to the windward side.

For every budget and every taste, for every tourist, visitor, back-packer, traveler, and globe-trotter seeking adventure or leisure, town or country, fine dining or food truck, mountains or beaches—O'ahu has it all.

Planning Your Trip

▶ WHERE TO GO

Waikiki

The quintessential O'ahu destination, Waikiki has beaches with gentle surf and warm water, great weather year-round, ocean activities, shopping, and dining, and is home to the majority of the hotels on the island. Waikiki's 2.5-mile strip of coastline is the stuff of legends. Not too far away is iconic landmark Diamond Head. The Honolulu Zoo and the Waikiki Aquarium exhibit local flora and fauna, while Kapi'olani Park is a beautiful green space in the city. Waikiki's bars and restaurants offer cuisine from around the world and a lively bar scene once the sun sets.

Honolulu

The economic and political center of the state, Honolulu is also the capital of Hawai'i. Best known for its historic district and Chinatown, Honolulu stretches from Honolulu International Airport to the ridges and valleys of the Ko'olau Mountains. Here you'll find stately government buildings like the Hawaii State Capitol and historic sites such as Washington Place and 'Iolani Palace. For museum enthusiasts, there's the Hawai'i State Art Museum and the Honolulu Museum of Art. Chinatown offers both fine art galleries and Pacific Rim cuisine.

North Shore

O'ahu's rural North Shore is all about beautiful beaches, diving, surfing, and snorkeling. The coastline is natural and unspoiled, and the beaches are the hallmark of tropical bliss. During winter, the North Shore attracts surfers from around the world to ride the powerful, barreling waves that break all along the coast. During summer, the ocean surface remains calm and flat, the perfect conditions for diving and snorkeling at Three Tables and Sharks Cove. Relax at Waimea Bay, take a walk through a botanical garden and historical cultural site at Waimea Valley, or drive up to Pupukea to visit the Pu'u O Mahuka Heiau, an ancient Hawaiian temple site.

Southeast and Windward

The southeast shore spans affluent Kahala to Makapu'u. Maunalua Bay offers a variety of water activities, from Jet Skiing and wakeboarding to surfing and diving. Sandy Beach is the best bodysurfing beach on the island.

From Makapu'u north to La'ie is the windward coast, hugging the spectacular verdant cliffs of the Ko'olau Mountains. The windward side is known for its numerous white sand beaches. Kailua has a beautiful crescent beach with fine sand and calm water, and the town is full of boutiques and restaurants. Hike up to Maunawili Falls, or along the Kawainui Marsh to see native Hawaiian waterfowl. Take the leisurely drive up the coast to the quiet town of La'ie, home of the Polynesian Cultural Center.

Central and Suburban

The Pearl Harbor Historic Sites are a must to grasp the history of Hawai'i and O'ahu and their role during World War II. Learn about O'ahu's agricultural past at the Dole Plantation and the Hawaii Plantation Village outdoor museum. Golf courses abound in the region, and there are isolated strips of windswept beaches from 'Ewa Beach to Kalaeloa.

Leeward

The arid leeward side runs from the Ko Olina Resort to Yokohama Bay and Ka'ena Point. Ko Olina has fine dining, a golf course, and four artificial seaside lagoons. The predominantly calm conditions of the leeward beaches means there is great visibility for snorkeling and diving. Hike out to Ka'ena Point State

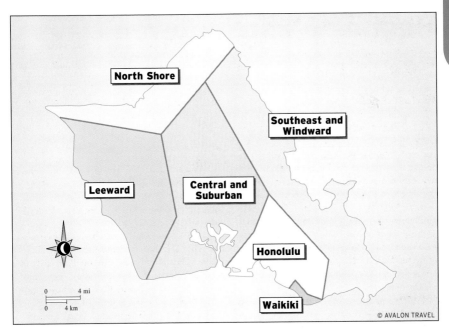

© AVALON TRAVEL

Park, the westernmost tip of the island, and look for Hawaiian monk seals, spinner dolphins, and several species of seabirds nesting in the sand dunes.

▶ WHEN TO GO

While the weather and water temperature remain comfortable all year long, O'ahu does experience a high tourist season from early December to late April. There is another busy time June-August, mirroring North America's summer. If you're planning on traveling in the high season, it's absolutely necessary to make reservations in advance. Don't stop making reservations once you arrive—it's best to make advance arrangements for outrigger canoe rides, catamaran trips, tours, spa services, nightly dinner, and lu'au shows several days beforehand. If you can make it to O'ahu during the off-season, you'll find a little more room to breathe, and rates will be lower.

O'ahu experiences slight changes in temperature during summer and winter. Summer temperatures reach into the low eighties and the air is more humid, while winter temperatures dip down to the mid-seventies with slightly higher rainfall. Remember that weather here is localized; it can be pouring rain on the windward side and sunny in Waikiki. Be prepared for passing showers anytime.

The south shore sees waves during the summer, from May till September, though they rarely exceed six feet on the face. If you're keen on catching the famous winter surf on the North Shore, swells start arriving in October, with the peak of the big wave action being November through February. The North Shore continues to have surf through April. If you plan on swimming in Waimea Bay or snorkeling and diving Sharks Cove and Turtle Bay, you'll want to visit the North Shore during the summer, when the ocean is flat and conditions are prime. North Pacific humpback whales visit near-shore waters from December through April.

Best of Oʻahu in Seven Days

The average stay on Oʻahu is about seven days. With sights and activities on all sides of the island, planning your days will help you take full advantage of your holiday. Let this suggested itinerary to the must-see locales and establishments be a jumping-off point for your travels. If you need more beach days during your stay, by all means, pencil yourself in for all you can handle.

Day 1

For most visitors, Waikiki will be home base. Spend the first day getting acclimated to the weather and acquainted with the surroundings right outside your hotel. Follow the Historic Waikiki Trail around town, a self-guided tour describing the history of the area.

Walk the beach path, stop at Waikiki Beach for a swim, stroll down Kalakaua Avenue and enjoy *pau hana* (happy hour) at The Shorebird, The Beach Bar at the Moana Surfrider, or on the upstairs deck at Tiki's.

After freshening up back at the hotel, head out for dinner at the Hau Tree Lanai, Sansei Seafood, or Top of Waikiki.

Day 2

Have breakfast in Waikiki at Kai Market while rush hour traffic subsides, then head to Honolulu's historic district. Start at the Hawaiʻi State Capitol then go next door and tour ʻIolani Palace. Visit the Kamehameha I Statue, Kawaikaʻo Church, and the Mission Houses Museum.

Next, head to Ala Moana Center or Aloha Tower Marketplace for lunch and shopping. Finish up the day in Chinatown. Stroll through fine art galleries like The ARTS at Marks Garage and the Pegge Hopper gallery. For Chinatown's premier Chinese restaurant, visit Little Village Noodle House. If you're looking for a sampling of Pacific Rim cuisine, stop by the Maunakea Marketplace Food Court. For upscale Eurasian dining try Indigo.

If you want to keep the party rolling, head into an Irish pub like J.J. Dolan's or Murphy's. If your vacation coincides with the first Friday of the month, save Honolulu for that day and be a part of Chinatown's lively First Friday celebration.

Day 3

Head to the southeast and windward shores,

rainbow over Honolulu

Makaha Beach, leeward coast

The Mokulua Islands are for the adventurous.

where there are a lot of ocean-related activities to consider. Start out by snorkeling Hanauma Bay. You'll need to get there before 9am to find a parking spot. If you prefer adventure sports, dive, Jet Ski, wakeboard, parasail, or deep-sea fish in Maunalua Bay.

If you prefer hiking, spend the morning on the 1,000-plus steps of the Koko Crater Trail, walking through the Koko Crater Botanical Garden, or making your way to the lighthouse at Makapu'u Point, a great vantage point for whale-watching.

Next, check out the pounding shore break at Sandy Beach, then drive up to Kailua for a relaxing afternoon. Have lunch at Kalapawai Market or Buzz's, then retreat to the beach. Bask on the fine white sand or rent a kayak and paddle out to Flat Island or all the way

to the Mokulua Islands. Alternatively, you can head north to paddle in Kahana Bay and visit the ancient fishponds.

If you have any steam left, take the meandering drive up Kamehameha Highway to La'ie town. You can grab dinner and a show at the Polynesian Cultural Center or choose one of the small local eateries along the coast. For the brave of heart, beeline for the La'ie Point State Wayside for cliff-jumping and magnificent views of the windward coast.

Day 4

Strike out early and be at the front of the line to see the Pearl Harbor Historic Sites. There are several memorials, museums, and sites to visit, so you can tailor your experience to your liking.

Aloha Tower, Honolulu

Ready to ride in an outrigger canoe?

Golfers should head to the 'Ewa Plain or up the central plateau and play one of several challenging courses. Or continue past 'Ewa out to Ko Olina, where you can play golf, relax in the seaside lagoons, and eat at one of the fine dining restaurants like Roy's or Ushio-Tei.

If hiking is more your style, get up early and drive out to Yokohama Bay on the leeward side. Known as the Ka'ena Point State Recreation Area, the natural reserve at the western tip of the island can't be missed for its rugged beauty and wildlife. On your way back, surf or relax at Makaha Beach, have dinner in Ko Olina, and watch the sunset from Paradise Cove.

Day 5

After being out and about for a few days, recalibrate by staying near home and take in the sights around Waikiki. Go up Diamond Head first thing in the morning and then have lunch at Bogart's or Diamond Head Cove Health Bar. Check out the Diamond Head beaches or head back across Kapi'olani Park to the Honolulu Zoo or the Waikiki Aquarium.

For live music during happy hour, head to Duke's Waikiki and hang out in the Barefoot Bar. Put in your reservation for dinner and enjoy a beachside meal watching the sunset over Waikiki Beach. If you're there on a Sunday, be a part of the festivities of Duke's on Sunday on the lanai.

Day 6

It's time to be North Shore-bound. For shopping, sightseeing, and dining, stop in historic Hale'iwa Town. Visit the art galleries and get a treat at Matsumoto Shave Ice.

Kayak or stand-up paddle the 'Anahulu River, then head north and explore Waimea Bay, Pipeline, and Sunset Beach for snorkeling in the summertime and wave-watching in the winter. During summer, snorkeling and diving at Three Tables and Sharks Cove are a must.

Continue north to Turtle Bay Resort for sunset drinks at the outdoor, oceanside Hang Ten Bar & Grill, then venture over to Lei Lei's for dinner on one of Turtle Bay's famous greens. If you're operating on a budget, skip Turtle Bay and drive to Kahuku Superette for some of the best *poke* on the island.

To add some adventure, shark dive from Hale'iwa Harbor, or take a glider ride or skydive in Mokule'ia. Catch a seaside polo match at Hawai'i Polo on Sunday afternoons during the summer. If your plans allow for dinner in Hale'iwa, don't miss Hale'iwa Joes.

Colorful shower trees, monkey pods, mesquite, and banyan trees line Kapi'olani Park.

Check out what's in the water at the Waikiki Aquarium.

Yokohama Bay is one of the most isolated and pristine beaches on the leeward coast.

Day 7

Soak up the sun and take advantage of all the ocean activities Waikiki has to offer. Stop by and chat with one of the beachboys about surfing or stand-up paddle lessons and surf iconic Waikiki surf breaks Queen's and Canoes. Take a ride and surf an outrigger canoe, snorkel in the Waikiki Marine Life Conservation District, hydrate under an umbrella on the beach and take a catamaran cruise off the Waikiki coast for a fresh perspective. If there's still daylight left, paddle back out for a second session.

Paradise Cove, Ko Olina

golf course at Turtle Bay Resort

Best Beaches

Tropical island destinations are often defined by the quality of their beaches. Luckily for O'ahu, the beaches are beautiful and varied from coast to coast. Different beaches have different types of sand, and combined with what's on the ocean floor, the water color glistens from deep blue to sparkling turquoise. Whether you're looking for recreation, isolation, or convenience, there's a beach that's just right for you, and these O'ahu spots are unmatched no matter what category they fall into.

Waikiki Beach and Kuhio Beach Park (pages 36 and 37)

Side by side in the middle of Waikiki's legendary shoreline, these two beaches present the essence of Waikiki: white sand framed by Diamond Head, historic hotels, and the sparkling blue Pacific. Queen's and Canoes surf breaks are just off the shore, catamarans and outrigger canoes line the beach, and sunbathers stretch out in all directions.

Waimea Bay Beach Park (page 117)

This marine protected area framed by rocks and boulders on both sides sees pods of spinner dolphins gracing the bay in the summer when the water is calm and perfect for swimming and snorkeling. Don't forget to leap off Jump Rock.

Sunset Beach (page 118)

This is the quintessential North Shore beach. The coarse sand made of tiny bits of coral and shells stretches out in both directions and is thick with tropical vegetation along the dune. Walk north to the point for an unspoiled view of the Wai'anae Mountains.

Sandy Beach Park (page 150)

Set along the dramatic volcanic southeast coast next to Halona Blowhole, Sandy Beach is a popular sunbathing locale with an infamous pounding shorebreak and the best bodysurfing on the island.

Makapu'u Beach Park (page 151)

On the southeastern tip of the island, Makapu'u offers a fine white sand beach and amazing views of the predominant headland, Ko'olau cliffs, and offshore islands. There is great snorkeling along the headland,

Kailua Beach offers clear water and ample ocean activities.

Sandy Beach draws body surfers and sun bathers.

Sunset Beach, North Shore

tidepools, and whale-watching during the winter.

Kailua Beach Park (page 154)
Fine white sand gently arcing up the coast for four miles; crystal clear water with a sandy bottom that's perfect for swimming, stand-up paddling, and kayaking; a grassy and shady park; rental outfitters and dining across the street—what isn't to love about Kailua Beach Park?

Moku Nui, Mokulua Islands (page 156)
Sometimes it's not about size, but perspective. This small sandy beach is on the leeward side of Moku Nui, the larger of the Mokulua Islands, just a quick kayak jaunt off the Lanikai shoreline. Witness amazing views

of mainland Oʻahu, spanning Makapuʻu to Kaneʻohe, from a vantage point not many others will see.

Kahana Bay Beach Park (page 156)
Set in a deep bay, the natural scenery here is breathtaking, the water is shallow and calm, and the peace and tranquility are tangible. It's perfect for families looking to escape the crowds.

Makaha Beach Park (page 215)
A classic venue on the leeward coast for taking in the sunset, Makaha has a wide beach, great wave, and is soaked in sun. When the water is calm, the area has a reef for snorkelers to explore and is great for swimming.

Kuhio Beach Park, Waikiki

Makapuʻu Beach

Best Snorkeling and Diving

Head to the right locales and you'll find that O'ahu's reefs teem with marine life: reef fish, green sea turtles, corals, rays, sharks, octopus, and many other endangered and endemic sea creatures only found in Hawaiian waters. Diving the wrecks, ledges, lava tubes, and deep-water rock formations only add to the diversity of ocean life. Remember, snorkeling and diving are contingent on the right ocean conditions--namely calm, clear water. If one side of the island has waves or is windy, the other side might be calm and flat, just right to get in the water and explore.

Waikiki Marine Life Conservation District (page 43)

This marine protected area located along Queen's Surf Beach offers the best snorkeling in Waikiki. Because the reef-covered area is protected, sealife thrives there, so you're sure to see an abundance of fish. It's also a favorite area for the famed *humuhumunukunukuapua'a*, so keep an eye out.

Three Tables (page 124)

Part of the Pupukea-Waimea Marine Life Conservation District, this area consists of three flat reef outcroppings that barely break the water's surface just 50 feet off the beach, and is a destination that snorkelers delight in exploring. The area teems with endemic marine life like puffer fish and reef squid.

Sharks Cove (page 124)

The premier shore diving area on the North Shore, Sharks Cove has interesting underwater topography like lava tubes, caverns, and walls. Since it is part of the Pupukea-Waimea Marine Life Conservation District, marine life is abundant here, and you're sure to see creatures like the spotted eagle ray, wrasse, and unicorn fish.

Waimea Bay (page 124)

During summer when the waves are flat, Waimea Bay has perfect conditions for snorkeling. Rock outcroppings at both ends of the bay attract marine life and pods of spinner dolphins frequent these waters.

Waimanalo (page 158)

With a mix of sand, rock, and reef bottom as a great backdrop for marine life, the shallow and beautiful waters along windward

Hanauma Bay has the best snorkeling on the south shore.

Three Tables is part of Pupukea-Waimea Marine Life Conservation District.

Waimanalo has crystal clear water.

Waimanalo beckon snorkelers to simply pull off the road and get in the water.

Hanauma Bay Nature Preserve (page 159)

This popular marine conservation area on the southeastern corner of the island is set in an arid cinder cone, creating a protected environment where hundreds of marine species thrive. Snorkel beyond the inner fingers of reef to escape the crowd.

China Walls (page 160)

A vertical wall dropping 75 feet off the southern side of Koko Head offers caves and ledges for divers to explore, and is a favorite area for endangered Hawaiian monk seals. During whale season, whale song can be heard echoing off the wall.

West Side Wrecks (page 220)

In the lee of the wind, the waters off the west side offer the most consistently ideal conditions for diving. In addition to ledges, arches, and rock formations, there are several wrecks to explore: a plane fuselage, a landing craft unit, an airplane, and a minesweeping vessel.

China Walls, Hawai'i Kai

Sharks Cove is the best destination for shore-diving on the North Shore.

Best Surfing

The sport of surfing was born in Hawai'i. Legendary Olympic gold medalist swimmer, original beachboy, and ambassador of aloha Duke Kahanamoku introduced surfing to the world on the sands of Waikiki and through traveling exhibitions in California and Australia. Be a part of that legacy and get on a board during your stay on O'ahu. Whether it's your first time or you're a lifelong surfer, there is year-round surf and the perfect wave to suit your skill level.

For Beginners

POPULARS AND PARADISE (PAGE 40)

Once you're comfortable with your feet in the wax, paddle out to Populars and Paradise for longer rides on Waikiki's outer reefs.

CANOES (PAGE 40)

No stay in Waikiki is complete without surfing famous Canoes surf break. A slow rolling wave, it's fun whether it's your first time or you can hang ten. Surfing Canoes is being part of the history of Waikiki.

CHUN'S REEF (PAGE 120)

A beautiful right breaking point on the North Shore, the slow breaking wave is perfect for beginners and even has small waves occasionally during the summertime.

TURTLE BAY (PAGE 122)

Slow rolling white-water breaks along the rugged point at Turtle Bay. With board rental and surf instructors on-site, it's a great place to give surfing a try and have your friends or family snap some pictures from the cliff.

WHITE PLAINS BEACH (PAGE 196)

This gentle beach break near 'Ewa is very similar to those found in Waikiki, but without the crowds, hotels, or outrigger canoes streaking through the surf. The waves are gentle and close to shore, perfect for beginners.

For Experts

ALA MOANA BOWLS AND KAISERS (PAGE 40)

Some of the best waves on the south shore are along a strip of reef in front of the Ala Moana Small Boat Harbor. Kaisers is a barreling right that breaks in extremely shallow water over sharp reef and Ala Moana Bowls is a long, fast

The rights at Populars break quite a ways off the beach, but are well worth the paddle.

Laniakea is a fast breaking right.

Canoes is Waikiki's premier wave for learning to surf.

left that local surfers keep under lock and key, coveting every barrel.

LANIAKEA (PAGE 120)
Just past Hale'iwa town on the North Shore, Laniakea is a long, right pointbreak. On the right swell, fast perfect waves grind down the point. Lani's, as it's often called, is surfable up to 20 feet on the face.

BANZAI PIPELINE (PAGE 121)
One of the most dangerous and deadliest waves on the planet, the Banzai Pipeline is a heavy, barreling left that detonates over shallow reefs and offers some of the best and biggest barrels in the world.

SUNSET BEACH (PAGE 121)
This powerful and unforgiving wave, no matter what size, is famous for separating the experts from the herd. The right boards, the right frame of mind, and stamina are a must to paddle out and surf the heaving walls of water that break along Sunset Beach.

MAKAHA (PAGE 218)
Makaha is a predominant right-hand point break, famous for its powerful surf, the characters in the lineup, and its backwash close to shore. Makaha breaks nearly all year long, on south, west, and north swells, and sees gigantic waves during the winter; it's the biggest surfable break on the leeward side.

The Banzai Pipeline is for experts only.   Turtle Bay has great waves for beginners.

Best Hikes

Just as Oʻahu shelters an underwater paradise, the majestic mountains and forests hold verdant treasures, best seen by getting out and hiking the ridges and valleys. There is a rich diversity of hiking trails, from shaded valleys leading to waterfalls to ridges overlooking coastline and valleys with views of neighbor islands on the clearest days. As you gain elevation, you'll see more of Oʻahu's endangered and native trees and shrubs, and hear the calls of the forest birds.

Diamond Head Summit Trail (page 47)

This hike inside a volcanic cinder cone offers a unique perspective of Oʻahu's geology and its military past. The summit offers sweeping views of the south shore.

Lyon Arboretum Trails (page 79)

Shaded, damp, and devoid of the crowds that flock to nearby Manoa Falls Trail, the vast network of trails at Lyon Arboretum introduces hikers to hundreds of different tropical plants and trees. The fragrant and bright blossoms of ginger and heliconia are everywhere, palms and canopy trees reign, vines and epiphytes grow in the trees, and a small waterfall is the prize in the back of the valley.

Waʻahila Ridge Trail (page 80)

With views of Manoa Valley, Palolo Valley, and the south shore, this ridge trail terminates at a massive peak at the back of Manoa Valley,

Mount Olympus. At nearly 2,500 feet in elevation, you'll find native vegetation including the slow growing *hapuʻu* fern.

Kuliʻouʻou Trails (page 168)

These valley and ridge trails reach a summit just above 2,000 feet and offer stunning views of Waimanalo and the windward coast, panning all the way to Diamond Head across Maunalua Bay.

Koko Crater Trail (page 168)

Far from a typical hike through the woods, this trail follows an old military railroad bed straight up the southern flank of a volcano to its precipice. With over 1,000 stairs hewn from railroad ties, this hike offers breathtaking summit views, a great workout, and a bit of military history

Kawainui Marsh (page 168)

A paved walking and bike trail that traverses

Native Hawaiian birds abound in the Kawainui Marsh.

the view of Diamond Head summit from inside the crater

Kuli'ou'ou Valley

Kawainui Marsh provides a great opportunity to see native Hawaiian waterfowl in one of the few remaining wetland habitats on O'ahu.

Maunawili Falls (page 168)

A popular, short hike just outside of Kailua in the shadow of Olomana, the trail follows Maunawili Stream to cascading Maunawili Falls where there's a deep swimming pool. There are also great views of the Ko'olau Mountains and Kane'ohe Bay.

'Aiea Loop Trail (page 196)

This shady loop trail traverses the foothills of the Ko'olau Range above Honolulu. It has views of the tallest peak of the range and unspoiled Halawa Valley with many different varieties of native Hawaiian trees along the trail. The trailhead is at a historic *heiau* site.

Ka'ena Point (page 222)

This hot and dry hike to Ka'ena Point, the western tip of the island, takes you along a rocky and rutted dirt road skirting a rugged and volcanic coastline with surf pummeling the cliffs. Whether you come from the North Shore or Yokohama Bay side, this natural preserve, home to nesting seabirds, native plants, and Hawaiian monk seals, will wow you.

Plan for light showers as you hike through Lyon Arboretum.

The three peaks of Olomana can be seen from the Maunawili Falls trail.

Best Historical and Cultural Sites

Learn about the culture and history of Oʻahu to understand its people and place in the modern world. Oʻahu's relatively short history has been tumultuous and prosperous, war-torn yet rich, as evident in its museums, historic places, and artifacts, each with a compelling story to tell.

ʻIolani Palace (page 83)
The only royal residence in the United States, this grand and regal palace was the official home of the monarch of the Hawaiian kingdom. Tours are offered of the lavishly furnished basement, first, and second floors.

Hawaii State Art Museum (page 85)
Located in the No. 1 Capitol Building in the Historic District of Honolulu, this fine art museum has four galleries featuring the finest collection of works by Hawaiian artists, including sculpture.

Mission Houses Museum (page 86)
This National Historic Landmark was the first wooden structure on Oʻahu. The museum includes two main structures as well as the first printing house in the islands.

Historic Chinatown (page 87)
With their vibrant mix of cuisine, culture, art, coffee galleries, and nightclubs, Chinatown's historic buildings are home to a curious mix of food and wares. The only way to experience Chinatown is to park the car and set out on foot, block by block.

Honolulu Museum of Art (page 88)
Oʻahu's premier fine art museum has amassed a collection including 50,000 pieces spanning 5,000 years featuring Asian, African, American, European, and Oceanic artifacts. There is also a theater, and its sister museum Spalding House in Makiki Heights holds a modern art collection. The entry fee is good for both museums on a same-day visit.

Bishop Museum (page 92)
Bishop Museum is the premier natural history

The Pearl Harbor Historic Sites are part of a national monument.

the sacred walls of Pu'u O Mahuka Heiau

Hawai'i State Art Museum

museum in the Pacific and the largest museum in the state of Hawai'i. It has seasonal rotating exhibits and an extensive collection of Hawaiian artifacts and cultural artifacts from peoples across the Pacific.

Pu'u O Mahuka Heiau (page 132)
Located on the Pupukea bluff overlooking Waimea Bay, this is the largest *heiau* on the island. The two-acre site has three- to six-foot stacked stone walls for three original enclosures and was connected to the thriving community that once inhabited Waimea Valley.

Pearl Harbor Historic Sites (page 200)
One of the most heavily visited areas in Hawai'i, the Pearl Harbor Historic Sites has free tours of the USS *Arizona* Memorial and paid tours of the USS *Bowfin* Submarine Museum and Park, the Battleship *Missouri*, and the Pacific Aviation Museum. The historic sites are part of the World War II Valor in the Pacific National Monument.

Kukaniloko Birthing Stones (page 203)
The Kukaniloko Birthing Stones are a group of about 40 large boulders clustered together on the central plain north of Wahiawa town that were of extreme importance to pre-contact Hawaiians. For some 800 years, the royal wives would come to this site to give birth to their children.

'Iolani Palace

Bishop Museum

Best for Honeymooners

O'ahu's beautiful natural treasures, luxurious accommodations, and varied cuisine make it the perfect destination for a romantic, activity-filled honeymoon. Take an early morning beach walk and soak in a warm sunrise, fill your day with activities to create long-lasting memories, and settle in with a romantic sunset and dinner. It's easy to do no matter what shore you're on.

Outdoor Adventures

The best part of a honeymoon is sharing new experiences and creating cherished memories. Celebrate outdoors by taking a horseback trail ride (page 129) in the hills above the North Shore.

For a chance to experience the most raw and beautiful natural preserve on the island, head out to Ka'ena Point State Park (page 226).

If sunsets are your passion, get out on the water in Waikiki and take a sunset catamaran cruise (page 45).

Scenic Strolls

Leave your shoes at the beach park and stroll beautiful Kailua Beach (page 154). Start at Kalama Beach Park in the middle of the beach, away from the crowds at the main beach park, and walk north to the end of the point. Enjoy the fine white sand and the crystal clear water splashing on your feet. This is a great locale for a sunrise stroll.

Surround yourself with colorful blossoms and bask in the fragrance at the Koko Crater Botanical Garden (page 176). At the entrance to the garden is a plumeria grove, a flower synonymous with Hawai'i. The grove begins to bloom in March, is in full bloom May-June, and then slowly sheds its flowers through fall. Stroll through the garden and explore the color, shapes, and smell of the beautiful flowers.

Couples Massage

Share the experience of pampering and deep relaxation with a deluxe spa package for two at the Kahala Spa (page 174), the pinnacle of luxury. The 3.5-hour Romance treatment includes a foot massage, body scrub, 90-minute full-body massage, facial, and floral immersion.

Spa Luana (page 131), located at Turtle Bay Resort on the beautiful North Shore, offers romantic couples massage treatments in an outdoor oceanside cabana, using local fruit and plant ingredients.

beautiful Kailua Beach

Nothing is more romantic than oceanfront accommodations.

North Shore sunset

Sunset Cocktails

There's only one establishment on the North Shore where you can relax at the water's edge and sip on a mai tai while watching the sun escape below the horizon, and that's the Hang Ten Bar & Grill (page 135) at Turtle Bay.

For a romantic sunset beverage in Waikiki, escape the bustle and get close and comfortable at the Hau Tree Lanai (page 61). Set right on Kaimana Beach, it offers amazing ocean views.

Fine Dining

Waikiki's Nobu (page 62) exudes romance. Modern in design, decor, and cuisine, the softly lit restaurant has an atmosphere of elegance. Its "New Style" Japanese cuisine of sushi and small, flavorful dishes is meant to be shared and savored.

Located in Waikiki's Royal Hawaiian is Azure (page 61), an exquisite fine-dining

seafood restaurant. Let sommeliers assist you in pairing the perfect wine with your meal, which you'll enjoy in beachfront dining cabanas.

Romantic Lodgings

At Turtle Bay Resort's beach cottages (page 242), you can fall asleep to the sound of waves rolling up the beach and rise to the view of sea turtles swimming in the surf, just footsteps from your lanai. It's the perfect setting for romance: The beach cottages are private, quiet, and stylish, and the view is breathtaking.

The Halekulani (page 238) is a hallmark of elegance and tranquility in bustling Waikiki. A beachfront property that somehow escapes the rush of traffic and busy footsteps, the hotel boasts fine-dining restaurants, SpaHalekulani, and light, airy, and stylish suites that exude comfort.

Have a massage for two at the Kahala Spa.   plumeria in bloom at the Koko Crater Botanical Garden

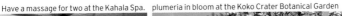

Best for Families

It takes activities of a more hands-on, interactive nature to keeps the kids excited and entertained. When traveling with the family, consider these sights and establishments to create the best experience for everyone of every age.

Sans Souci Beach (page 38)

Just outside of Waikiki proper, this swath of sandy beach is perfect for families with small children. An outer reef blocks waves from reaching the shore, and the water is clear, calm, and shallow, with the best conditions for kids at low tide.

Honolulu Zoo (page 51)

With plants and animals emphasizing tropical ecosystems and the African Savannah, the Honolulu Zoo is a must do for families. From large mammals to small reptiles and a host of birds, the zoo also offers a children's interactive petting zoo and a massive jungle gym.

Waikiki Aquarium (page 52)

Grab the family and escape the sun and heat at the Waikiki Aquarium. Get up close and personal with marine life that calls the Pacific region home. Get to know what's swimming around O'ahu, visit the monk seals, and get your hands wet petting some of the reef's smaller sea creatures.

Sea Life Park (page 178)

By Makapu'u, Sea Life Park is an aquatic park specializing in education and interaction with sealife. At the park you can swim with dolphins and even take a dorsal fin ride. Guests can also swim with sharks, sea lions, or rays. There are even child-oriented animal encounters.

Kualoa Ranch (page 180)

A real outdoor adventure, this working 4,000-acre ranch offers horseback rides, ATV rides, Jeep tours, kayak tours, and tours of rainforests and fishponds. They also have educational experiences like hula instruction.

Dole Plantation (page 203)

Learn about O'ahu's role in pineapple production at the Dole Plantation. Explore the living garden maze, take a train ride, visit the plantation gardens, and have lunch and a frosty pineapple treat.

Aston Hotels

Aston Hotels & Resorts has several hotels and condominiums in Waikiki that are perfect for families, like the Aston at the Waikiki Banyan (page 234) and the Aston Waikiki Beach Tower (page 238). They offer multiple-bedroom condominiums with full kitchens at reasonable rates.

residents of the Honolulu Zoo

WAIKIKI

White sandy beaches, swaying palm trees, surfers, stand-up paddle surfers, and outrigger canoes share the lineup at the famous Canoes and Queen's surfing breaks. Swimmers and sunbathers grace the shoreline for a refreshing dip—with an average daytime high temperature in the low 80s and water temperature in the mid-70s. It's no wonder Waikiki has long been a coveted destination for world travelers seeking the enchantment of a tropical oasis. But make no mistake, while the surf and sun rarely disappoint, you'll be hard pressed to find peace, solitude, or tranquility on Waikiki's narrow beaches, busy avenues, or in its packed restaurants.

A scant 2.5 miles of shoreline on the South Shore between Diamond Head and the Ala Wai Small Boat Harbor, Waikiki pulses year-round with the footsteps of visitors from all over the world marching up and down Kalakaua and Kuhio Avenues and sinking their toes in the sand. Lined with high-rise hotels, condominiums, and apartment buildings, Waikiki is a complete destination, a beachside hamlet with all the amenities of city life within its mesmerizing embrace: shopping, dining, nightlife, health, fitness, spas, and, of course, ocean sports and activities. The Honolulu Zoo and the Waikiki Aquarium are a must for families. Kapiʻolani Park is a runner's delight, and tai chi and yoga are commonplace under the park's flowering canopy trees.

As cliché as it might sound, make sure to take a surf lesson or go on a canoe ride with a beachboy to become a part of a Waikiki tradition that harks back a century to the father of

© KEVIN WHITTON

WAIKIKI

HIGHLIGHTS

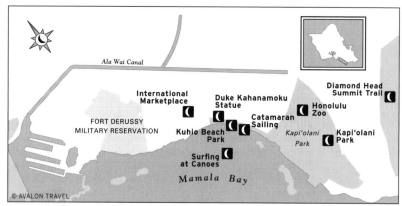

LOOK FOR ◖ TO FIND RECOMMENDED SIGHTS, ACTIVITIES, DINING, AND LODGING.

◖ **Kuhio Beach Park:** Visit the famous Duke Kahanamoku Statue, relax under a palm tree, lay out on the beach, rent a surfboard, or take a canoe or catamaran ride (page 37).

◖ **Surfing at Canoes:** No stay in Waikiki is complete without surfing. Whether it's your first time getting your feet on the wax or you've been surfing your entire life, be a part of the legacy of surfing in Hawai'i and paddle out to Canoes for a wave or two (page 40).

◖ **Catamaran Sailing:** Take a break from the crowd on the beach and get out on the open water on one of Waikiki's catamarans. The sunset sails on the bigger boats offer a particularly good time (page 45).

◖ **Diamond Head Summit Trail:** Combine O'ahu's unique volcanic geography, military history, and a short hike that will get your heart pumping and you've got the Diamond Head

Summit Trail, home to the best views in Waikiki (page 47).

◖ **Honolulu Zoo:** The Honolulu Zoo showcases the African savannah, the Asian and American tropical forest and the Pacific Islands in a great family outing (page 51).

◖ **Kapi'olani Park:** It's Waikiki's outdoor gym. Play tennis, go for a run, stretch out with beachside yoga, or just throw down a blanket and enjoy lunch under flowering canopy trees (page 52).

◖ **Duke Kahanamoku Statue:** Pay homage to the original ambassador of aloha, the man who grew up in Waikiki and brought the sport of surfing to the world (page 53).

◖ **International Marketplace:** Duck into the shade under the banyan trees and into the International Marketplace, your one-stop shop for all the Hawaiiana kitsch you can handle (page 55).

modern-day surfing and original ambassador of aloha Duke Kahanamoku. Across Waikiki, *pau hana* (happy hour) is celebrated every day with food and drink specials, and live music, to welcome the sunset. Once the sun goes down,

Waikiki takes on a whole new tempo. The sidewalks of Kalakaua Avenue teem with street performers and swell with curious onlookers, and the clubs and bars welcome patrons till four in the morning.

Waikiki is not without its blemishes, and the town can get rough and rowdy in the cool hours of early morning. Prostitution is illegal, but tolerated on Kuhio Avenue; homelessness is ever-present; theft and muggings occur; and bar fights spill out onto the sidewalks after hours. But if you keep your eyes focused on the surf and sun, it's easy to find the paradise Waikiki is famous for.

PLANNING YOUR TIME

For first-time O'ahu travelers and many returning visitors, Waikiki is the perfect home base. It's easy to take a day trip anywhere around the island and make it back in time for dinner. It's also the ideal locale to relax at the water's edge in very close proximity to your accommodations. To experience the gamut of Waikiki's sights and activities, set aside a day to spend in the Diamond Head area in addition to the time you plan for beach activities and shopping in Waikiki proper.

ORIENTATION

Waikiki is framed by the Ala Wai Canal to the north and west, Diamond Head to the east, and the beautiful Pacific Ocean to the south. Most streets in Waikiki are one-way thoroughfares: **Kalakaua Avenue,** the main drag, runs east to Diamond Head, **Ala Wai Boulevard** runs west, and in between them, **Kuhio Avenue** has two-way traffic east and west. Residents generally define directionality in relation to towns or major landmarks.

Beaches

Waikiki's narrow beaches are generally packed shoulder to shoulder with people, or umbrella to umbrella, for most of the day. In the heart of Waikiki, the towering hotels have been built right to the water's edge, leaving anywhere from 20 to 50 feet of beach for public use. If a leisurely walk along the beach is your fancy, the feat is best accomplished during the first few hours after sunrise or after 6pm, when most people have made their way back to their hotel to prepare for dinner. It's not uncommon for the moon to rise over Diamond Head while the sun is still setting in the west. To get away from the crowds altogether, find a patch of sand along Diamond Head's seaside cliffs and revel in the fact that a short, steep walk down a gravelly path will deter most visitors.

DUKE KAHANAMOKU BEACH

At the west end, or 'Ewa (EH-va) side of Waikiki, is **Duke Kahanamoku Beach,** one of the wider beaches in Waikiki. Fronting the Hilton Hawaiian Village and Beach Resort, it stretches from the Ala Wai Small Boat Harbor to the Hilton's catamaran pier. A shallow outer reef with great waves keeps the inner waters calm and very kid friendly. There's even an artificial ocean-fed lagoon between the beach and the hotel, the perfect spot to try out stand-up paddle surfing without having to worry about ocean chop or currents. The lagoon does have a synthetic feel to it though, especially apparent in its coarse compacted shoreline that makes sand play an all-out construction job. Kahanamoku Beach was recognized in 2012 as Number 3 on Dr. Beach's Best Beaches in America list.

There is a beach path that runs the length of Waikiki, but if you're coming from Kalakaua Avenue, you'll have to trek down Lewers Street, Beach Walk, or Saratoga Road to reach the sand. There is public beach access on the west side of the Outrigger Reef. Once you hit the beach path, keep walking west till you pass the catamaran pier. If you're coming by car, there is free parking in the Ala Wai Small Boat Harbor.

FORT DERUSSY BEACH

Just east of the catamaran pier, **Fort DeRussy Beach** runs all the way to the Outrigger Reef. Now a clean and tidy public beach and manicured park shaded by canopy trees, this military

WAIKIKI

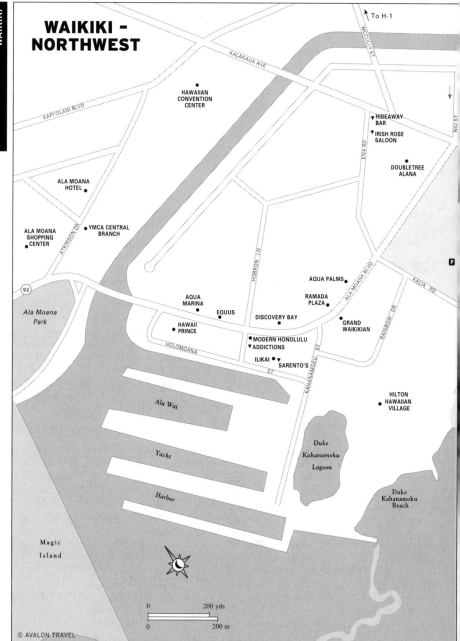

WAIKIKI - NORTHWEST

To H-1

MCCULLY ST

KALAKAUA AVE

NIU ST

HAWAIIAN
CONVENTION
CENTER

KAPI'OLANI BLVD

▼ HIDEAWAY BAR
▼ IRISH ROSE SALOON

ENA RD

DOUBLETREE ALANA

ALA MOANA HOTEL

ATKINSON DR

YMCA CENTRAL BRANCH

ALA MOANA SHOPPING CENTER

HOBRON LN

ALA MOANA BLVD

KALIA RD

P

92

AQUA PALMS

Ala Moana Park

AQUA MARINA

RAMADA PLAZA

EQUUS

DISCOVERY BAY

GRAND WAIKIKIAN

RAINBOW DR

HAWAII PRINCE

HOLOMOANA

● MODERN HONOLULU
▼ ADDICTIONS

ILIKAI ● ▼

SARENTO'S

KAHANAMOKU ST

HILTON HAWAIIAN VILLAGE

Ala Wai

Duke Kahanamoku Lagoon

Yacht

Duke Kahanamoku Beach

Harbor

Magic Island

| 0 | 200 yds |
| 0 | 200 m |

© AVALON TRAVEL

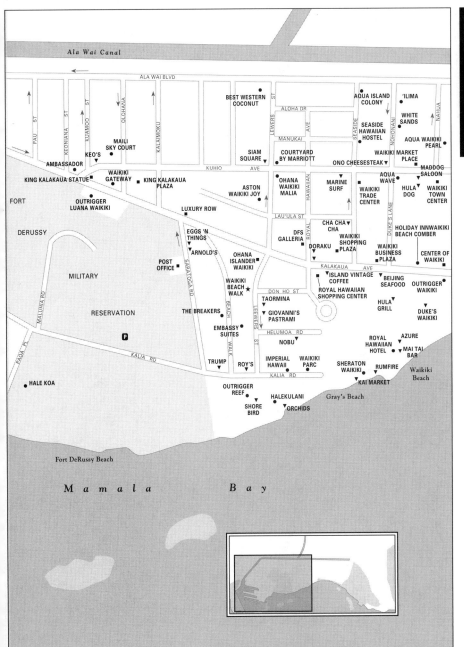

Ala Wai Canal

ALA WAI BLVD

PAU ST
KEONIANA ST
KUAMOO ST
OLOHANA ST
KALAIMOKU

BEST WESTERN COCONUT
ALOHA DR
LEWERS ST
MANUKAI
AVE
SEASIDE ST
NOHONANI
NAHUA

AQUA ISLAND COLONY
'ILIMA
WHITE SANDS
SEASIDE HAWAIIAN HOSTEL
AQUA WAIKIKI PEARL

MAILI SKY COURT
KEO'S
SIAM SQUARE
COURTYARD BY MARRIOTT
WAIKIKI MARKET PLACE
ONO CHEESESTEAK
MADDOG SALOON

AMBASSADOR
KING KALAKAUA STATUE
WAIKIKI GATEWAY
KING KALAKAUA PLAZA
KUHIO AVE
OHANA WAIKIKI MALIA
MARINE SURF
AQUA WAVE
WAIKIKI TRADE CENTER
HULA DOG
WAIKIKI TOWN CENTER

FORT
OUTRIGGER LUANA WAIKIKI
ASTON WAIKIKI JOY
HAWAIIAN
LAU'ULA ST

DERUSSY
LUXURY ROW

EGGS 'N THINGS
DFS GALLERIA
ROYAL
CHA CHA CHA
WAIKIKI SHOPPING PLAZA
DUKE'S LANE
HOLIDAY INN WAIKIKI BEACH COMBER

POST OFFICE
ARNOLD'S
OHANA ISLANDER WAIKIKI
DORAKU
WAIKIKI BUSINESS PLAZA
CENTER OF WAIKIKI

MILITARY
SARATOGA RD
KALAKAUA AVE
ISLAND VINTAGE COFFEE
BEIJING SEAFOOD
OUTRIGGER WAIKIKI

RESERVATION
WAIKIKI BEACH WALK
DON HO ST
ROYAL HAWAIIAN SHOPPING CENTER
HULA GRILL
DUKE'S WAIKIKI

MALUHIA RD
THE BREAKERS
TAORMINA

BEACH WALK
GIOVANNI'S PASTRAMI
HELUMOA RD
ROYAL HAWAIIAN HOTEL
AZURE
MAI TAI BAR

EMBASSY SUITES
NOBU
LEWERS ST

PAOA PL
KALIA RD
TRUMP
ROY'S
IMPERIAL HAWAII
WAIKIKI PARC
SHERATON WAIKIKI
RUMFIRE
Waikiki Beach

HALE KOA
KALIA RD
KAI MARKET

OUTRIGGER REEF
SHORE BIRD
HALEKULANI
ORCHIDS
Gray's Beach

Fort DeRussy Beach

M a m a l a   B a y

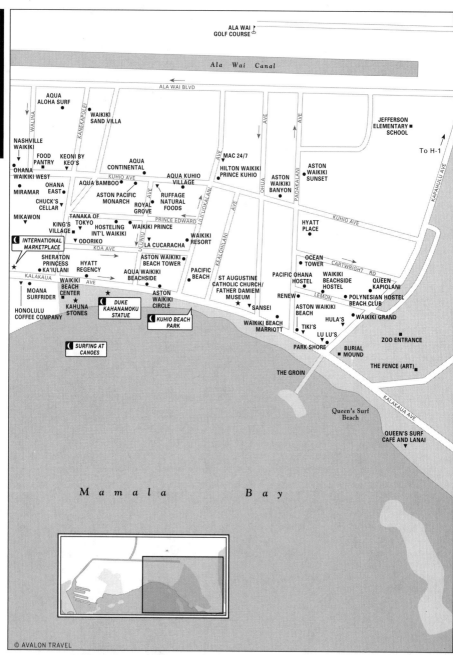

© AVALON TRAVEL

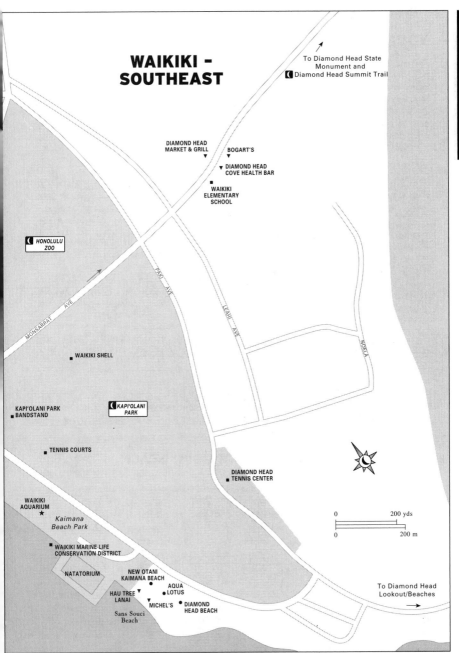

WAIKIKI - SOUTHEAST

To Diamond Head State
Monument and
Diamond Head Summit Trail

DIAMOND HEAD
MARKET & GRILL

BOGART'S

DIAMOND HEAD
COVE HEALTH BAR

WAIKIKI
ELEMENTARY
SCHOOL

HONOLULU
ZOO

PAKI AVE

LEAHI AVE

NOELA

MONSARRAT AVE

WAIKIKI SHELL

KAPI'OLANI PARK
BANDSTAND

KAPI'OLANI
PARK

TENNIS COURTS

DIAMOND HEAD
TENNIS CENTER

WAIKIKI
AQUARIUM

Kaimana
Beach Park

0   200 yds

0   200 m

WAIKIKI MARINE LIFE
CONSERVATION DISTRICT

NATATORIUM

NEW OTANI
KAIMANA BEACH

AQUA
LOTUS

HAU TREE
LANAI

MICHEL'S

DIAMOND
HEAD BEACH

Sans Souci
Beach

To Diamond Head
Lookout/Beaches

WAIKIKI

YOUR BEST DAY IN WAIKIKI

There is so much to do in Waikiki, from outdoor activities like surfing, stand-up paddling, snorkeling, and hiking, to shopping, dining, or simply relaxing on the beach under an umbrella. Of all the activities on offer, some tap into the history and character of Waikiki, which have evolved to make Waikiki the iconic and unique place that it is today.

- Wake up early and walk, run, bike, taxi, or bus to the **Diamond Head State Monument.** Hike through the extinct Diamond Head crater to the summit and take in the entire south shore from your morning perch.

- On your way back to Waikiki proper, stop at **Diamond Head Cove Health Bar** for a delicious acai bowl. If you'd rather have eggs or a bagel, try **Bogart's Café** next door.

- After refueling, you'll want to head back to the beach and partake in Waikiki's ample ocean activities. If you snorkel, post up at **Queen's Surf Beach** and check out the fish and reef in the marine protected area. If you surf or stand-up paddle, head straight to **Kuhio Beach Park** or **Waikiki Beach,** where you can rent a board and paddle out into the legendary Waikiki surf at **Canoes** or **Queen's.**

- As afternoon rolls around, freshen up back at the hotel and head back outside and cruise the shops on Kalakaua Avenue while being entertained by the street performers. Stop by the **International Marketplace** to pick up all sorts of Hawaiiana goodies for your friends and loved ones back home.

- Is it five yet? Happy hour, better known as *pau hana* in the islands, beckons you into one of Waikiki's many dining establishments. Your best bet is to choose one with an ocean view—think oceanfront hotel. If you'd rather be on the water for sunset, hop on one of the **catamaran cruises** along the beach for a 1.5-hour sail.

- For dinner, immerse yourself in the beach culture of Waikiki and head to **Duke's Waikiki** for an amazing beachfront steak and seafood meal with the best sunset views. Make sure to order a Hula Pie after dinner. If sushi is your game, try **Doraku Sushi** in the Royal Hawaiian Shopping Center.

reservation was one of several shore batteries on Oʻahu during WWII and served as an R&R locale for soldiers during the Vietnam War. The beach fronts the Hale Koa hotel, which caters strictly to armed forces personnel and their families, and the U.S. Army Museum, and has a distinct military presence and vibe. It's also known for its calm inner waters perfect for swimming or snorkeling and volleyball courts. An open-air parking lot across from Fort DeRussy Beach Park on Kalia Road is a relatively safe place to park for access to the beach. The rates are average for Waikiki standards at $3 per half hour, and they offer military discounts.

GRAY'S BEACH

Continuing east, the beach ends, and a raised cement walking path on top of the armored shoreline provides transport to **Gray's Beach,** a nook of coarse, imported sand in between the Halekulani and Sheraton Waikiki Hotel. There is also beach access from Kalia Road between the two hotels.

WAIKIKI BEACH

Widened in the spring of 2012, **Waikiki Beach** is half of the heart of Waikiki. Stretching from the Royal Hawaiian to the Moana Surfrider, the first two hotels in Waikiki, this is prime real estate for visitors and the sand fills up quickly with beachgoers. This strip is lined with beach service providers and beachside bars and dining. Because of the sand bottom off Waikiki Beach, the water is a translucent aqua-green and perfect for swimming, stand-up paddling, or just floating on a fluorescent blow-up mat. There is a sandbar just offshore from the Royal Hawaiian that people wade or float out to in order to play in the knee-deep

© KEVIN WHITTON

Duke Kahanamoku Beach

water and small surf. For snorkeling, there's not much to see in the way of marine life, save for the occasional green sea turtle. The famous surf spot Canoes breaks quite a ways offshore, and while this part of the beach does have small shorebreak—quite exciting for the kids—the inner waters are calm and sheltered from the prevailing trade winds.

The easiest way to get to Waikiki Beach is to walk down the shore from Kuhio Beach to the east. Otherwise, make your way through one of the big hotels on the beach to access the world-famous sand, sparkling waters, and iconic view of Diamond Head. Parking in Waikiki is very expensive, whether you valet or self-park at one of the hotel parking garages. Your best bet is to park in the Waikiki Shell parking lot, which is free, and walk down Kalakaua Avenue. There is also free parking on the *makai* side (ocean side) of Kalakaua Avenue from Kapahulu Avenue all the way down to Diamond Head. Since landing one of the coveted free parking spots is hard to do, there is also metered parking on the *mauka* side (mountain side) of Kalakaua Avenue along

Kapi'olani Park for a reasonable $0.25 per half hour.

◖ KUHIO BEACH PARK

Stretching from the east side of the Moana Surfrider to the concrete pier where Kapahulu Avenue intersects Kalakaua Avenue, **Kuhio Beach Park** is the other half to the thumping heart of Waikiki. It has a snack bar, restrooms and showers at the west end, two lagoons for sheltered swimming, grassy knolls for relaxing in the shade under a palm tree, ample beach services, and one of the best waves in Waikiki—Queen's. Just as on Waikiki Beach, you'll want to arrive early to stake a claim in the sand with a beach towel or chair.

Kuhio Beach Park is the hub of surfing in Waikiki, with the forgiving waves of Queen's and Canoes breaking fairly close to shore by Hawai'i standards. You'll find a host of beachboys in red shorts stoked to rent surfboards, stand-up paddle surfboards, bodyboards, and floating mats. They also offer surf lessons and outrigger canoe rides. Along the beach

© KEVIN WHITTON

Kuhio Beach Park, the heart of Waikiki

park you'll also find the iconic statue of Duke Kahanamoku adorned in lei and the statue of Prince Kuhio, as well. Once again, it's best to find parking around Kapiʻolani Park and walk to Kuhio Beach Park. The beach park is closed 2am-5am.

QUEEN'S SURF BEACH

On the east side of the concrete pier, **Queen's Surf Beach** offers two things you won't find anywhere else in Waikiki: a No Surfboard zone and the Waikiki Marine Life Conservation District. Demarcated by buoys on the east side of the concrete pier, just off the shoreline, the No Surfboard zone sees small waves roll across the shallow waters and up the beach. While action of the water would be great for bodyboarding, the ocean floor is sharp, flat reef with the odd coral head, so swimming and body surfing are not a good idea.

On the east side of the jetty, the Waikiki Marine Life Conservation District stretches to the Waikiki War Memorial Natatorium's crumbling western wall. With fishing forbidden in this 76-acre marine conservation area and calm, shallow inner waters, this healthy reef ecosystem offers the best snorkeling in Waikiki.

Kapiʻolani Park, with its wide-stretching banyan trees, runs the length of the beach. There are restrooms, showers, and a hip shoreline café open for breakfast, lunch, and dinner. The Waikiki Aquarium is at the Diamond Head end of the park. Publics is the main surfing wave along the beach, a dangerous left that breaks along a shallow reef of odd-shaped coral heads that rise above sea level on an extremely low tide. The beach and park area at Publics, where the beach ends, is a favorite for LGBT visitors. The park is also home to many of Waikiki's homeless population. Parking is available along Kalakaua Avenue and around Kapiʻolani Park.

SANS SOUCI BEACH

A small patch of sand between the eroding Waikiki War Memorial Natatorium and the New Otani Kaimana Beach Hotel, **Sans Souci Beach**, also known as **Kaimana Beach,**

© KEVIN WHITTON

Sans Souci is the perfect beach for snorkeling, swimming, and for the kids.

is a favorite spot for residents seeking easy access to a family-friendly beach and park without the hassle of getting in and out of Waikiki. There's limited free parking, restrooms, an outdoor shower at the beach, and indoor showers at the natatorium. In front of the natatorium is great for snorkeling, and swimmers take advantage of a wide, deep channel through the reef out to a wind sock fixed on its outer corner. Four laps from the beach to the wind sock is roughly a mile. The water is very calm, making it the perfect locale for children of all ages.

MAKALEI BEACH PARK

If you're in the mood to escape Waikiki and find solace on your own slice of beach, **Makalei Beach Park** is the best option within Waikiki. Only the quaint park is visible from Diamond Head Road. Tucked back behind some houses in the southwest corner of the park, the beach is a quiet, small strip of sand no more than 100 feet long favored by residents and surfers attracted to Suicides surf break. It's also best to

visit on a low tide, when more sand is exposed. Once you are in the water, the seafloor is entirely reef, so ocean life abounds, but choppy conditions and strong currents are prevalent in this area. There are no lifeguards, so exercise caution when snorkeling and swimming off the beach. There are a shower and picnic tables in the beach park. To get there, park around Kapiʻolani Park and walk east up Diamond Head Road. The entrance to the beach park is signed.

DIAMOND HEAD BEACH PARK

At the base of Diamond Head's seaside cliffs are some of the best beaches on the South Shore for escaping the crowds and enjoying the island's natural scenery. There's parking on both sides of Diamond Head Road and a paved footpath that cuts down the cliff. At the bottom of the path, **Diamond Head Beach Park** stretches out in both directions. The shoreline is lined with shells and sea glass, and there are tidepools on the west end of the beach. There are several surf breaks along the reef, but the pervasive trade winds, strong ocean currents, wind chop, and extremely shallow patches of reef make snorkeling and swimming dangerous. The beach below Diamond Head is a great spot for a romantic winter season stroll as the sun sets straight off Waikiki. Diamond Head Beach Park is closed 10pm-5am.

Surfing

Surfing is synonymous with Waikiki. Not only did Hawaiians invent the sport of surfing, but the legendary Duke Kahanamoku—original beachboy, Olympic gold-medalist swimmer, and the father of modern-day surfing who hailed from Waikiki—introduced the fluid sport to the world. The surf breaks that Duke made famous riding on heavy wooden boards are the same spots that surfers seek out today. While the waves are biggest, best, and most consistent during summer, June till September, Waikiki has the potential to see surf at any time during the year. Whether you are a longboarder, shortboarder, experienced, novice, or first-timer, Waikiki has a number of breaks that suit all abilities. Just remember that proper surfing etiquette applies at all breaks, and with so many people in the water, safety and respect for others are of the utmost importance. When in doubt, don't go out.

ALA MOANA BOWLS TO KAISER'S

Ala Moana Bowls is a fast, hollow left that is heavily guarded by a seasoned crew of local surfers. The wave breaks into the mouth of the Ala Wai Small Boat Harbor and is best viewed from across the channel on Magic Island. **Kaiser's** is a predominant right that breaks over a very shallow reef shelf. With a tight takeoff zone and a pack of hungry locals, it's also best left to the residents. If you plan on surfing in this area, it's best to surf the stretch of reef between the two spots, known as **Rockpile.** Good for both shortboarding and longboarding, the fast lefts break over sharp, shallow reef and allow for a quick cover up if you're lucky. Paddle out from the small swatch of beach fronting the parking lot (with designated free and paid parking), but avoid the areas of very shallow reef straight out from the beach. There are some slow whitewater rollers on the inside perfect for beginner surfers.

FOURS TO POPULARS

Straight out from the U.S. Army Museum, on the east side of a deep channel, is **Fours,** a wave that only comes alive when the surf gets big. Just to the east of Fours, way out over the outer reef, is **Threes,** a perfect right that breaks best on a low tide and holds it shape at all sizes. Threes is a favorite with local surfers and gets very crowded. To the east of Threes is **Paradise,** a surf zone with big, rolling, shifty peaks. It's a favorite for longboarders and stand-up paddle surfers. Continuing east, the next break is a favorite for all board riders—**Populars.** Locally referred to as Pops, this long right breaks over a sand-covered reef and can handle big surf. When the trade winds are stiff, Pops does get choppy.

◖ CANOES

Canoes is straight out from the west end of Kuhio Beach Park. It breaks both right and left and has several takeoff zones. A slow rolling longboard wave, Canoes is perfect for beginners. Start off slow on the inside catching the whitewater till you learn to stand up and balance on the board. Once you're more confident and comfortable, sit out the back with a mix of locals, beachboys, and people from all around the world sharing in this Hawaiian tradition. Canoes is very crowded with all types of watercraft, from 12-foot longboards to canoes and catamarans. Stay aware and by all means, if something large is coming your way, don't be a deer in the headlights, paddle out of the way.

WAIKIKI BEACHBOYS

If there's something about Waikiki that sets it apart from other tropical sea destinations, it's the Waikiki beachboys. Hailing back a century, the beachboy culture has evolved with the changing face of tourism in Hawai'i, but the gentlemen in the red shorts still practice the same core values of sharing the sports of surfing, outrigger canoe riding, and aloha with visitors.

After Calvinist missionaries decimated the Hawaiian culture in the 19th century, the sport of surfing, a purely Hawaiian endeavor, was nearly extinguished. It was seen as sinful because of how much skin was shown while surfing. Only a few surfers remained at the end of the century, namely legendary waterman and three-time Olympic gold medalist Duke Kahanamoku and a few of his friends. As the first wave of wealthy American tourists arrived on steamers in the early decades of the 20th century, these few surfers took it upon themselves to entertain the visitors, teaching them how to surf, ride canoes, and relax and have a good time in general. In essence, they created a way to earn a living surfing year-round on the beach at Waikiki. These first visitors came to Hawai'i for extended stays and were able to develop relationships with the beachboys, who became their tour guides and a bridge to the Hawaiian culture and a different lifestyle. After giving surfing lessons during the day, the beachboys entertained their guests with ukulele, song, and libations at night, a hedonistic lifestyle by all accounts.

The fun was curtailed by WWII, and as travel and tourism have changed since then, so too have the beachboys. With the ease and affordability of flying across the Pacific, a vacation to Waikiki is accessible for so many more people, not just the wealthy elite. Today, with thousands of visitors flocking to the beach daily, the beachboys focus on surfing and outrigger canoe surfing and have shifted roles from entertainers and tour guides to beach services. While only a few of Waikiki's beachboys can still trace their ties back to the original beachboys, any beachboy can still show you how to have the time of your life in Waikiki's gentle surf.

QUEEN'S

Queen's, also called Queen's Surf, is one of the best waves in Waikiki. Straight off the beach from the east end of Kuhio Beach Park, before the lagoon, it's best for longboarding. Professional and amateur contests are often held here. The perfect turquoise rights draw a host of the best longboarders in Hawai'i, who hang ten down the line with style and ease. Queen's is usually very crowded, and if there's any swell in the water, Queen's is breaking. Because of the tight takeoff zone and thick crowd, beginners should stick to Canoes.

PUBLICS TO TONGG'S

Just on the east side of the rock jetty off Queen's Surf Beach, way off the beach on the outer reef, **Publics** is a long left that breaks over shallow, sharp, and irregular-shaped coral heads. Sound inviting? For longboarders, the long, sloping wave offers a chance to get out of the thick crowds in the heart of Waikiki. The wave is best ridden at high tide when the coral heads are submerged. On low tide, the coral heads go dry, and the wave breaks right over them. The break can get choppy from its exposure to the trade winds, and on big south swells, the waves can get quite big and the currents very strong. A lifeguard in the tower on the beach can assist you with ocean conditions.

To the east of Kaimana are two breaks best for longboarding on the outer reef: **Old Man's** is on the left side of the channel and **Tongg's** just up the reef. These soft, sloping waves offer respite from the Waikiki crowds, but keep an eye peeled for coral heads.

DIAMOND HEAD

On the west end of Diamond Head, off Makalei Beach Park, is a left for experts only called **Suicides.** It's windy, quite a ways offshore, and subject to strong currents. Below the Diamond Head Lookout parking lots are several good breaks, the two most popular being **Lighthouse** and **Cliffs.** At the bottom of the trail down the cliff is a deep channel through the reef. From the beach, to the right of the channel is Lighthouse, a fast and powerful right for experts only. On the left of the channel is Cliffs, several peaks along the reef that break both right and left and are suited for all types of board riders. Diamond Head can get very windy as the trade winds blow right across the break, and is a favorite for kiteboarders and sailboarders during the extreme conditions.

OUTFITTERS

Koa Board Sports (2420 Koa Ave., 808/923-0189, www.koaboardsports.com, 10am-6pm daily) has a huge selection of longboards and shortboards available for rent. Rates go from $20 for a half day, $25 for one day (overnight), to $50 for two days. You can also change the board anytime the shop is open. **Hans Hedemann Surf Adventures** (2586 Kalakaua Ave., 808/924-7778, www.hhsurf.com, 8am-5pm daily) is located in the Park Shore Hotel between Starbucks and the hotel lobby. The surf school specializes in surf lessons out at Publics. You will have to carry a soft-top longboard from the retail outlet to the break, about a 10-minute walk. They also offer stand-up paddle lessons, guided surf adventures, and surfboard rentals.

If you prefer to rent your board right on the beach, or take a lesson with one of Waikiki's famous beachboys, then you'll want to check out some of Waikiki's vetted beach services. **Faith Surf School** (www.faithsurfschool.com),

operated by the legendary Moniz family, offers their expertise at several beach locations: the Outrigger Reef (2169 Kalia Rd., 808/924-6084), the Outrigger Waikiki (2335 Kalakaua Ave., 808/926-9889), and the Sheraton (2255 Kalakaua Ave., 808/922-4422). They rent longboards starting at $20 per hour and offer 1.5-hour group lessons for $60 and private lessons for $125.

Aloha Beach Services (808/922-3111, http://alohabeachservices.com, 8am-4pm daily), serving guests since 1932, has a small palapa, but a lot of boards, in between the Outrigger Waikiki and the Moana Surfrider. They rent longboards for $15 per hour and $5 each additional hour and have one-hour group lessons for $40 and private lessons for $80. They also have a photo package with the group lesson and rent beach umbrellas, chairs, and air mats and rings. Aloha Beach Services accepts cash only.

You'll find **Star Beachboys** (no phone, 8am-4pm daily) at the west end of Kuhio Beach Park, by the concession stand and the bathrooms. They rent 8- to 10-foot longboards for $10 per hour and 11- to 12-foot boards for $15 per hour with a $5 charge for each additional hour. They also have one-hour group lessons for $40 and private lessons for $75. On the sand just to the east of the Duke Kahanamoku statue and at the far eastern end of Kuhio Beach Park are the **Hawaiian Ocean Waikiki** (808/721-5443) beachboys. They have one-hour group lessons for $40 and two-hour private lessons for $100. They also rent longboards starting at $10 per hour and shortboards for $15 per hour, with $5 each additional hour or $35 for a half day. You can also rent beach chairs and umbrellas, as well.

Other Water Sports

SNORKELING

The snorkeling in Waikiki is decent at best anytime of year. Overuse and overfishing for decades have led to the decline in the number of species and fish in the nearshore waters, and all that fine white sand over the reef, which gives the water its light, crystal color, leaves little shelter for reef dwellers. Patience, and the luck of being in the right place at the right time, can yield some great underwater exploring.

Duke Kahanamoku and Fort DeRussy Beach

Since the near-shore waters off **Duke Kahanamoku Beach** and **Fort DeRussy Beach** are not heavily used, the potential to encounter marine life is definitely heightened. The water is shallow, waist- to chest-deep, all the way out to the waves breaking at Threes and Fours, and the bottom is a mix of reef and sand. As an added bonus, you won't have to keep your eye out for surfers, swimmers, canoes, or catamarans, so you can stay focused on what fish you can find.

Waikiki Marine Life Conservation District

The **Waikiki Marine Life Conservation District,** located along Queen's Surf Beach from the jetty to the Waikiki War Memorial Natatorium's western wall, is hands down the best snorkeling in Waikiki. The 76-acre marine conservation area is a regulated and patrolled no-take zone, where fishing or removing of any sea creature is illegal. The protection has allowed a plethora of reef-dwelling vertebrates and invertebrates to thrive. The shallow inner waters are generally calm, but heavy trade winds can texture the surface. Look for bonefish, funny face fish, wrasse, puffer fish, eel, and yellow tang. Chances are you'll even catch a glimpse of the sleek *humuhumunukunukuapua'a.*

Diamond Head

The near-shore waters off the beaches of Diamond Head are great for snorkeling, but more suited for experienced snorkelers and swimmers. The reefs at Diamond Head attract all sorts of marine life, including sharks and the endangered Hawaiian monk seal. Shallow water and lots of nooks and crannies in the sharp reef make for great habitat, but beware of extremely shallow areas of reef, strong currents, and wind chop. Snorkeling is best in winter when the waves are small to nonexistent.

Outfitters

Whether you purchase your own snorkel gear or rent equipment is for you to decide. Renting allows you to travel without lugging around cumbersome snorkel gear, while owning gives you the luxury of a custom fit only your mouth knows. **Aqua Zone Scuba Diving & Snorkeling** (2552 Kalakaua Ave., 866/923-3483, www.aquazonescuba.com, 8am-5pm daily), in the Waikiki Beach Marriott, rents and sells gear and is a short walk from the Waikiki Marine Life Conservation District. They rent complete snorkel sets starting at $10 for 24 hours, $20 for three days, and $25 for five days.

Snorkel Bob's (702 Kapahulu Ave., 808/735-7944, www.snorkelbob.com, 8am-5pm daily), just outside of Waikiki on Kapahulu Avenue, sells equipment and rents complete sets, snorkels, fins, flotation, and wetsuits. They rent several different sets of snorkeling gear. The most basic starts at $2.50 per day and $9 per week.

Nearly all the beach services at the beachfront hotels rent and sell snorkel gear and most **ABC Stores** sell complete sets as well.

SCUBA DIVING

Once you get offshore from Waikiki, the seafloor slowly sinks away and the water becomes a rich, deep blue. At these greater depths are a few great dive sites, from reefs to shipwrecks.

Offshore, the water teems with life, and turtles, eels, triggerfish, octopus, and a host of other reef fish abound. Diving off Waikiki is a year-round pursuit, weather and wave permitting.

In the heart of Waikiki you'll find two PADI diver centers. **Waikiki Diving Center** (424 Nahua St., 808/922-2121, www.waikikidiving. com) dives two wrecks and 10 different sights right off Waikiki. With 32 years of experience, they offer dives for every type of diver, rent and sell equipment, and offer PADI certification. Two-tank beginner dives start at $109, wreck dives start at $99, and PADI certification courses start at $250. **Aqua Zone Scuba Diving & Snorkeling** (2552 Kalakaua Ave., 866/923-3483, www.aquazonescuba.com) is in the Waikiki Beach Marriott. They offer free pool lessons for beginners and rusty divers and daily boat dives for all levels. They offer two levels of PADI certification and provide daily snorkel tours, equipment rental and sales. Two-tank boat dives with rental equipment start at $129. Both Waikiki Diving Center and Aqua Zone dive numerous locations outside of Waikiki as well.

STAND-UP PADDLING

Long before stand-up paddling became a full-fledged sport, a few of the Waikiki beachboys were known to cruise around the lineups kneeling or standing up on longboards and paddling with their canoe paddles. Now the equipment has been refined and stand-up paddling is popular both for surfing and flat-water paddling, each a full-body workout. **Paradise, Populars,** and **Canoes** are the go-to surf breaks for stand-up paddle surfing in Waikiki. If you prefer to just paddle and check out the water from a different perspective, get away from the crowds by paddling out beyond Canoes and **Queen's** and explore. Make your way to **Publics** and paddle in with the wind at your back. You'll be amazed that even at 10-15 feet deep, you'll still be able to see the bottom.

Faith Surf School (www.faithsurfschool. com) rents stand-up paddle boards from the Outrigger Reef (2169 Kalia Rd., 808/924-6084), Outrigger Waikiki (2335 Kalakaua Ave., 808/926-9889), and Sheraton (2255 Kalakaua Ave., 808/922-4422) starting at $25 for one hour and going up to $70 for all day. They also have stand-up paddle lessons starting at $65 up to $125 for a 1.5-hour private lesson. **Aloha Beach Services** (808/922-3111, http://alohabeachservices.com, 8am-4pm daily), between the Outrigger Waikiki and the Moana Surfrider, rents stand-up paddle boards for $30 for the first hour and $10 each additional hour. Their lessons start at $60 and go to $80 for a private one-hour lesson. In Kuhio Beach Park, **Star Beachboys** (no phone, 8am-4pm daily) rent boards for $20 for the first hour and $10 for the second. Nearby, **Hawaiian Ocean Waikiki** (808/721-5443, 8am-4pm

---

STAND-UP PADDLING VS. STAND-UP PADDLE SURFING

Stand-up paddle surfing, also known as SUP, is a relatively new sport in the surfing world. Originally used by Waikiki beachboys who would rest on their knees on their big longboards and use a canoe paddle to get around, today's stand-up paddle boards are high-tech, light, and very stable. Stand-up paddle boards range 9-12 feet long, are thick and wide, and made from epoxy resin. Surfers stand with their feet parallel, like a skier, in the center of the board and use a long paddle to accelerate forward. With a little practice, it's easy to pick up the technique rather quickly. Stand-up paddle boards are great for flat-water paddling (distance paddling) and for surfing. Stand-up paddle surfing is a great workout, from your core to your legs and arms, and it affords a great perspective looking down over the reef. Because the boards are so big, though, only experienced stand-up paddlers should try surfing waves, as the boards are hard to maneuver and can be very dangerous for others in the water.

daily) rents stand-up paddle boards for $25 for the first hour and $10 for each additional hour.

BODYBOARDING

While you can bodyboard any of the waves around Waikiki, there are a two areas where bodyboarders tend to congregate. Just off the cement pier at the east end of Kuhio Beach Park is a break called Walls, where warbley waves break over very shallow reef and wash over the lagoon wall. To the east of the pier, along Queen's Surf Beach, is a specially marked No Surfboard zone. The waves here break over some shallow coral heads along the fringe reef and roll all the way to the shore.

Aloha Beach Services (808/922-3111, http://alohabeachservices.com, 8am-4pm daily), **Star Beachboys** (Kuhio Beach Park, no phone, 8am-4pm daily), and **Hawaiian Ocean Waikiki** (Kuhio Beach Park, 808/721-5443, 8am-4pm daily) rent bodyboards for $5 per hour or $20 per day.

OUTRIGGER CANOEING

The outrigger canoe is one of the defining facets of Hawaiian culture. After all, it is how early Polynesian voyagers first arrived in these islands. Before surfboards came along, native Hawaiian fishers would stand up and "surf" their canoes back to shore. Outrigger canoe paddling and surfing have remained popular in Hawai'i to this day, and Waikiki offers the only place on O'ahu you'll be able to hop into a real six-person outrigger canoe with a professional rudder operator to guide you through the surf.

Faith Surf School (www.faithsurfschool.com) runs six-person canoes at $25 each for three waves, with locations at the Outrigger Reef (2169 Kalia Rd., 808/924-6084), the Outrigger Waikiki (2335 Kalakaua Ave., 808/926-9889), and the Sheraton (2255 Kalakaua Ave., 808/922-4422). **Aloha Beach Services** (808/922-3111, http://alohabeachservices.com, 8am-4pm daily) runs eight-person canoes for $15 each for two waves. In Kuhio Beach Park **Star Beachboys** (no phone, 8am-4pm daily) canoe rides are $15 per person for three waves, and **Hawaiian Ocean Waikiki**

(808/721-5443, 8am-4pm daily) runs a four-person canoe at $15 each for two waves.

◖ CATAMARAN SAILING

There are seven catamaran cruises that launch from the beach and sail the waters off Waikiki almost every day, weather dependent, from Ala Moana to Diamond Head. The boats are different sizes and cater to different interests (some of the catamaran tours are known locally as the "booze cruise"), but the tours all offer a beautiful perspective of Waikiki, the city skyline, and the verdant Ko'olau Mountains from out at sea.

Waikiki Cruises (no phone, 2-passenger min., 6-passenger max., $20 per person) operates a 24-foot catamaran from the beach fronting the Outrigger Reef. Known for its fluorescent pink sail, the cat sails for one hour Monday-Saturday. First sail launches at 10:30am and the last sail departs around 3pm. You'll need to bring your own refreshments on board and make reservations from the beach.

Waikiki Rigger (808/922-2210, www.

a Waikiki Cruises catamaran

© KEVIN WHITTON

waikikirigger.com, $30 pp), a championship racing catamaran, also launches from the beach fronting the Outrigger Reef. Their High Speed Tradewind Sail departs at 11am, 1pm, and 3pm on Tuesday, Thursday, Saturday, and Sunday, and 1pm and 3pm on Monday, Wednesday, and Friday. Nonalcoholic beverages are $1, cocktails are $3. The daily Sunset Sail ($42 pp) departs at 5pm and offers complimentary beverages. Waikiki Rigger also has a 2.5-hour Aquatic Eco Tour ($51 pp) combining sailing and snorkeling. The 44-foot **Maita'i Catamaran** (808/922-5665, www.leahi.com) seats 47 people comfortably and departs from the beach between the Sheraton Waikiki and the Halekulani hotels. The 90-minute Tradewind Sail ($28 adults, $14 children) leaves the beach at 11am, 1pm, and 3pm. Beverages start at $3. There is a two-hour Underwater Adventure Sail ($45 adults, $27 children) at 10:30am on Monday, Wednesday, and Friday. The Sunset Mai Tai Sail ($39 adults, $19 children) is aptly named for its stocked bar and free beverages. It departs at 5pm. On selected nights the Maita'i offers a Mahina Moonlight Sail ($39 adults, $19 children); times may vary. Children three and under are free on all trips.

On Waikiki Beach you'll find three catamaran operators. In front of the Royal Hawaiian is the **Kepoikai II** (no phone, http://kepokai.com), a 42-foot cat operating in Waikiki for more than 35 years. Their one-hour sail begins at 10:30am daily for $20 per person. Last sail is at 6pm during the summer. On board they sell $1 mai tais, $2 beer, juice, soda, and water. You'll need to make reservations or bookings from the beach.

The **Manu Kai** (808/554-5990) beaches in front of the Outrigger Waikiki and offers one-hour trips ($25 pp with alcoholic beverages, $20 pp without). The 43-foot catamaran's last sail ($30 pp) is at 5:30pm and is a 1.5-hour trip. Right next to the Manu Kai you'll find the famous yellow and red **Na Hoku II** (no phone, www.nahokuii.com, $30 pp with alcoholic beverages, $25 pp without). They offer 1.5-hour trips, and the first leaves the beach at 11:30am. They also have a sunset sail that departs at 5:30pm. Both of these boats have a 49 person maximum capacity and fill up quickly. If you're planning a weekend sunset sail, it's best to make a reservation at least a few days in advance.

At Kuhio Beach Park you'll find the **Mana Kai** (no phone, $20 pp), which holds up to 27 passengers, but will sail with just six. The crew does not serve any beverages, but you are welcome to bring your own. The first one-hour sail departs at 9:30am, and the last sail is around 6pm, depending on the season.

PARASAILING

Parasailing offers the thrill of hang gliding while affixed by a prescribed length of line to a boat motoring across the warm Pacific Ocean. The parachute can soar up to 1,000 feet above the ocean, and as you can imagine, it really is a bird's-eye view. **Hawaii Active** (808/871-8884 or 866/766-6284, www.hawaiiactive.com) is an easy way to book a parasailing trip. There are four options for line length and time in the air, starting with the 300-foot line for 5-7 minutes for $44 per person, up to a 1,000-foot line for 10-12 minutes for $77.

Hiking, Biking, and Bird-Watching

HIKING

You won't need a pair of hiking boots during your stay in Waikiki, even if you do plan on trekking the two "trails" on offer: the Diamond Head Summit Trail inside the Diamond Head crater, or the Waikiki Historic Trail that encircles the region.

Diamond Head Summit Trail

The **Diamond Head Summit Trail** is inside the Diamond Head crater, an extinct tuff cone volcano that erupted about 300,000 years ago, and is part of the **Diamond Head State Monument** (www.hawaiistateparks.org, 6am-6pm daily, $5 per vehicle, $1 walk-in visitor). The historic trail, built in 1908, climbs 560 feet from the crater floor to the summit in just 0.8 miles. The steep trail up the inner southwestern rim of the crater is a combination of concrete walkway,

Look for these surfboard markers along the Waikiki Historic Trail.

© KEVIN WHITTON

switchbacks, stairs, uneven natural terrain, and lighted tunnels. Inside the semiarid crater is hot and rather dry, so bring plenty of water and sun protection. Along the hike you'll see remnants of O'ahu's natural and military history, punctuated by the breathtaking views of the entire South Shore from the observation station at the summit. Plan on 1.5-2 hours round-trip. The entrance to the Diamond Head State Monument is off Diamond Head Road between Makapu'u Avenue and 18th Avenue. The last entrance to hike the trail is 4:30pm. Visitors must exit the park by 6pm. To get there by bus, use route 22, 23, or 24.

Waikiki Historic Trail

The self-guided **Waikiki Historic Trail** (www.waikikihistorictrail.com) takes you throughout Waikiki, covering fascinating historical, geological, and cultural sights with tidbits about Waikiki past and present. Informative surfboard markers at viewing areas correspond to a prescribed map and program available online. Print out a copy of the map and guide to take with you or use a personal electronic device while on the go. You can follow the order of sights in the program or just visit those areas you prefer. The trail begins at Queen's Surf Beach, hugs the coast to the west (the most scenic section of the trail), rounds up to the Ala Wai Canal and follows Kalakaua Avenue back into the heart of Waikiki. At a normal walking pace, the trail takes about two hours to complete.

BIKING

Since bicycles are prohibited on Waikiki sidewalks and the busy avenues of Waikiki, sans bike lanes, are not exactly bike-friendly for those wishing to get around on two wheels, biking is best suited to near and around **Diamond Head** where traffic is lighter and moves a bit slower. Biking to the Diamond Head lookout and beaches will also alleviate the

A DAY AT DIAMOND HEAD

Diamond Head, named Le'ahi in Hawaiian, is the tuff cone of an extinct volcano that erupted approximately 300,000 years ago. Today, the profile of Diamond Head as seen from Waikiki has become an iconic image that conjures up all the beauty and lore of Hawai'i. However, there's more to do at this natural wonder than just take a picture for prosperity sake. Here are a few great ways to explore Diamond Head:

· The **Diamond Head Summit Trail** is the most heart-pumping trail in Waikiki. The summit hike climbs 560 feet inside the volcano, from the crater floor to the rim. It is as much a walk through a natural museum as it is a window to O'ahu's military role in the 20th century: Diamond Head's panoramic view made it the perfect site for coastal defense; five artillery batteries were installed in the crater. The views at the summit lookout are breathtaking and span the entire South Shore.

· Whether you walk, run, or drive to the **Diamond Head Lookout** on Diamond Head Road, it's a great place to relax for a spell and take in the scenery. Mansions line the beach to the east out to rugged Black Point, surfers and windsurfers ride the waves below and sailboats and barges cruise the Pacific in the distance. From December through May, humpback whales can be seen breaching, spouting, and playing off the coast from this vantage point. There's even a working lighthouse on the edge of the cliff.

· Located on Diamond Head Road in between the lookout and Kapi'olani Park, **Le'ahi Beach Park** is a quiet, seaside spot that is a great retreat for a picnic or simply to unwind and gaze out at the ocean. There is no beach at this park, as the surf rushes up against a rock wall protecting the oceanside estates, but there is a nice shaded area, and the park is seldom used.

· To experience Diamond Head in its entirety, take the short paved path down the cliff and take a walk on the beach. There are tidepools at both ends of the beach and straight out from lookout up above is the surf spot called **Cliffs.** It's a great wave for longboarding, and the view from the water, looking back up at magnificent Diamond Head, is something most people don't get to see.

· The **Diamond Head Tennis Center,** a 10-court tennis complex, is nestled up against the west side of the outer crater wall. There's nothing like hitting the ball back and forth with the ever-present Diamond Head as your teammate.

task of finding parking and allow more time for exploring and enjoying your surroundings. You can circumnavigate Diamond Head easily by traveling from Diamond Head Road to Monsarrat Avenue (a great place to stop for a beverage and a bite to eat) to Paki Avenue and then back to Diamond Head Road.

Hawaiian Style Rentals (2556 Lemon Rd., 808/946-6733, www.hawaiianstylerentals.com, 8:30am-5:30pm daily) rents bicycles with helmet, lock, map, front pouch, and rear rack starting at $20 per day and $10 per day for three days or more. You'll also find bicycle rentals at **Adventure Rentals** (159 Kaiulani Ave., 808/924-2700, 8am-5:30pm daily) and **Big Kahuna Motorcycle Tours**

and Rentals (407 Seaside Ave., 808/924-2736 or 888/451-5544, www.bigkahunarentals.com, 8am-5pm daily).

BIRD-WATCHING

On the east end of Waikiki, on the Diamond Head-side of where Kapahulu and Kalakaua Avenues intersect, **Kapi'olani Park** (www.kapiolanipark.net) is the place to spot birds in Waikiki. Look up in the trees for green parrots, several types of waxbills, northern and red-crested cardinals, spotted and zebra doves, and the yellow-fronted canary. Look in the grass for the cute Java sparrow, Pacific golden plovers, cattle egrets, and the sassy common myna.

© KEVIN WHITTON

running path, Kapi'olani Park

Running and Tennis

RUNNING

Kapi'olani Park (intersection of Kapahulu and Kalakaua Avenues) and **Diamond Head** are a runner's delight, and the area is host to myriad walking events and marathons throughout the year, the most famous being the Honolulu Marathon held annually in December. Kapi'olani Park has a paved path circling the perimeter of the park, a two-mile circumference. Run under the bright and colorful white, yellow, and sherbet flowers of the shower trees, and through the aerial roots and trunks of a banyan tree. There is also an exercise station near the Kapi'olani Park Tennis Courts.

If you would like to get a little closer to the ocean during your jog, there is a seaside paved trail stretching from Queen's Surf Beach to the natatorium. Cut through Kaimana Beach Park back to the sidewalk on Kalakaua Avenue and follow it to Diamond Head Road. From here you can access Kapi'olani Park or run up Diamond Head Road to the lookout.

The Running Room (819 Kapahulu Ave., 808/737-2422, www.runningroom.com, 10am-7pm Mon.-Fri., 10am-5pm Sat.-Sun.) has a wide selection of footwear, apparel, accessories, and info about what's new in O'ahu's running and racing community.

TENNIS

The **Diamond Head Tennis Center** (3908 Paki Ave.) is on the east end of Kapi'olani Park. This 10-court public complex, resurfaced in 2012, is a favorite for local and visiting players. Because of the demand for court time, games are limited to 45 minutes if others are waiting. There are restrooms, shaded benches, and clocks for each court to keep track of playing time. The public courts are free, but unlit, so playing hours are subject to daylight. The parking lot for the courts is open from 6am-7pm daily.

Across the park on Kalakaua Avenue, at the east end of Queen's Surf Beach, are the **Kapi'olani Park Tennis Courts** (5am-midnight daily). These four public courts light up once the sun goes down, so you can play tennis until midnight. The courts are open during park hours, 5am-midnight daily, and the same rules of court etiquette as at Diamond Head Tennis Center apply.

Yoga and Spas

YOGA

Two key aspects of island life are physical activity and relaxing, two pastimes that seem at odds until you consider yoga. There are several yoga studios, indoors and out, for centering yourself through stretching and breathing.

Open Space Yoga (3046 Monsarrat Ave., 808/232-8851, www.yogaopenspace.com) offers hot yoga in their second floor Diamond Head Studio. Opened in 2011, Open Space Yoga offers visitors two weeks unlimited yoga for $60 and single classes for $17. You can even book classes online.

Another option for hot yoga in Waikiki proper is **Waikiki Hot Yoga** (2345 Kuhio Ave., 808/277-9935, www.waikikihotyoga.com). Inside the Miramar at Waikiki Hotel on the fifth floor, the classes are designed with the beginner in mind. Single classes run $25, and class packages start at $170 for 10 classes.

If you're keen to practice yoga out of doors in Kapi'olani Park just steps from Queen's Surf Beach, check out **Yoga with Christine** (808/927-7335, www.yogachristine.com, 9am-10am Mon.-Fri.). What you give up in privacy you'll get back in scenery. Certified instructor Christine Okamoto leads classes, conducted in English and Japanese, under a tree near lifeguard tower 2F.

SPAS

Several high-end hotels offer spa services. **SpaHalekulani** (2199 Kalia Rd., 808/931-5322, www.halekulani.com/living/spahalekulani, 9am-8pm daily) in the luxurious Halekulani hotel incorporates Polynesian therapeutic rituals into their award-winning services. They offer a full range of custom massage treatments, and their services include professional salon staff. One-hour experiences start at $140;

facials start at $140. They have special spa offerings for teenagers 11-15, and their complete packages start at $390.

The **Abhasa Waikiki Spa** (2259 Kalakaua Ave., 808/922-8200, www.abhasa.com, 9am-9pm daily) offers private garden cabanas nestled in the secluded Royal Grove Courtyard of the Royal Hawaiian. The outdoor tropical garden setting is a one-of-a-kind spa experience in Waikiki. Massages and facials start at $135 for 50 minutes, and packages begin at $260.

Next door at the Outrigger Waikiki on the Beach you'll find the **Waikiki Plantation Spa** (2335 Kalakaua Ave., 808/926-2880, www.waikikiplantationspa.com, 9am-7pm daily) in the hotel's penthouse on the 17th floor offering a different, expansive perspective with views of Waikiki Beach and the Pacific Ocean. Stylized with elements of a traditional Zen rock garden, the full service spa also offers private fitness programs to highlight the spa experience. Massages start at $115 for 50 minutes, facials begin at $120 for 50 minutes, packages start at $250, and the spa also features a host of body polishes and wraps, like the popular Papa'ala, which uses cooling aids to help heal sunburns—$100 for the 50-minute treatment.

Set in the historic Moana Surfrider, Waikiki's first hotel, **Moanalani Spa** (2365 Kalakaua Ave., 808/237-2543, www.moanalanispa.com, 8am-8pm daily) combines traditional Hawaiian healing with steam rooms, dry saunas, and water therapy areas with ocean views, along with all the other standard spa services. Moanalani also caters to couples treatments, with two private ocean front lanai. Massage and facials start at $145 for 50-minute sessions, and spa packages begin at $245.

The **Na Ho'ola Spa** (2424 Kalakaua Ave., 808/923-1234, http://waikiki.hyatt.com/hyatt/

pure/spas, 7:30am-9pm daily) is located on the fifth floor of the Hyatt Regency Waikiki. The two-story, 10,000 square-foot spa has 16 treatment rooms that evoke the sense of Waikiki, a dry sauna, and steam showers. Massages and body treatments start at $140 for 50 minutes, 50-minute facials begin at $145, and spa packages start at $275.

Sights

◖ HONOLULU ZOO

Only a mere 2,392 miles from the nearest zoo, the **Honolulu Zoo** (151 Kapahulu Ave., 808/971-7171, www.honoluluzoo.org, 9am-4:30pm daily, $14 adults, $8 military adults, $6 children 3-12 with an adult, $4 military children with an adult, children 2 and under free) is a must-see in Waikiki. The plant and animal collections emphasize Pacific tropical ecosystems and are organized into three ecological zones: the African savannah, the Asian and American tropical forest, and the Pacific Islands. Mammals and birds are the spotlight here, with just a few reptiles on display, including a handful of Galapagos tortoises, a Komodo dragon, and dangerous-looking gharials. There's an expanded Indian elephant enclosure, opened in 2012 for the two playful inhabitants; the orangutans, Rusty and Violet, sleep mostly during the day; and the zebras, giraffes, hippos, and rhinoceroses on the savannah are a major draw. The baboons are quite interactive as well. The kids will love the massive jungle gym by the snack bar and the Sumatran tiger area. Right next door is the Keiki Zoo, with a crawl-through circular koi fish tank, lizards, farm animals, and a goat petting area.

There are several after-hours events at the

© KEVIN WHITTON

giraffe at the Honolulu Zoo

zoo, as well. Twilight Tours are on Friday and Saturday evenings. The guided, two-hour walk is a great chance to see who wakes up after everyone has left, and the Dinner Safari is a buffet and a two-hour guided night tour. Every Wednesday during the summer, The Wildest Show Summer Concert Series is a fun family event featuring local musicians. Check the website for the schedule. If you plan on returning to the zoo more than once during your stay or visit Oʻahu several times a year, consider an annual pass. There are several levels of membership, but the average family can take advantage of the Chimpanzee Family membership: unlimited entrance and benefits for one year for two adults and up to four children under 18. There is pay parking lot for the zoo on Kapahulu Avenue, $1 per hour and the kiosks accept credit cards or coins only, no bills. Free parking is located at the Waikiki Shell parking lots across Monsarrat Avenue on the *makai* side (ocean side) of the zoo.

WAIKIKI AQUARIUM

Situated on 2.35 acres right on the shoreline in Kapiʻolani Park, the **Waikiki Aquarium** (2777 Kalakaua Ave., 808/923-9741, www.

ART ON THE ZOO FENCE

Fancy yourself an art aficionado? Maybe you'd like to take home a piece of art to remember Hawaiʻi. **Art on the Zoo Fence** (www.artonthezoofence.com, Sat.-Sun. 9am-4pm) is a great outdoor venue where you can check out a range of art, from photography to postcards to paintings, and speak with the artists, as well. A tradition in Waikiki for over 50 years, artists hang their works from the exterior of the zoo fence along Monsarrat Avenue. Stroll under the towering banyan trees, peruse the art, and engage the artists. It's not uncommon for the artists to be painting on-site.

---

waquarium.org, 9am-4:30pm daily, $9 adults, $6 military, students, seniors, $4 youth 13-17, $2 children 5-12, children 4 and under free) has a number of beautiful collections focusing on the South Pacific and Hawaiian marine communities. With your paid admission you receive a free audio tour wand, which gives insight and information for all the different collections. The aquarium has both indoor and outdoor viewing areas. Inside you'll find displays showcasing the marine life around the different islands and the creatures living in different marine ecosystems, from the intertidal zone to the open ocean. Corals, giant clams, colorful reef-dwelling fish, predators like sharks, trevally, and groupers, jellyfish, chambered nautilus, and even a gold American lobster (only one in 30 million American lobsters show this genetic disposition) are some of the curious residents at the aquarium. Outside you'll find the monk seal, a tidal pool with fish that reflect the marine life around Waikiki, an interactive area where people can hold hermit crabs and other little creatures, and a serene grassy open space under palm trees right next to the ocean for the kids to run around on and get some energy out or to sit and enjoy a snack.

The Waikiki Aquarium also has a signature summer concert series on the lawn that draws a more mature crowd than the zoo's summer concert series. Ke Kani O Ke Kai: The Sound of the Ocean starts in June and runs through August. Check the website for the latest schedule and information. Parking at the aquarium is very limited. Park along Kalakaua Avenue, the ocean side is free and the mountain side is metered parking, $0.25 per half hour.

◖ KAPIʻOLANI PARK

Kapiʻolani Park (intersection of Kapahulu and Kalakaua Avenues, www.kapiolanipark. net) is the oldest public park in Hawaiʻi, established in 1877 by King David Kalakaua, monarch of Hawaiʻi. What was once marshland and lagoons is now a 300-acre expanse of grass, sports fields, canopy trees, and running trail. The park attracts all types of sports,

© KEVIN WHITTON

The Diamond Head Lighthouse is still active.

from rugby and cricket to soccer and softball and has four lit tennis courts. It's a hub for picnics, birthdays, large family gatherings, and barbecues. The park also draws runners and walkers who circle it on the 3-mile running path. The park is the best spot for birdwatching on the South Shore, and birders set up binoculars and cameras to spy on the avian parkgoers in the mature shower trees, mesquite, and banyans.

The **Waikiki Shell,** an outdoor concert venue, and the Victorian-style **Kapi'olani Bandstand,** built in the late 1890s, are in close proximity, just across from the zoo. The park hosts festivals all year long to celebrate culture, food, and community, such as the Korean Festival and the Ukulele Festival. The park extends across Kalakaua Avenue, all the way to the beach. There is free parking along Monsarrat Avenue by the Waikiki Shell and the bandstand, along Paki Avenue, and on the ocean side of Kalakaua Avenue. There are parking meters (10am-6pm daily, $0.25/30 min., 4-hour limit) on the mountain side of Kalakaua Avenue.

DIAMOND HEAD LOOKOUT

Where Kalakaua Avenue and Paki Avenue meet at the east end of Kapi'olani Park, Diamond Head Road begins its easy climb to the **Diamond Head Lookout.** At the apex, there are two designated areas to pull off the road and park right at the edge of the cliff for spectacular views up and down the coast. Keep in mind that the Waikiki Trolley and tour buses of all sizes also stop at the lookouts, so sometimes they are tranquil and uncrowded, while at other times they are infiltrated by mobs of visitors, taking pictures shoulder to shoulder. The tour buses will block any parked cars from leaving, but on the bright side, they usually don't stay long. From the lookout you can see the waves crashing on shallow reefs to the west, the surfers at Diamond Head's popular surf spots, and **Black Point** to the east, its rugged coastline fringed by palm trees and mansions.

Just before the first parking area on the ocean side of Diamond Head Road, coming from Waikiki, is the **Diamond Head Lighthouse** (3399 Diamond Head Rd.). First constructed in 1899, then rebuilt in 1917, the lighthouse still uses its original Fresnell lens, and its beacon can be seen more than 18 miles out to see. The Lighthouse Keeper's dwelling, where the lighthouse is situated, is a private residence, the quarters of the commander of the Fourteenth Coast Guard district. A gate restricts access to the lighthouse, but its close proximity to the gate, approximately 30 feet, still makes for a Kodak moment.

◖ DUKE KAHANAMOKU STATUE

"The Father of Modern Surfing," Duke Paoa Kahanamoku, is immortalized in a larger than life bronze statue on the sidewalk fronting Kuhio Beach. Hang lei from his outstretched arms, pose with a loved one in front of Duke, and have someone snap a picture—a stop at the Duke statue is a must in Waikiki. Duke is the embodiment of Waikiki, of ocean recreation, and of aloha. Mornings are best to avoid the crowd and to catch the sunlight illuminating the statue. Duke grew up near the Hilton

THE LEGACY OF DUKE

Born Duke Paoa Kahinu Mokoe Hulikohola Kahanamoku on August 24, 1890, Duke grew up in Waikiki near what is now the Hilton Hawaiian Village. In the course of his childhood on the beach, Duke quickly became a skilled waterman, mastering surfing, outrigger canoe paddling, and swimming. As one of the original Waikiki beachboys, Duke shared his passions with wealthy, upper-class tourists from the U.S. mainland, and by doing so saved the sport of surfing from near extinction. A champion swimmer, Duke won his first gold medal at the 1912 Olympics in Stockholm, Sweden. In 1912 he also traveled to Southern California to give swimming and surfing exhibitions, introducing surfing to America. In 1914, he traveled to Sydney, Australia, for more exhibitions and turned the Aussies on to surfing as well. In the 1920 Olympics in Antwerp, Belgium, he won two more gold medals in swimming. Duke's success and early relationships as a beachboy opened doors for him in the Hollywood film industry, where he played in nearly 20 films from 1925 until 1967. He also served as the sheriff of Honolulu from 1932 to 1961. Known as the original ambassador of aloha, Duke is immortalized in Hawai'i for sharing the sport of surfing with the world and embodying the aloha spirit throughout his life.

Hawaiian Village and was an accomplished surfer, canoe paddler, and Olympic gold-medalist swimmer. As Hawai'i's first ambassador of aloha, Duke spread the sport of surfing around the world, traveling to the U.S. mainland and Australia for surfing exhibitions. Later in life he became a Hollywood star and held elected office in Honolulu for 29 years.

U.S. ARMY MUSEUM OF HAWAI'I

Located on Fort DeRussy Beach, the **U.S. Army Museum of Hawai'i** (808/955-9552, http://hiarmymuseumsoc.org, 9am-5pm Tues.-Sat., free) highlights O'ahu's military history. The museum is actually inside Battery Randolph, a massive concrete coastal defense structure with reinforced walls up to 12 feet thick. The battery was constructed in 1911 to house two 14-inch guns, part of a system set up to protect Honolulu Harbor from invasion.

The battery was rendered obsolete by the rise of the aircraft carrier in WWII. Audio tours are available for $5. The museum validates parking tickets for the Fort DeRussy Parking Facility directly across the street.

DAMIEN MUSEUM

Across from Kuhio Beach is St. Augustine Catholic Church, a David among the high-rise Goliaths. Look for its angular, oxidized green roof resembling a series of A-frames. The **Damien Museum** (130 Ohua Ave., 808/923-2690, 9am-3pm Mon.-Fri., free) is housed in a separate building to the rear, displaying photos and other artifacts of Father Damien, the Belgian priest who humanely cared for the lepers of Kalaupapa, Moloka'i, until his own death from complications of leprosy. Although entrance is free, donations are gratefully accepted because they are the museum's only source of revenue.

Shopping

◖ INTERNATIONAL MARKETPLACE

The nucleus of Hawaiiana kitsch, the **International Marketplace** (2330 Kalakaua Ave., 808/971-2080, www.internationalmarketplacewaikiki.com, 10am-9pm daily), between Dukes Lane and Kailulani Avenue, spanning from Kalakaua Avenue all the way back to Kuhio Avenue, is a gathering of carts, vendors, and stores all under one far-reaching banyan tree. Magnets, bikini-girl lighters, tiki salt and pepper shakers, toy ukuleles, coral necklaces, pearls, aloha prints, quilts, wood carvings, the list goes on and on; it's a one-stop-shopping haven of fun, Hawaiian-themed goodies for all your friends and relatives back home. Check it out on your way out of town and don't forget to haggle.

ROYAL HAWAIIAN CENTER

The **Royal Hawaiian Center** (2201 Kalakaua Ave., 808/922-2299, www.royalhawaiiancenter.com, 10am-10pm daily), in the heart of Waikiki on Kalakaua Avenue, stretches from Lewers Street to the Outrigger Waikiki hotel. Here you'll find a mix of high-end retailers—clothing, accessories, and jewelry—surf shops and aloha wear, boutiques, beauty products, and food and drink from coffee to cocktails. If you're looking for local-style luggage and backpacks, check out **DaKine** (808/921-0373) on the second floor of building B. For women's swimwear, **Allure Swimwear** (808/926-1174) is located on the first level of building C. For those visiting Waikiki for romance, visit **Princesse Tam-Tam Lingerie** (808/922-3330) on the third level of building A for fine to moderate French lingerie. For glam accessories and premium denim and leather, find **Remix Hawaii** (808/922-3119) on the first level of building C. With more than 110 shops and restaurants, there's even an **Apple Store** (808/931-2480) for your tech needs. Big-name stores front Kalakaua Avenue, but there is a parallel walkway through the mall with a host of other stores, a great way to get out of the sun. A small outdoor performance area with hewn stone seats under a banyan tree leads to a beautifully landscaped Hawaiian botanical garden and into the Royal Hawaiian hotel courtyard.

LUXURY ROW

Just to the west of the Royal Hawaiian Center on Kalakaua Avenue, on the mountain side of the street, is **Luxury Row** (2100 Kalakaua Ave., 808/541-5136, www.luxuryrow.com, 10am-10pm daily). The name says it all. At Luxury Row you'll find high-end international brands like **Coach** (808/924-1677), **Chanel** (808/971-9011), **Tiffany & Co.** (808/926-2600), **Yves Saint Laurent** (808/924-6900), **Bottega Veneta** (808/923-0800), and **Gucci** (808/921-1000).

The International Marketplace is the king of Hawaiiana kitsch.

© KEVIN WHITTON

ART GALLERIES

Art abounds in Waikiki, with Hawaiian, ocean, and nature themes being the most prevalent. **Wyland Galleries Waikiki** (270 Lewers St., 808/924-1322, www.wyland.com, 10am-10pm daily) features Wyland's signature ocean art and is the most comprehensive Wyland source in Hawai'i. Also on Lewers Street in the Waikiki Beach Walk shops is the **Peter Lik Gallery** (226 Lewers St., 808/926-5656, www.lik.com/galleries/waikiki.html, 10am-11pm daily), featuring bold prints from landscape photographer Peter Lik. Inside the Outrigger Waikiki on the Beach (2335 Kalakaua Ave.) you'll find **Tabora Gallery** (808/922-5400, 8am-11pm daily) with originals from seascape painter Roy Tabora. **Sand People** (2369 Kalakaua Ave., 808/924-6773, www.sandpeople.com, 9:30am-9:30pm daily), next door to the Outrigger in the Moana Surfrider, is a quaint gift shop with ocean-themed trinkets, art, and clever gift ideas like vintage signs and surf art.

FARMERS MARKETS

There are three farmers markets in the heart of Waikiki. Two are operated by **Mahiku Farmers' Markets** (808/225-4002, www.mahikufarmersmarket.com): every Thursday 4pm-8pm in the International Marketplace (2330 Kalakaua Ave.) food court, and at King's Village (131 Kaiulani Ave.) every Monday and Friday 4pm-9pm. There is also a rooftop farmers market at the **Royal Hawaiian Center** (2201 Kalakaua Ave.) on Tuesday 4pm-7:30pm, located on the fourth floor on the west side of the shopping center.

Entertainment and Events

NIGHTLIFE

Lu Lu's (2586 Kalakaua Ave., 808/926-5222, www.luluswaikiki.com, 7am-2am daily) serves breakfast, lunch, and dinner, but is more widely known as a place to hang out, have a beer, and enjoy their second-story view. Right on the corner of Kalakaua and Kapahulu Avenues, it's the spot for people-watching.

Maddog Saloon (2301 Kuhio Ave., 808/924-3400, www.MaddogSaloonWaikiki.com, 10am-4am daily) is a great after-hours bar (after 2am) with dartboards and pool tables.

In the International Marketplace, **Lava Rock Lounge** (2330 Kalakaua Ave., 808/921-9978, www.lavarockloungewaikiki.com, 11am-4am daily) is dark and perfect for a quiet place to watch sports. With TVs throughout, pool tables, a good liquor selection, and good service, you might even find time to relax on a couch and play Wii.

The Hideaway Bar (1913 Dudoit Ln., 808/949-9885, 6am-2am daily) is a famous little dive that prides itself on being the first establishment in Waikiki to start serving alcohol fresh and early at 6am. It's also notorious for interesting characters.

For a more upscale bar experience check out **Rum Fire** (2255 Kalakaua Ave., 808/922-4422, www.rumfirewaikiki.com, 11am-12:30am Fri.-Sat., 11am-midnight Sun.-Thurs.) in the Sheraton Waikiki. Set by the infinity pool, the food is globally influenced to complement the cocktails.

Next door at the Royal Hawaiian is the **Mai Tai Bar** (2259 Kalakaua Ave., 866/716-8109, www.royal-hawaiian.com/dining/maitaibar, 10am-midnight daily). Right on the beach, the views are exquisite, and there are a couple of cabanas to lounge under. The food and drink are on the expensive side.

The **Irish Rose Saloon** (478 Ena Rd., 808/947-3414, www.irishrosesaloon.com, 6am-2am daily) is a great Irish pub with live and loud rock and roll and a great selection of Irish whiskey, of course. Smoking is still allowed in the Irish Rose, which you'll either love or hate. **Nashville Waikiki** (2330 Kuhio Ave., 808/926-7911, www.nashvillewaikiki.com, 4pm-4am daily) is Waikiki's only country-and-western bar, complete with line dancing. Open till early morning, a military favorite, and located along the more seedy part of Kuhio Avenue, it is notorious for fights and skirmishes.

Arnold's Beach Bar & Grill (339 Saratoga Rd., 808/924-6887, 10am-2am daily) is a kitschy throwback to the 1950s. It's warm and cozy, the service is friendly, and the drinks are priced just right.

One of the only true nightclubs in Waikiki, **Addiction Nightclub** (1775 Ala Moana Blvd., 808/943-5800, http://addictionnightclub. com, 10:30pm-3am Thurs.-Sat.) is in the chic Modern Honolulu hotel. DJs, dancing, bottle service—check the website for who's spinning while you're in town.

On the second floor of the Waikiki Grand hotel, **Hula's Bar & Lei Stand** (134 Kapahulu Ave., 808/923-0669, www.hulas.com, 10am-2am daily) is Waikiki's premier gay and lesbian bar. Famous for its open-air lanai and beautiful views from the rail, they have DJs and dancing, daily drink specials, and a limited menu of entrées and appetizers. Check their website for a complete monthly events calendar.

LU'AU AND REVUES

There are two traditional lu'au in Waikiki. The Hilton Hawaiian Village's (2005 Kalia Rd., 808/949-4321, www.hiltonhawaiianvillage.com) **Waikiki Starlight Luau** is an outdoor lu'au featuring traditional Hawaiian, Tahitian, and Samoan live music and dance, as well as traditional lu'au fare with accompanying dishes for the less adventurous like huli huli chicken and Hawaiian fried rice. Held Sunday through Thursday (weather permitting) on the rooftop of the Mid-Pacific Conference Center, the two-hour show begins at 5:30pm with general seating for $102 adult, $51 children 4-11, and premier seating for $125 adult, $62.50 children 4-11. Children under 3 are free. The premier seating includes a fresh orchid lei greeting, preferred table seating closest to the stage, and first dibs at the buffet. All prices include two complimentary beverages. The Sheraton Princess Kaiulani (120 Kaiulani Ave., 808/922-5811,

www.princess-kaiulani.com) hosts **Creation: A Polynesian Journey** a lavish and dramatic lu'au and show featuring Hawaiian legend, Samoan and New Zealand dance, and modern hula. Creation shows five nights a week (closed Monday and Wednesday) starting at $110 adult, $82.50 for children 5-12, for the basic dinner show package. There is also a deluxe dinner show package for a higher rate, as well as a cocktail show package for $65 adult and $48.75 children 5-12.

The Royal Hawaiian (2259 Kalakaua Ave., 808/923-7311, www.royal-hawaiian.com) has a plated lu'au dinner and show held on the Ocean Lawn called **'Aha'aina,** a cultural journey through time. The special dinner is served Monday evenings 5:30pm-9pm for $175 adult, $97 for children 5-12. There is a nominal charge for children under 5 years.

If you're in the mood for an evening revue with cocktails, check out **Society of Seven** (2335 Kalakaua Ave., 808/923-7469, www.societyofseven.com) on the second floor of the Outrigger Waikiki on the Beach. The show presents Broadway hits, pop music favorites with artists in full costume, and also skits and original pieces as well. The show runs Tuesday

STREET PERFORMERS

Once the sun sets over Waikiki, the streets teem with people shopping, walking to dinner (or just waiting for a table), and strolling the main drag, simply enjoying the warm tropical night. Taking advantage of this makeshift nightly audience, Waikiki's street performers line the mountain side of the 2300 block of Kalakaua Avenue, wrapping around Kaiulani Avenue and up to King's Village. Break-dancers, spray paint artists, portrait artists, musicians, and gold- and silver-painted mimes entertain for a drop in the hat. Some of the acts draw quite a crowd, so if you're on the move and don't want to get caught up in the melee, it's best to walk on the other side of the street.

through Saturday with two seatings: a show and dinner option at Hula Grill starting at 5:30pm or simply the show and cocktails at 7:30pm.

LIVE MUSIC AND CONCERT VENUES

The Waikiki Shell (2805 Monsarrat Ave., www.blaisdellcenter.com/venues/waikikishell.html) in Kapi'olani Park is Waikiki's premier concert venue and draws all sorts of performers and musicians. The outdoor, shell-shaped amphitheater has an acoustically sophisticated stage to help amplify music and sound, which reaches all the way to the Pacific Ocean with remarkable clarity. With seating and an expansive lawn area, the Shell is the perfect venue for twilight concerts. There is a free parking lot at the Shell and ample free and paid parking around the park. The Waikiki Shell events schedule is posted online.

A good portion of the restaurants and bars in Waikiki, especially the ocean-front establishments, have live music during *pau hana* and at night, usually a solo guitarist and singer or duo playing a mix of island-style classic rock peppered with a few island lounge classics. By far, the most popular free concert in Waikiki is **Duke's on Sunday.** From 4pm-6pm every Sunday at Duke's Waikiki (2335 Kalakaua Ave., 808/922-2268, www.dukeswaikiki.com) in the Outrigger Waikiki hotel, Hawaiian rock legend Henry Kapono plays a lively 2-hour rock-and-roll set of his own hits and classic rock covers done in his own style. Known as the "Wild Hawaiian," he draws residents and visitors alike to Duke's lower lanai, right on the sand, to catch the show, dance, and enjoy a few beverages in the afternoon sun. Kapono plays every Sunday unless he's on tour, in which case

there are several other noteworthy bands in the lineup that put on a great show.

FESTIVALS AND EVENTS

There is no shortage of cultural events, festivals, and parades throughout the year that close down Kalakaua Avenue to vehicular traffic and bring out the live music and food vendors to invoke a celebratory atmosphere.

Spring

The **Waikiki Spam Jam** (www.spamjamhawaii.com) goes off at the end of April with two stages on Kalakaua Avenue with live music, food vendors, and a party till 10pm celebrating local Hawaiian culture. On May 1 **Lei Day** is celebrated with a colorful parade of flowers.

Summer

June is packed full of festivals: the **Honolulu Pride Parade and Celebration** (http://honoluluprideparade.blogspot.com) is in early June, the **Pan-Pacific Festival** (www.pan-pacificfestival.com) is a three-day event celebrating Pacific Rim culture with performances, food, events, and a parade, and the **Kamehameha Day Floral Parade** should not be missed if you're in Waikiki on June 11. In late July, the **Ukulele Festival** (www.ukulelefestivalhawaii.org) is a local favorite, when local and international ukulele talents entertain at the Kapi'olani Bandstand. **Duke's Oceanfest** (http://dukesoceanfest.com) is a weeklong series of ocean events in late August celebrating ocean sports and the legacy of Duke Kahanamoku. Competitions in longboarding, paddle boarding, swimming, tandem surfing, surf polo, beach volleyball, and other events go down from sunrise to sunset along Kuhio Beach Park.

Food

COFFEE

Honolulu Coffee Company (2365 Kalakaua Ave., 808/533-1500, ext. 4, www.honolulucoffee.com, 6am-10pm daily) can be found at the Moana Surfrider, but right on the sidewalk of Kalakaua Avenue, so you don't need to enter the hotel to find it. They have a wide variety of bagels, breads, and pastries and several tables, even sidewalk window seats.

Upstairs in the Royal Hawaiian Shopping Center, on the second floor, you'll find **Island Vintage Coffee** (2201 Kalakaua Ave., 808/922-2299, www.islandvintagecoffee.com, 6am-11pm daily), serving 100 percent Kona coffee, prepared foods, bakery treats, and àìaì bowls. They also have a nice lanai where you can enjoy your coffee and snack.

© KEVIN WHITTON

Located in the International Marketplace, Hank's Haute Dogs are more a meal than a snack.

QUICK BITES AND CAFÉS

Giovanni's Pastrami (227 Lewers St., 808/923-2100, www.giovannipastrami.com, 10am-10pm daily, $9-23) is a great New York-style deli and sports bar. With choice ingredients to nosh, 17 TVs, breakfast served till midnight, and a weekday happy hour 3pm-6pm, it's a great place to watch the game and have a sandwich and beer in style.

At **Ono Cheesesteak** (2280 Kuhio Ave., 808/923-8080, www.onocheesesteak.com, open 24 hours daily, $4-10) you know what you're getting—a Philly cheesesteak. They have chicken, beef, and vegetarian sandwiches with steak fries, curly fries, or onion rings anytime you can handle.

A toasted hole in the bun, tropical relishes, and one-of-a-kind garlic lemon sauces on a polish sausage make **Hula Dog** (2301 Kuhio Ave., 808/924-7887, www.huladoghawaii.com, 8am-midnight daily, $7) a snack, or meal, to experience. Doubling as a sports bar, during football season they open at 6am.

Mac 24/7 (2500 Kuhio Ave., 808/921-5564, www.mac247waikiki.com, open 24 hours daily, $14-28) serves so many different purposes in Waikiki. It's a bar, it's a club, it's a restaurant, and it's a breakfast joint. Find it inside the Hilton Waikiki Beach Hotel and see if you're up to the pancake challenge—eat three, 14-inch pancakes topped with a slew of fixings in under 90 minutes for free breakfast, prizes, and bragging rights.

◖ **Hank's Haute Dogs** (2330 Kalakaua Ave., 808/924-9933, www.hankshautedogs.com, 10am-4pm Mon.-Fri., 11am-5pm Sat.-Sun., $5-8) is a boutique hot dog joint that turns tube steak into a gourmet feast. Built upon the traditions of the Chicago hot dog, Hank's has placed their own spin on their dogs via toppings and sauces. They also feature special sausages made in-house. If you like hot dogs, try the Fat Boy.

What's the perfect meal in Waikiki? How

© KEVIN WHITTON

Be prepared to wait in line for a stack of pancakes from Eggs 'n Things.

about an afternoon surf at Publics and then dinner at **Queen's Surf Café & Lanai** (2701 Kalakaua Ave., 808/924-2233, 7am-7pm Mon.-Wed., 7am-9pm Thurs.-Sat., 7am-8pm Sun., $9-15) overlooking Queen's Surf Beach and the beautiful waves that peel along the reef. Open-air seating right on the beach and good food—what could be better? Live music Thursday through Sunday and beach barbecue Friday and Saturday starting at 5:30pm— that's what.

Bogart's Café (3045 Monsarrat Ave., 808/739-0999, 6am-6:30pm Mon.-Fri., 6am-6pm Sat.-Sun., $6-21) is a great little breakfast spot for escaping the bustle of Waikiki proper. The eggs, bagels, pancakes, waffles, and coffee are the perfect breakfast options after a walk or run across Kapi'olani Park.

From homemade cakes, salads, and dips to cold sandwiches, local food, and burgers right off the grill, **Diamond Head Market & Grill** (3575 Campbell Ave., 808/732-0077, www.diamondheadmarket.com, 6:30am-9pm daily, $5-17) has a little bit of everything on offer.

The grill has a walk-up window on the exterior of the building. Be prepared for a bit of a wait at lunch, as the food is popular with locals and visitors alike. And check out all the bakery delights inside. The scones are beyond delicious, if there are any left.

BREAKFAST

Eggs 'n Things (343 Saratoga Rd., 808/923-3447, www.eggsnthings.com, 6am-2pm, 5pm-10pm daily, $8-17) is an extremely popular breakfast joint serving American-style breakfast with a few local style variations. Meat, eggs, pancakes, waffles, and even crepes are the crux of the menu. They serve dinner as well. There is also a location on Kalakaua Avenue, called the **Waikiki Beach Eggspress** (2464 Kalakaua Ave., 808/926-3447, 6am-2pm, 5pm-10pm daily, $8-17), which has an interesting seating method. First you'll have to wait in line to order, then you wait in line to get seated, and then sometimes you'll have to wait a little longer for your food to arrive. With an average wait of 30-40 minutes from the moment it opens, it's apparent Eggs 'n Things has developed quite a following.

STEAK AND SEAFOOD

The **Hau Tree Lanai** (2863 Kalakaua Ave., 808/921-7066, http://kaimana.com/hautreelanai.htm, 7am-2pm, 5:30pm-9pm daily, $30-52) is a quaint open-air restaurant right on Sans Souci Beach, nestled under the canopy of a distinctive hau tree growing on the property for more than a century. In fact, American author Robert Louis Stevenson enjoyed its shade in the early 1900s as a place where he could relax and put pen to paper. Serving breakfast, lunch, and dinner, they offer traditional American and Asian-influenced cuisine.

Azure (2259 Kalakaua Ave., 808/923-7311, www.azurewaikiki.com, 5:30pm-9pm daily, $26-52) is the pinnacle of fine seafood dining. Set inside the Royal Hawaiian, it serves the freshest seafood there is, hand selected from the Honolulu fish auction every morning. The focus is on high-heat aromatic herb-roasted and Hawai'i regional preparations with bright tropical flavors. Sommeliers can assist in selecting the perfect wine for your dinner. Azure has beachfront dining cabanas in addition to the dining room and a traditional six-course degustation menu with samplings of the chef's signature dishes and wine pairings.

Tired of ordering a steak and finding it not done to your liking? Then the **Shore Bird** (2169 Kalia Rd., 808/922-2887, http://shorebirdwaikiki.com, 7am-2am daily, $16-30), a beachfront restaurant in the Outrigger Reef, is your calling. At the Shore Bird's Famous Grill, you can cook your own steak, chicken, or fish. They also serve breakfast and lunch, and have a late night menu with classic bar food.

Roy's (226 Lewers St., 808/923-7697, http://royshawaii.com, 11am-9:30pm Mon.-Thurs., 11am-10pm Fri.-Sun., $15-45) has Hawaiian fusion wired, and the quality of ingredients, consistency, and service are exceptional. They are open for appetizer service 11am-5pm and offer a prix fixe menu with a sampling of all the favorites in additional to a well-balance offering of meat and fish entrées, as well as sushi.

Orchids (2199 Kalia Rd., 808/923-2311, www.halekulani.com/living/dining/orchids, 7:30am-10pm daily, $28-60) is located inside the Halekulani hotel. As the name suggests, colorful orchids abound, and the restaurant opens out to a breathtaking view of the Pacific Ocean unencumbered by beach umbrellas or sunbathers. Their Sunday brunch is punctuated by a three-meat carving station, something you won't find at most Waikiki breakfast buffets, and their signature dinner entrée is a light onaga (snapper) Orchids-style, with sesame oil, shoyu, and ginger. They also offer a lunch menu.

◗ **Kai Market** (2255 Kalakaua Ave., 808/921-4600, www.sheraton-waikiki.com/dining/kai, 6am-11am, 5:30pm-9:30pm daily, breakfast $22-29, dinner $55-58) prides itself on locally sourcing all their products and ingredients, from the baked-goods to their meat and produce. Kai Market is inside the Sheraton Waikiki, and both breakfast and dinner are buffet style. Kids 5 and under eat free anytime, and children 6-12 eat for half price.

Top of Waikiki (2270 Kalakaua Ave., 808/923-3877, http://topofwaikiki.com, 5pm-9:30pm daily, starting at $37) is truly a unique dining experience. On the top floor of the Waikiki Business Plaza, the three-tiered round restaurant slowly revolves 360 degrees per hour, offering guests a complete view of O'ahu's glowing South Shore. An open sit-down bar provides an additional level for viewing the sights. Great Pacific Rim cuisine and nightly happy hour specials—5pm-7pm and 9pm-11pm—complete the experience.

◗ **Duke's Waikiki** (2335 Kalakaua Ave., 808/922-2268, www.dukeswaikiki.com, 7am-12:30am daily, $15-33) is a must, whether its for the breakfast buffet, lunch, dinner, or just cruising in the Barefoot Bar and watching the surfers out at Canoes and Queen's. Decorated with historic and recent pictures of the Waikiki beachboys and surf nostalgia, the relaxed, beachside atmosphere complements the excellent food and service. They have live music Monday through Thursday in the bar 4pm-6pm, and Friday through Sunday the show moves out to their lower lanai under the sun, the highlight being Duke's on Sunday, featuring Henry Kapono (unless he's on tour). For dinner, make reservation or be prepared to wait up to an hour during busy times, which isn't that bad if you retire to the bar and relax till your table is ready.

Hula Grill (2335 Kalakaua Ave., 808/923-4852, www.hulagrillwaikiki.com, 6:30am-10pm daily, $20-34), in the Outrigger Waikiki and just upstairs from Duke's, is a great steak and seafood option if you don't have the time to wait for a table downstairs. With comfortable, Hawaiiana home decor and live music nightly 7-9pm, they provide a comfortable ambience in which to savor several fish specialties including the popular Macadamia Nut Crusted, as well as the succulent Filet Steak Kiana, their take on the steak Diane. Hula Grill has a great Aloha Hour 4pm-6pm with half-off selected menu and drink items.

Chuck's Cellar (150 Kaiulani Ave., 808/923-4488, www.chuckshawaii.com/cellar.html, 5:30pm-10pm daily, starting at $20) offers an all-you-can-eat salad bar with every entrée, but the real draw for Chuck's Cellar is live jazz Thursday through Sunday. The decor, and a little jazz flute, will take you back in time.

In the Aston Waikiki Beach Hotel on the second floor overlooking Kuhio Beach Park, **Tiki's Grill & Bar** (2570 Kalakaua Ave., 808/923-8454, http://tikisgrill.com, 10:30am-2am daily, $24-29) is a locally owned and operated establishment with tasty lunch and dinner menus serving regional and Pacific Rim cuisine. Their ingredients are locally sourced, and they partner with local farmers for the freshest produce, as well as following a Green Program in all aspects of their business. Catch Hawaiian Hula Nights every Thursday 5pm-11pm featuring traditional and contemporary Hawaiian music, hula, and food and drink specials on their open lanai.

Michel's (2895 Kalakaua Ave., 808/923-6552, http://michelshawaii.com, 5:30pm-9pm Mon.-Thurs. and Sun., 5:30pm-10pm Fri.-Sat., $40-75) is the pinnacle of French haute cuisine in Waikiki and has been recognized as the "Best Restaurant for Romance" since 1985. Overlooking a beautiful stretch of reef and ocean closer to Diamond Head and away from the Waikiki crowds, their stunning setting, live music, and delectable menu are worth the price for a truly special occasion. They also offer a chef's choice six-course tasting menu.

MEXICAN

Cha Cha Cha (342 Seaside Ave., 808/923-7797, 11am-midnight Mon., Wed.-Sun., 11am-2am Tues., $10-16) is a great change of pace for your palate. A cross between Mexican and Caribbean, with jerk side by side on the menu with nachos and fish tacos, they also have a few great homemade salsas to accompany their meals. Doubling as a tequileria, try 'em all and get your name on the wall.

ITALIAN

Perched at the top of the Ilikai hotel, **Sarento's** (1777 Ala Moana Blvd., 808/955-5559, www.sarentoswaikiki.com, 5pm-10:30pm Sun.-Thurs., 5pm-midnight Fri.-Sat., $24-42) has magnificent views of Waikiki and Honolulu's skyline. Fine Italian dining with a Mediterranean flair is accompanied with live piano music and great service.

Taormina (227 Lewers St., 808/926-5050, http://taorminarestaurant.com, 11am-10pm Sun.-Thurs., 11am-11pm Fri.-Sat., $17-49) serves Sicilian cuisine in a fine dining setting. With fresh fish and homemade breads and pastas for their specials, they offer over 125 wines for the perfect pairing. A favorite is the Fresh Pasta Nero "Frutti Di Mare."

JAPANESE

No detail has been left unexplored at **Nobu** (2233 Helumoa Rd., 808/237-6999, www.no-burestaurants.com, 5:30pm-10pm Mon.-Thurs. and Sun., 5:30pm-10:30pm Fri.-Sat., $3-48), where the architecture and interior help create an intimate and elegant setting, and the innovative and award-winning "New Style" Japanese cuisine is unmatched. A sophisticated seafood-centric menu covers a range of hot and cold dishes, sushi and sashimi, complete dinners, and kushiyaki and tempura. Their happy hour (5pm-7pm Sun.-Thurs.) has drink and food specials that could suffice for a meal by themselves, though it's only available in the bar and lounge area.

Serving contemporary, inventive sushi and Asian-influenced dishes, **◖ Sansei Seafood Restaurant and Sushi Bar** (2552 Kalakaua Ave., 808/931-6286, www.sanseihawaii.com, 5:30pm-10pm Mon.-Thurs. and Sun., 5:30pm-1am Fri.-Sat., starting at $8) is one of the most popular sushi restaurants in Waikiki. With its handful of award-winning sushi creations, the à la carte menu is perfect for sampling the gamut. They have a popular early bird special 5:30pm-6pm Sunday and Monday with half-off most of the menu (people line up early at the door) and half-off drink specials 10pm-1am Friday and Saturday.

Odoriko (2400 Koa Ave., 808/923-7368, http://odorikohawaii.com, 6am-midnight daily, $4-50) serves up traditional Japanese cuisine for breakfast, lunch, and dinner, as well as offering an assortment of fresh seafood and sushi—even live Maine lobster. If you're not feeling like fish, they also have hot pot entrées like shabu-shabu or sukiyaki. Odoriko has private party and karaoke rooms for rent by the hour starting at $30.

Tanaka of Tokyo (131 Kaiulani Ave., 808/922-4233, www.tanakaoftokyo.com, 5:30pm-11pm daily, $19-95) is a Japanese seafood and steak house teppanyaki restaurant where the food is prepared by master chefs on tabletop grills. It's a fun and relaxed atmosphere with excellent food and service. The Shogun Special, with tenderloin, lobster tail and sea scallops is a house favorite. Find them on the third floor of King's Village.

Doraku Sushi (2233 Kalakaua Ave., 808/922-3323, http://dorakusushi.com, 11:30am-11pm Mon.-Thurs., 11:30am-2am Fri.-Sat., 11:30-midnight Sun., $4-44) features izakaya dining, where dishes are brought

to the table throughout the meal to share. On the menu you'll find hot and cold dishes as well as a beautiful assortment of specialty sushi rolls, sashimi, and soups and salads. A relaxing and enjoyable experience.

CHINESE

For fine Chinese seafood dining check out **Beijing Chinese Seafood Restaurant** (2301 Kalakaua Ave., 808/971-8833, www.beijing-hawaii.com, 11:30am-2:30pm, 5pm-9:30pm daily, $35-92). Specializing in set dinner menus with a variety of delectable seafood creations paired with entrées including duck, chicken, and beef, this place won't let you leave hungry. Their lunch menu features a range of steamed dumplings.

THAI

Keo's Thai Cuisine (2028 Kuhio Ave., 808/951-9355, www.keosthaicuisine.com, 7am-10pm daily, $13-20) is an internationally known and award-winning restaurant that has great prices for the quality of the food, the chic atmosphere, and a colorful tropical garden interior. The owner sources many of his ingredients from his two North Shore farms.

Keoni by Keo's (2375 Kuhio Ave., 808/922-9888, www.keonibykeos.com, 4pm-10:30pm daily, $11-18) is Keo's sister restaurant and has Thai and Western cuisine on the menu.

Siam Square (408 Lewers, 808/923-5320, www.siamsquaredining.com, 11am-10:30pm daily, $10-15) is a great little Thai place located upstairs from the ABC Store on the corner—look for the small sign. It's clean and comfortable with good food, as well.

KOREAN

Mikawon (2345 Kuhio Ave., 808/924-3277, 10am-10pm daily, $11-28) is a little hard to find, which makes it all the better. At the very back of the International Marketplace, and actually part of the Miramar hotel (there is an entrance from both sides), the tiny restaurant has family-style seating and yakiniku grills at the tables. The menu is very diverse with a host of delicious entrées.

HEALTH FOOD

◖ Diamond Head Cove Health Bar (3045 Monsarrat Ave., 808/732-8744, www.diamond-headcove.com, 10am-8pm Mon. and Fri-Sat., 10am-11pm Tues.-Thurs., and Sun., $5-13) is a small juice and kava bar that also serves fresh omelets, hummus, salads, and is famous for their hearty and healthy aìai bowls. The staff is friendly, the food is fresh and delicious, and surf art, posters, and decorations fill every space on the walls and ceiling, creating a cool hangout to beat the midday heat. The Cove, as it's known by local patrons, stays open late for Kava Nights, Tuesday through Thursday, when they turn the lights low and let the live musicians set the mood.

One of the few places in Waikiki that caters to vegetarians and vegans, **Ruffage Natural Foods** (2443 Kuhio Ave., 808/922-2042, 9am-6pm daily, $5-10) has simple but great sandwiches, salads, burritos, and other prepared foods (they do have meat options, too). They also sell health foods as well as blend great smoothies.

MARKETS

Food Pantry (2370 Kuhio Ave., 808/923-9831, 9am-5pm Mon.-Fri.) is the closest thing to a proper grocery store in Waikiki. It's also notorious for being ridiculously expensive, which can also be called the price of convenience.

Information and Services

MAIL

While most of the hotels offer outgoing mail service, Waikiki has a **post office** (330 Saratoga Rd., 808/973-7517, 9am-4:30pm Mon.-Fri., 9am-1pm Sat.). There is an Automated Postal Center for after-hours business or if you want to avoid the line.

MEDICAL

Should you be in need of medical service, there are several options for care: **Straub Doctors on Call** (808/971-6000 or 808/923-9966 for Japanese-speaking doctors) for emergencies and "house calls" to your hotel, 24 hours a day; **Kuhio Walk-in Medical Clinic** (2310 Kuhio Ave., Ste. 223, 808/924-6688, 9am-4pm Mon.-Fri., 9am-1pm Sat.) at the corner of Nahua in Waikiki; **Urgent Care Clinic of Waikiki** (2155 Kalakaua Ave., Ste. 308, 808/924-3399, www.waikikiclinic.org, 8:30am-7pm daily) in the ANA Kalakaua Building, with lab and x-ray capabilities; **The Medical Corner** (1860 Ala Moana Blvd., #101, 808/943-1111, www.themedicalcorner.com, 8am-4:30pm Mon.-Fri., 9am-noon Sat.) for minor emergencies; and **Waikiki Health Center** (277 Ohua Ave., 808/922-4787, www.waikikihc.org, 8:30am-7pm Mon. and Wed., 8:30am-6:30pm Tues., Thurs.-Fri., 8:30am-12:30pm Sat.), for low-cost care. **Kuhio Pharmacy** is the only full-service pharmacy in Waikiki, with two locations: one on Kuhio Avenue (2330 Kuhio Ave., 808/923-4466, 9am-5pm Mon.-Fri. for prescriptions), attached to the Ohana Waikiki West Hotel on the ground level, and the other on Kalakaua Avenue (1922 Kalakaua Ave., 808/942-1922, 9am-5pm Mon.-Fri. for prescriptions).

LIBRARY

Internet access is available at the **Waikiki-Kapahulu Public Library** (400 Kapahulu Ave., 808/733-8488, http://hawaii.sdp.sirsi.net/custom/web, 10am-5pm Tues., Wed., Fri., Sat., noon-7pm Thurs.) on the outskirts of Waikiki on the corner of Kapahulu Avenue and Ala Wai Boulevard. Visitors need a valid HSPLS library card to use an Internet computer. Three-month visitor cards are available for $10. You can reserve Internet computer time online or in person. You can also find printed bus schedules and browse titles online for availability. Closed Monday and Tuesday.

GAS

There is one gas station in Waikiki proper, **Aloha Island Mart** (2025 Kalakaua Ave., 808/942-0075). The convenience store and the pumps are open 24 hours a day. You can also fill up near the Diamond Head businesses at the **Aloha Island Mart** (3203 Monsarrat Ave., 808/735-5333).

Getting There and Around

BY CAR

If you didn't pick up a rental car at the airport and find you would like to make use of a vehicle during your stay, there are national big-brand companies in Waikiki as well as several smaller independent firms that rent vehicles including sedans, four-wheel drives, SUVs, and convertibles. **Thrifty** (2002 Kalakaua Ave., 808/971-2660, www.thrifty.com, 7am-8pm daily) and **Dollar** (2002 Kalakaua Ave., 808/952-4264, www.dollar.com, 7am-8pm daily) share a lot at the west end of Waikiki. Among the independent companies are **VIP (Very Inexpensive Prices) Car Rentals** (234 Beach Walk, 808/922-4605, www.vipcarrentalhawaii.com, 7am-5pm daily) and **Paradise Rent-A-Car** (1837 Ala Moana Blvd., 808/946-7777; 151 Uluniu Ave., 808/926-7777; http://paradiserentacarhawaii.com, 8am-5pm daily).

The most distinctive cars in Waikiki are the sports cars and luxury imports available from **Hawaii Luxury Car Rentals** (2025 Kalakaua Ave., 808/222-2277, www.hiluxurycarrentals.com, 8am-5pm daily). This company has a fleet of American and European classic cars, like the Viper, Corvette, Porsche, Cadillac Escalade, H2 Hummer, BMW, and the only Prowler for rent in Hawai'i, all at the Aloha Gas Station. Rates start at $250 per day for the Prowler. They offer multiple day discounts and welcome customers 21 and over.

BY BUS

Many popular island destinations and attractions are reachable via the Honolulu public bus system, called **TheBus** (www.thebus.org), either directly from Waikiki or from the Ala Moana Shopping Center bus depot after a short ride from Waikiki. Routes 19 and 20 will get travelers to the airport in Honolulu; Diamond Head can be reached via buses running on Routes 22, 23, and 24.

BY TAXI AND LIMOUSINE

There are several taxicab companies that service Waikiki. **Star Discount Taxi Service** (808/942-7827, www.startaxihawaii.com) offers a $30-or-less flat rate to or from the Honolulu International Airport from any Waikiki hotel and has discount flat-rate fares for a variety of O'ahu destinations; **TheCAB** (808/422-2222, www.thecabhawaii.com) operates 24 hours a day, 365 days a year; **Honolulu Taxi Service** (808/699-9999, http://honolulu-taxi.com) has door-to-door service; and for **Honolulu Taxi Cab** (808/741-7545), call one hour ahead for best service.

Limos are a great way to get around in style and are popular for wedding parties and transfer to and from the airport. **Duke's Limousine** (808/738-1878, www.dukeslimo.com) has a fleet of limos with varying carrying capacity and rates starting at $60 per hour with a two-hour minimum. **Hawaii Limo** (808/294-1124, http://hawaiilimo.org) has rates that start at $75 per hour for six passengers, flat rates for airport service, and offers a five-hour circle island tour for $300. **Platinum Limousine Hawaii** (808/739-0007, www.platinumlimousinehawaii.com) operates 24 hours a day, seven days a week, and with award-winning service and high-end, showy luxurious vehicles, they've built quite a star-studded clientele. Rates start at $85 per hour for the eight-passenger Lincoln Towncar limo with a two-hour minimum, or a three-hour minimum on Sunday.

BY MOTORCYCLE AND MOPED

For rentals, try **Big Kahuna Motorcycle Tours and Rentals** (407 Seaside Ave., 808/924-2736 or 888/451-5544, www.bigkahunarentals.com, 8am-5pm daily), where rentals run $50-180 for four hours, with full-day and weekly rentals available. **Cruzin Hawaii** (1980 Kalakaua Ave., 808/945-9595 or 877/945-9595, www.cruzinhawaii.com, 8am-6pm daily) rents Harley-Davidsons at its shop near the Ambassador Hotel, $79-99 for three hours, $99-149 all day, with 24-hour, three-day, and weekly rates available. **Paradise Rent-A-Car** (1837 Ala Moana Blvd., 808/946-7777; 151 Uluniu Ave., 808/926-7777; http://paradiserentacarhawaii.com, 8am-5pm daily) also rents Harleys. And **Chase Hawaii Rentals** (355 Royal Hawaiian Ave., 808/942-4273, www.chasehawaiirentals.com; 138 Uluniu Ave., 808/348-6070; 8am-6pm daily) has over 30 models of Harley-Davidsons for rent, as well as sport bikes and cruisers.

Mopeds and motor scooters are common across the island and a great way to get around, but accident statistics prove they are quite dangerous. Even though there is no helmet law in Hawai'i, motorcycle and moped riders should always wear one. **Big Kahuna Motorcycle Tours and Rentals** (407 Seaside Ave., 808/924-2736 or 888/451-5544, www.bigkahunarentals.com, 8am-5pm daily) rents mopeds starting at $25 for four hours and larger scooters starting at $65 for four hours, with full-day and weekly rentals available. **Chase Hawaii Rentals** (355 Royal Hawaiian Ave., 808/942-4273; 138 Uluniu Ave., 808/348-6070; www.chasehawaiirentals.com, 8am-6pm daily) rents Vespas starting at $79 for 10 hours and $99 for 24 hours. **Paradise Cruisers** (2413 Kuhio Ave., 808/926-2847, http://paradisecruisershawaii.com, 8am-8pm daily) rents mopeds and scoot cars, and you can also find mopeds and scooters at **Adventure on 2 Wheels** (1946 Ala Moana Ave., 808/944-3131, 8am-4pm daily; 2552 Lemon Rd., 808/921-8111, 8am-5pm daily).

HONOLULU

The capital of the Hawaiian Islands since 1845, Honolulu means "sheltered bay" in the Hawaiian language. Honolulu is the political, cultural, and economic center of Oʻahu and the state of Hawaiʻi, thanks largely to Honolulu Harbor's commercial port and the Honolulu International Airport. Its over 400 high-rises create a skyline in stark contrast to the verdant backdrop of forested ridges and valleys. Honolulu combines the hustle, convenience, and abundance of a major city and an ethnically diverse population of 350,000 people with a history made unique by its architecture and thriving neighborhoods.

Just east of Pearl Harbor, Honolulu is defined by its city center, the economic heart of the county and state. Containing the Hawaii state capitol building that neighbors ʻIolani Palace, the only royal residence in the United States, the historic district is beset by towering skyscrapers. It gives way to Chinatown, a relic of Oʻahu's whaling, migrant worker, and war-torn past. Today, Chinatown is chock-full of art galleries, nightclubs, bars, and some of Oʻahu's best restaurants.

Honolulu's neighborhoods spread out in all directions and are as dynamic as the rainbows that hang over the mountains. Manoa Valley is home to the University of Hawaiʻi and Lyon Arboretum at the back of the valley. Kaimuki is known for its shopping and restaurants. Kakaʻako's industrial spaces have become the bastion for a burgeoning urban art scene, and Ala Moana Beach Park affords expansive grassy space, great waves, and a calm swimming area on the inside of the reef.

© KEVIN WHITTON

HONOLULU

HIGHLIGHTS

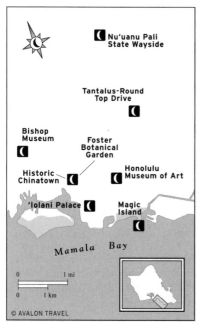

LOOK FOR **(** TO FIND RECOMMENDED SIGHTS, ACTIVITIES, DINING, AND LODGING.

(**Magic Island:** This manicured park is shaded with beautiful trees, and jogging paths wind beneath the branches. There's a protected beach and lagoon where *keiki* can safely play. Beautiful views along the coast make it perfect for a seaside picnic (page 73).

(**'Iolani Palace:** The only royal residence in the United States, this grand and stately pal-

ace sits on 11 grassy acres with beautiful shade trees (page 83).

(**Historic Chinatown:** Chinatown is a hub for international dining, art, nightlife—and for Chinese food and goods, of course (page 87).

(**Honolulu Museum of Art:** Hawai'i's most prestigious art museum, with over 50,000 pieces spanning 5,000 years, was established in 1927. The museum's holdings include Asian, European, American, and African works of art (page 88).

(**Foster Botanical Garden:** Century-old trees, palms, orchids, and cycads, curious leafy plants that date back to prehistoric times, can all be found in this majestic spot (page 88).

(**Nu'uanu Pali State Wayside:** Partake in the grandeur of the Ko'olau Mountains and the tropical beauty of Kane'ohe Bay. The lookout is at the summit of the historic route from Honolulu to the windward side; it's a beautiful spot to get a close-up view of the vertical cliffs of the Pali (page 89).

(**Tantalus-Round Top Drive:** This leisurely, scenic drive winds up the Tantalus Crater to beautiful Pu'u 'Ualaka'a Park at the top of the cone. The view scans Diamond Head, Punchbowl Crater, and greater Honolulu (page 90).

(**Bishop Museum:** The premier cultural and natural history museum in the Pacific, this venue explores Hawaiian culture and history, the peoples of other Polynesian and Pacific cultures, and the natural history of the islands. It also features a planetarium and interactive Science Adventure Center (page 92).

PLANNING YOUR TIME

Many of the activities in Honolulu, whether sightseeing in the Historic District or hiking in the Ko'olau Mountains, require at least a half day's time. Mix in a meal or two and you have a packed day.

When heading downtown to see the Historic

District, leave early to beat the hot midday sun, since the best option is walking to the different buildings and museums. Downtown metered street parking has a two-hour time limit, so when its time to get back to the car, head over to Chinatown, park in one of the municipal lots, and explore the small, historic city blocks. Plan on saving your appetite for eating in Chinatown, as the diversity of cuisine here will make your head spin.

For an art day, start out at the Honolulu Museum of Art. With your paid admission you'll also get entry at the Honolulu Museum of Art Spalding House in Makiki Heights, featuring contemporary art and a botanical garden. Stop by the Hawai'i State Art Museum, which is free to the public, to check out the finest work from top local artists, then hop over to Chinatown for a walking tour of art galleries and dinner on Bethel Street and Nuuanu Avenue.

After a day in the city center, you might enjoy a little peace and quiet. To attain such solace in nature, go for a hike in Manoa Valley or at Wa'ahila Ridge State Park, then grab a bite to eat at one of the casual BYOBs in Kaimuki. If you need to expand your horizons, take the windy drive up Tantalus or Round Top Drives to Pu'u 'Ualaka'a Park and relax with views of Honolulu and Diamond Head. If you feel like walking, there are several trailheads in the vicinity.

Honolulu might be urban, but it still has beaches. Spend the morning swimming, surfing, or stand-up paddling at Ala Moana Beach Park, then head across the street to Ala Moana Center for shopping and dining.

ORIENTATION
Downtown
Downtown is the epicenter of Honolulu, and the financial and political center of the island and the state. Within downtown are the Historic District, comprised of the state capitol, 'Iolani Palace, government buildings and offices, as well as other historical and cultural buildings. To the immediate west of the historic district is the financial district, where high-rise office buildings perch along one-way streets.

Chinatown
Just west of the financial district is the historic Chinatown neighborhood, which stretches from Vineyard Boulevard to the north, to Aloha Tower along the harbor, with the Nu'uanu Stream as its western border. Chinatown is home to a curious mix of bars, hip ethnic restaurants, Chinese and Pacific Rim cuisine, Chinese grocery stores, small local eateries, art galleries, and chic coffee shops.

Kaka'ako
At the forefront of the urban art scene, much of Kaka'ako is industrial, especially the streets southeast of downtown. Young artists have transformed the area into an explosion of color and art, and drab building walls are now radiant and expressive. In addition to colorful building exteriors, art galleries, coffee shops, and restaurants, Kaka'ako also has a green waterfront park. Kaka'ako stretches toward the mountains all the way to the H-1 freeway.

Ala Moana
Dominated by Ala Moana Beach Park, Magic Island, and Ala Moana Center, the Ala Moana neighborhood straddles the gap between Kaka'ako, Waikiki, and the McCully residential neighborhoods to the east. This central area for shopping encompasses several other malls are located to the west, along Ward Avenue.

Greater Honolulu
Honolulu is a sprawling metropolis with many neighborhoods stretching out in all directions from downtown. Some are industrial, others are urban, and some are in the valleys and on the mountains behind the city.

In the mountains directly behind downtown Honolulu, you'll find **Nu'uanu,** defined by residential neighborhoods stretching from the north side of Chinatown and downtown back through Nu'uanu Valley.

To the east of Nu'uanu, on the mountain side of Interstate H-1, is **Punchbowl,** which consists of the old neighborhoods surrounding Punchbowl Crater.

Northeast of Punchbowl is the verdant **Makiki** neighborhood, which snakes up the mountains.

Heading east takes you to the upscale neighborhood of **Manoa,** which stretches from deep

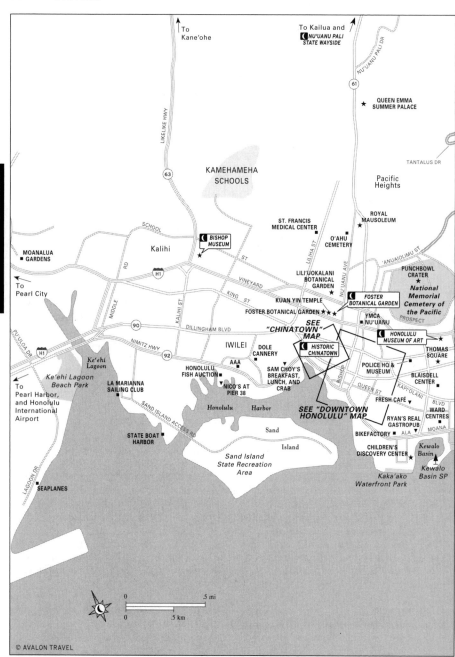

GREATER HONOLULU

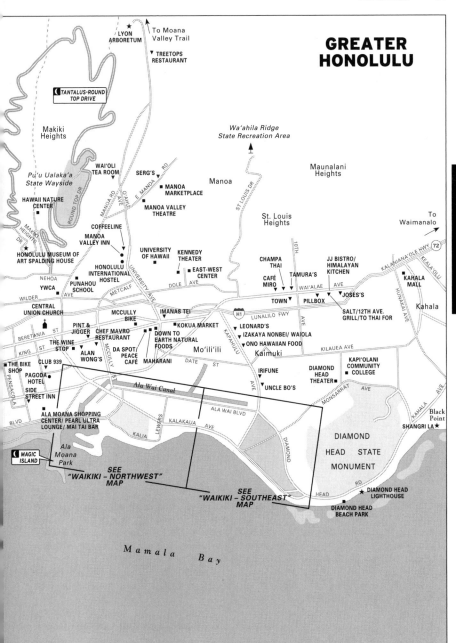

HONOLULU

LYON ARBORETUM

To Moana Valley Trail

TREETOPS RESTAURANT

TANTALUS-ROUND TOP DRIVE

Wa'ahila Ridge State Recreation Area

Makiki Heights

Maunalani Heights

Pu'u Ualaka'a State Wayside

WAI'OLI TEA ROOM

SERG'S

Manoa

HAWAII NATURE CENTER

MANOA MARKETPLACE

MANOA VALLEY THEATRE

St. Louis Heights

To Waimanalo

COFFEELINE

MANOA VALLEY INN

UNIVERSITY OF HAWAII

KENNEDY THEATER

CHAMPA THAI

JJ BISTRO/ HIMALAYAN KITCHEN

KAHALA MALL

HONOLULU MUSEUM OF ART SPALDING HOUSE

HONOLULU INTERNATIONAL HOSTEL

EAST-WEST CENTER

CAFÉ MIRO

TAMURA'S

NEHOA

YWCA

PUNAHOU SCHOOL

DOLE

WAI'ALAE

Kahala

WILDER

CENTRAL UNION CHURCH

TOWN

PILLBOX

JOSES'S

SALT/12TH AVE. GRILL/TO THAI FOR

BERETANIA

MCCULLY BIKE

IMANAS TEI

LUNALILO FWY

PINT & JIGGER

CHEF MAVRO RESTAURANT

KOKUA MARKET

LEONARD'S

THE WINE STOP

KING

DOWN TO EARTH NATURAL FOODS

IZAKAYA NONBEI/ WAIOLA

ONO HAWAIIAN FOOD

KILAUEA AVE.

THE BIKE SHOP

CLUB 939

ALAN WONG'S

DA SPOT/ PEACE CAFÉ

MAHARANI

Mo'ili'ili

Kaimuki

KAPI'OLANI COMMUNITY COLLEGE

PAGODA HOTEL

DATE

IRIFUNE

DIAMOND HEAD THEATER

SIDE STREET INN

Ala Wai Canal

UNCLE BO'S

MONSARRAT

ALA MOANA SHOPPING CENTER/ PEARL ULTRA LOUNGE/ MAI TAI BAR

ALA WAI BLVD

Black Point

SHANGRI LA

BLVD

KALAKAUA AVE

MAGIC ISLAND

Ala Moana Park

KALIA

DIAMOND HEAD STATE MONUMENT

SEE "WAIKIKI – NORTHWEST" MAP

SEE "WAIKIKI – SOUTHEAST" MAP

DIAMOND HEAD LIGHTHOUSE

DIAMOND HEAD BEACH PARK

M a m a l a   B a y

HONOLULU

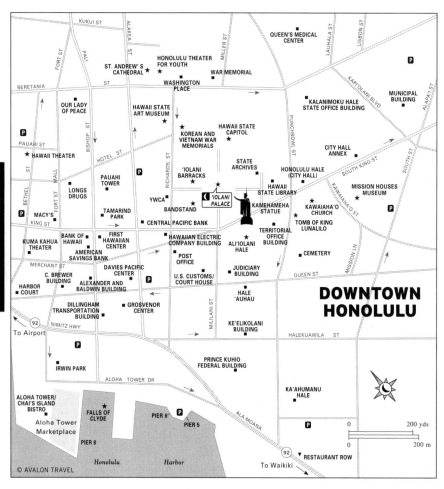

in Manoa Valley to the University of Hawai'i at Manoa.

To the east and south are the old, congested neighborhoods of **Kaimuki,** where you'll find ample shopping and dining on Waialae and Kapahulu Avenues.

Just to the west of Kaimuki is **Mo'ili'ili,** another predominantly residential area with some shops and dining along King and Beretania Streets.

To the west of downtown Honolulu and Nu'uanu lie the local communities of **Kalihi** and Kalihi Valley. There is also a small area to the south of Kalihi called **Iwilei,** known for its seafood restaurants on Pier 38 in Honolulu Harbor.

Sand Island, south of downtown Honolulu across the harbor, is an industrial port with an oceanfront state recreation area.

To the west is the airport, and inland from the airport are the **Salt Lake** and **Moanalua** communities.

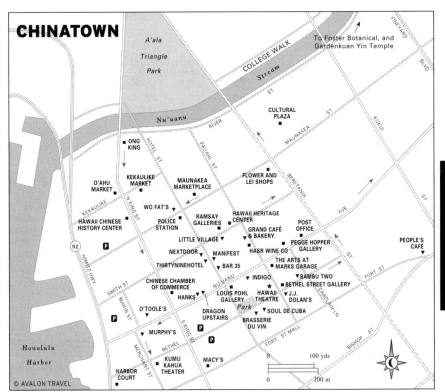

Beaches

Bustling Honolulu Harbor stretches along much of Honolulu's coastline, and only a few beaches fall within its borders. Not to mention, the beach parks in Honolulu are more park than actual sandy beach. The beach parks draw big crowds all summer long when there's surf along the south shore, while the weekends seem to be crowded all year long. The city beaches and parks are also the stomping grounds of many of Honolulu's pervasive homeless population.

ALA MOANA
◖ Magic Island

Magic Island is an artificially constructed peninsula that creates the western flank of the Ala Wai Canal and Small Boat Harbor. This grassy park with shade trees, walking paths, restrooms, and outdoor showers also includes a tranquil *keiki* beach at the end of the point. It's blocked from the waves by towering rock jetties and framed in all around by beach, making it a perfect place for the kids to play and swim safely. The jetties are constructed so that fresh ocean water can flow in and out of the lagoon without creating currents or waves. During the summer months, a wave known as Bomburas breaks beyond the jetty at the end of the point.

There is ample parking, but it does fill up during the summer and on weekends when

YOUR BEST DAY IN HONOLULU

While there are many neighborhoods that comprise Greater Honolulu, most of what appeals to visitors is centrally located in the downtown vicinity. For most visitors based out of Waikiki, plan your Honolulu day around avoiding the daily rush-hour traffic to maximize your time.

- Instead of rushing immediately into the historic district in the morning and getting caught in traffic, head to **Lyon Arboretum** in Manoa Valley and explore the extensive trail system, bird watch, and learn about native Hawaiian plants. If you'd like to be closer to downtown, try **Foster Botanical Garden** just outside of Chinatown.

- Next, visit the historic district and take in the **Hawai'i State Capitol** and **'Iolani Palace,** the only royal residence in the United States.

- For lunch, head to the **Ala Moana Center,** where you can grab lunch in the comfortable, open-air **Mai Tai Bar** on the upper lanai of the mall. Or, head into Kaka'ako, where you can find hip and unique shops and restaurants.

- A visit to the **Honolulu Museum of Art** is a must in the afternoon. If you have your own transportation, take advantage of the free same-day admission to the Spalding House in Makiki Heights, a museum of contemporary art.

- For dinner, head back into Chinatown and peruse the many restaurants and bars. Whether you're after Chinese food from **Little Village Noodle House,** French cuisine at **Brasserie Du Vin,** or pizza from Irish pub **J.J. Dolan's,** Chinatown has you covered.

people turn out en masse with barbecue grills and tents to take advantage of the beautiful weather. To get to Magic Island, turn onto Ala Moana Park Drive from Ala Moana Boulevard where it intersects Atkinson Drive. After you pass the first right bend in the road, the parking lot is on the left, and it's free. The lot and park are closed 10pm-4am daily.

Ala Moana Beach Park

Connected to Magic Island, but on the west side of the peninsula, is **Ala Moana Beach Park.** Ala Moana Beach is a 4,000-foot-long, rather straight strip of sand falling into an artificial channel that runs along the entire beach. Buoys demarcate a swimming lane and one for stand-up paddling. Across the channel is a very shallow reef that stretches way out to the waves washing up on the sharp coral. There are many surf breaks along the outer reef, all the way across the beach park. A rectangular park, with busy Ala Moana Boulevard on one side and the beach on the other, has a tide-fed stream meandering through it with a pond at each end. There are many shade trees, lots of picnic tables and barbecue areas, facilities, a

snack bar, tennis courts, a community center, and lots of parking along Ala Moana Park Drive, which intersects Ala Moana Boulevard at both ends of the park. Parking can get crazy during the summer when the surf is up and on the weekends when the park is packed with families. Be sure you don't use one of the designated lifeguard parking spots. Parking is free, but the park is closed 10pm-4am daily.

SAND ISLAND
Sand Island State Recreation Area

Wedged between the Honolulu International Airport's reef runway and Honolulu Harbor sits Sand Island. The expansive, but aesthetically challenged **Sand Island State Recreation Area** (808/832-3781, www.hawaiistateparks. org, sunrise-sunset daily) is on its south shore. There is a camping area, park, picnic areas, restrooms and outdoor showers, and a steep sandy beach that stretches from the island's western point, nearly to the harbor channel entrance. Since the beach and park are in an industrial zone and the park is littered with bits of rubbish, paradise isn't the first thing that

© KEVIN WHITTON

Magic Island has a protected beach perfect for families.

comes to mind here. Planes zoom overhead on a regular basis. The large, rectangular sand trappers exposed on both ends of the beach could be a safety hazard for small children. Still, there are a few decent surf breaks off the beach if you're looking to get away from the crowds at Ala Moana Beach, and the area is popular with local families on the weekends. To get to the beach, turn onto Sand Island Access Road from North Nimitz Highway and follow this to the end. Parking is free. The gated parking lot is locked when the recreation area is closed.

Water Sports

SURFING, BODYSURFING, AND STAND-UP PADDLING

The surf breaks in Honolulu come alive during the summer months, when south swells generated by storms in the southern hemisphere travel thousands of miles to Hawaiian waters. And the breaks are usually crowded with bodyboarders, shortboarders, and longboarders.

Bomburas is a predominant left that breaks at the top of Magic Island, with the white water pushing right into the jetty. When the surf is big enough, the waves break far enough out to round the point and swing into the bay on the Ala Moana side. The wave breaks best on a low tide. You'll have to paddle out and in through a gap in the jetty across the *keiki* pool, timing the white water on the way in so you don't get pushed into the rocks.

The reef that stretches across Ala Moana Beach has a handful of waves that break on different conditions. Some of the more shallow breaks are preferred by bodyboarders, and some waves don't start breaking until the surf is breaking above head high. Two of the more popular waves that are easy to pick out from shore are **Concessions** and **Big Rights**.

© KEVIN WHITTON

Sand Island is popular with locals for fishing, surfing, and weekend camping.

Toward the west side of the beach, in front of the concession stand, there is a sandy path in the reef that leads straight out in between the two breaks. You'll see surfers walking in and out in knee-deep water along the channel. The break to the east is Concessions, a right and left breaking wave that gets pretty shallow if you go right. To the west of the channel in the reef is Big Rights, a predominant right that gets pretty hollow, and surfers will try to nab one of the fast barrels. Park along Ala Moana Park Drive.

There is a channel that runs parallel and spans Ala Moana Beach entirely designated as a swimming and stand-up paddling zone. Buoys demarcate lanes. The water is flat and calm, even when it's windy because the reef protects it from the surf. It's a great place to learn how to paddle or to paddle for exercise.

There are a couple of breaks along Kewalo Basin Park as well, the most popular being a left and right peak called **Kewalo's.** The left breaks into the Kewalo Basin channel that the boats use to access the harbor. The right breaks into shallow and sharp reef. Kewalo's is often

crowded since it's a favorite break for school-age kids when class is out. There are a few more breaks along the reef to the east that are usually less crowded. Access the water by carefully climbing down the seawall and paddling out over the reef. Keep in mind you'll have to come in by climbing up the seawall, which can be a challenge when the surf is big and the surges are pushing up and pulling away from it with force.

There are two small parking lots, showers, and restrooms in Kewalo Basin Park. To get to Kewalo Basin, you'll need to be driving east on Ala Moana Boulevard. Once you pass Ward Avenue, take the second right turn into the harbor. If you come to the signal at Ala Moana Park Road, you've missed it. Follow the road past all the boats and tour operators. It bends right at the park, and the two parking lots are just ahead on the right.

Across the Kewalo Basin Harbor channel, fronting Kakaʻako Waterfront Park and the Kewalo Marine Laboratory, is Oʻahu's only strictly bodysurfing wave, **Point Panic.** It is against the law and punishable by a fine to

© KEVIN WHITTON

Ala Moana Beach offers surfing over the outer reef and a designated swimming and stand-up paddle zone along the inner lagoon.

surf the break with a board. Point Panic is a beautiful, barreling right off the rocky point. There is no beach in this area. However, there are restrooms, showers, and a small parking lot at the end of Ahui Street.

Flies is a lumpy, soft wave that breaks in front of the seawall along Kakaʻako Waterfront Park. There are several right and left breaking peaks that break best on a low tide, as the backwash can be a bit much on a higher tide. It is a good break for novice surfers intimidated by the crowds at other spots. Watch how the local surfers enter and exit the water. To get to the waterfront, park at the end of Ahui Street.

Outfitters
Hawaiian South Shore (320 Ward Ave., #112, 808/597-9055, www.hawaiiansouthshore.com, 10:30am-7pm Mon.-Sat.) is a complete surf shop in the Ala Moana/Kakaʻako area, right by Ala Moana Beach. They sell surf-related apparel, accessories, new shortboards and longboards, and rent shortboards and longboards

for $25 per day. **Blue Planet** (540 Ward Ave., 808/596-7755, www.blueplanetsurf.com, 10am-6pm daily) is just up the street and still conveniently close to Ala Moana Beach. They sell new and used longboards, shortboards, stand-up paddle boards, and accessories. They also offer long-term surfboard rentals (two or more days) starting at $40, long-term stand-up paddle rental starting at $75, and 90-minute private stand-up paddle lessons for $90.

Surf Garage (2716 S. King St., 808/951-1173, www.surfgarage.com, 10am-7pm Mon.-Sat., 11am-5pm Sun.) and **Aloha Boardshop** (2600 S. King St., 808/955-6030, www.alohaboardshop.com, 10am-6:30pm Mon.-Sat., 11am-5pm Sun.) are right next to each other at the intersection of University Avenue and King Street. Check out Surf Garage for longboards, stand-up paddle boards, and accessories. Aloha Boardshop has a ton of shortboards, new and used, as well as longboards and surf accessories for sale.

Closer to Waikiki and Diamond Head in

the Kapahulu area, **RV's Ocean Sport** (3348 Campbell Ave., 808/732-7137, http://rvsocean. com, 11am-5:30pm daily) is the place for used longboards and shortboards. The small shop is wall-to-wall boards, and they also specialize in ding repair.

Hawaiian WaterSports (415 Kapahulu Ave., 808/739-5483, www.hawaiianwatersports. com, 9am-5pm daily) specializes in the sale and rental of strong and light epoxy boards. They offer shortboards, longboards, and stand-up paddle boards. Surfboards rent for $29 for 24 hours, $149 for seven days, and stand-up paddle boards go for $69 for 24 hours and $350 for seven days. Group surfing lessons start at $99 for two hours, and private lessons are $179 for two hours. They surf breaks are around Diamond Head. Stand-up paddle lessons start at $99 for two-hour group lessons and $179 for two-hour private lessons.

DIVING

Diving Honolulu waters is all about exploring shipwrecks and finger reefs. The YO-257 and San Pedro wrecks are home to whitetip reef sharks, eels, and green sea turtles with deep-water reef fish on the surrounding reefs. The Sea Tiger wreck, rumored to be a forcibly retired smuggling vessel, rests in a protected area. Look for white-spotted eagle rays, large puffer fish, and filefish. There is also an area of finger reefs called Turtle Canyons that is home to a number of eel species, reef fish, and turtles. Most of the dive charters leave from Kewalo Basin.

Kaimana Divers (1051 Ala Moana Blvd., 808/772-1795, www.waikikiscuba.com, 7am-8pm daily) two-tank boat charters start at $89 including tanks and weights. Gear rental is $5 per piece or $10 full set. They also have a 10-dive package with everything included for $495. In addition to charters, they offer intro dive, private, standard, and advanced open-water courses starting at $125.

Dive Oahu (1085 Ala Moana Blvd., 808/922-3483, http://diveoahu.com, 8am-3pm daily) offers two-tank charters with Waikiki hotel pickup and drop-off, gear, tanks, and weights included in the rate: $129 standard, $385

five-day unlimited package. They also offer PADI online scuba courses and have a full dive shop.

Also in Kewalo Basin is **Rainbow Scuba** (1086 Ala Moana Blvd., 808/224-7857, http:// rainbowscuba.com, 7am-5pm daily). Their rates include Waikiki hotel transportation, light snacks and water on the charter, two tanks, and full gear rental. They offer two-site beginner dives for $100 for first-time divers, certified divers charter to one wreck site and one reef site for $110, and PADI certification courses starting at $275.

Breeze Hawaii Diving Adventures (3014 Kaimuki Ave., 808/735-1857, http://breeze-hawaiidiving.com, 7am-5pm daily) has a retail shop in the Kapahulu area and offers two-tank boat charters for $115, three-tank charters for $172, one-tank night dives $149, and two-tank sunset/night dives for $200. They also have three levels of PADI beginner dive courses.

While **Pearl Harbor Divers** (725 Auahi St., 808/589-2177, http://pearlharbordivers.com, 9am-6pm Mon.-Fri., 8am-5pm Sat.-Sun.) has dive charters available only on the leeward side, they do have scuba courses in Honolulu. They offer NAUI certification starting at $379 group and $449 private.

FISHING

The bulk of the fishing charters are found in Kewalo Basin, where they can easily access the deeper south shore waters. If you're interested in shoreline fishing, you can cast from anywhere along the seawall at Kaka'ako Waterfront Park or from the beach at Sand Island.

Magic Sport Fishing (1125 Ala Moana Blvd., 808/596-2998, www.magicsportfishing.com) runs a 50-foot Pacifica Sportfishing Yacht out of Kewalo Basin and provides everything except lunch and beverages. The captain has over 20 years of experience commercial fishing in Hawaiian waters, and they will divvy up a small portion of fish per person on shared trips and larger portions for private charters. With up to six passengers, eight-hour full-day shared trips run $200 per person, private trips $975. There are also half-day private charters for $775.

Sea Verse Sport Fishing (1125 Ala Moana Blvd., 808/262-5587, http://seaversesportfishing.com), with a 44-foot twin-engine vessel equipped for angling and trolling, runs private half-day trips for $700, three-quarter-day trips for $750, and full-day private charters for $900. Full-day shared charters are $200 per person. They also offer bottom fishing trips.

Operating since 1985, **Tradewind Charters** (1125 Ala Moana Blvd., 808/973-0311, www.tradewindcharters.com) has a variety of vessels for different types of fishing expeditions, from 40-foot sailing yachts to a 65-foot sportfishing yacht, and they offer two different fishing expeditions: catch-and-release reef fishing and deep-sea sportfishing. Their private reef fishing charter includes snorkeling and sightseeing and for one to six people, starts at $595 for three hours, $795 for four-and-a-half hours, $995 for six hours, and $1,195 for eight hours. Their private deep-sea charters for one to six people start at $895 for four hours, $1,095 for six hours, and $1,295 for eight hours.

Aikane Sport Fishing (866/920-0979, www.aikanesportfishing.com) has shallow-water fishing charters for trevally and snappers or deep-sea fishing charters for big game fish like wahoo, mahimahi, blue marlin, and yellowfin tuna. They have a 42-foot Ocean Yacht and 38-foot Bertram Sportfisher. The shallow-water charters start at $500 for four hours and go to $625 for eight hours; the deep-sea big game fishing charters start at $650 for four hours and go to $990 for 10 hours.

Established in 1950, **Maggie Joe Sport Fishing** (1025 Ala Moana Blvd., 808/591-8888, www.maggiejoe.com) has a fleet of boats designed to catch big game fish like blue marlin, yellowfin tuna, mahimahi, and skipjack tuna. They have half-day to full-day private and shared trips as well as night shark fishing for $550. Their biggest boat, a 53-foot Custom Sport Fishing Yacht, starts at $890 for a three-quarter day and $933 for a private, full-day charter. Full-day shared charters are $179 per person, and half-day shared charters are $150 per person. Bananas are not permitted onboard due to superstition.

Hiking, Biking, and Bird-Watching

HIKING
Makiki
The **Makiki-Tantalus** hike is an eight-mile loop that circles Tantalus Peak and is a great way to see a few different valleys and Ko'olau peaks up close. The trail is known for songbirds and some native Hawaiian flora. Look for the native white hibiscus and *'ohi'a 'ahihi*, with clusters of delicate red flowers. The hike takes advantage of the Kanealole Trail, at the trailhead, then connects in succession to the Makiki Valley Trail, the Nahuina Trail, the Kalawahine Trail, the Pauoa Flats Trail, the Manoa Cliff Trail, the Moleka Trail, and back to the Makiki Valley Trail as it rounds Tantalus. The junctions are marked well. To get to the trailhead, from Makiki Street heading north, bear left on Makiki Heights Drive. As the road switches back to the left, continue straight on an unnamed paved road into the Makiki Forest Recreation Area and past the Hawai'i Nature Center. Park on the side of the road by the gate. There is a native plant identification guide available in the nature center office for a small fee.

Manoa
In the back of rainy Manoa Valley are a myriad of trails all within **Lyon Arboretum** (3860 Manoa Rd., 808/988-0456, www.hawaii.edu/lyonarboretum, 8am-4pm Mon.-Fri., 9am-3pm Sat.). These trails are designed to take you through the different sections of the arboretum, so there's a wealth of interesting and colorful exotic, tropical, and native Hawaiian plants and trees everywhere you look. You could hike for a half day and not walk the same trail twice there's so much area to cover.

The trails range from wide and dry to narrow, muddy, and graded. They are marked with numbers on wooden stakes that correspond to a trail map, which you can pick up in the visitor center. The main trail through the arboretum terminates at a small waterfall. Be prepared for mud, rain, and mosquitoes. Lyon Arboretum has its own free, private parking lot by the visitor center. Follow Manoa Road all the way to the back of the valley, past the houses, past Paradise Park, and turn onto the arboretum's private drive before the end of the road.

Also in the rear of Manoa Valley are several of the 18 trails that comprise the Honolulu *mauka* trail system. **Manoa Falls** is a great introduction to the area, a short 0.8-mile hike with a gradual grade under canopy and through lush foliage, up to a small waterfall and pool. Manoa is famous for its pervasive mist, so the trail can be muddy and crossed with roots in some sections. This is a popular hike, so it is well used, especially on the weekends. To get to the trailhead, either park on Manoa Road just before it narrows at the intersection with Wa'akaua Street, or continue driving on Manoa Road till you reach Paradise Park, where $5 flat-rate parking is available. If you prefer to park for free in the nearby neighborhood, tack on a quarter-mile walk just to reach the trailhead. From the paid parking lot, continue on foot on the gravel road until it becomes the Manoa Falls Trail. The trail follows Waihi Stream to the falls and pool.

Kaimuki

At the top of Saint Louis Heights, in Kaimuki, you'll find a hike with views of Manoa Valley and Palolo Valley, terminating on top of Mount Olympus, a massive peak at the back of Manoa Valley. The **Wa'ahila Ridge Trail** begins in a stand of Cook pines—a misnomer since they are actually columnar araucaria, native to New Caledonia. The hike along the ridgeline is perfect for novices, but once you find the narrow trail that ascends to the summit, the route is more suited for intermediate hikers. At the 2,486-foot summit, in addition to breathtaking views, you'll find a thicket of native vegetation, including slow-growing *hapu'u* ferns. The hike is 6 miles round-trip. To get to the trailhead, park in the **Wa'ahila Ridge State Recreation Area** (www.hawaiistateparks.org, 7am-7:45pm daily Apr.-early Sept., 7am-6:45pm daily early Sept.-Mar.) by following Saint Louis Drive to nearly the top of the rise and turning left on Ruth Place. There are restrooms, drinking fountains, and picnic tables by the parking lot. Parking is free, but the gate is locked when the recreation area is closed.

MOUNTAIN BIKING

While there are a plethora of trails all around O'ahu, mountain biking is prohibited on most of them. Fortunately for those looking to go off road on two wheels, there are a handful of mountain biking trails on the North Shore and the southeast and windward sides. Mountain biking is prohibited on all Honolulu area trails, but the big name local bicycle shops are all in town.

Outfitters

The Bike Shop (1149 S. King St., 808/596-0588, www.bikeshophawaii.com, 9am-8pm Mon.-Fri., 9am-5pm Sat., 10am-5pm Sun.) is

---

EXCEPTIONAL TREES

In 1975, the Hawai'i state legislature passed Act 105, The Exceptional Tree Act. The law recognizes the ecological and cultural significance and value of trees deemed exceptional and establishes the protection of designated trees. What is an exceptional tree? Exceptional trees on O'ahu must have historic or cultural value or meet certain criteria of age, rarity, location, size, aesthetic quality, and endemic status. Exceptional trees are marked with a gold or silver plaque that identifies their scientific and common name and county of origin. There are over 150 exceptional trees on O'ahu. Find the complete list of exceptional trees and their location at www.honolulu.gov.

© KEVIN WHITTON

Manoa Falls

a full-service rental, retail, and repair shop in the Kaka'ako neighborhood. They rent mountain bikes for $85 per day, road bikes starting at $40 per day, and seven-speed city bikes for $20 day. If you need racks for your rental car, they charge $5 per day.

The **BikeFactory** (740 Ala Moana Blvd., 808/596-8844, http://bikefactoryhawaii.com, 10am-7pm Mon.-Fri., 9am-5pm Sat., 11am-5pm Sun.), also in Kaka'ako, sells bicycles and accessories, but does not rent equipment. And in Mo'ili'ili, **McCully Bicycle and Sporting Goods** (2124 S. King Street, 808/955-6329, http://mccullybike.com, 9am-8pm Mon.-Fri., 9am-6pm Sat., 10am-5pm Sun.) sells bicycles of all shapes and sizes, as well as other sporting goods like fishing gear, tennis rackets, and athletic shoes. They do not rent bicycles, however.

BIRD-WATCHING
Bird-watching in Honolulu is all about finding the forest birds along the **Ko'olau Range trails,** including the **Lyon Arboretum trails.** Most of the birds are introduced species, like the shama thrush and the red-billed leiothrix, but beautiful nonetheless. The shama thrush is black on top with a chestnut-colored chest and a long, black and white tail and is able to mimic other birds' songs. There are few native forest birds remaining on O'ahu in accessible places, but this region is a great place to look for the red *'apapane,* which likes to feed on nectar from *'ohi'a lehua* blossoms, and *'amakihi,* a yellow Hawaiian honeycreeper with a black, curved beak.

HONOLULU

Golf and Tennis

GOLF
Kaimuki
The **Ala Wai Golf Course** (404 Kapahulu Ave., 808/296-2000, www1.honolulu.gov/des/golf/alawai.htm), on the mountain side of the Ala Wai Canal, is the closest golf course to Waikiki and a local favorite for a quick round of golf. The 18-hole course is flat and has views of Diamond Head and the Ko'olau Range. Greens fees are $52 daily for 18 holes and $26 daily for twilight or nine holes. Golf cart fees are $20 for 18 holes, $10 for nine holes.

Moanalua
Even though Hawai'i's oldest golf course, **Moanalua Golf Club** (1250 Ala Aolani St., 808/839-2311, www.mgchawaii.com), is a private club with membership benefits, access is open to the public. Built in 1898, the nine-hole course can be played as an 18-hole course by utilizing different sets of tees. The Moanalua Stream winds through the challenging course, set along the slopes of Moanalua, creating natural hazards. There are views of Diamond Head and the Honolulu skyline. Greens fees start at $45.

TENNIS

Public tennis courts can be found throughout the greater Honolulu area. **Kaimuki Community Park** (3521 Waialae Ave., 808/733-7351) has two courts, but the parking can be a hassle. There is free parking on 10th Avenue, metered parking on Waialae Avenue, or if those options are exhausted, park on 10th on the north side of Waialae. **Makiki District Park** (1527 Keeamoku St., 808/522-7082) has four courts, and **Manoa Valley District Park** (2721 Kaaipu Ave., 808/988-0580, www1.honolulu.gov/parks) has five courts. Both **Ala Moana Park** (1201 Ala Moana Blvd., 808/592-2288) and **Ala Moana Tennis Park** (1135 Hoolai St., 808/524-6626) have 10 courts each.

Yoga and Spas

YOGA
Manoa

In the Manoa Marketplace, **Iyengar Yoga** (2752 Woodlawn Dr., 808/382-3910, www.manoayoga.com) strives to promote physical health and mental poise. This type of yoga makes frequent use of props to adjust the body into the different poses. Single beginner classes are $12, and single intermediate classes are $15. They also offer yoga for kids at $30 for four classes.

Kaimuki

Bikram Yoga Honolulu (1120 12th Ave., 808/737-5519, www.bikramyogahonolulu.com) is no-nonsense hot yoga. Their second-floor studio has showers, locker rooms, and a naturally lit classroom. These are silent classes, so no talking during the session. Single classes are $20, and they offer seven days of unlimited yoga for $50.

Also in Kaimuki, **Dahn Yoga** (3569 Harding Ave., #B, 808/738-5522, www.dahnyoga.com) is a holistic health center offering classes in dahn yoga, a variety of mind and body exercises, tai chi, and meditation. One-hour classes start at $10. There is another studio in Kakaʻako (401 Kamakee St., 808/596-9642).

Moili'ili

Purple Yoga (2615 S. King St., 808/944-8585, www.purpleyoga.com) specializes in ashtanga yoga, as well as in vinyasa, pregnancy, and mom and baby yoga. They encourage students to go at their own, comfortable pace. Single classes are $18, five classes are $80, and 10 classes are $135.

SPAS
Downtown

Heaven on Earth Salon & Day Spa (1050 Alakea St., 808/599-5501, www.heavenonearthhawaii.com, 9am-7pm Mon.-Fri., 8am-5pm Sat., 10am-4pm Sun.) is a full-service salon and spa located in the heart of downtown Honolulu. In addition to their complete set of services, they offer signature spa packages of skin body treatments, or you can create your own. Massages start at $88 for 50 minutes and $118 for 80 minutes, facials start at $80 for 50 minutes, and 50-minute body treatments are $95. The spa packages range from 80 minutes

---

ICE IN HONOLULU?

A great way to cool off in the Salt Lake area is to lace up some ice skates and glide around Oʻahu's only ice-skating venue, **Ice Palace** (4510 Salt Lake Blvd., 808/487-9921, www.icepalacehawaii.com). Complete with DJ and light show, they also have a closed-off section of the rink with special "walkers" that slide on the ice to help beginners get the hang of skating. Check the monthly schedule for public skating days and hours, as these do change for classes and sporting events. Generally, public skating is 9am-3pm, and admission is $8.90.

to four hours and start at $210. They also have gentlemen's spa services like facials, manicures, pedicures, and waxing.

Ala Moana

On the third floor in the Ala Moana Center is **Hoʻala Salon and Spa** (1450 Ala Moana Blvd., 808/947-6141, http://hoalasalonspa.com, 9am-9pm Mon.-Sat., 10am-7pm Sun.), a full-service salon and spa using natural and eco-sensitive products from Aveda. The award-winning spa is a quiet respite from the bustle of the mall and town. Their signature massage care ranges from 25 to 90 minutes, 50-minute therapies start at $100, 75 minutes start at $150. They have an extensive menu of facials, 25 minutes start at $65 and 60 minutes start at $125. Hoʻala Spa also offers nail, hand, and foot care, spa body treatments, and hair care, as well as a 50- or 75-minute pregnancy massage.

Elements Spa and Salon (1726 Kapiolani Blvd., #206, 808/942-0033, www.elementshawaii.com, 10am-8pm Mon.-Fri., 9am-6pm Sat., 10am-6pm Sun.) is right across from the Hawaii Convention Center and specializes in custom offerings, including tea service, foot treatment, mini facials, and scalp massages with their full-service salon and spa treatments. They provide three basic massages and several specialty massages like shiatsu, hot stone, and deep tissue. The basic massages are $50 for 30 minutes, $85 for 60 minutes, and $110 for 90 minutes. Their specialty massages start at $100 for 60 minutes. They also have a couples massages starting at $165 for 60 minutes. Facials start at $85 for 60 minutes, and they offer series rates for both facials and massages. Elements provides salon, nail, waxing, and bridal services.

Sights

DOWNTOWN
◖ ʻIolani Palace

Set on a grassy 11 acres, shaded by canopy trees in the heart of the Capitol District, **ʻIolani Palace** (364 S. King St., 808/522-0822, www.iolanipalace.org, 9am-5pm Mon.-Sat.) is the second royal palace to grace the grounds. The building, with its glass and ironwork imported from San Francisco and its Corinthian columns, is the only true royal palace in America. ʻIolani Palace, begun in late 1879 under orders of King Kalakaua, was completed in December 1882 at a cost of $350,000. It was the first electrified building in Honolulu, having electricity and telephones even before the White House in Washington, D.C. The palace served as the official residence of the monarch of Hawaiʻi until the overthrow of the Hawaiian kingdom in 1893. It then became the main executive building for the provisional government, with the House of Representatives meeting in the throne room and the Senate in the dining

room, until 1968. It has since been elevated to a state monument and National Historic Landmark.

Through the first floor of this palace runs a broad hallway with a grand stairway that leads to the second story. On the east side of the building is the large and opulent Throne Room, the scene of formal meetings and major royal functions. On the west side are the smaller Blue Room, an informal reception area, and the dining room. The upstairs level was the private residence of the king and his family. It also has a wide hallway, and on each side are bedrooms, sitting rooms, a music room, and office. The basement held servants' quarters, the kitchen, and offices of certain government officials. On the palace grounds you'll find the Coronation Pavilion, which originally stood directly in front of the palace, but was later moved to where it stands today as a bandstand for the Royal Hawaiian Band, and a raised earthen platform, the original site of the royal mausoleum, which was later moved out along the Pali Highway.

HONOLULU

© KEVIN WHITTON

'Iolani Palace is the only royal residence in the United States.

'Iolani Palace has docent-guided tours and self-guided tours of the first and second floors, both with self-guided exploration of the basement gallery. One-hour tours enter the palace every 15 minutes. Reservations are required for the **guided tour** (808/522-0832, palace-tickets@iolanipalace.org, Tues. and Thurs. 9am-10am, Wed., Fri.-Sat. 9am-11:15am, $20 adults, $6 children ages 5-12), but not for the **self-guided audio tour** (9am-5pm Mon., 10:30am-5pm Tues. and Thurs., noon-5pm Wed. and Fri.-Sat., $12 adults, $5 children ages 5-12, $1 fee for the audio recording). The **Basement Gallery exhibits** (9:30am-5pm Mon.-Sat., $7 adults, $3 children) are another option for touring. Tickets are also sold at the 'Iolani Barracks (9am-4pm Tues.-Sat.), behind the palace. Also in the barracks is the palace gift shop and bookstore (8:30am-4pm Mon.-Sat.).

There is limited metered parking on the palace grounds. From South King Street, turn left onto Likelike Street, a one-way drive, just before the major Punchbowl Street intersection.

Turn left through the decorated gate onto the palace grounds.

Hawaii State Capitol

Directly behind 'Iolani Palace sits the unique **Hawaii State Capitol** (415 S. Beretania St., 808/587-0478, www.capitol.hawaii.gov), built in 1969. The structure is a metaphor for Hawai'i: the pillars surrounding it are palms, the reflecting pool is the sea, and the cone-shaped rooms of the Legislature represent the volcanoes of Hawai'i. The walls are lined with rich *koa* wood from the Big Island and further graced with woven hangings, murals, and two gigantic, four-ton replicas of the State Seal hanging at both entrances. The inner courtyard has a 600,000-tile mosaic and standing at the *mauka* entrance to the building is a poignant sculpture of Saint Damien of Molokai, while the statue *The Spirit of Lili'uokalani* fronts the building on the ocean side. The State Legislature is in session for 60 working days starting on the third Wednesday in January. The legislative session opens with dancing,

© KEVIN WHITTON

HONOLULU

The state capitol was designed to reflect Hawai'i's volcanic origins.

music, and festivities, and the public is invited. Peek inside, then take the elevator to the fifth floor for outstanding views of the city. There is also a Korean-Vietnam War Memorial paying tribute to those that died in the two wars.

Washington Place

Begun in 1841 by Captain John Dominis, **Washington Place** (320 S. Beretania St., 808/536-8040, www.washingtonplacefoundation.org) is best known as the home of Queen Lili'uokalani and her husband, John Owen Dominis, son of Captain Dominis. The Greek revival mansion was both Queen Lili'uokalani's home and also her prison beginning in 1893, when the Hawaiian kingdom was overthrown. She resided at Washington Place till her death in 1917. In 1918 the home became the official residence of governors of Hawai'i. The mansion was converted into a museum in 2001, and a new governor's mansion was built behind it. Washington Place is still used for state dinners and official functions and remains the official residence of the governor. The mansion is on the mountain side of Beretania Street, directly across from the Hawaii State Capitol.

St. Andrew's Cathedral

Just to the west of Washington Place is **St. Andrew's Cathedral** (229 Queen Emma Sq., 808/524-2822, www.thecathedralofstandrew.org). Construction started in 1867 as an Anglican church, but wasn't really finished until 1958. Many of its stones and ornaments were shipped from England, and its stained-glass windows, especially the large contemporary-style window on the narthex end, the bell tower, and its pipe organ, touted as the largest pipe organ in the Pacific, are of particular interest. Hawai'i's monarchs worshiped here, and the church is still active. There is a free guided tour following the 10:30am Sunday service. After the service, simply wait below the pulpit for a docent. There is limited public parking on church grounds during the week.

Hawai'i State Art Museum

The **Hawai'i State Art Museum** (250 S. Hotel

© KEVIN WHITTON

HONOLULU

The Hawai'i State Art Museum features Hawai'i's finest artists.

was used to cast this second one. The original now stands in the tiny town of Kapa'au, in the Kohala District of the Big Island, not far from where Kamehameha was born. The Honolulu statue was dedicated in 1883, as part of King David Kalakaua's coronation ceremony. Its black and gold colors are striking, but it is most magnificent on June 11, King Kamehameha Day, when 18-foot lei are draped around the neck and the outstretched arms. The third stands in Washington, D.C., dedicated when Hawai'i became a state.

St., #2, 808/586-0900, http://hawaii.gov/sfca/ HiSAM.html, 10am-4pm Tues.-Sat.) is on the second floor of the No. 1 Capitol District Building and has four galleries: the Diamond Head Gallery, the Ewa Gallery, the Sculpture Lobby, and the Sculpture Garden. The exhibitions highlight the finest collection of work by Hawai'i artists and the gallery displays rotate regularly. The museum gift shop is on the first floor.

King Kamehameha I Statue

The statue of King Kamehameha I is centered in a roundabout near the junction of King and Mililani Streets. Running off at an angle is Merchant Street, the oldest thoroughfare in Honolulu. This statue is much more symbolic of Kamehameha's strength as a ruler and unifier of the Hawaiian Islands than as a replica of the man himself. It is one of three. The original, lost at sea near the Falkland Islands en route from Paris where it was bronzed, was later recovered, but not before the insurance money

Kawaiaha'o Church

The **Kawaiaha'o Church** (957 Punchbowl St., 808/522-1333, www.kawaiahao.org) was built between 1836 and 1842. The first Christian church in Hawai'i, its New England-style architecture was crafted from 14,000 coral slabs, quarried by hand from local reefs. King Liholiho and his wife Queen Emma, who bore the last child born to a Hawaiian monarch, wed at the church, and on June 19, 1856, Lunalilo, the first king elected to the throne, took his oath of office in the church. Lunalilo is buried in a tomb at the front of the church, along with his father, Charles Kana'ina, and nearby lies the grave of his mother, Miriam Kekauluohi. In the graveyard at the rear of the church rest many members of the Parker, Green, Brown, and Cooke families, early missionaries to the islands. Most are recognizable as important and influential people in 19th-century Hawaiian history. Hidden away in a corner of the grounds is an unobtrusive adobe building, the remains of a schoolhouse built in 1835 to educate Hawaiian children. Kawaiaha'o holds beautiful Christmas services with a strong Polynesian and Hawaiian flavor, and Hawaiian-language services are given here every Sunday, along with English-language services.

Mission Houses Museum

The days when tall ships with tattered sails bore in God-fearing missionary families dedicated to Christianizing the savage islands are alive in the halls and buildings of the **Mission Houses**

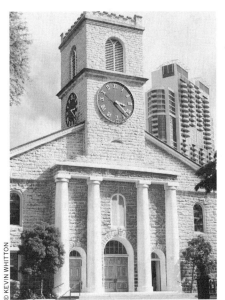

© KEVIN WHITTON

Kawaiahaʻo Church is constructed of coral blocks hewn from nearby reefs.

Museum (553 S. King St., 808/447-3910, www.missionhouses.org, Tues.-Sat. 10am-4pm), now a registered National Historic Landmark. Set behind Kawaiahaʻo Church, the complex includes two main houses, a printing house annex, a research library, and a gift shop. The printing office was the first in the islands just as the Frame House is the oldest wooden structure in Hawaiʻi. One-hour guided tours are offered every hour 11am-3pm; admission is $10 adults, $6 students.

CHINATOWN
◖ Historic Chinatown

Chinese immigrants came to Hawaiʻi in the 1800s as the first contract laborers for the burgeoning sugar industry. They established a vibrant community with herb shops, restaurants, temples, and retail outlets in what is now **historic Chinatown.** Today, Chinatown is a vibrant mix of art galleries, coffeehouses, upscale restaurants, bars and clubs, outdoor markets, and quick and delicious ethnic food

restaurants. It also has a seedy side of homeless sleeping in doorways, prostitution, and fights spilling out of dive bars onto the sidewalk, which gives the historic neighborhood depth and character.

The best way to see Chinatown is to park the car and explore the streets on foot. Chinatown is relatively small, and the square grid of streets makes it easy to get around quickly. There are six municipal parking lots across Chinatown, which have the best rates. There is one on River Street, one on Maunakea Street, two on Smith Street, and two on Bethel Street.

On the east side of Chinatown, Fort Street Mall is a pedestrian area dominated by take-out restaurants and mingling students from Hawaii Pacific University as they wait for classes. The art galleries are generally on the east end of Chinatown, on Smith Street, Nuʻuanu Avenue, and Bethel Street. The cuisine on offer in Chinatown is truly international, from Irish and Cuban to French and Mediterranean, much of which is found on Bethel Street. But the main draw, traditional Chinese fare, is easily found. The wealth of Chinese establishments are on Smith and Maunakea Streets. Noodle shops and Chinese restaurants merely complement the variety of Asian food found in the **Maunakea Marketplace Food Court,** on the corner of Maunakea and Hotel Streets. Chinese, Thai, Korean, Vietnamese, and Filipino plates are served from small market stalls with family-style seating available for enjoying the myriad flavors. Just across Beretania Street, on the outskirts of Chinatown, is the **Chinatown Cultural Plaza Center,** a small indoor mall with gift and herb shops, as well as a host of small eateries. There is paid parking at the plaza, as well.

Chinatown has an abundance of historical buildings dating back to the early 20th century, like the **Hawaii Theatre** on Bethel Street, which opened in 1922. The upper-story facades of the buildings along Hotel Street, between Bethel and Maunakea Streets, still retain vestiges from the World War II era. There is also the **Hawaii Kuan Yin Temple** on the mountain side of Vineyard Boulevard at the entrance to

Foster Botanical Garden. The temple is dedicated to the Chinese deity of compassion.

KAKA'AKO
Honolulu Museum of Art
With a rich history dating back to its opening in 1927, the **Honolulu Museum of Art** (900 S. Beretania St., 808/532-8700, http://honolulumuseum.org, 10am-4:30pm Tues.-Sat., 1pm-3pm Sun.) has a collection of 50,000 pieces spanning 5,000 years of Asian art and textiles, American and European painting and decorative art, works on paper, and traditional works from Africa, Oceania, and the Americas. Within its earthy, revival mission-style architecture, the museum also houses a library, an education wing, a contemporary gallery, a café, and a 280-seat theater. Admission is $10 adult, $5 children 4-17, children 3 and under free. The fee also covers the Honolulu Museum of Art Spalding House for same day entry.

Parking can be a bit tricky. There is metered street parking on the blocks around the museum, but make sure to check for time restrictions. The museum maintains two parking lots: the Honolulu Museum of Art School lot behind the Honolulu Museum of Art School with entrances on Beretania Street and Young Street ($3 with validation for four hours), and the Kinau Street Lot (1035 Kinau St., 4:30pm-11pm Mon.-Fri., 10am-11pm Sat.-Sun., free). There are five spaces at the museum for visitors with disabilities.

Kaka'ako Waterfront Park and Kewalo Basin Park
Kaka'ako Waterfront Park is a 35-acre expanse of grassy rolling hills that runs to the water's edge on the west side of Kewalo Basin. There are restrooms, picnic tables, and a paved jogging path, but no sandy beach. If you want to jump in the water, there are cement steps that scale down the rocky jetty wall.

On the eastern flank of Kewalo Basin is **Kewalo Basin Park,** a small, coastal refuge with shade trees, restrooms, picnic tables, great views of the ocean, and a couple of popular surf breaks. If you've chartered a boat out of Kewalo Basin for diving or fishing, the park is the perfect place to kill some time before or after your tour. There are two small parking lots, which often fill up on the weekends.

Children's Discovery Center
The **Children's Discovery Center** (111Ohe St., 808/524-5437, www.discoverycenter-hawaii.org, 9am-1pm Tues.-Fri., 10am-3pm Sat.-Sun.), at Kaka'ako Waterfront Park, is an interactive, hands-on children's museum and activity center focused on learning and discovering through play. The center has six exhibits, one for visitors five years and younger and five for older children. They can learn about their bodies, role play to discover how a community functions, find out about Hawaiian history and culture, as well as cultures beyond Hawaiian shores, and explore and understand the importance of rainforests. Admission is $10 general, $6 senior citizen, children under one year are free.

NU'UANU
Foster Botanical Garden
Wedged between the H-1 freeway and downtown's skyscrapers **Foster Botanical Garden** (50 N. Vineyard Blvd., 808/522-7066, www1.honolulu.gov/parks/hbg/fbg.htm, 9am-4pm daily) finds itself in an unlikely area for abundant greenery. But once you set foot into the garden, you'll be mesmerized by the lush foliage and incredibly tall trees and all things urban will melt away. Since some of the trees in the collection were planted back in 1853, when the grounds were the residence of German physicist and botanist William Hillebrand, the enormity of the trees on the main lawn are a wonder of nature. There are 26 "Exceptional Trees" on the 13.5-acre property, and the garden boasts indoor and outdoor orchid sections, a palm section, as well as a cycad garden. Cycads are curious leafy plants that date back 200 million years to the Jurassic period. Admission is $5 general, 13 and older, $1 children 6-12, and children 5 and under are free. The garden has ample parking.

HONOLULU

© KEVIN WHITTON

Foster Botanical Garden features many of Honolulu's "Exceptional Trees."

Queen Emma Summer Palace

Hanaiakamalama, today known as the **Queen Emma Summer Palace** (2913 Pali Hwy., 808/595-3167, http://daughtersofhawaii.org, 9am-4pm daily), was King Kamehameha IV and Queen Emma's summer retreat from 1857 to 1885. Today the historic landmark is a museum set on beautifully landscaped grounds. Admission is $6 per adult and $1 per child. They also offer docent-led tours of the 19th-century home. To get to the palace, take the Pali Highway exit from the H-1 freeway. The palace is on the east side of the highway.

◖ Nu'uanu Pali State Wayside

Better known as the Pali Lookout, the **Nu'uanu Pali State Wayside** is on the Honolulu side of the tunnels on the Pali Highway. The lookout has amazing views of Kane'ohe Bay, Kailua, and the Ko'olau Range. The lookout is often windy. If you're feeling adventurous, there is a ramp that leads down to the Old Pali Road, which you can walk along till it is literally swallowed up by vegetation and decay.

PUNCHBOWL
National Memorial Cemetery of the Pacific

The **National Memorial Cemetery of the Pacific** (2177 Puowaina Dr., 808/532-3720, 8am-6:30pm daily Mar.-Sept., 8am-5:30pm daily Oct.-Feb.) is inside Punchbowl Crater. Established in 1949, the cemetery is a memorial to those who served in the U.S. Armed Forces and is listed on the National Register of Historic Places. Spreading across 112 acres, the beautiful, solemn grounds are a quiet place good for reflection. There is a small office and restrooms located at the entrance open 8am-4:30pm Mon.-Fri., and at the back of the cemetery, behind the main memorial, are restrooms and a pathway that leads to a magnificent viewing area on the crater rim overlooking Honolulu.

There are several ways to reach the cemetery and many signs around the crater indicating the way. From the H-1 freeway eastbound, take the Pali Highway exit, turn right on Iolani Avenue immediately after crossing the bridge,

National Memorial Cemetery of the Pacific

© KEVIN WHITTON

then take the next left onto Lusitana Street. Bear right onto Puowaina Drive and follow the signs. One-lane roads curve through the cemetery.

MAKIKI
◖ Tantalus-Round Top Drive

One of only two roadways in Hawai'i listed on the National Register of Historic Places, **Tantalus Drive** and **Round Top Drive** meet at the **Pu'u 'Ualaka'a State Wayside** on top of a cinder cone with amazing views of Honolulu, from Diamond Head to Pear Harbor, including Manoa Valley. Tantalus Drive approaches the wayside park from the west, while Round Top Drive comes in from the east. A round-trip on the winding roads is about 20 miles. The leisurely drive passes hillside homes, is thick with vegetation, and often quite narrow. If you're easily carsick, this is a drive you'll probably want to avoid. Reach Tantalus Drive from Auwaiolimu Street via Nehoa Street. Reach Round Top Drive from Makiki Street via Nehoa Street. You can also take Makiki Street, to Makiki Heights Drive, to Tantalus Drive. The wayside park is also the trailhead for several forest hiking trails and known for auto theft, so be sure not to leave any valuables in your vehicle, even if you're just stopping for a few minutes to take in the view.

Honolulu Museum of Art Spalding House

Formerly the Contemporary Museum, the **Honolulu Museum of Art Spalding House** (2411 Makiki Heights Dr., 808/526-0232, http://honolulumuseum.org, 10am-4pm Tues.-Sat., noon-3pm Sun., $10 adults, $5 children 4-17, children 3 and under free) was gifted the entire contemporary art collection, covering from the 1940s to present, in 2011. The museum is set on three and a half acres of terraced, sculpture, and botanical gardens. Admission also covers entry to the Honolulu Museum of Art for same-day entry. There is a one-hour docent-led walking tour at 1:30pm Tuesday through Sunday, and the museum is free to the public the first Wednesday of each month.

SAILOR JERRY

Hawai'i is socially and culturally accepting of tattoos on the whole. After all, tattooing is engrained in Polynesian, and Hawaiian, culture. So it comes as no surprise that the father of the traditional Americana tattoo style, Sailor Jerry, practiced his art and gained his international acclaim working from a small shop on Smith Street in Chinatown.

Born Norman Keith Collins in 1911, Sailor Jerry joined the Navy at age 19 and, after his time at sea and abroad, fell in love with the imagery of Southeast Asia and the Hawaiian Islands. He settled in Hawai'i in the 1930s and cemented his reputation as the best tattoo artist in Chinatown during World War II, when sailors docking at Aloha Tower were flocking to Chinatown for booze, hookers, and tattoos. Sailor Jerry established paradigms in tattooing for cleanliness and sterilization, pigments producing bright colors, and a technique and style that is still mimicked to this day.

Sailor Jerry passed away in 1973 and is buried in the National Memorial Cemetery of the Pacific in Punchbowl Crater. Most important, Sailor Jerry passed on an appreciation for the tattoo as a legitimate form of art to be cultivated and collected. And as for his small shop on Smith Street, it's still a tattoo studio to this day.

HONOLULU

Parking is also free. From Nehoa Street, turn onto Makiki Street, then take Makiki Heights Drive at the fork.

MANOA
University of Hawai'i at Manoa
On University Avenue, just off the H-1 freeway, the **University of Hawai'i at Manoa** is a beautiful, compact campus with mature landscaping and fascinating architecture spanning decades. Founded in 1907, UH Manoa holds the distinction of being a land-, sea-, and space-grant research institution, with nine colleges rounding out their academic programs. Of particular interest on campus are the trees planted across its 320 acres. Stop by the botany department and pick up their **Campus Plants** pamphlet. It has a map of the campus and identifies the myriad unique and unusual plants, making for a lovely walk. Also noteworthy is the art department's two free art galleries. The **University of Hawai'i Art Gallery,** off the main foyer, features local and international artists and thematic exhibitions in many different media. The **Commons Gallery,** upstairs, rotates exhibitions on a weekly basis and allows students to experiment with exhibition design and display. And don't miss the giant baobab tree on the west side of the art building—a natural work of art.

To get to UH Manoa, take the University Avenue exit from the H-1 freeway from either direction. There is free parking in the neighborhoods surrounding campus, requiring a bit of a walk, or there is paid meter parking on campus. You can access on-campus parking lots from East West Road, from Dole Street, or on Maile Way from University Avenue. A great time to visit is mid-May to mid-July, when the Summer Session is in, but the campus is rather empty.

Lyon Arboretum
Nestled in the back of verdant and often misty Manoa Valley, **Lyon Arboretum** (3860 Manoa Rd., 808/988-0456, www.hawaii.edu/lyonarboretum, 8am-4pm Mon.-Fri., 9am-3pm Sat.) is a 194-acre botanical garden in a tropical rainforest setting. With over 5,000 tropical plants and a vast network of trails, you'll have the opportunity to see heliconias, gingers, aroids, native Hawaiian plants, and one of the largest collections of palms in Hawai'i. Initially established as a watershed restoration project in 1918, the garden is shaded with a variety of far-reaching canopy trees, their trunks laden with bromeliads, moss, and ferns. With the arboretum receiving an average of 165 inches of precipitation annually, you should

HONOLULU

© KEVIN WHITTON

Verdant Lyon Arboretum is a great place to spot forest birds.

be prepared for long periods of rain, mud, and mosquitoes. Bring binoculars for spotting birds. Pick up a trail map at the Visitor Center and take the time to explore the smaller trails off the main artery that winds back up the valley.

To get to Lyon Arboretum, follow Manoa Road all the way back into the valley, past Paradise Park, and turn left onto the arboretum's private drive before the end of the road. There's a parking lot after a couple switchbacks. The Visitor Center also has a very nice bookstore focusing on conservation, biology, and botany.

KALIHI
◖ Bishop Museum

The premier natural and cultural history institution in the Pacific and the largest museum in the state, **Bishop Museum** (1525 Bernice St., 808/847-3511, www.bishopmuseum.org, 9am-5pm Wed.-Mon.), the Hawai'i State Museum of Culture and Natural History, was founded in 1889 by Charles Reed Bishop, in honor of his late wife, Princess Bernice Pauahi Bishop. It was erected as a bastion for her extensive collection of Hawaiian artifacts and royal family heirlooms as the last descendant of the royal Kamehameha family. The museum also has an extensive library and archives for research purposes.

Bishop Museum has both rotating and mainstay exhibits. Hawaiian Hall utilizes its three floors to explore the different realms of Hawaiian culture from the gods and legends to the customs of daily life. Polynesian Hall, which opened in 2013, represents the peoples of Pacific cultures across Polynesia, Micronesia, and Melanesia. And the Abigail Kinoiki Kekaulike Kahili Room honors the kings of the Hawaiian monarchy and displays their *kahili,* feather standards, and other heirlooms. The Science Adventure Center has interactive exhibits focusing on Hawai'i's volcanic origins and environment. It's a great installation to let the kids get hands-on and explore every nook and cranny. From the amazing collection of Pacific seashells to the planetarium, Bishop

FARMERS' MARKETS

Honolulu has a rich farm-to-table restaurant culture as restaurants are sourcing their produce directly from local farmers. With the popularity of farmers' markets, anyone can get on board and find fresh local produce and prepared foods. Check out these farmers' markets in Honolulu:

- **KCC Farmers' Market:** 4303 Diamond Head Rd., Kapi'olani Community College Parking Lot C, 4pm-7pm Tuesday, 7:30am-11am Saturday

- **Ala Moana Farmers' Market:** 1450 Ala Moana Blvd., Ala Moana Center upper deck by Sears, 4pm-7pm Tuesday, 8am-noon Saturday

- **Honolulu @ Night:** 777 Ward Ave., Neal Blaisdell Concert Hall, 4pm-7pm Wednesday

- **Kaka'ako Makai Community Cultural Marketplace:** corner of Ilalo and Ahui Sts., 4:30pm-8pm Friday, 9am-2pm Saturday

- **Manoa Marketplace:** 2752 Woodlawn Dr., 7pm-11pm Sunday, Tuesday, and Thursday

Museum explores Hawai'i's culture through many different disciplines.

Admission is $17.95 adult, $14.95 senior and children age 4-12, children 3 and under are free. To get there from the H-1 freeway, take the Likelike Highway and turn right on Bernice Street.

MOANALUA
Moanalua Gardens

A large grassy park shaded by famous monkeypod trees with canopies creating beautiful, cooling shade, **Moanalua Gardens** (1352 Pineapple Pl., 808/839-5334, www.mgf-hawaii.org, 7:30am-sunset daily) is a 24-acre privately owned reserve open to the public during daylight hours. It is also the site of the home of Prince Lot Kapuaiwa, who later became King Kamehameha V. The Prince Lot Hula Festival is held at Moanalua Gardens every summer. From the Moanalua Freeway H-201, take the Puuloa Road exit toward Tripler Hospital. Turn right immediately after the exit sign into the gardens. The exit is from the off-ramp.

Shopping

DOWNTOWN
Aloha Tower Marketplace

Aloha Tower, a lighthouse that has welcomed ships into Honolulu Harbor since 1926, is the backdrop of the **Aloha Tower Marketplace** (1 Aloha Tower Dr., 808/566-2337, www.aloha-tower.com, 9am-9pm Mon.-Sat., 9am-6pm Sun.). Here you'll find dining, shopping, and a festive atmosphere at one of Honolulu's iconic landmarks.

Check out Ann's Fashion (808/545-1017), which sells aloha wear, sarongs, sundresses and other relaxing beachwear. Imperial Galley (808/529-8866) specializes in Asian-inspired art, apparel, accessories, and home decor. Or for unique gifts, stop by the Aloha Candles kiosk. It's full of colorful and intricately hand-carved candles and other Hawaiiana gift ideas.

ALA MOANA AND KAKA'AKO
Ala Moana Center

Ala Moana Center (1450 Ala Moana Blvd., 808/955-9517, www.alamoanacenter.com, 9:30am-9pm Mon.-Sat., 10am-7pm Sun.) is the world's largest open-air shopping center with over 290 stores and restaurants. The mall is conveniently located near Waikiki and features high-end international clothiers and jewelers, along side popular brand-name stores. Department stores **Macy's** (808/941-2345),

Neiman Marcus (808/951-8887), and **Nordstrom** (808/953-6100) surround the open-air central mall area. At the heart of the mall is an auditorium with seating on multiple mall levels where daily hula performances and other shows are put on.

For technical athletic wear for yoga, running, dancing, and other aerobic pursuits, check out **Lululemon Athletica** (808/946-7220, www.lululemon.com/honolulu/alamoanacenter) on the second floor, Nordstrom wing. Also on the second level, right by Sears, is **Na Hoku** (808/946-2100, www.nahoku.com), a local jewelry store featuring island-themed jewelry, stones, and pearls. **Shirokiya** (808/973-9111, www.shirokiya.com), next to Macy's on the second floor, is like a Japanese mall within the mall. There are food and confections, a beer garden, Japanese goods, health care needs, as well as toys, trinkets, and other wares.

If you're in need of a bikini, on the first level is **San Lorenzo Bikinis** (808/946-3200, www.sanlorenzobikinis.com) with all the best in Brazilian bikini fashion. For local surfwear, **Hawaiian Island Creations** (808/973-6780, www.hicsurf.com) is on the first floor by Sears, and **Town and Country Surf Design** (808/973-5199, www.tcsurf.com) is on the third floor, Sears wing. And for authentic Hawaiian quilts and accessories, head up to the Ho'okipa Terrace and check out **Hawaiian Quilt Collection** (808/946-2233, www.hawaiian-quilts.com).

If you're looking for a great used bookstore in the Kaka'ako area, check out **Jelly's** (670 Auahi St., 808/587-7001, www.jellyshawaii.com, 10am-7pm Mon.-Sat., 10am-6pm Sun.). Not only do they have a great selection of fiction, nonfiction, and children's books, but you'll also find used LPs, CDs, and videos.

Ward Warehouse

Just a couple blocks west of Ala Moana Center is a small, two-story open-air mall called **Ward Warehouse** (1050 Ala Moana Blvd., 808/591-8411, www.wardcenters.com, 10am-9pm Mon.-Sat., 10am-6pm Sun.), part of a conglomerate of five open-air malls in the immediate vicinity.

Ala Moana Center

© KEVIN WHITTON

For the musician on the go in Honolulu, **Island Guitars** (808/591-2910, www.islandguitars.com) is a one-stop shop for new, used, and vintage fretted instruments. **Native Books/Na Mea Hawaii** (808/596-8885, www.nativebookshawaii.com) has locally made gifts, clothing, food, and art, as well as a complete collection of books about Hawai'i and the Pacific. If you're looking for surf apparel or wetsuits, check out **Xcel Wetsuits** (808/596-7441, www.xcelwetsuits.com). And if you're in the mood for a specialty beer, wine, or liquor, the **Liquor Collection** (808/524-8808, http://liquorcollection.com) is a must.

CHINATOWN

If you're interested in picking up a bottle of wine, stop by **HASR Wine Co.** (31 N. Pauahi St., 808/535-9463, www.hasrwineco.com, 10am-8pm Mon.-Fri., 10am-5pm Sat.-Sun.). They have a very knowledgeable staff and offer wine tastings Tuesday and Friday (5pm-7pm).

KAIMUKI

Kapahulu Avenue is a hub for dining and shopping. The mile-long stretch, running from Leahi Avenue by the fire station nearly up to the H-1 freeway, has plenty of places to grab a quick bite, sit-down restaurants, clothing stores, sporting goods stores, coffee shops, and a supermarket. There are even two tattoo parlors on the strip.

The Clothes Chick (415 Kapahulu Ave., 808/739-2442, http://theclotheschick.com, 10am-9pm daily) is a designer resale and consignment shop with chic clothes and accessories located next to a gas station. Parking is in the rear of the building. **Glam Rok** (449 Kapahulu Ave., 808/732-6278, http://glamrokhawaii.com, 10:30am-6pm daily) is a small, resale and consignment boutique specializing in designer jeans and handbags and trendy clothes in Hee

Hing Plaza next to the bank. Free parking is available under the two-story center. **Bailey's Antiques and Aloha Shirts** (517 Kapahulu Ave., 808/734-7628, http://alohashirts.com, 10am-9pm daily), next to another gas station up the street, is a score if you're looking for Hawaiiana wear and decoration. Along with over 15,000 aloha shirts in stock—new, used, and vintage—they also sell antiques like figurines, jewelry, postcards, and Hawaiian music LPs. **Peggy's Picks** (732 Kapahulu Ave. Ste. 1, 808/737-3297, Mon.-Sat. 11am-7pm) is an eclectic shop with Hawaiiana and other collectibles from around the world, furniture, jewelry, and curious odds and ends. Limited street parking is available.

Waialae Avenue also has retail outlets worth a stop. **Drift Boutique** (3434 Waialae Ave., #4, 808/284-1177, 1pm-6pm Mon.-Sat.) between 8th and 9th Avenues is a beach girl boutique selling unique locally handmade jewelry, bathing suits, and specialty accessories. If you're crafty, check out **Bead It** (1152 Koko Head Ave., 808/734-1182, http://ibeads.com/kaimuki.htm, 10am-6pm Mon.-Sat., noon-4pm Sun.). They have a full range of beads, gemstones, books, chains, tools, and they also offer classes. **Gecko Books & Comics** (1151 12th Ave., 808/732-1292, 11am-7pm Sun.-Tues., 10am-9pm Wed.-Sat.) is right off Waialae Avenue and packed with books and comics. The owner is extremely knowledgeable and helpful.

MOILI'ILI

If you're just in the mood for a nice bottle of wine, stop by **The Wine Stop** (1809 S. King St., 808/946-3707, www.thewinestophawaii.com, 10am-9pm Mon.-Thurs., 10am-10pm Fri.-Sat., 11am-7pm Sun.). This quaint beer and wine boutique has an in-store sommelier to help with your wine selection or pairings.

HONOLULU

Entertainment and Events

NIGHTLIFE
Chinatown

On Nuuanu Avenue, **The Dragon Upstairs** (1038 Nuuanu Ave., 808/526-1411, www.thedragonupstairs.com, 7pm-2am) is a warm and classy jazz club located above Hank's Café. They also feature world music. For a different beat, check out **O'Toole's Irish Pub** (902 Nuuanu Ave., 808/536-4138, http://otoolesirishpub.com, 10am-2am daily). The pub has live Irish, folk, and reggae music and is also a cigar bar where smoking is allowed inside.

On Bethel Street you'll find **Bambu Two Cafe** (1144 Bethel St., 808/528-1144, www.bambutwo.com, 2pm-2am Mon.-Sat.), a café and martini bar with indoor and outdoor seating. They serve $3.50 martinis all day, every day.

On Hotel Street, check out **Thirtyninehotel** (39 N. Hotel St., 808/599-2552, www.thirtyninehotel.com, 4pm-2am Tues.-Sat.). This upstairs art gallery and indoor/outdoor bar serves tapas and is a great place to relax outside and listen to live music or DJs. Right next door on the street level is the aptly named **Nextdoor** (43 N. Hotel St., 808/548-6398, http://nextdoorhnl.com, 8pm-2am Wed.-Sat.). A two-story combination nightclub and creative arts venue, Nextdoor is as versatile as its acts, ranging from a cinema house to a dance hall, but it's best known as a music venue. There are full-service bars upstairs and downstairs, with VIP bottle service and table reservations upstairs. Also on the same block is **Bar 35** (35 N. Hotel St., 808/537-3535, www.bar35.com, 4pm-2am Mon.-Fri., 6pm-2am Sat.), a warm and modern spot featuring hundreds of international beers, indoor and patio bars, daily happy hour specials, DJs, and live music. They also have table reservations and bottle service, and serve fusion-gourmet pizzas and simple tapas. **Manifest** (32 N. Hotel St., 808/523-7575, http://manifesthawaii.com, 8am-10pm Mon., 8am-2am Tues.-Fri., 10am-2am Sat.) also holds valuable real estate on Hotel Street. A coffee shop by day, Manifest is a sophisticated cocktail bar after dark and a venue for artists of all mediums. Live music includes hip-hop, bluegrass, punk, and everything in between.

Kaka'ako

Pint + Jigger (1936 S. King St., 808/744-9593, www.pintandjigger.com, 4:30pm-midnight Sun. and Tues.-Thurs., 9am-1:30am Fri.-Sat.) is a modern public house designed to offer creative pairing of cuisine, beer, and cocktails, within a relaxed atmosphere. Along with 21 beers on tap that change regularly, specialty cocktails, and a menu that also teeters to reflect the selection of libations, this bar also takes into account atmosphere with bar seating, table seating, beer gardens, and shuffleboard.

Ala Moana

One of the premier night clubs on O'ahu is on the Ho'okipa Terrace at the top of Ala Moana Center. **Pearl Ultralounge** (1450 Ala Moana Blvd., 808/944-8000, www.pearlhawaii.com, Tues.-Fri. 11am-1am daily) offers a luxury lounge experience with cuisine, live music, and dancing. Reservations for VIP bottle service are

the Pearl Ultralounge at the top of Ala Moana Center

© KEVIN WHITTON

taken at 10:30pm and held for 30 minutes. The dress code is strictly enforced.

Also on the Hoʻokipa Terrace is a lively open-air bar called the **Mai Tai Bar** (1450 Ala Moana Blvd., 808/947-2900, www.maitaibar. com, 11am-1am daily). They offer daily *pau hana* specials (4pm-7pm), nightly happy hour pricing (9:30pm-12:30am), and beer specials all day during football season. The appetizers and entrées have local flair, and they also have island-style live music for happy hour every night (8pm-11pm).

Rumors (410 Atkinson Dr., 808/955-4811, 5pm-3am Fri., 5pm-3am Sat.), located in the Ala Moana Hotel, has a more relaxed atmosphere focusing on the music and dancing. They play everything from hip-hop to hits of the '70s, '80s, and '90s.

THE ARTS

Chinatown is the home of Honolulu's art scene, and there are nearly 20 art galleries that support and promote the local artists comprising Honolulu's art community. **The ARTS at Marks Garage** (1159 Nuuanu Ave., 808/521-2903, www.artsatmarks.com, 11am-6pm Tues.-Sat.) is the heartbeat of Chinatown's art scene. With 12 major exhibits and performances, lectures, screenings, and workshops, Marks has transformed the Chinatown community through the arts. **Ong King Art Center** (184 N. King St., http://ongking.com) has carved out a niche for performance art. Whether it be through spoken word, poetry, live music, or visual art, Ong King encourages creative risk taking. **Pegge Hopper** (1164 Nuuanu Ave., 808/524-1160, http://peggehopper.com, 11am-4pm Tues.-Fri., 11am-3pm Sat.) has been a mainstay in Chinatown, her gallery open since 1983. Famous for her paintings and drawings of Hawaiian women, her gallery features her own work, as well as guest artists from time to time. **Bethel Street Gallery** (1140 Bethel St., Ste. G-4, 808/524-3552, www.bethelstreetgallery.com, 11am-4pm Tues.-Fri., 11am-3pm Sat.) is Hawaiʻi's largest artist owned and operated gallery, showcasing top artists in different medium.

THEATER
Downtown

On the grounds of the Honolulu Museum of Art, **Doris Duke Theatre** (900 S. Beretania St., 808/532-8700, http://honolulumuseum. org) screens independent, documentary, and international films, performances and concerts in a 280-seat venue. For families, the **Honolulu Theatre for Youth** (229 Queen Emma Sq., 808/839-9885, www.htyweb.org) is the perfect introduction to the dramatics for kids preschool through high school. The professional company presents a full season of plays every year. Another community theater in downtown Honolulu, **Kumu Kahua Theatre** (46 Merchant St., 808/536-4441, http://kumukahua.org) features Hawaiian playwrights and plays about life in Hawaiʻi.

Chinatown

The **Hawaii Theatre** (1130 Bethel St., 808/528-0506, www.hawaiitheatre.com) is an old vaudevillian theater dating back more than 90 years and listed on the National Register of Historic Places. Today, the restored multipurpose arts

HONOLULU

PUBLIC ART

At first glance, the industrial zone in Kakaʻako, between Ala Moana Boulevard and Kapiolani Boulevard, can be a mind-numbing experience. Auto repair Quonsets, warehouses, and homogeneous industrial edifices appear crushed together with little regard for open space. But young urban artists are gentrifying this industrial zone with imagery and color, free for all to see, sparking a renaissance of cafés, art studios, and galleries.

Artists are taking art outside and have created murals of varying sizes all over the exterior of buildings in parts of Kakaʻako, mostly in the urban graffiti style. Just drive slowly down Queen Street between Cooke Street and Ward Avenue and check out all the public art. Now that you know what to look for, go explore and find more.

center is a stage for concerts, film, musicals, and ballets. Just the allure and grandeur of the theater complements any performance.

Kaka'ako

The Neil S. Blaisdell Concert Hall (777 Ward Ave., 808/768-5400, www.blaisdellcenter.com) is the premier performing arts theater for the Honolulu Symphony and the Hawaii Opera Theatre. With 2,158 seats, a balcony, and a proscenium stage, the theater accommodates many traveling Broadway productions as well.

Manoa

Located on the UH Manoa campus, **Kennedy Theatre** (1770 East-West Rd., 808/956-7655, www.hawaii.edu/kennedy) showcases productions from the university's department of theater and dance. The 620-seat mainstage theater shows Asian productions, Western productions, and contemporary works, including dance performances.

Set back in Manoa Valley, the **Manoa Valley Theatre** (2833 East Manoa Rd., 808/988-6131, www.manoavalleytheatre.com) is Honolulu's Off-Broadway playhouse. The semiprofessional theater showcases mainstream contemporary plays and musicals from Broadway, Off-Broadway, and major regional theaters.

Kaimuki

The oldest performing arts center in Hawai'i, **Diamond Head Theatre** (520 Makapuu Ave., 808/733-0277, www.diamondheadtheatre.com) opened in 1915. The historic theater shows six mainstage theatrical productions each season, including five major musicals. The theater has been dubbed the Broadway of the Pacific.

CINEMA

If you're in the mood for a box office smash, there are two major movie theaters in Honolulu. In Kaka'ako, the **Ward Stadium 16 Cinema** (1044 Auahi St., 808/594-7044, www.consolidatedtheatres.com, $11) may be found in Ward Center. Matinee (before 4pm) showings cost $8.75. Add $4 for 3-D films. In Iwilei,

you've got the **Regal Dole Cannery Stadium 18 and IMAX** (735 Iwilei Rd., 808/528-3653, www.fandango.com), a participating theater in the Hawai'i International Film Festival.

FESTIVALS AND EVENTS

The **Neil S. Blaisdell Center** (777 Ward Ave., 808/768-5400, box office 808/768-5252, www.blaisdellcenter.com) spans a city block and includes the multipurpose circular arena for concerts, shows, and sporting events; the concert hall; and the exhibition hall for expos, fairs, and events.

The **Honolulu Museum of Art** (900 S. Beretania St., 808/532-8700, http://honolulumuseum.org, 10am-4:30pm Tues.-Sat., 1pm-3pm Sun.) hosts **ART after DARK,** a monthly art party exploring different themes on rotating exhibit in the museum, like the art of tattoo or celebrating *Hina matsuri* (Girls' Day in Japan) through elaborate dolls, 6pm-9pm on the last Friday of the month, January through October . Admission is $10.

With myriad bars, nightclubs, restaurants, and art galleries, it's no wonder Chinatown is also the hub of outdoor events. Chinatown hosts annual Chinese New Year, Halloween, St. Patrick's Day, and Cinco De Mayo Festivals, as well as the famous **First Friday.** On the first Friday of every month, people gather in the streets of Chinatown and in the galleries,

---

100 MILES ON TWO WHEELS

The **Honolulu Century Ride** (www.hbl.org, late Sept.) is the largest cycling event on O'ahu. It's not so much a race, but rather an untimed challenging ride to pedal 100 miles from Kapi'olani Park, around Koko Crater, up to Swanzy Beach in Ka'a'awa, then back to Kapi'olani Park. Road closures go into effect for the safety of the thousands of local, national, and international riders who show up to participate.

museums, and art studios to celebrate the vibrant art scene. The festive event includes live music and street entertainment, and bars and restaurants cater to the crowds. Festivities begin around 6pm.

January-March

The **Honolulu Festival** (808/926-2424, http://honolulufestival.com) is a cultural event focusing on Pacific Rim cultures. The three-day festival has educational programs, activities, and performances, like cultural dances and traditional art demonstrations. The finale is a parade down Kalakaua Avenue and a spectacular fireworks display over Waikiki.

The **Hawaii Collectors Expo** (777 Ward Ave., 808/768-5400, box office 808/768-5252, http://hawaiicollectorsexpo.wix.com) in late February features all kinds of art, antiques, and collectibles. With its Hawaiiana, colored glass, handmade aloha shirts, Star Wars figurines, this three-day expo at the Neil S. Blaisell Exhibition Hall is a favorite of local residents. There is a small entrance fee.

April-June

Memorial Day weekend is celebrated in Honolulu with the annual **Lantern Floating Hawaii** (www.lanternfloatinghawaii.com) festival on Magic Island. On the holiday itself, people from all corners of world write remembrances and prayers on specially prepared floating lanterns to be placed in the Ala Wai Canal at dusk. The sight of over 3,000 floating lanterns is a powerful and moving experience.

On King Kamehameha Day, June 11, the **King Kamehameha Celebration Floral Parade** (www.kamehamehadaycelebration.org/floral-parade.html) is not to be missed. Beginning at 'Iolani Palace with a lei draping ceremony at the King Kamehameha statue, the parade marches slowly to Kapi'olani Park, with a beautiful display or culture, color, and flowers.

The **Islandwide Spring Crafts & Foods Expo** (777 Ward Ave., 808/768-5400, box office 808/768-5252, www.islandwidecraft-expos.com/public/public/index4.htm) is the state's largest craft fair. Over 200 artisans and food vendors come together at the Blaisdell to share their handmade goods and cuisine. There is also a larger Christmas show. Entrance fees apply.

July-September

The biennial **Hawaiian Islands Vintage Surf Auction** (777 Ward Ave., 808/768-5400, box office 808/768-5252, http://hawaiiansurfauction.com) takes place at the Blaisdell every other July on odd years. The auction draws vintage surf collectors from all over the world, and the items on auction, everything from old surf movie posters to vintage surfboards, are on display for all to see.

Also in July, the **Prince Lot Hula Festival** (1352 Pineapple Pl., 808/839-5334, http://moanaluagardensfoundation.org) at Moanalua Gardens is the largest noncompetitive hula event in Hawai'i. The daylong display is very popular and honors Prince Lot Kapuaiwa, who

HONOLULU

FIRST FRIDAY GALLERY WALK

What kicked off in 2003 as a cultural community revival of the art scene in Honolulu has become one of the most attended, and most popular, monthly events on O'ahu. In doing so, **First Friday** has transformed Chinatown into a community with a hip, vibrant art culture supporting myriad galleries, studios, cafés, and restaurants sponsoring local art and artists as a community.

First Friday, a campaign initiated by The ARTS at Marks Garage, is a free, self-guided gallery walk 5pm-9pm every first Friday of the month. Chinatown galleries and studios present art exhibits, and live entertainment and refreshments abound for the thousands of art enthusiasts who descend upon the area to celebrate art in all its forms. Visit www.artsatmarks.com, where you'll find a link to a Chinatown gallery map.

helped to revive hula by carrying on the tradition through parties at his home, which is located at the gardens.

The **Hawaii Food & Wine Festival** (www.hawaiifoodandwinefestival.com) is a four-day epicurean delight featuring the specialties of over 50 internationally renowned master chefs and wine and spirit producers. The festival takes place across Honolulu and Ko'olina in September. Check the website for details.

October-December
Every year in early December, over 20,000 runners from around the world flock to Honolulu to participate and compete in the **Honolulu Marathon** (3435 Waialae Ave., Ste. 200, 808/734-7200, www.honolulumarathon.org). Ala Moana Boulevard between Ala Moana Beach Park and Ala Moana Center is transformed into the starting line, where runners begin their 26.2-mile trek to Hawai'i Kai and back to finish in Waikiki.

Downtown's Historic District, at Honolulu Hale, hosts **Honolulu City Lights** (www.honolulucitylights.org) in December. The Christmas celebration of lights is punctuated by huge statues decorating the exterior of the building, most notably, Shaka Santa.

Food

DOWNTOWN
Hawaiian
On the outskirts of downtown Honolulu is a long-established Hawaiian food joint called the **People's Cafe** (1300 Pali Hwy., 808/536-5789, 10am-8pm Mon.-Sat., 10am-5pm Sun., $6-12). Just *makai* of the Pali Long's parking lot, look for the bright red neon sign for this small restaurant having all the favorite Hawaiian combos plus some extras like salted meat and kimchi.

American
For a delicious burger and seasonal brews overlooking Honolulu Harbor, check out **Gordon Biersch** (1 Aloha Tower Dr., 808/599-4877, www.gordonbiersch.com, 11am-midnight Sun.-Thurs., 11am-1am Fri.-Sat., $12-24). They have a wide variety of beers on tap and live music Wednesday through Saturday.

CHINATOWN
Honolulu's Chinatown is chock-full of restaurants providing regional cuisine from all over the globe. Just about every other storefront is a restaurant or serves food in some fashion.

Tea
For a quaint and quiet afternoon tea, stop in at the unpretentious **Tea at 1024** (1024 Nuuanu Ave., 808/521-9596, www.teaat1024.net, 11am-2pm Tues.-Fri., 11am-3pm Sat.). Relax in the charming teahouse, don a special hat from the hat stand, and choose your china for tea time.

Asian
For a sampling of cuisine from China, Korea, Vietnam, Thailand, and the Philippines, duck inside the **Maunakea Marketplace Food Court** (1120 Maunakea St., 808/524-3409). In the center of the shopping complex that spans the small city block are vendors with stalls lined up shoulder to shoulder and family-style seating in the middle. The air is thick with the sweet smells of seafood and spices from different countries mingling together. Most vendors offer their food bento or plate lunch style.

Chinese
In historic Chinatown, **Little Village Noodle House** (1113 Smith St., 808/545-3008, http://littlevillagehawaii.com, 10:30am-10:30pm Mon.-Fri., 10:30am-midnight Sat.-Sun., $7-13) is the quintessential Chinese restaurant for grabbing a bite. With over 100 menu items covering meat, poultry, seafood, rice, and noodle dishes, the family-friendly restaurant has every palate covered.

Pacific Rim

For exceptional Pacific Rim cuisine, check out **Indigo** (1121 Nuuanu Ave., 808/521-2900, www.indigo-hawaii.com, 11:30am-midnight Tues., 11:30am-1:30am Wed.-Sat., $22-34), a very popular, award-winning restaurant with Eurasian-influenced fare. They also boast over 70 wines to pair with the dishes, as well as desserts. They serve lunch and dinner, and after the dining room closes, the bar carries on with the festivities.

Irish Pubs

J.J. Dolan's (1147 Bethel St., 808/537-4992, www.jjdolans.com, 11am-2am Mon.-Sat., $16-19) is an Irish pub serving delicious New York pizza. With a full bar and a selection of Irish whiskey, this small pub can get pretty rowdy when there is a packed house.

Murphy's Bar & Grill (2 Merchant St., 808/531-0422, http://murphyshawaii.com, 11:30am-2am Mon.-Fri., opens at 4pm Sat.-Sun., $11-19) has a separate bar and dining room under one historic roof. The menu features a combination of bar food, burgers, and Irish food. The bar favors Irish whiskey and draught beer, with shuffleboard on offer.

Cuban

On Bethel Street you'll find **Soul De Cuba Cafe** (1121 Bethel St., 808/545-2822, http://souldecuba.com, 8am-8pm daily, $10-24). The authentic flavorful and rich Cuban fare is prepared from family recipes passed down through generations. The classic Cuban dish *ropa vieja* is a Honolulu favorite. If you stop by for lunch, the Cuban sandwiches are also extremely delicious.

French

Brasserie Du Vin (1115 Bethel St., 808/545-1115, brasserieduvin.com, 11:30am-10pm Sun.-Thurs., 11:30am-midnight Fri.-Sat., $11-26) is a French restaurant with a casual and rustic environment offering indoor and patio seating. The seasonal menu includes small dishes, entrées, artisan cheeses, charcuterie, and classic French desserts. They also have food and drink specials during happy hour (4pm-6pm Mon.-Sat.).

KAKA'AKO
Quick Bites

For coffee, sandwiches, quick bites, breakfast foods, and Internet access, stop in at **Fresh Café** (831 Queen St., 808/688-8055, http://freshcafehi.com, 8am-11pm Mon.-Sat., 9am-6pm Sun., $5-9), where the ingredients are locally sourced. Fresh Café is the center of the Kaka'ako urban art scene revival, and hip art decorates the walls of the establishment as well as the walls of the buildings surrounding it. They also have a performance space in the back of the restaurant for live music and art shows. Check their website for the calendar of events.

Steak and Seafood

On the second floor of Ward Center you'll find a great steak and seafood restaurant. **Ryan's Grill** (1200 Ala Moana Blvd., 808/591-9132, www.ryansgrill.com, 11am-midnight daily, $13-21) has a varied menu with small and big salads, pasta and pizza, sandwiches, and steak and seafood options. They also have a relaxing bar area and beautiful views of Ala Moana Beach Park.

Gastropub

In the Ward Farmer's Market, **REAL a gastropub** (1020 Auahi St., 808/596-2526, www.realgastropub.com, 2pm-2am Mon.-Sat., $3-12) is spearheading the gastropub trend in Honolulu with smart combinations of flavors in their tapas-style menu items, designed for sampling. You can combine your choice with one of over 200 bottled beers, imported from all over the world, and 24 rotating taps. They also have a full bar and wine.

MANOA
Quick Bites

For a coffee, some home-cooked quick bites, and lots of reading material, stop in at **Coffeeline Campus Coffeehouse** (1820 University Ave., 808/778-7909, 8am-2pm Mon.-Fri., 8am-noon Sat.-Sun.). In the back of the YWCA building on University Ave., across from UH Manoa, look for the stairs on the south side of the building leading up to Coffeeline's patio, complete with tables, couches, and more reading material than you can handle. There is free parking behind the building.

Tea

Wai'oli Tea Room (2950 Manoa Rd., 808/988-5800, www.thewaiolitearoom.net, 10:30am-8:30pm Mon.-Fri., 8am-3:30pm Sat.-Sun., $8-14) is a sophisticated restaurant and bakery set in a historic dwelling among beautiful landscaping. Enjoy breakfast, lunch, or dinner with sandwiches, salads, quiche, homemade soup, and of course, afternoon tea.

Hawaiian

Deep in the valley, by the Manoa Falls trailhead and Lyon Arboretum, is a restaurant set among the trees of Manoa's verdant rainforest. **Treetops Restaurant** (3737 Manoa Rd., 808/988-6838, www.thetreetopsrestaurant. com, 11am-2pm Mon.-Fri., opens at 10:30am Sat.-Sun., $7-16) serves both a weekday and a weekend buffet lunch, perfect for a post-hike meal.

Mexican

For authentic Mexican food, stop in at **Serg's Mexican Kitchen** (2740 E. Manoa Rd., 808/988-8118, 11am-9pm Mon.-Sat., 8am-8pm Sun., $4-16). With open-air, family-style seating and mariachi music, this BYOB joint is the spot for a quick taco or a sit down meal with a big group.

KAIMUKI
Quick Bites
Rainbow Drive-In (3308 Kanaina Ave., 808/737-0177, www.rainbowdrivein.com, 7am-9pm daily, $6-8) has served choice plate lunches since 1961, always at a reasonable price. Protein, rice, and gravy never tasted so good.

Steak and Seafood
On Waialae Avenue are a handful of popular restaurants. **Town** (3435 Waialae Ave., 808/735-5900, www.townkaimuki. com, 7am-9:30pm Mon.-Thurs., 7am-10pm Fri.-Sat., $16-26) serves breakfast, lunch, and dinner. The hip spot, with modern art decor, is a mix between Hawai'i regional and Italian cuisine, all with the focus of serving organic, fresh, and locally sourced ingredients. They have a full bar, or you can BYOB for a corkage fee of $15. Limited street parking is available, but there is a small parking lot behind the restaurant as well.

Café Miro (3446 Waialae Ave., 808/734-2737, www.cafemirohawaii.com, Tues.-Sun. 5:30pm-10:30pm, $43-54) is an exquisite steak and seafood restaurant with mostly French cuisine, serving a three-course prix fixe menu and a four-course Chef's Special menu. Think oysters, lamb, duck, scallop, abalone, and steak, each drizzled in an appropriate sauce.

12th Ave Grill (1145 12th Ave., 808/732-9469, www.12thavegrill.com, 5:30pm-9pm Mon.-Thurs., 5:30pm-10pm Fri.-Sat., $25-30) is just off Waialae Avenue and offers award-winning contemporary American cuisine and a commitment to locally sourced and seasonal ingredients. A well-selected wine list and scratch bar pair nicely with the flavorful fare. The small dining room is intimate, yet comfortable.

Salt (3605 Waialae Ave., 808/744-7567, http://salthonolulu.com, 5:30pm-midnight daily, $6-25) is another popular Waialae Avenue establishment. Salt Kitchen and Tasting Bar offers an extensive wine list from around the world, signature cocktails, and a variety of beers, paired with eccentric *pupu*-style dishes meant to be shared using locally sourced ingredients. You'll find local rabbit, oysters, salads, cheese boards, and salted, dried, and cured meats, or you can just get a burger.

On Kapahulu is a popular and often packed **Uncle Bo's** (559 Kapahulu Ave., 808/735-8311, www.unclebosrestaurant.com, 5pm-2am daily, $12-27). Combining American bistro with Pacific Rim cuisine, Uncle Bo's is a small, modern, but casual restaurant. They have an extensive *pupu* menu, as well as serving steak, seafood, pasta, and pizza. Be prepared for a bit of wait on the weekends, and if the bar is full, that means you'll have to stand outside.

Award-winning chef Colin Nishida creates Hawaiian-style comfort food, served as complete meals or *pupu* style, inside the Prudential Locations building in an offshoot of the famous Side Street Inn in Kaka'ako called **Side Street Inn on Da Strip** (614 Kapahulu Ave., 808/739-3939, http://sidestreetinn.com, 3pm-midnight daily, $12-22). The restaurant has family-style seating with a touch of fine dining, and the portions are quite large and designed to be shared.

Hawaiian

For authentic Hawaiian food, check out **Ono Hawaiian Food** (726 Kapahulu Ave., 808/737-2275, 11am-8pm Mon.-Sat., $6-22). The family-run restaurant is small and cozy, with just a few tables. Be prepared to wait outside during peak hours.

Thai

On Waialae Avenue there are two consistent picks for Thai food. **Champa Thai** (3452 Waialae Ave., 808/732-0054, www.champathai.com, 11 am-2pm and 5:30pm-9:30pm Mon.-Sat., 5pm-9pm Sun., $7-13) is a BYOB restaurant that serves lunch and dinner and offers sit-down or take-out service. There is street parking available in the neighborhood and four parking spaces behind the restaurant. **To Thai For** (3571 Waialae Ave., 808/734-3443, www.itstothaifor.com, 10:30 am-9:30pm Mon.-Sat., 5pm-9pm Sun., $9-20) has a basic Thai menu through which you can combine the dish with the protein of your liking.

Japanese

On Kapahulu Avenue are three noteworthy Japanese restaurants. **Irifune** (563 Kapahulu Ave., 808/737-1141, 11:30 am-1:30pm and 5:30pm-9:30pm Tues.-Sat., $10-15) is a curious hole-in-the-wall with some of the best ahi on O'ahu. The entire menu consists of some combination of garlic and ahi, served with local-style sides. This restaurant is very popular,

and on the weekends you can expect a wait. They do have a bench outside. Park across the street in the pay parking lot, or there is street parking in the neighborhood behind the restaurant.

Tokkuri Tei (611 Kapahulu Ave., 808/732-6480, http://tokkuri-tei.com, 11 am-2pm and 5:30pm-midnight Mon.-Fri., 5:30pm-midnight Sat., 5pm-10:30pm Sun., $4-50) is a popular izakaya restaurant offering traditional Japanese food with French influence and local uniqueness. With its sushi bar or table seating and an extensive sake and spirits selection, it will take several visits sample the wealth of food on all 13 pages of the menu. It's located on the second floor of Hee Hing Plaza, and there is valet parking under the plaza. Reservations are necessary.

At the opposite end of Kapahulu Avenue, just off the main drag, is another top-notch izakaya establishment offering traditional Japanese fare. **Izakaya Nonbei** (3108 Olu St., 808/734-5573, 5pm-11:30pm Mon.-Thurs., 5pm-1:30am Fri.-Sat., 5pm-10:30pm Sun., $6-25) is a small restaurant with a sushi bar and shared and private seating. They have a vast selection of sake and beer, but they are known for their frozen sake.

Mexican

Jose's Mexican Cafe & Cantina (1134 Koko Head Ave., 808/732-1833, www.joseshonolulu.com, 11am-10pm Mon.-Sat., 11am-9pm Sun., $14-25) serves up simple Mexican food with seafood, beef, and pork specialties, and even a few egg dishes. They have happy hour weekdays 3pm-6pm and a selection of Mexican beers and different styles of margaritas, mixed either for a glass or a pitcher.

Indian

Himalayan Kitchen (1137 11th Ave., #205, 808/735-1122, 11am-2pm and 5:30pm-10pm Tues.-Fri., 5:30pm-10pm Sat.-Mon., $11-22) serves Nepali and Indian cuisine in a small restaurant with indoor and patio seating. This second-story BYOB is a local favorite and often packed with those seeking their variety

HONOLULU

of vegetarian and meat dishes. The entrance to the restaurant is in an alcove between a gift store, a barbecue joint, an Italian restaurant, and a salon. There is a paid parking lot with ample parking.

Sweets and Treats

You can grab a delicious pastry, dessert, or cup of coffee on Waialae Avenue at **JJ Bistro & French Pastry** (3447 Waialae Ave., 808/739-0993, 9am-9pm Mon.-Thurs., 9am-9:30pm Fri.-Sat., noon-8pm Sun., $5-19). They also have pizza, pasta, sandwiches, and à la carte entrées. If you're down for an old-fashioned ice cream cone, stop by the **Pill Box** (1133 11th Ave., 808/737-4966, 9am-9pm Mon.-Fri., 9am-5pm Sat., 9pm-11pm Sun.). This full-service neighborhood pharmacy has friendly staff, books, and the best ice cream in town. There are a couple spaces out front on 11th Avenue, or you can park in the paid parking lot behind the building. If you're quick and can get your ice cream within the 15-minute grace period, parking is free.

On Kapahulu Avenue, residents and visitors flock to **Leonard's Bakery** (933 Kapahulu Ave., 808/737-5591, www.leonardshawaii.com, 5am-11pm daily) in record numbers, often backing up traffic on Kapahulu while they wait for a parking stall in the small parking lot out front. Look for the neon sign and the line out the door. Leonard's is famous for its *malasadas* and doughnuts, but also has delicious pastries, cookies, bread, pies, and wraps. For shaved ice, head to **Waiola Shave Ice** (3113 Mokihana St., 808/735-8886, 10:30am-7:30pm daily). It's tucked away right off Kapahulu Avenue, across from Safeway.

Markets

Tamura's Fine Wines & Liquors (3496 Waialae Ave., 808/735-7100, http://tamurasfinewine.com, 9:30am-9pm Mon.-Sat., 9:30am-8pm Sun.) not only has one of the best selections of beer, wine, and spirits for the best prices in Honolulu, but they also have prepared foods, cheeses, specialty groceries, and are famous for their fresh *poke*.

© KEVIN WHITTON

Leonard's Bakery, the mecca of *malasadas*

MOILI'ILI
Health Food

Down To Earth (2525 S. King St., 808/947-7678, www.downtoearth.org, 7:30am-10pm daily) is an all-vegetarian, natural, and organic food store with a deli, salad bar, hot foods, and smoothies. Parking is on the roof behind the store. Take the alley right past the entrance and turn up the ramp.

Kokua Market (2643 S. King St., 808/941-1922, www.kokua.coop, 8am-9pm daily) is a natural food store co-op on the other side of University Avenue from Down To Earth. They have bulk foods and natural and organic groceries, but the real draw is the deli, with hot and cold items. The menu includes raw, vegan, macrobiotic, and natural meats options. There are also freshly baked desserts. Parking is behind the store from Kahuna Lane.

An oasis of charm and natural food on busy and urban King Street, **Peace Cafe** (2239 S. King St., 808/951-7555, www.peacecafehawaii.com, 11am-9pm Mon.-Sat., 11am-3pm Sun., $9-11) serves vegan home cooking in a comfortable setting. Within its eclectic decorating scheme, Peace Cafe has sandwiches, salads, stews, and prepared goods like granola for the taking.

Japanese

Sometimes the restaurants that are the hardest to find turn out to be the best. This is the case at **Imanas Tei** (2626 S. King St., 808/941-2626, 5pm-11:30pm Mon.-Sat., $6-10). Tucked away behind the 7-11, the traditional Japanese menu is a favorite with locals, as well as the chanko nabe, a hearty seafood stew. There are only a few designated parking stalls for Imanas Tei, so if they're full, you'll need to park at Puck's Alley around the corner off University Avenue; the plaza has a paid parking lot.

Indian

Cafe Maharani (2509 S. King St., 808/951-7447, http://cafemaharanihawaii.com, 5pm-10pm daily, $14-16) is an award-winning casual restaurant blending natural ingredients and a host of spices to create some of the most sought after Indian food in Honolulu.

Mediterranean

Da Spot (2469 S. King St., 808/941-1313, 10:30am-9:30pm Mon.-Sat., $6-10) is a roomy Mediterranean café that is completely open to King Street from the front. They offer vegetarian fare, including Thai and Egyptian cuisine and desserts, as well as rustic salads and prepared foods like mango salsa, imported cheeses, olives, and hummus. Take a seat and take advantage of Internet access with your meal.

Steak and Seafood

For modern fine dining on the best in Hawai'i regional cuisine, **Chef Mavro** (1969 S. King St., 808/944-4714, www.chefmavro.com, 6pm-9pm Tues.-Sun., $75-165) offers the quintessential experience. The French-influenced cuisine is award-winning and the ingredients are locally sourced. Seasonal menus are geared toward wine pairings. Children must be 5 years of age or older, and attire is aloha casual.

Renowned chef specializing in Hawai'i regional cuisine Alan Wong pairs fine dining with fresh and local ingredients at his flagship restaurant **Alan Wong's** (1857 S. King St., 808/949-1939, www.alanwongs.com, 5pm-10pm daily, $30-50). Locally raised beef and sustainable seafood combined with O'ahu farm fresh produce are served up with a completely local flair. In addition to entrées, they offer two set multicourse tasting menus available with wine pairings.

In the same vein of Hawai'i regional cuisine and locally sourced ingredients, **Side Street Inn** (1225 Hopaka St., 808/591-0253, http://sidestreetinn.com, 2 pm-2am daily, $12-22) has transformed over the years from a little hole-in-the-wall with exceptional food to a big-hole-in-the-wall with phenomenal cuisine where local and international chefs go to eat. With the full bar and large portions served *pupu* style, this is a great place to share the experience of food and drink with family and friends.

IWILEI
Seafood

In the Honolulu Harbor area, seafood is the main attraction. **Nico's at Pier 38** (808/540-1377, http://nicospier38.com, 10am-4pm and 5pm-9pm Mon.-Sat., 10am-4pm Sun., $13-17) is both a fish market and restaurant. They serve Hawaiian-style seafood with a French twist—gourmet food with plate lunch delivery. The open-air restaurant also has a full bar. From Nimitz Highway, access Pier 38 from Alakawa Avenue.

Sam Choy's Breakfast Lunch and Crab (580 N. Nimitz Hwy., #1, 808/545-7979, http://samchoyhawaii.com, 7am-9pm Mon.-Thurs., 7am-10pm Fri., 8am-10pm Sat., 8am-9pm Sun., $16-40) is a local favorite, serving up big portions of Hawaiian-style seafood with gourmet flair. They also have a local brewing company right next door for fresh, handcrafted beers to complement the seafood. Their Sunday brunch buffet, complete with carving and omelet stations, is also a big draw.

On the way out to Sand Island is one of the few real tiki bars still in operation. **La Mariana** (50 Sand Island Access Rd., 808/848-2800, www.lamarianasailingclub.com, 11am-9pm daily, $14-42) is a steak and seafood restaurant located in the La Mariana Sailing Club. Nestled at the edge of Ke'ehi Lagoon, the restaurant is a veritable museum of Hawaiiana treasures and collectibles, with an unmatched ambience from the warm glow of colorful lights, wood decor, and the grin of tikis all around.

Information and Services

VISITOR CENTER

The **Hawaii Visitors and Convention Bureau** (2270 Kalakaua Ave., Ste. 801, 808/524-0722 or 800/464-2924, www.gohawaii.com) manages the official visitor center for O'ahu and has all manner of maps, brochures, travel tips and activity ideas.

LIBRARY

Internet access is available at the **Kaimuki Public Library** (1041 Koko Head Ave., 808/733-8422, www.librarieshawaii.org), the **McCully-Moiliili Public Library** (2211 S. King St., 808/973-1099, www.librarieshawaii.org), the **Manoa Public Library** (2716 Woodlawn Dr., 808/988-0459, www.librarieshawaii.org), and the **Hawaii State Library** (478 S. King St., 808/586-3500, www.librarieshawaii.org). Visitors need a valid HSPLS library card to use an Internet computer. Three-month visitor cards are available for $10. You can reserve Internet computer time online or in person. You can also find printed bus schedules, too.

MAIL

Post offices in Honolulu are located in Kaimuki (1130 Koko Head Rd., 808/737-8937), Manoa (2754 Woodlawn Dr., Ste. 7-101, 808/532-5689) in the Manoa Marketplace, Moili'ili (2700 S. King St., 808/275-8777), Ala Moana (1450 Ala Moana Blvd., 808/532-1987) in the Ala Moana Center, and downtown (335 Merchant St., 808/532-1987).

Getting There and Around

GETTING THERE
By Air

All commercial flights to Oʻahu are routed to the **Honolulu International Airport** (300 Rodgers Blvd., 808/836-6411, http://hawaii.gov/hnl), as are most other flights with neighboring island as their final destinations. The Honolulu International Airport has three terminals: the Overseas Terminal accommodates international and mainland flights, the Interisland Terminal handles Hawaiian Airlines flights, and the Commuter Terminal handles the small interisland carriers. There is a free intra-airport shuttle service for getting around the airport, and ground transportation is available just outside the baggage claim areas on the lower level, along the center median, where you can get a taxi, catch a shuttle to a rental car agency office, board TheBus, or pick up the other private shuttle buses that ferry visitors to Honolulu, Waikiki, and beyond. The airport is a mere 10 miles from Waikiki, and six miles from downtown Honolulu.

GETTING AROUND
By Car

Urban community planning was not top of mind for state officials as Honolulu grew and expanded up and out. Two-way roads suddenly change to one way only, roads curve and bend with the geography, narrow neighborhood roads have street parking that blocks an entire lane, and it can be extremely frustrating to find a freeway on-ramp. Add to this confusion rush hour traffic and contra flow, and you're sitting in literally the worst traffic in the United States. Don't be too discouraged, though, because with proper planning and an up-to-date road map, the adventure of getting around Honolulu can be quite exciting.

The H-1 freeway runs east/west through Honolulu at the base of the Koʻolau Mountains. Ala Moana Boulevard, which becomes Nimitz Highway, Route 92, parallels the H-1 along Honolulu Harbor. Beretania Street is a one-way, westbound thoroughfare that also parallels the H-1, and King Street, once you enter Chinatown, becomes an eastbound thoroughfare parallel to Beretania. Beretania and King Streets are a great way to get across town without using the freeway. From downtown, King Street forks after the Historic District. If you take the right fork, Kapiolani Boulevard, you'll go by Ala Moana Center and can turn right on Kalakaua Avenue to get into Waikiki. On the other side of the mall, Ala Moana Boulevard runs along the coast and will put you directly into Waikiki.

From the H-1 freeway westbound coming into downtown, take the Vineyard Boulevard exit and turn left at the first signal, Punchbowl Street. This will take you right into the Historic District. From the H-1 freeway eastbound, you can exit on Pali Highway and take a right, which will put you directly in downtown. Chinatown is a couple blocks to the west. You can also exit on Punchbowl Street, which puts you again in the Historic District.

Making the most of your time in Honolulu will mean working with the daily tide of traffic. Typical rush hour traffic is 5am-8am, when people flood into downtown from the east and west and the H-1 freeway slows to a crawl. Kapiolani Boulevard and Nimitz Highway are modified with an extra contra flow lane and there are turning restrictions. In the afternoon, rush hour starts up again for 3pm-6:30pm, contra flow lanes are added in the opposite direction for traffic to flow out of town, and the H-1 freeway again slows to a crawl. With limited freeway on-ramps, entire side streets will back up for blocks as cars jam onto the H-1. Plan your meals during these periods, or activities where you'll be out of the car and off the road for an extended period of time.

Dealing with parking in Honolulu is another matter in itself. The historic district has metered street parking, which is free on Sundays and holidays, and downtown and Chinatown have ample structure parking. For the best rates, look for the Chinatown municipal parking lots; there are several. You can also park in the high-rises downtown, but the rates are much higher.

By Bus

TheBus (808/848-4500, www.thebus.org) provides islandwide transportation, including transportation from the airport. If you're planning on riding the bus from the airport to your hotel, keep in mind that your bags have to be able to fit under the seat or on your lap without protruding into the aisle. There are several bus stops on the second level of the airport on the center median. Route Nos. 19, 20, and 31 access the airport, and Route No. 19 eastbound will take you to Waikiki.

There are nine transit centers on O'ahu. The major Honolulu transit centers are the Ala Moana Center Bus Stops, the Alapai Transit Center in downtown, and the Kalihi Transit Center. Fares are $2.50 for adults, $1.25 children ages 6-17, children 5 and under are free if they sit on an adult's lap. The Visitors Pass, a four consecutive day pass, is $25 with unlimited use. Call or visit their website for route information, maps, and timetables.

NORTH SHORE

Just 30 miles from Honolulu is the famed North Shore, the big city's polar opposite. Local surfers appropriately make the distinction and have coined the regions "town" and "country." With an average of 30 inches of rainfall annually, the North Shore is an escape to a natural haven and a simpler, almost hedonistic lifestyle. It's all about the beaches, diving, fishing, and, of course, surfing.

From the northernmost tip of the island to Ka'ena Point to the west, the North Shore's coastline looks more like a backwards L, or even the open jaws of a shark, and captures the powerful open-ocean swells that track across the Pacific during the northern hemisphere's winter. That's the reason for the enormous, powerful surf that pounds the reefs from October through April. Save for the town of Hale'iwa, the gateway to the North Shore, and Turtle Bay Resort, this area has remained undeveloped, a mix between residential housing and farmland. Locals have taken great pride in their grassroots efforts to establish a marine protected area along Waimea Bay, Three Tables, and Sharks Cove, and to preserve the bluff known as Pupukea-Paumalu that frames the quaint North Shore community.

Along the extreme northern stretch of the North Shore, you'll find world-class surf spots like Laniakea, Waimea Bay, the Banzai Pipeline, and Sunset Beach. Because of the quality and sheer number of surf breaks, this part of the North Shore is known as the "Seven Mile Miracle." Hale'iwa, sitting just off the Kamehameha Highway at the bottom of the

© KEVIN WHITTON

HIGHLIGHTS

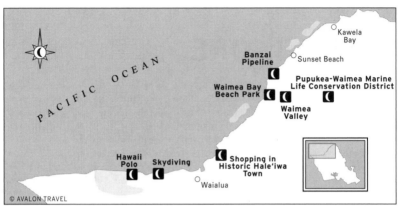

© AVALON TRAVEL

LOOK FOR ◖ TO FIND RECOMMENDED SIGHTS, ACTIVITIES, DINING, AND LODGING.

◖ **Waimea Bay Beach Park:** One of the most beautiful beaches on the North Shore, this expansive sandy shore yields to turquoise water that is home to reef fish, spinner dolphins, and green sea turtles. Swim and snorkel the calm waters in summer, or watch surfers ride enormous waves in winter (page 117).

◖ **Banzai Pipeline:** Watch expert surfers attempt to ride the barrel at one of the most dangerous breaks in the world (page 121).

◖ **Pupukea-Waimea Marine Life Conservation District:** Comprised of Waimea Bay, Three Tables, and Sharks Cove, this mile-long protected shoreline is where marine life abounds. It is the best area for snorkeling and shore diving on the North Shore (page 124).

◖ **Skydiving:** Skydiving operators in

Mokule'ia offer a once-in-a-lifetime opportunity to tandem skydive on the North Shore, affording you a bird's-eye view of paradise (page 129).

◖ **Waimea Valley:** Part verdant tropical botanical garden, part restored ancient cultural site, Waimea Valley is a bastion of beauty and education (page 132).

◖ **Shopping in Historic Hale'iwa Town:** Hale'iwa is the official gateway to the North Shore and has a vibrant history in agriculture and surfing. The quaint town is packed with clothing boutiques, surf shops, and art galleries (page 133).

◖ **Hawaii Polo:** Enjoy the camaraderie and festive atmosphere of a polo match by the sea. Bring the family, spread out a blanket, open the cooler, and enjoy a perfect summer afternoon (page 135).

pineapple fields, is where you'll find shopping, dining, dive and surf rental outfitters, and the famous Matsumoto Shave Ice. Waialua and Mokule'ia comprise the western side of the North Shore and offer quieter, less visited beaches and the rare opportunity to watch polo during the summer months. To those who wish

to jump out of a plane and skydive in paradise: Head this way.

PLANNING YOUR TIME

No matter if it's summer or winter, rain or shine, the North Shore shouldn't be missed and can't be rushed. Take advantage of all the

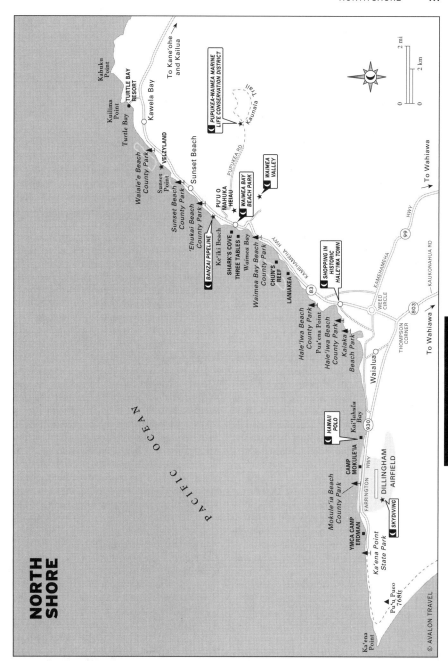

NORTH SHORE

NORTH SHORE

PACIFIC OCEAN

Ka'ena Point

Pu'u Pueo
768ft

Ka'ena Point
State Park

YMCA CAMP
ERDMAN

Mokule'ia Beach
County Park

■ SKYDIVING

DILLINGHAM
AIRFIELD

FARRINGTON HWY

CAMP
MOKULE'IA

■ HAWAII
POLO

Kai'aluhulu
Bay

930

Waialua

803

THOMPSON
CORNER

WEED
CIRCLE

To Wahiawa

KAUKONAHUA RD

99

To Wahiawa

HWY

KAMEHAMEHA

83

■ SHOPPING IN
HISTORIC
HALE'IWA TOWN

Kaiaka
Beach Park

Hale'iwa Beach
County Park

Pua'ena Point

Hale'iwa Beach
County Park

KAMEHAMEHA HWY

LANIAKEA ■

CHUN'S
REEF ■

Waimea Bay Beach
County Park

Waimea Bay

■ WAIMEA
VALLEY

■ WAIMEA BAY
BEACH PARK

PUU O
MAHUKA
HEIAU

THREE TABLES ■

SHARK'S COVE ■

Ke'iki Beach

■ BANZAI PIPELINE

'Ehukai Beach
County Park

Sunset Beach
County Park

Sunset
Point

★ VELZYLAND

Sunset Beach

Waiale'e Beach
County Park

Turtle Bay

Kuilima
Point

● Kawela Bay

TURTLE BAY
RESORT

Kahuku
Point

To Kane'ohe
and Kailua

■ PUPUKEA-WAIMEA MARINE
LIFE CONSERVATION DISTRICT

PUPUKEA RD

Kaunala Trail

0   2 mi

0   2 km

© AVALON TRAVEL

natural beauty and ocean activities on offer and plan for a full-day trip to the region. The 33-mile drive from Waikiki to the North Shore, taking the most direct route across the central plateau, will last an hour if all goes well and traffic is light. If your stay on O'ahu is during the summer, drive up in the morning and snorkel in the Pupukea-Waimea Marine Life Conservation District, at Waimea Bay, Three Tables, and Sharks Cove. Park at Three Tables, which is between the other two, and utilize the walking trail to visit all three locales without moving the car. Grab a quick lunch at Ted's Bakery at Sunset Beach or at one of the numerous establishments in Hale'iwa, then head out to Mokule'ia for Hawaii Polo, skydiving, or a glider ride. If the mountains are more your style, take a trail ride on Pupukea or in Kahuku, then head to Turtle Bay for a sunset cocktail at the Hang Ten Bar, right on Kuilima Point.

During the winter the North Shore has a completely different vibe, as powerful waves push across the reefs and surfers flock to the beaches. Snorkeling and diving are out of the picture, as turbulent white water sweeps across the reefs, but watching the surf and the talented surfers taking it on can be mesmerizing. Check out the action at Waimea Bay, Pipeline, and Sunset Beach. Take a break during the day to drive to Kahuku and visit Kahuku Superette for some fresh *poke* and rice, then head back to the beach to eat while wave-watching. Enjoy dinner in Hale'iwa before setting out back to Honolulu.

For a longer, but more scenic trip to the North Shore from Waikiki, follow the Likelike Highway to Kane'ohe and drive up the windward coast in the morning. The roughly 45-mile drive will take about an hour and a half as the sun rises over the east side. The mellow, gently meandering drive will put you in the right mood for a relaxing day on the North Shore.

If you're looking for an O'ahu destination where you can spend a portion of, , or your entire, stay surrounding yourself in a rural, coastal setting far removed from the city, then a vacation rental along the North Shore Beaches or a room at Turtle Bay Resort are great options. Just be aware that it will take a bit more time and planning for sightseeing and activities in most other island regions.

ORIENTATION
Hale'iwa

As you descend from the pineapple and coffee fields, the first town you'll come to is Historic Hale'iwa Town, the official gateway to the North Shore. On either side of town, Kamehameha Highway makes a detour through Hale'iwa. If you want to pass around Hale'iwa and continue up the coast, stay on the Joseph P. Leong Highway bypass.

Hale'iwa is full of places to eat, markets, and clothing, souvenir, and surf shops, as well as art galleries. Sportfishing, shark tour, and scuba operators are congregated in Hale'iwa Harbor, which has lovely beaches on both sides, though they are better for surfing and stand-up paddling rather than swimming or snorkeling. The 'Anahulu River empties out by the harbor and beaches, offering potential for stand-up paddling upriver.

Just to the west of Hale'iwa, between the Wai'anae Mountains and the coast as you head toward Ka'ena Point, are **Waialua** and **Mokule'ia.** Both are sleepy rural agricultural communities. Farrington Highway rejoins the coast through Mokule'ia, where if it's not too windy, the beaches are nice, the water is crystal clear, and solitude surrounds you. Mokule'ia offers polo matches on Sunday afternoons in the summer, skydiving throughout the year, and a seaside hike in a natural reserve at the end of the road to the western tip of the island.

North Shore Beaches
The North Shore Beaches comprise an immaculate stretch of coastline along Kamehameha Highway from **Laniakea,** just past Hale'iwa town, to the legendary **Sunset Beach** to the north. Spinner dolphins frolic in Waimea Bay, sea turtles feed off the shoreline rocks, and reef fish abound along the **Pupukea-Waimea Marine Life Conservation District,** which

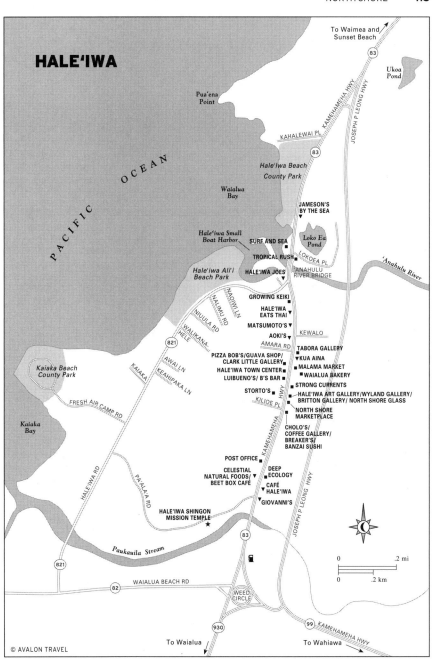

HALE'IWA

To Waimea and
Sunset Beach

83

Ukoa
Pond

Pua'ena
Point

KAHALEWAI PL.

KAMEHAMEHA HWY

JOSEPH P LEONG HWY

83

Hale'Iwa Beach
County Park

P A C I F I C   O C E A N

Waialua
Bay

JAMESON'S
BY THE SEA ▼

Hale'iwa Small
Boat Harbor

SURF AND SEA ■

Loko Ea
Pond

'Anahulu River

TROPICAL RUSH ■

LOKOEA PL.

Hale'iwa Ali'i
Beach Park

HALE'IWA JOES ■

ANAHULU
RIVER BRIDGE

NAOWILN

GROWING KEIKI ■

NALIMU RD.

HALE'IWA
EATS THAI ▼

MATSUMOTO'S ▼

NIUULA RD.

AOKI'S ▼

KEWALO

WALIKANA.
HELE

AMARA RD.

TABORA GALLERY ■

821

▼KUA AINA

AWAI LN

PIZZA BOB'S/GUAVA SHOP/
CLARK LITTLE GALLERY ■

■ MALAMA MARKET

KAIAKA

KEAHIPAKA LN

HALE'IWA TOWN CENTER ■

■ WAIALUA BAKERY

Kaiaka Beach
County Park

LUIBUENO'S/ B'S BAR ■

■ STRONG CURRENTS

STORTO'S ■

■HALE'IWA ART GALLERY/WYLAND GALLERY/
BRITTON GALLERY/ NORTH SHORE GLASS

KILIOE PL.

FRESH AIR CAMP RD.

■NORTH SHORE
MARKETPLACE

KAMEHAMEHA HWY

Kaiaka
Bay

CHOLO'S/
COFFEE GALLERY/
BREAKER'S/
BANZAI SUSHI

POST OFFICE ■

HALE'IWA RD.

PA'ALA'A RD.

CELESTIAL
NATURAL FOODS/ ▼
BEET BOX CAFÉ

DEEP
ECOLOGY ▼

CAFÉ
▼ HALE'IWA

JOSEPH P LEONG HWY

▼GIOVANNI'S

HALE'IWA SHINGON
MISSION TEMPLE ★

Paukauila Stream

83

821

82

WAIALUA BEACH RD.

WEED
CIRCLE

0   .2 mi

0   .2 km

930

To Waialua

99   KAMEHAMEHA HWY

To Wahiawa

© AVALON TRAVEL

YOUR BEST DAY ON THE NORTH SHORE

Surf, sun, and beaches—the rural North Shore is all about leaving behind the city and tapping into the laidback atmosphere. Just remember, the North Shore can be very different depending if it's summer or winter.

- Drive up the H-2 freeway, through the central plateau. You'll be able to see the extent of O'ahu's agriculture base—pineapple fields as far as the eye can see. Head directly to the **Pupukea-Waimea Marine Life Conservation District,** the best snorkeling on the North Shore. Whether you post up at Waimea Bay, Three Tables, or Sharks Cove, or visit all three, you'll be amazed at the underwater beauty of the area. Snorkeling is best in the summertime.

- If it's winter during your stay, check out the waves at **Waimea Bay, Pipeline,** or **Sunset Beach.** They attract professional surfers from around the world. The action is spectacular, especially once the waves get really big.

- Stop in at **Ted's Bakery** for lunch, local style, or head out to Kahuku, just a few miles farther north, and visit **Kahuku Superette** for some of the best *poke* on the island.

- Outdoor activities are the hallmark of the North Shore. If you're daring, try **skydiving** in Mokule'ia. If staying on land suits you better, there are two outfitters that offer horseback rides in the verdant mountains above the North Shore beaches.

- During the summer, you can also spend the afternoon stand-up paddling the **'Anahulu River** in Hale'iwa Town or try a shore dive at Sharks Cove or Three Tables.

- For dinner, try **Hale'iwa Joe's** if you're in Hale'iwa town. If you're closer to the northern tip of the island, stop by Turtle Bay Resort and have a great meal at the local favorite, **Lei Lei's.**

includes Three Tables and Sharks Cove just north of Waimea Bay, some of the best snorkeling and scuba diving on the island. In the summer, the calm water along this stretch of coast is perfect for swimming and snorkeling, but in the winter, powerful surf draws expert surfers from around the world in search of giant waves at Waimea Bay and Sunset Beach and the awe-inspiring barrels of the Banzai Pipeline. While the most popular beaches might be busy with tourists hopping off buses all year long, a short walk up or down the beach will easily remove you from the melee and most of your cares or worries. For meals you'll mostly find food trucks along the highway, and for accommodations, vacation rentals are the only way to go, save for the only hostel in the region at Three Tables. Sunsets are remarkable from this stretch of coast.

Turtle Bay

Turtle Bay is the area along Kamehameha Highway from **Kawela Bay** to **Kahuku,** the old sugar town. This region sits at the northern tip of the island and is prone to wind and rain throughout the year. The Turtle Bay Resort on **Kuilima Point** dominates the area, with surf and golf being the main attractions, along with the bars and restaurants that many residents and visitors along the North Shore Beaches make the short drive to indulge in.

Just to the east of Turtle Bay is Kahuku, with a nine-hole golf course of its own. Locals prefer the affordable fees and relaxed atmosphere at the Kahuku course to the resort's professional course. Kahuku is also home to a little market with some of the best *poke* on O'ahu. There is a working ranch here offering horseback trail rides for all levels of riders.

Beaches

The North Shore beaches are some of the finest on the island. With the natural backdrops of the Pupukea-Paumalu escarpment along the northern portion of the coast and the Wai'anae Range behind Hale'iwa stretching to Ka'ena Point, natural beauty catches your eye in every direction. Ample vegetation separates the sand from the beachfront property, and the coast is broken up by interesting rock and reef rock formations, sandy bays and rugged points.

The North Shore also has two distinct personalities: benign and tranquil during the summer, from May until September; and powerful and fierce in the winter, from October to April. This duality is caused by powerful storms in the North Pacific that send swell thousands of miles across open ocean, straight to the Hawaiian Islands. The North Shore reefs absorb this energy as giant waves that pound the coast, breaking up to 50 feet from crest to trough. During high surf events in the winter, the water is closed to swimming, and lifeguards monitor the spectators on the beach, as well as the surfers in the water, to make sure everyone is safe. During the biggest swell events, the beaches are closed as well.

On the other hand, summer provides perfect conditions for swimming, snorkeling, and diving. The ocean remains generally calm and flat, and the beaches are at their widest. Sunsets are also better during this time as the sun tracks farther west on the horizon.

HALE'IWA
Ali'i Beach Park

There is a small beach, framed in by rocks, at both sides of **Ali'i Beach Park,** just to the west of the Hale'iwa Small Boat Harbor, where Hale'iwa town intersects the coast. These area great place for the kids to jump around in the small shorebreak. Ali'i Beach Park also has a community center, restrooms, and a large, shaded grassy park with palm trees, picnic tables, and shrubs along the vegetation line that offer shade. If there are waves breaking along the outer reef, there is a strong and dangerous rip current that sweeps across the beach. From Kamehameha Highway, turn onto Haleiwa Road, and the beach park is past the entrance to the boat harbor. There is ample parking.

Hale'iwa Beach Park

On the other side of the harbor entrance and the 'Anahulu River, across the famous Rainbow Bridge, is **Hale'iwa Beach Park.** The water is a bit murky and the sand somewhat silty from the rivermouth, but the calm waters here are a favorite for kayakers and stand-up paddlers, where you can choose to paddle in the ocean or forge up the 'Anahulu River. There is parking on the side of the road or in the designated parking area. To the north of the parking lot is a big grassy area and restrooms. The beach park is beside Kamehameha Highway. The parking lot and restrooms are closed 10pm-6am daily.

Pua'ena Point Beach Park

You'll have a different experience all together in **Pua'ena Point Beach Park** to the immediate north of Hale'iwa Beach Park. From Kamehameha Highway, turn onto Kahalewai Place and drive to the parking lot at the end. From there walk through the ironwood trees to the small cove. The beach has lots of shade and is a great place to explore in and out of the water. Snorkel the inner waters with their a mix of sand and reef bottom, or you can walk up the beach to the rocky outcropping of Pua'ena Point.

Mokule'ia Beach Park

Situated on the western flank of the North Shore, **Mokule'ia Beach Park** is a quiet, uncrowded beach across from the Dillingham Airfield. The sand is narrow, but stretches out in both directions with interesting nooks and crannies along the coast. There are shrubs along the beach and some trees for shade to

© KEVIN WHITTON

Haleʻiwa Beach Park is perfect for stand-up paddling.

the east. Mokuleʻia Beach Park is great for a long walk on the beach or relaxing in the sun. It's in the path of the trade winds, so it can get blustery. If you plan on swimming or snorkeling, the conditions are best with light winds. There are showers and portable toilets at the beach park along Farrington Highway, close to the end of the road. The parking lot is closed 7pm-7am daily.

NORTH SHORE BEACHES
Laniakea

Famous for the turtles that rest in the sand and feed off of the rocky shelf at the water's edge, **Laniakea** is a beautiful stretch of beach once you get away from the hordes of people that jam onto the small pocket of sand where the majority of the turtles rest. Park in the dirt parking lot on the mountain side of Kamehameha Highway just north of a ranch with horses. Cross the road with extreme caution. Tour buses of all sizes stop here and direct people to the northern corner of the beach. The turtles, however, feed along the rocks that run

the length of the beach, so walk to the south to escape the melee. Where the beachfront properties begin at the southern end of the beach, the sand widens and there are beautiful views of the Waiʻanae Mountains and the western side of the North Shore. If you plan on swimming or snorkeling, this is also the best place to enter and exit the water. The farther south you walk along the beach, the better the chance of finding seclusion.

Chun's Reef

A beautiful spot for a beach day, **Chun's Reef** is the next beach north of Laniakea, but without the tour buses and crowds. The wide sandy beach has tidepools in the southern corner up against the rocky point, and the water right off the beach is a bit deeper here and more suitable for swimming and snorkeling. The beach gets wider to north end of Chun's and is lined with tall ironwood trees, providing ample shade. Little waves break over the reef quite a distance offshore almost all year long, so it's a great place for beginners to surf in the summer. It's also a

© KEVIN WHITTON

Waimea Bay Beach Park

favorite area for stand-up paddle surfers. Park in the dirt on the mountain side of the road across from the beach. There are lifeguards, but no facilities at Chun's.

◖ Waimea Bay Beach Park

At the mouth of the Waimea River and Waimea Valley is the scenic **Waimea Bay Beach Park.** The tight bay is lined with beautiful white sand, and the water is crystal clear, perfect for swimming and snorkeling. There are rocky points on both sides of the bay, while the center is all sand, producing light blue water. Stand-up paddle across the bay, relax on the beach, or jump off the famous Jump Rock, a 20-foot-tall rock spire right off the beach. Spinner dolphins and green sea turtles are frequent visitors. Park in the designated parking area, but if it's full, there is paid parking in Waimea Valley, which is about a ten-minute walk to the beach. Use the white pedestrian bridge to cross the river and access the beach park, which has restrooms, showers, picnic areas, and a grassy park. The beach park is closed 10pm-5am daily.

Three Tables

Once you round Waimea Bay, the first beach you come to heading north is **Three Tables,** named after three flat reef platforms that rise above the ocean surface just off the beach. This is part of the Pupukea-Waimea Marine Life Conservation District, a protected area where fishing is illegal. The resulting copious amounts of reef fish in the water mean the main draw here is snorkeling. Three Tables has a quaint beach with shallow water stretching between rock outcroppings. Perfect for families, there are shade trees on the beach and picnic tables up by the bike path. There are a few parking spaces in front of the beach on the side of Kamehameha Highway, or you can park in the parking lot just to the north of Three Tables. Turn into the lot at the Pupukea Road traffic signal. There are restrooms here as well, though they are notoriously dingy.

Ke'iki Beach

On the north side of the prominent reef rock point that frames in Sharks Cove, **Ke'iki Beach** is the place to go if you're looking for solitude. The beach stretches out to the north, and even though the name might change every quarter mile, its still one beautiful ribbon of sand with aquamarine water pushing up against it. The water gets deep rather quickly, so it's also great for swimming and snorkeling. From the highway, turn onto Keiki Road and look for parking. There is also intermittent parking along Kamehameha Highway on the ocean side. Follow one of the designated public access paths to the beach. There are no facilities and no shade here.

'Ehukai Beach Park

Across from Sunset Elementary School is a small parking lot for **'Ehukai Beach Park.** Walk through the small park toward the lifeguard tower and onto the sand. To the immediate left is the world-famous **Banzai Pipeline** surf break. If it's summer, the water is beautiful and clear, but there will be no waves. To the right is 'Ehukai Beach, which stretches north up to Rocky Point. Swimming is great up and down the beach, which is lined with palms and shrubs offering midday shade. During the summer, the snorkeling is better on the Pipeline side

JUMP IN!

In the mid-1900s, sand mining at Waimea Bay unearthed a large rock in the sand. Today that rock is at the water's edge and stands about 20 feet high. People flock to the rock, aptly named **Jump Rock,** to take the plunge into the turquoise water below. The ascent is gradual, starting from the sand to Jump Rock's highest point. Most people jump off the east side. North Shore surfers actually practice a balled-up type of belly flop to better prepare themselves for any unfortunate wipeouts during the upcoming winter's extra-large surf. If the main jumping point is a bit too high for your liking, the very end of the rock, farthest out into the bay, is only about six feet high.

of the park where there is a wide shelf of reef, canyons, and caves to explore. 'Ehukai Beach Park has restrooms and showers, and there are additional public restrooms across the street in front of the school. The beach park is closed 10pm-5am daily.

Sunset Beach

To the north of Sunset Elementary School, homes line the ocean side of Kamehameha Highway, and the beach is hidden from view. But once you pass a gas station, **Sunset Beach** is all you see. A wide swath of sand from the highway to the water's edge, Sunset is also famous for its big waves during the winter, but its natural beauty is splendid, waves or not. In the summer, it's perfect for swimming and snorkeling, or you can stand-up paddle up and down the coast from here for a good look at the shore. Take a walk up the point to the north for a great view back toward Hale'iwa. There is parking on the ocean side of the highway, along the bike path. If you luck into one of these spots, it's pleasant enough to relax, have a snack or some coffee, and watch the ocean sparkle. During the winter, it's also a great vantage point for whale-watching. There is another parking lot on the mountain side of the highway where you'll find restrooms and showers.

TURTLE BAY
Kawela Bay

One of the most protected and secluded bays on the North Shore, **Kawela Bay** shelters a small strip of sand and a calm lagoon protected by an outer reef between Sunset Beach and Turtle Bay. it's great for snorkeling, swimming, and getting away from it all. Park on the side of the highway across from the fruit stand and walk through the trees to the beach.

Kuilima Point

Kuilima Point, today known as **Turtle Bay,** is the site of the Turtle Bay Resort, a dramatic coastline, and a sandy beach. To the west of the resort and rugged Kuilima Point is a sand and rock beach that stretches to the eastern point of

© KEVIN WHITTON

'Ehukai Beach

Kawela Bay. Walk the beach at low tide when there is more sand or snorkel over rock and reef. On the immediate east side of the point and the main resort is a small protected cove great for families and for swimming, but you'll have to share it with the other hotel guests. Farther east of the small bay is a beach seldom visited even though it sits right next to the resort. Walk along the sand or relax under some trees. The reef is shallow right up to the shore, so this is not the best spot for swimming. Visit the beach when the winds are light, as the trade winds blow straight on shore and get quite blustery. Turtle Bay is a great stop if you're looking for a little beach time followed by lunch or dinner.

To get to Kuilima Point from the Kamehameha Highway, turn onto Kuilima Road and follow it to the main resort parking lot. There is beach access on both sides of the main resort tower.

Surfing

The North Shore is synonymous with surfing. Dubbed the "Seven Mile Miracle," this area has more high-quality surf breaks packed into the scenic coastline from Hale'iwa to Turtle Bay than in any other place in the world. The powerful waves draw surfers from around the world, and for over three decades professional surfing's elite world tour has wrapped up the title season at the infamous Banzai Pipeline.

The waves on the North Shore are also some of the most dangerous, and deadliest, in the world. With huge breaks, strong currents, and shallow reefs, even top athletes are not immune to severe injury or death. Because of these and other factors, only expert surfers should paddle out. There are lifeguards posted at most North Shore beaches; check with them for ocean conditions and safety. If you're having doubts

© KEVIN WHITTON

Turtle Bay

about the waves and your ability, it's best to have a seat on the beach, enjoy the spectacle, and live to surf another day on a different wave.

HALE'IWA
Hale'iwa Break
Located in Hale'iwa town to the west of the harbor, **Hale'iwa** breaks off Ali'i Beach. A peak when it's small, the wave becomes exponentially more dangerous the larger it gets, breaking as a predominant right. The fast waves closeout over a very shallow inside reef ledge known as the Toilet Bowl. A strong rip current is a staple at Hale'iwa. Paddle out from the west side of the beach, to the left of the Toilet Bowl section.

Pua'ena Point
Pua'ena Point is one of smaller and softer waves on the North Shore, just to the north of the 'Anahulu River. It has both right and left breaking waves and is friendly for longboarders when it's small. The waves can still get big at Pua'ena, but it doesn't happen that often. Paddle straight out from the beach. The

parking lot can be a bit suspect, so don't leave any valuables in plain sight.

NORTH SHORE BEACHES
Laniakea
Best on north swells, **Laniakea** is a right pointbreak that breaks over flat reef and sand. Depending on the direction of the swell, the wave is one of the longest on the North Shore. Expert surfers tend to sit up at the point, while novice surfers and longboards prefer the inside section off the south end of the beach. Paddle out from the south end of the beach. Laniakea is to the immediate north of a ranch, and there is a long dirt parking lot on the mountain side of Kamehameha Highway.

Chun's Reef
Just north of Laniakea, the next beach and surf spot you can see from the highway is **Chun's Reef.** Chun's is a soft breaking right point, but also has a fast breaking left at the top of the sandy point that most often closes out. Chun's is a favorite wave for beginners, longboarders,

and kids. It's one of the most user-friendly waves on the North Shore. Keep in mind that even though the wave itself is good for learning, the shallow bottom is still dangerous, since it's covered by a sharp, flat reef. Chun's is one of the few breaks on the North Shore that also has very small waves in the summer.

Leftovers

At the next small break in homes along the highway where you can see the water you'll find a wave called **Leftovers**. The wave is a left that breaks into deep water, so there is a defined channel where you can paddle out. A right also breaks off the peak on the very outside. The inside section covers an extremely shallow and sharp reef. Getting in and out of the water can also be an obstacle, as the beach is covered with rocks and large boulders that stretch out into the water.

Waimea Bay

A big wave spot that only starts to break when the waves are 15 to 20 feet on the face, **Waimea Bay** is the only chance for many to see waves of this size, a feat of nature that should not be missed if the bay is breaking. The shorebreak is also something to see, as huge waves barrel and detonate in spectacular fashion in inches of water. Parking at Waimea fills up quickly when the waves are big. There is limited additional parking along the highway on the west side of the bay heading west, or you can pay to park at Waimea Valley, just past the turn off to Waimea Bay. You could also park by Three Tables and Sharks Cove and walk back along the highway. Many spectators watch and snap photos from the railing above the rocks on the east side of the bay.

◖ Banzai Pipeline

The **Banzai Pipeline** is one of the most dangerous waves in the world. Guarded closely by a territorial crew of local surfers, Pipeline is one of those waves where visiting surfers will find it more to their advantage to sit on the beach and watch its grandeur rather than test their mettle. Breaking just 75 yards off the beach, Pipeline is a spectator's delight. Massive round and hollow lefts explode over a shallow reef, and brave surfers try to place themselves as deep as possible inside the barrel, hoping to emerge out the end on their feet. On the sand, you can feel the waves break on the beach and sense the tension and emotion in the water. Park in the 'Ehukai Beach Park parking lot or along the highway. Pay attention to the sporadic No Parking signs.

'Ehukai

Also accessible from 'Ehukai Beach Park is the North Shore's only beach break, **'Ehukai**. Depending on the sand and the swells, the waves can break right or left and range from phenomenal shape to junky and lumpy surf.

Sunset Beach

Sunset Beach offers one of the most powerful and dangerous waves in the world, breaking from Sunset Point all the way into the bay. Strong currents and closeout sets are the hallmark of Sunset, along with a dredging inside section called **The West Bowl**, which breaks closest to the beach. A wave for experts only, when the water is gigantic, you'll find surfers attempting to ride the mountainous fluid walls. Bring binoculars to catch all the action way out to sea.

SURFING THE SEVEN MILE MIRACLE

In the surf world, the stretch of coastline from Hale'iwa to Kuilima Point is known as the **Seven Mile Miracle.** Unlike anywhere else on planet, the North Shore has just the right combination of geography, geology, wind, weather, and swell to make it one of the most sought after surfing destinations in the world. The quality, consistency, size, and sheer number of surf breaks along the seven-mile stretch are unmatched. This is truly a surfer's paradise.

NORTH SHORE

© KEVIN WHITTON

The surf at Waimea Bay doesn't start breaking until the waves reach at least 20 feet.

TURTLE BAY
Kuilima Point

Kuilima Point, known locally as **Turtle Bay,** is a funky, soft wave that breaks along a sharp reef outcropping into deep water. Since the break is just off Kuilima Point, where the Turtle Bay Resort is situated, you can literally watch the surfers from Turtle Bay's pool bar. The inside has soft rolling white water that is perfect for beginners. You can also rent longboards at the resort. The beach and water are open to the public. Paddle out from the rocky shore in front of the bungalows.

OUTFITTERS

Hale'iwa town is full of surf shops that sell apparel, boards, and surf accessories. **Hawaiian Island Creations** (66-224 Kamehameha Hwy., 808/637-0991, www.hicsurf.com, 10am-6pm Mon.-Sat., 9:30am-5pm Sun.) and **Wave Riding Vehicles** (66-451 Kamehameha Hwy., 808/637-2020, www.waveridingvehicles.com, 9am-7pm daily) are two local surf brands with retail shops, and **Xcel** (66-590 Kamehameha Hwy., 808/637-6239, www.xcelwetsuits.com, 9am-5pm daily) is a local wetsuit company where you can find all manner of wetsuits to stay warm and protect yourself from the sun. **Surf N Sea** (62-595 Kamehameha Hwy., 808/637-9887, http://surfnsea.com, 9am-7pm daily) not only has apparel and new and used boards for sale, but they also rent shortboards and longboards by the hour, day, and week. Shortboards are $5 the first hour, $3.50 each additional hour, $24 daily, and $120 weekly; longboards are $7 the first hour, $6 each additional hour, $30 daily, and $150 weekly. Right across the street is **Tropical Rush** (62-620 Kamehameha Hwy., 808/637-8886, 9am-7pm daily). They sell apparel, new surfboards, and gear, and rent boards by the hour, day, and week.

Hawaii Eco Divers (61-101 Iliohu Pl., 808/499-9177, www.hawaiiecodivers.com, 7:30am-9pm daily) offers surf tours for experienced surfers and lessons for beginners. The surf tours include personalized surf coaching and a video of the session, $150 for a morning

© MICHELLE WHITTON

The Banzai Pipeline is one of the most exciting and dangerous waves in the world.

session or $250 all day for a group of up to three surfers. Surfboards are not included. Their surf lessons run $100 for a three- to four-hour session focusing on catching and riding waves. The lesson rate includes boards and transportation. **Sunset Suratt Surf Academy** (808/783-8657, http://surfnorthshore.com) gives beginner surfing and stand-up paddling lessons. With an arsenal of boards and vans, they drive to where the surf is best suited for learning. Book online.

Located across from Sharks Cove, **North Shore Surf Shop** (59-053 Kamehameha Hwy., 808/638-0390, 10am-7:30pm daily) has a huge selection of shortboards, new and used, and carries a lot of the professional surfers' used boards. They rent shortboards for $25 daily, $60 for three days, $125 weekly, and $300 for a month; longboards are $30 daily, $75 for three days, $140 weekly, and $300 for a month. They also have a retail location in the town of Haleʻiwa.

At Turtle Bay Resort you can rent boards at **Hans Hedemann Surf** (57-091 Kamehameha Hwy., 808/447-6755 or 808/293-7779, www. hhsurf.com, 8am-5pm daily). They rent shortboards and longboards for $15 per hour, $40 for four hours, $50 all day, $60 overnight, $35 each additional day, and $250 per week. Two-hour private lessons go for $150, semi-private lessons are $125, and group lessons, for up to four surfers, are $75. All equipment is included.

SNORKEL VS. SURF

While Hawai'i's slight seasonal changes in temperature and precipitation might not be apparent to visitors who only stay a week or two at a time, there is one natural phenomenon that strikingly differentiates summer and winter on the North Shore—waves! During Hawai'i's winter, October-April, and sometimes into spring, storms in the North Pacific create very large, open ocean swells that track toward the equator, passing by the state and expending the wave energy on the reefs and beaches. This is great news for surfers, who follow these swells closely and live to surf the powerful waves, which can break up to 60 feet on the face during the biggest surges on the outermost reefs. For snorkelers and divers, high surf is a worst-case scenario.

Once summer rolls around, the tables turn. From May to September, the North Shore becomes a tranquil swimmer's paradise. The waves usually remain flat the entire period, the sand settles, and the water becomes crystal clear. Snorkelers and divers revel in the conditions, and the focus on the North Shore shifts from the waves above the surface to the exploration of its underwater world.

Snorkeling and Diving

NORTH SHORE BEACHES

During the summer, from May to September, when the ocean is flat, the North Shore Beaches are an amazing place to snorkel. With a mix of rocks, reef, sand, calm waters, and favorable winds, just about anywhere you jump in the water will have some interesting underwater topography, coral, and marine life.

◖ Pupukea-Waimea Marine Life Conservation District

The most abundant marine life is found at **Three Tables, Sharks Cove,** and **Waimea Bay,** which comprise the **Pupukea-Waimea Marine Life Conservation District.** Established in 1983 to conserve and replenish marine species at Three Tables and Sharks Cove, the reserve was expanded in 2003 to include Waimea Bay, covering 100 acres of coastline about a mile long. Fishing or the taking of any marine species is strictly prohibited in the area. Look for wrasse, surgeonfish, reef squid, puffer fish, the spotted eagle ray, palani, unicorn fish, harlequin shrimp, and frogfish, just some of the creatures that inhabit the area. Waimea Bay is also known for pods of spinner dolphins that frolic in the middle of the bay.

There are boat dives and shore dives available on the North Shore. The shore dives explore Three Tables and Sharks Cove, where there are flourishing reefs teeming with endemic fish and lava tubes, caverns, and walls to explore. The boat dives provide access to the extraordinary underwater topography and pristine offshore reefs of the North Shore Beaches: Atlantis is an area full of trenches, valleys, walls, and lava tubes, and Cathedrals has rock formations, reefs, and caverns where turtles, eels, and whitetip reef sharks are common; Grand Canyon is a drift dive along the North Shore Beaches where you'll find sponges hanging from the ledges and trevallies and rays in the deep water; two reef sites, Nanny's Reef and Nautilus Reef, are 40-foot dives with a plethora of marine life. Diving the North Shore during the winter is contingent on the size of the surf.

OUTFITTERS

Surf N Sea (62-595 Kamehameha Hwy., 808/637-9887, http://surfnsea.com, 9am-7pm daily) in Hale'iwa is the North Shore's most complete surf and dive shop. They sell new gear, rent beach and ocean-related gear and accessories, and even lead shore and boat dives.

© KEVIN WHITTON

Sharks Cove is part of the Pupukea-Waimea Marine Life Conservation District.

They rent dive equipment by the piece at a daily or weekly rate. For snorkel gear, they rent by the piece or in a set, the latter runs $6.50 for four hours, $9.50 daily, and $45 weekly. Their guided dives are operated by **Hawaii Scuba Diving,** which offers shore and boat dives as well as certification courses. Their morning dives are for certified divers, while the afternoon charters to shallow reef sites are open to any level diver. One-tank shore dives are $75 for certified divers and $95 for noncertified; two-tank shore dives are $100 certified, $125 noncertified; one-tank night dives are $100; two-tank boat dives are $140. PADI diving certification courses are $375 for Open Water Diver, $295 for Advanced Open Water Diver, and $650 for Divemaster.

Deep Ecology (66-456 Kamehameha Hwy., 808/637-7946 or 800/578-3992, www.oahuscubadive.com, 8am-6pm Mon.-Sat., 8am-5pm Sun.) also has a retail dive center in Haleʻiwa town. Their shop also has clothing and ocean art for sale, and they sell dive and snorkel equipment. They rent snorkel sets for $12

daily and $60 weekly, with 2 days free rental. They also rent complete two-tank scuba sets for $60 daily and $300 weekly with two days free rental. For diving charters, boat dives and night boat dives are $145, shore dives are $109, night shore dives are $95, intro dives are $109, and boat intro dives are $159. Gear is included in the price, and they will give discounts if you have your own equipment. Deep Ecology also has a broad range of PADI certification courses.

Hawaii Eco Divers (61-101 Iliohu Pl., 808/499-9177, www.hawaiiecodivers.com, 7:30am-9pm daily), operating from Haleʻiwa Harbor, specializes in personalized small group shore dives. Two-tank shore dives or one-tank night dives for certified divers are $89, and one-tank shore dives for noncertified divers are $99. All gear is included in the rate along with snacks, refreshments, and photos of the dives. They will also shoot a video of your dive for $75.

If you get to Sharks Cove and discover you really want to snorkel but don't have any gear, then you're in luck: Right across the street is

North Shore Surf Shop (59-053 Kamehameha Hwy., 808/638-0390, 10am-7:30pm daily). They rent complete snorkel sets for $15 daily and $30 for three days. They also have rash guards for rent for $5, which are great for sun protection while you're snorkeling.

Other Water Sports

STAND-UP PADDLING AND FISHING

Hale'iwa is the hub of stand-up paddling and kayaking on the North Shore, largely because of the **'Anahulu River** and the protected and calm waters off **Hale'iwa Beach Park.** You can access the shoreline in the small parking lot next to Surf N Sea or along Hale'iwa Beach Park. From there, you can paddle around the shallow rivermouth, north to Pua'ena Point and beyond, or head upriver for a smooth and mellow ride.

On the North Shore, stand-up paddling is popular at **Waimea Bay, Laniakea,** and **Chun's Reef.** The conditions are best in the summer when the ocean surface is flat. Chun's and Laniakea often have very small waves in the summer, so you can even try surfing the stand-up board.

In Hale'iwa, **Surf N Sea** (62-595 Kamehameha Hwy., 808/637-9887, http://surfnsea.com, 9am-7pm daily) rents single kayaks for $7 the first hour, $5 for each additional hour, $20 for a half day, and $75 for a full day. Their weekly rate is $300. Stand-up paddle boards rent for $10 for the first hour, $8 for each additional hour, and $40 for a full day. The weekly rate is $200. They also rent water bikes and pedal boats and have the distinction of being situated on the bank of the river mouth for easy ocean access.

Hawaii Eco Divers (61-101 Iliohu Pl.,

© KEVIN WHITTON

Many people stand-up paddle the 'Anahulu River in Hale'iwa.

808/499-9177, www.hawaiiecodivers.com, 7:30am-9pm daily) offers a two-hour Haleʻiwa Beach and River Tour all year long for $79. In the summer they also have a three-hour Waimea Bay Tour for $109 and a four-mile drift Sunset Beach to Waimea Bay Tour for $125. Snorkeling gear is included for both summer tours.

At the Turtle Bay Resort **Hans Heddeman Surf** (57-091 Kamehameha Hwy., 808/447-6755 or 808/293-7779, www.hhsurf.com, 8am-5pm daily) rent stand-up paddle boards for $25 per hour, $50 for three hours, $80 all day, $100 overnight, $50 each additional day, and $400 per week. Two-hour private lessons go for $150, semiprivate lessons are $125, and group lessons, up to four surfers, is $75. All equipment is included.

FISHING

During the summer, spearfishing is common along the North Shore, where reef fish and octopus are the desired take. The conditions are prime during this season with the calm, flat ocean surface. Shoreline fishing is also common from Mokuleʻia out to Kaʻena Point and along the beach south of Laniakea. Remember that the area from the west side of Waimea Bay to the north side of Sharks Cove is a marine protected area and fishing or taking any marine species is strictly prohibited. Fishing gear is available in Haleʻiwa at **Haleiwa Fishing Supply** (66-519 Kamehameha Hwy., 808/637-9876, 10am-8pm daily).

The North Shore is very favorable for sportfishing with deep water offshore and strong currents from the northwest that continually bring in bait and game fish. Several deep-sea sportfishing operators are located in the Haleʻiwa Small Boat Harbor if you're interested in fishing for big game fish like wahoo, mahimahi, tuna, and marlin.

Chupu Charters (66-105 Haleiwa Rd., Slip 312, 808/637-3474, www.chupu.com) operates a 53-foot Hatteras with amenities like air-conditioning, a custom Pompanetter fighting chair, and top-of-the-line rods and reels. Bait, tackle, ice, and fish packaging supplies are provided. They offer full-day shared charters for $250, full-day private charters for $850, morning half-day private charter $700, afternoon half-day private charter $750. Private charters have a maximum of six passengers.

Sport Fishing Hawaii (808/721-8581 or 808/450-7601, www.sport-fishing-hawaii.com) operates a 47-foot Hatteras and charges for $650 for half-day charters and $825 for the full-day, 10-hour charter. They have a six-passenger limit.

Kuuloa Kai (66-195 Kaamooloa Rd., 808/637-5783, www.kuuloakai.com) has private charters for up to six anglers and lets you take home enough fish for a couple dinners. They offer full-day charters for $800 and half-day charters for $700.

H2O Adventures Hawaii (808/864-3102, www.h2oadventureshawaii.com) has five-hour deep-sea trolling charters for $500 and eight-hour charters for $700, with a four-passenger maximum. They also offer four-hour bottom fishing charters for $400 and six-hour trips for $600 with a maximum of six passengers.

Hiking, Biking, and Bird-Watching

HIKING

You can hike to **Ka'ena Point,** the western tip of the island, from the North Shore. About five miles round-trip, the route follows an old dirt road to the point. It is a dry, windswept, but extremely beautiful hike with views of the North Shore the entire way out. Once you reach the nature reserve at the end of the point, cross through the special predator-proof fence to see seabird nesting grounds, monk seals, spinner dolphins, and possibly humpback whales if you're hiking from November to March. Drive to the end of Farrington Highway, past Mokule'ia, park, and proceed on foot. Bring plenty of water. There are no facilities in the area.

At the very end of Pupukea Road is **Kaunala Trail** (6 mi loop), which runs through the verdant gulches and across the ridges of the Ko'olau foothills above Pupukea. The trail is wide and well graded with a slight elevation gain. There are great views of the North Shore on the return route. Drive to the end of Pupukea Road and park on the side of the road. Follow the dirt road past the Boy Scout camp and go around the locked gate. The trail is not far ahead to the left of the dirt road. This trail is open on weekends and holidays.

The **Kealia Trail** (7 mi round-trip) is an intermediate hike that climbs the cliff behind Mokule'ia to a summit in the Wai'anae Range. The prize is an overlook of beautiful Makua Valley. After hiking about 4 of the 19 switchbacks you'll find amazing views of the entire North Shore, as well as native trees and shrubs along the trail. To get to the trail, take Farrington Highway through Mokule'ia. As you pass the end of the airport runway, look for an access gate in the fence and turn left. It's open 7am-6pm daily. Go past the runway and park in the lot in front of the control tower. Walk toward the mountain and go through the gate in the fence and immediately turn left.

BIKING

The **North Shore Bike Path** stretches from Waimea Bay to Sunset Beach. Much of the trail is shaded, and there are several ocean views along the way. Most of the trail is flat, great for a leisurely cruise or a more relaxing way to beach hop without having to worry about parking.

If you prefer going off-road, mountain bike out to Ka'ena Point on the **Ka'ena Point Trail,** an old railroad bed which is now a dirt road that hugs the coast around the point, a five-mile round-trip. The road is rough and rocky, there is no shade, and the surroundings are arid. Conversely, the scenery of the coastal dunes, the rugged shoreline, and the beautiful water is amazing. In the winter months, huge swells can wrap around the point creating a cooling sea mist from the white water crashing against the rocks.

In Hale'iwa you can rent bikes at **Surf N Sea** (62-595 Kamehameha Hwy., 808/637-9887, http://surfnsea.com, 9am-7pm daily) for $10 per hour, $20 daily, and $100 weekly. Across from Sharks Cove, the **North Shore Surf Shop** (59-053 Kamehameha Hwy., 808/638-0390, 10am-7:30pm daily) rents cruisers for $15 per day. **Hele Huli Rental** (57-091 Kamehameha Hwy., 808/293-6024, www.turtlebayresort.com) at Turtle Bay Resort rents bikes for $10 for one hour, $20 for two hours, or $25 per day. **North Shore Bike Rentals** (888/948-5666, www.north-shorebikerentals.com) is a bike rental and delivery service. They deliver cruisers to any location from Mokule'ia to Velzyland. They rent cruisers for $19 a day, children's bikes for $10 a day, tandem bikes for $29 a day, pull carriers for $12 a day, and adult cruisers with a pull carrier for $28 a day. For three-day minimum rentals they waive the $10 delivery charge. Free helmets and locks are included with rental.

BIRD-WATCHING

The **James Campbell National Wildlife Refuge** (66-590 Kamehameha Hwy., 808/637-6330, www.fws.gov/jamescampbell) is two separate sections of wetland habitat in between Turtle Bay and Kahuku, 164 acres in total. The wetlands are dedicated to the recovery of Hawai'i's endemic waterfowl, primarily the endangered Hawaiian stilt, Hawaiian moorhen, Hawaiian coot, and the Hawaiian duck. The 126-acre Ki'i Unit is open to the public during the nonbreeding season, October to February. Also utilizing the wetlands is the bristle-thighed curlew. Guided tours are offered twice per week, on Thursday afternoons and Saturday mornings on the first two Saturdays of the month and in the afternoon on the last two Saturdays of the month. Reservations are required.

Adventure Sports

SHARK DIVING

There are two shark diving tour operators out of Hale'iwa Harbor. They travel three to four miles offshore and drop a metal shark cage in the water, where guests dive in to see Galapagos, tiger, hammerhead, and other sandbar sharks from a safe underwater vantage point. The tours are weather dependent, and no diving experience is required. If you're lucky, you'll see spinner dolphins, turtles, and even humpback whales during your time at sea. **North Shore Shark Adventures** (808/228-5900, www.hawaiisharkadventures.com) offers two-hour tours throughout the day for $120 adult, $60 children 3-13 years old. If you require transportation from Waikiki, they charge $55. **Hawaii Shark Encounters** (808/351-9373, www.hawaiisharkencounters.com) offers tours for $105 and $75 for children under 12 years old.

HORSEBACK RIDING

The North Shore is a rural enclave from Kahuku to Mokule'ia, and farms and ranches are common along the coast. Up on Pupukea, overlooking Waimea Valley and the North Shore is **Happy Trails Hawaii** (59-231 Pupukea Rd., 808/638-7433, www.happytrailshawaii.com). Their trails meander through forest, ranch land, and tropical orchards, offering panoramic mountain and ocean views. Two-hour tours are $99, and one-hour tours are $79. Riders must be at least six years old. **Gunstock Ranch** (56-250 Kamehameha Hwy., 808/293-2026, http://gunstockranch.com), just outside of Kahuku, is a family owned and operated working ranch at the base of the Ko'olau Mountains. They have a network of trails and tours for all riding levels with mountain terrain and beautiful ocean views stretching all the way down the windward coast to Kane'ohe Bay. Their Scenic Ride is a 90-minute guided ride suitable for all skill levels for $89; the Keiki Experience is a 30-minute horse experience and ride for children ages 2-7 years old for $39; the Advanced Trail Ride is a one-hour ride with trotting and cantering during the ride for $109, and previous riding experience is required. They also offer a Moonlight Ride, a Picnic Ride, a Sweetheart Ride, a Sunset Ride, and a Dinner Sunset Ride.

◀ SKYDIVING

What could be more exhilarating than seeing the entire island of O'ahu, all at once, from 20,000 feet? Jumping out of the plane that took you that high and parachuting back to earth. **Skydive Hawaii** (68-760 Farrington Hwy., 808/637-9700 or 808/945-0222, www.skydivehawaii.com) operates from Dillingham Airfield in Mokule'ia and specializes in tandem skydiving for first-time jumpers, but their services also extend to experienced skydivers and skydiving students. They make three jumps a day and offer a free shuttle service from several points in Honolulu. Tandem skydiving from 12,000 feet is $225, from 14,000 feet is $250, and from 20,000 feet (the highest tandem sky-dive in Hawai'i) is $998. Skydivers must be at least 18 years old. You can also find similar rates and services literally right next door at **Pacific Skydiving Hawaii** (68-760 Farrington Hwy., 808/637-7472, www.pacificskydiving-hawaii.com).

GLIDER FLIGHTS

For those who would rather stay inside an air-craft, yet still partake of those same views of the North Shore and beyond, **Hana Hou Air** (808/222-4235, www.hanahouair.com) of-fers 20-minute scenic glider flights above the Wai'anae Mountains along the North Shore for $100. Reservations are required. Also accessing the Dillingham Airfield is **Honolulu Soaring** (808/637-0207, www.honolulusoaring.com). They have several planes in their fleet and offer scenic as well as acrobatic glider flights. The av-erage visibility is 30 to 40 miles. One-passenger scenic flights start at $79 for 10 minutes and go to $215 for 60 minutes. Two-passenger scenic flights start at $128 for 10 minutes and go to $390 for 60 minutes. One-passenger acrobatic flights start at $165 for 15 minutes and go to $285 for 60 minutes. Combination scenic and acrobatic flights are also available.

Golf and Tennis

GOLF

Turtle Bay Resort (57-091 Kamehameha Hwy., 808/293-6000 or 800/203-3650, www.turtlebayresort.com/hawaii_golf) is the premier golf destination on the North Shore with two 18-hole championship courses, the **Palmer Course** and the **Fazio Course.** One of the best courses on O'ahu, the Palmer Course is set across natural wetlands, with its sig-nature 17th hole right on the coast. At 180 acres, there are no interruptions from homes or resort amenities. Rates for the Palmer Course are $174 till noon, $140 noon-2pm, $105 2pm-4pm, and $84 after 4pm, which include fees, golf cart, practice balls, and bottled water. The Fazio Course is more forgiving than the Palmer Course and has a walker-friendly layout set among native Hawaiian palms along the coastline. It is designed for short game play. Rates includ-ing fees, golf cart, practice balls, and bottled water are $115 till noon, $95 noon-2pm, $75 2pm-4pm, and $50 after 4pm. Walking rates are $90 till noon, $70 noon-3pm, and $25 after 3pm. Add $35 to the rate for the course you play in the morning to create a 36-hole package. The resort also has complete prac-tice facilities including target greens, chip-ping area, bunkers, and putting greens. You can contact the pro shop to reserve tee times at 808/293-8574.

For a more relaxed and informal round of golf, visit the **Kahuku Golf Course** (56-501 Kamehameha Hwy., 808/293-5842, www1.honolulu.gov/des/golf/kahuku.htm). The nine-hole sporty, seaside course is a walking-only course that can be challenging due to pre-dominantly windy conditions. The greens fee for two nine-hole rounds is $30, twilight or just nine holes is $15. Golf club rental is $12, and handcarts are available for $4.

TENNIS

Public tennis courts can be found on the North Shore at **Sunset Beach Neighborhood Park** (59-360 Kamehameha Hwy., 808/638-7051), which has two courts, and in Waialua at **Waialua District Park** (67-180 Goodale Rd., 808/637-9721), which has four courts. These courts are free to anyone. **Turtle Bay Resort** (57-091 Kamehameha Hwy., 808/293-6000 or 800/203-3650, www.turtlebayresort.com) has a four-court tennis complex. The courts are open 7am-9pm daily. The fee is $25 per hour, and resort guests get one hour per day for free. They also offer clinics and private lessons and rent rackets for $8 and a bag of balls for $4. Call 808/293-6024 to reserve a court.

Yoga and Spas

YOGA

With the focus on healthy living that comes with the ocean-influenced recreational lifestyle of the North Shore, yoga studios abound. In Waialua you'll find **Bikram Yoga North Shore** (67-208 Goodale Ave., 808/637-5700, www.bikramyogahawaii.com), which warms and stretches the muscles. The drop-in rate is $15, one week unlimited is $50, and a 10-class card is $130. **The North Shore Yoga Co-op** (67-174 Farrington Hwy., 808/561-9639, http://northshoreyoga.org) is a donation-based yoga co-op located at the Weinberg Community Center in Waialua. Students are asked to donate what they feel is appropriate for the instruction and their means. The co-op offers several types of yoga, like vinyasa, yin yoga, yoga for surfers, restorative yoga, and pregnancy yoga. Check the online schedule for class times, complete class list, and descriptions.

Along the North Shore Beaches, **Paumalua Yoga** (59-540 Kamehameha Hwy., 808/221-4258, www.paumaluyoga.com) operates from the Sunset Beach Recreation Center. They lead donation-based hatha, vinyasa, yoga for athletes, and keiki yoga classes. In addition, they offer private and semiprivate yoga instruction at their Pupukea studio, or they can come to you. Private rates start at $75 for one 60-90 minute session. The **North Shore Wellness Retreat** (59-142 Kamehameha Hwy., 808/638-8137, http://surfintoyoga.com) offers vinyasa flow, pranayama, yin yoga, and hatha flow classes, as well as Surf Into Yoga, their signature class led by professional surfer Rochelle Ballard. The drop-in rate is $10. They also have wellness packages that combine yoga, surfing, spa treatments, and a healthy meal, which start at $130. If you're up at **Turtle Bay Resort** (57-091 Kamehameha Hwy., 808/293-6000 or 800/203-3650, www.turtlebayresort.com), they have different types of yoga, Zumba, and other fitness classes for $10 per session. The monthly calendar is online.

SPAS

Spa Luana (57-091 Kamehameha Hwy., 808/447-6868 or 808/293-6000, www.turtlebayresort.com, 8am-8pm daily) is Turtle Bay Resort's luxurious spa. Located in your choice of one of six treatment rooms or an outdoor oceanside cabana, their signature services use local fruit and plant ingredients to complement the spa's relaxing tropical atmosphere. Seaside single massages start at $165 for 50 minutes and $325 for couples. They have nine types of massage on the menu, starting at $135 for 50 minutes; six body treatments starting at $135 for 50 minutes; facials and skin care enhancements starting at $135 for 50 minutes; spa treatment packages and salon services are also available.

At the **North Shore Wellness Retreat** (59-142 Kamehameha Hwy., 808/638-8137, http://surfintoyoga.com), the choice is yours whether to relax inside in the Spa Room or outdoors in their lush tropical garden. They offer three types of massage starting at $90 for 60 minutes and $130 for 90 minutes. They also offer light body energy work, acupuncture, polarity treatment, body scrubs for $75, and 60-minute facials starting at $80.

NORTH SHORE

© KEVIN WHITTON

Spa Luana is situated right on Kuilima Point.

Sights

PU'U O MAHUKA HEIAU

Located on the Pupukea bluff right above Waimea Bay and covering two acres, **Pu'u O Mahuka Heiau** is the largest *heiau* on O'ahu. Three- to six-foot stacked stone walls are what remain of the original three enclosures thought to have been built in the 17th century. The structure was integral to the social, political, and religious systems for the once thriving Waimea Valley community. The *heiau* has views of Waimea Valley and the North Shore. There are dirt walking paths around the structure and interpretive signage, but no water or facilities. Follow the trail to the edge of the cliff for a unique view of Waimea Bay. To get there, drive up Pupukea Road and take the first right turn after the switchbacks. The paved road is rough and narrow, so drive slowly and be aware of oncoming vehicles.

◖ WAIMEA VALLEY

Waimea Valley (59-864 Kamehameha Hwy., 808/638-7766, www.waimeavalley.net, 9am-5pm daily) is one of O'ahu's last partially intact *ahupua'a* (land division stretching from the mountain to the sea), and is part botanical garden and part native Hawaiian cultural site. Once a thriving native Hawaiian community based around the river running down the valley to the sea, it offered sustenance in many forms for native Hawaiians. Today, Waimea Valley is home to many collections of tropical plants, but it is most famous for the hybrid hibiscus collection at the front of the garden and the ginger and heliconia collection at the back of the valley. Peacocks run wild through the gardens, and native birds are common along the stream. There are several native Hawaiian historic living sites along the three-quarter-mile paved trail back to the waterfall and pool.

General admission is $15 for adults and $7.50 for children ages 4-12 and seniors 60 and over. Golf cart transportation from the ticket booth to the waterfall is available for $4 one way and $6 round-trip. They also have several guided hikes led by staff on Thursday and Saturday. Reservations must be made at least three days in advance for these, and additional fees apply. Check the website for the detailed information about the guided hikes.

Shopping

HALE'IWA
【 Historic Hale'iwa Town

Historic Hale'iwa Town is packed full of restaurants and shops, most within a comfortable walking distance. Art galleries, surf shops, souvenir shops, and clothing and swimwear boutiques line Kamehameha Highway through this old seaside town established at the turn of the 20th century.

In the **North Shore Marketplace** (66-250 Kamehameha Hwy.) on the south end of town you'll find **Wyland Galleries** (808/637-8729, www.wyland.com, 10am-8pm Mon.-Thurs., 10am-9pm Fri.-Sat., 10am-7pm Sun.), featuring a handful of acclaimed artists with works based on ocean and outdoor themes, **Britton Gallery** (808/637-6505, www.brittongallery. com, 10am-6pm daily), with prints, sculpture, jewelry, and Hawaiiana decor from 35 island artists, and **North Shore Glass** (808/780-1712, www.northshoreglass.com, 11am-4pm daily) where they blow glass on-site. For women's swimwear check out **North Shore Swimwear** (808/637-7000, www.northshoreswimwear. com, 10am-6pm daily).

Directly north of the Marketplace is **Haleiwa**

NORTH SHORE

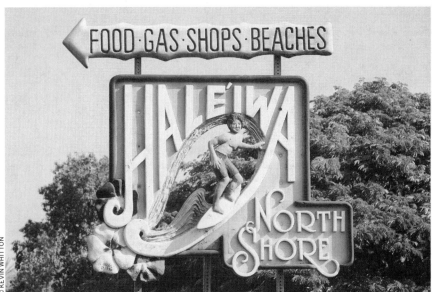

© KEVIN WHITTON

Welcome to Historic Hale'iwa Town.

© KEVIN WHITTON

Hale'iwa Farmers Market is held in Waimea Valley.

NORTH SHORE

Art Gallery (66-252 Kamehameha Hwy., 808/637-3368, www.haleiwaartgallery.com, 10am-6pm daily), Hale'iwa's oldest gallery. They feature the work of 30 island artists in media from oil and watercolor to bronze and embroidery.

In the heart of Hale'iwa, in the **Hale'iwa Town Center,** you'll find **Clark Little Gallery** (66-165 Kamehameha Hwy., 808/626-5319, www.clarklittlephotography.com, 10am-6pm Mon.-Sat., 10am-5pm Sun.) featuring the underwater and wave photography of award-winning local photographer Clark Little. Next door is the boutique clothing and beach shop **Guava Shop** (66-165 Kamehameha Hwy., 808/637-9670, 10am-6pm daily). And at the north end of town is a popular children's store, the **Growing Keiki** (66-051 Kamehameha Hwy., 808/637-4544, http://thegrowingkeiki.com, 10am-6pm daily).

They have unique clothes, locally published children's book, and handmade wooden toys.

For local farm-fresh produce and prepared foods, **Hale'iwa Farmers Market** (59-864 Kamehameha Hwy., 808/388-9696, http://haleiwafarmersmarket.com, 3pm-7pm Thurs.) is a grassroots community market held at Waimea Valley, rain or shine. They also have live music and free arts and crafts for the kids.

Waialua

If you're in Waialua, head to the old Waialua Sugar Mill, where the **North Shore Soap Factory** (67-106 Kealohanui St., 808/637-7627, www.hawaiianbathbody.com, 9am-6pm Mon.-Fri., 8:30am-6pm Sat., 10am-5pm Sun.) specializes in premier Hawaiian bath and body products, the cornerstone being their own handmade and natural soaps.

Entertainment and Events

NIGHTLIFE

Hale'iwa has two popular bars that draw the crowds at night, but also double as restaurants by day. Located in the North Shore Marketplace, **Breakers** (66-250 Kamehameha Hwy., 808/637-9898, www.restauranteur. com/breakers, 8am-2am daily, $11-24) serves breakfast, lunch, and dinner, but the surf-themed restaurant is best known for its full bar and relaxed beach vibe. Packed with surf memorabilia and one of the few places in Hale'iwa that stays open late, it often hosts big parties and has live music. Next to Longs in the Hale'iwa Town Center, **B's Bar and Grinds** (66-197 Kamehameha Hwy., 808/744-4125, www.bsbarandgrinds.com, 11am-2am daily, $12-24) is a full bar that serves lunch and dinner, a mix of sandwiches, steak, seafood, and appetizers, with a late-night menu running till midnight.

Many people on the North Shore venture to **Turtle Bay Resort** (57-091 Kamehameha Hwy., 808/293-6000 or 800/203-3650, www. turtlebayresort.com) to visit the only outdoor bar where you can grab a drink and watch the surf, the **Hang Ten Bar & Grill** (808/293-6000, 10am-10pm daily, $8-19), better known as the Pool Bar. Stiff mai tais and other tropical drink concoctions are their specialty. Situated right on the point, this is a great place for a sunset beverage. Inside the resort there is **Surfer, The Bar** (808/293-6000, 6pm-midnight daily, $12-24), a modern mixed-media bar centered around surfing and its legacy on the North Shore. Along with a light food menu, they offer tropical drinks, wine by the glass, and a bunch of local beers. Check out Talk Story Wednesday, where prominent figures in the surf industry share their stories for the crowd. Video and live music also add to the experience.

FESTIVALS AND EVENTS
◖ Hawaii Polo
Experience the fun and sport of seaside polo in beautiful Mokule'ia. **Hawaii Polo matches** (http://hawaii-polo.org, 2pm Sun. Apr.-Sept., $10 adults, children 12 and under free) are held on Sundays April through September. Game day feels like a giant tailgate party, as people pull their vehicles right up to the field and open blankets under the ironwood trees. Bring a cooler full of food and beverage and enjoy a few chuckers. Gates open at noon.

Haleiwa Arts Festival
The **Haleiwa Arts Festival** (62-449 Kamehameha Hwy., www.haleiwaartsfestival. org, July, free) is a weekend-long annual event that takes place at Hale'iwa Beach Park in the middle of July. The festival features the works of over 100 artists for exhibition and purchase, and has live musical and cultural entertainment, art demonstrations, and children's art activities. Food vendors accompany the open-air festival.

Vans Triple Crown of Surfing
For six weeks every winter, from early November through late December, the **Vans Triple Crown of Surfing** (www.triplecrownofsurfing.com, Nov.-Dec.) takes over the North Shore. This professional surfing event is comprised of three contests, the first at Ali'i Beach Park in Hale'iwa, the second at Sunset Beach, and the final one at the Banzai Pipeline. An international field of hundreds of competitors, as well as a cadre of hungry locals, battle it out on the biggest and best days of surf during the holding period for each event. Spectators flock to the beach to watch the action, some of the best surfing in the world. There are food vendors, restrooms, drinking water, souvenirs, and giveaways at each event. With limited parking and an influx of people on the North Shore, expect driving delays and plan to either pay for parking or park and walk quite a distance, especially during the Pipeline event.

© KEVIN WHITTON

It doesn't get better than seaside polo on a Sunday afternoon.

NORTH SHORE

Food

HALE'IWA
Coffee

In the North Shore Marketplace, the **Coffee Gallery** (66-250 Kamehameha Hwy., 808/637-5355, www.roastmaster.com, 6:30am-8pm daily) is a popular stop for coffee, both brewed and roasted beans. They have a great selection of bakery goods and sell local coffee by the pound. They also offer free wireless Internet for customers at the rustic covered patio seating or outdoor benches.

Quick Bites

Kua Aina (66-160 Kamehameha Hwy., 808/637-6067, www.kua-aina.com, 11am-8pm daily, $7-10) is great for the standard burger and fries combo.

Storto's (66-215 Kamehameha Hwy., 808/637-6633, 8am-6pm daily, $5-12) is the go-to sandwich deli in Hale'iwa. The friendly staff makes big sandwiches for big appetites. For a normal serving, order a half sandwich, and don't forget the papaya seed dressing.

Cafe Haleiwa (66-460 Kamehameha Hwy., 808/637-5516, 7am-1:45pm daily, also 6pm-9:30pm Tues.-Sat., $4-10) is a delicious pancakes and eggs breakfast restaurant with Mexican specialties and a signature mahimahi plate.

In the mood for shrimp? Visit **Giovanni's** (66-472 Kamehameha Hwy., 808/293-1839, www.giovannisshrimptruck.com, 10:30am-5pm daily, $4-13) shrimp truck. The white truck is an icon on the North Shore, and they've been serving up shrimp plates since 1993. They have three shrimp plates to choose from and a hot dog for the *keiki*. They also have another truck in Kahuku by the old sugar mill that stays open till 6:30pm.

THE EDDIE

Waimea Bay is home to the iconic **Quiksilver In Memory of Eddie Aikau,** an annual one-day event that honors the late North Shore waterman Eddie Aikau and the surfers who dedicate their lives to riding giant waves. Eddie was the first official lifeguard at Waimea Bay and a revered big wave surfer. In 1978, Eddie was selected to help crew a Polynesian voyaging canoe, a cultural expedition bound for Tahiti. When the canoe encountered treacherous seas outside the Hawaiian Islands and capsized, Eddie struck out fearlessly on a paddleboard back to Hawai'i to save his stranded crew. He was never seen again.

Since 1985, The Eddie is staged every year to test the strongest and best big wave surfers in the spirit of Eddie's courageous selflessness. The invitational has some impressive criteria, the waves must be at least 20-feet for the entire day of competition. Because of this minimum wave height requirement, The Eddie has only run eight times in 27 years. The waiting period is from December through February and as the saying goes on the North Shore, "The Bay calls the day."

Steak and Seafood

Overlooking the Hale'iwa Harbor, right by the Rainbow Bridge, is **Haleiwa Joes** (66-011 Kamehameha Hwy., 808/637-8005, http://haleiwajoes.com, 11:30am-9:30pm daily, $19-40). Joes serves up fresh and delicious seafood with Hawaiian-influenced Pacific Rim preparations. They also have meat selections and great salads. Indoor and patio seating are available or sit in the bar for a more casual experience with the full benefits of the menu. Make reservations to avoid the wait.

Across from Hale'iwa Beach Park and overlooking the Hale'iwa Harbor as well, **Jameson's By The Sea** (62-540 Kamehameha Hwy., 808/637-6272, www.restauranteur.com/jamesonshawaii, 11am-9:30pm Mon.-Fri., opens at 9am Sat.-Sun., $20-37) offers fresh local seafood with indoor and patio seating. Though the decor is a bit outdated, it is a romantic spot to eat and watch the sunset.

Pacific Rim

◖**Hale'iwa Eats Thai** (66-079 Kamehameha Hwy., 808/637-4247, http://haleiwaeatsthai.com, noon-9pm Mon.-Thurs., noon-9:30pm Fri.-Sun., $12-18) is a BYOB that has a religious local following. Don't be in a rush though; every order is made fresh, and there can be a bit of a wait for a table in the compact one-room restaurant. The flavorful Thai cuisine is consistent and delicious. Try a refreshing Thai iced tea with your meal.

For sushi, **Banzai Sushi** (66-246 Kamehameha Hwy., 808/637-4404, www.banzaisushibarhawaii.com, noon-9:30pm daily, $6-48) in the North Shore Marketplace is the go-to joint. Sit at a table or try the floor seating for an authentic Japanese experience on a finely decorated outdoor covered lanai. The fish is fresh, the rolls are inventive, and they have a list of premium sake. They have vegan options on the menu as well as large party sushi combinations. The tempura avocado is a treat, as is the live music often on hand.

Pizza

A staple in Hale'iwa town for nearly four decades, **Pizza Bob's** (66-145 Kamehameha Hwy., 808/637-5095, http://pizzabobshawaii.com, 7am-9pm Sun.-Thurs., 7am-10pm Fri.-Sat., $11-30) is a casual pizza parlor serving breakfast, lunch, and dinner. They have indoor and patio seating and nightly specials on food and drinks. They also have burgers and pasta in addition to signature and build-your-own pizzas.

Mexican

◖ **Luibueno's** (66-165 Kamehameha Hwy., 808/637-7717, http://luibueno.com,

© KEVIN WHITTON

Hale'iwa Eats Thai

11am-10:30pm daily, $6-29) serves authentic Mexican and Latin seafood, something that's hard to find on O'ahu. The restaurant decor is modern and colorful, the atmosphere is lively, and they source their ingredients locally, including the fish that comes right off the boat at Hale'iwa Harbor.

Cholo's (66-250 Kamehameha Hwy., 808/637-3059, www.cholosmexican.com, 9:30am-9pm Sun.-Thurs., 9:30am-9:30pm Fri.-Sat., $10-15), in the North Shore Marketplace, is a popular eatery, but more for the tequila bar rather than the food, which is the standard taco, burrito, chimichanga affair.

Health Food

Celestial Natural Foods (66-445 Kamehameha Hwy., 808/637-6729, 9am-6pm Mon.-Fri., 10am-6pm Sat.-Sun.) has been the premier health food grocer in Hale'iwa since 1974. They carry organic and natural foods, organic and local produce, vitamins, cosmetics, and other natural and healthy products.

In the back of the store, the **Beet Box Café** (66-443 Kamehameha Hwy., 808/637-3000, www.thebeetboxcafe.com, 9am-5pm Mon.-Sat., 9am-4pm Sun., $6-11) offers an extensive organic vegetarian menu for breakfast and lunch. Egg dishes served all day, and acai bowls, soup, sandwiches, salads, smoothies, and raw organic vegetable juice are all possibilities.

Sweets and Treats

Established in 1951, **Matsumoto Shave Ice** (66-087 Kamehameha Hwy., 808/637-4827, www.matsumotoshaveice.com, 9am-6pm daily) is an integral part of the history of quaint Hale'iwa town. They have developed a huge following for ices over the years. The result is a long line that snakes around the building just to get a cup of the Hawaiian treat. Be prepared to wait quite a while, especially on the weekends and during the summer. Originally a sundries store, they still have souvenirs, snacks, and items like sunscreen and sunglasses.

Just a couple storefronts away is **Aoki's**

© KEVIN WHITTON

A crowd lines up at Matsumoto Shave Ice.

Shave Ice (66-117 Kamehameha Hwy., 808/637-7017, http://aokishaveice.com, 11am-6:30pm daily). Opened in 1981, Aoki's also serves ice cream, smoothies, shakes, and has snacks and gifts. You'll also find a line at Aoki's for their delicious shaved ice made with homemade syrups, but not quite as long as at Matsumoto.

The **Waialua Bakery** (66-200 Kamehameha Hwy., 808/341-2838, 10am-5pm Mon.-Sat.) has much more than just baked goods. The locally owned bakery also has juices, a long list of smoothies, and fresh sandwiches. Much of their produce is from the family farm in Mokule'ia.

Markets

Malama Market (66-190 Kamehameha Hwy., 808/637-4520, 7am-8pm Mon., 1pm-8pm Tues., 8am-10pm Wed., 11am-9pm Thurs., 7am-10pm Fri., 10am-9pm Sat.-Sun.) is the big brand grocery store in the heart of Hale'iwa with alcohol, produce, dry goods, meats, and groceries.

NORTH SHORE BEACHES AND TURTLE BAY
Quick Bites

Sharks Cove Grill (59-712 Kamehameha Hwy., 808/638-8300, www.sharkscovegrill.com, 8:30am-8:30pm daily) is right across from Sharks Cove and enjoys great ocean views. The food truck serve breakfast, smoothies, and lunch all day, and is known for the grilled skewer plates. They have a few covered tables to take in the view while you eat.

Across from Sunset Beach, **Ted's Bakery** (59-024 Kamehameha Hwy., 808/638-5974, www.tedsbakery.com, 7am-8pm daily) provides homemade bakery goods, pies, salads, burgers, sandwiches, and plate lunches. Expect a wait of 30 minutes during the lunch rush if you order hot food.

Steak and Seafood

When North Shore locals celebrate a big occasion, they go to **Lei Lei's Bar and Grill** (57-049 Kuilima Dr., 808/293-2662, www.turtlebayresort.com/explore/restaurants/lei_leis_bar,

7am-10pm daily, $22-36). The open-air restaurant and bar has indoor and patio seating, just steps away from the Fazio Golf Course. They serve rich and savory fresh seafood cuisine with Hawaiian favorites like ahi *poke*. The prime rib is also a favorite, as is the escargot appetizer. Lei Lei's is open for breakfast, lunch, and dinner.

Markets

The Pupukea **Foodland** (59-720 Kamehameha Hwy., 808/638-8081, www.foodland.com, 6am-11pm daily) is the only grocery store on the North Shore. Luckily, the big brand grocery store has everything on premises: produce, meat, groceries, alcohol, and a deli with great made-to-order sandwiches. Expect higher prices, even by Hawai'i standards.

Kahuku Superette (56-505 Kamehameha Hwy., 808/293-9878, 6am-10pm daily), across from Kahuku High School, is known and treasured for the fresh *poke*, Hawaiian favorites like lomi lomi salmon, and marinated raw meats. They also have alcohol and beverages, beach gear and fishing supplies, and a bare-bones assortment of snacks and groceries.

Information and Services

VISITOR INFORMATION

The **North Shore Chamber of Commerce** (66-434 Kamehameha Hwy., 808/637-4558, www.gonorthshore.org) is a great place to find detailed visitor information or get a firsthand recommendation. The building is across from the Post Office on the south end of Hale'iwa town. They also host a 90-minute walking tour of Historic Hale'iwa Town at 3pm Wednesday and at 9:30am Saturday for $10 per person. Reservations are required.

LIBRARY

Internet access is available at the **Waialua Public Library** (67-068 Kealohanui St., 808/637-8286, www.librarieshawaii.org) and the **Kahuku Public Library** (56-490 Kamehameha Hwy., 808/293-8935). Visitors need a valid HSPLS library card to use an Internet computer. Three-month visitor cards are available for $10. You can reserve Internet computer time online or in person. You can also find printed bus schedules, too.

MAIL

There are full-service **post offices** in Hale'iwa (66-437 Kamehameha Hwy., 808/637-1711) and in Waialua (67-079 Nauahi St., 808/637-2754).

Getting There and Around

GETTING THERE
By Car

To get to the North Shore, you can either take Kamehameha Highway, Route 83 on the windward coast, or travel the H-2 up the middle of the island. At Wahiawa the freeway ends and becomes Wilikina Drive through Schofield Barracks, which turns into Kaukonahua Road and then finally becomes Farrington Highway as you pass Waialua and drive out to Mokule'ia at the end of the road.

Or, as the H-2 ends, you can take the Wahiawa off ramp, exit 8, which puts you on\ Kamehameha Highway through Wahiawa. Kamehameha Highway continues through the town of Hale'iwa, across the North Shore, and back down the windward side. You can bypass Hale'iwa on the Joseph P. Leong Highway, Route 83.

By Bus

You can get to the North Shore from Honolulu

via **TheBus** (808/848-5555, www.thebus.org) on Routes 55 and 88A, both of which traverse the windward coast.

GETTING AROUND

During the Vans Triple Crown of Surfing and periods of high surf on the North Shore, traffic can slow to a crawl from Hale'iwa to Sunset Beach. There are several notorious choke points along this stretch. Traffic backs up at Laniakea, Chun's Reef, Waimea Bay, and Sunset Beach. Look out for pedestrians crossing the highway. The weekends are notorious for stop-and-go traffic from Hale'iwa through Chun's Reef.

If the waves are extremely large and Waimea Bay is breaking, traffic gets crazy around the bay as people try to pull off the road to get a view and take photos. Parking on the mountain side of the road is illegal, and there is only limited space on the ocean side shoulder of the highway. It's much safer to park around Sharks Cove and walk back to the bay for photos. Parking laws are strictly enforced in the area.

On the North Shore, parking along the highway is haphazard at best. Be sure not to block residential driveways and be aware of No Parking signs and bus stops. The No Parking signs have arrows pointing in the direction of the area where it is illegal to park, and No Parking areas are strictly enforced.

For those looking to leave the car parked for a bit, **TheBus** (808/848-4500, www.thebus.org) offers Route 76, which travels between Waialua and Hale'iwa.

NORTH SHORE

SOUTHEAST AND WINDWARD

The windward side of O'ahu, the eastern shore of the island, spans the entire length of the Ko'olau Mountain Range. It's known for its ample rainfall, the lush and dramatic corduroy cliffs of the Ko'olaus, and the chance to pull off the winding Kamehameha Highway right to the water's edge. Windward towns, save for Kailua and Kane'ohe, are primarily residential and historically rooted in agriculture and aquaculture: *kalo lo'i,* banana plantations, papaya, and fishponds. A drive up the windward coast is a trip back in time, with weathered wooden fruit stands offering family farm goods. It's a leisurely drive that should be enjoyed at every turn in the road.

Kailua and Kane'ohe have developed into major population centers and desirable destinations, each with its own draw. Kailua is full of hip shops, restaurants, and some of the best fine, white sand beaches on O'ahu. It's also known for kitesurfing and kayaking, with several islets just offshore. Kane'ohe town definitely caters to locals with its dining and shopping services, but there are more than enough reasons for a visit with the Ho'omaluhia Botanical Garden and the famous Kane'ohe Bay Sandbar, perfect for a half-day kayaking adventure.

The southeast corner of O'ahu is one of the drier locales of the island. Makapu'u and Sandy Beach are O'ahu's premier bodysurfing beaches, and Makapu'u offers a short hike to its lighthouse and prime whale-watching opportunities during the humpback whales' annual stay in the Hawaiian Islands from November to March. The coastline is dramatic, as the island

© KEVIN WHITTON

HIGHLIGHTS

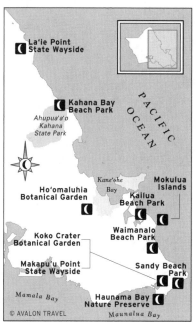

LOOK FOR **(** TO FIND RECOMMENDED SIGHTS, ACTIVITIES, DINING, AND LODGING.

(Sandy Beach Park: The powerful break at Sandy Beach is infamous and the place to test your mettle as it detonates right on the sand (page 150).

(Waimanalo Beach Park: White sand beach, ironwood trees, calm water, and an empty beach: Waimanalo has everything you need (page 153).

(Kailua Beach Park: Kailua Beach Park is the destination for ocean activities like swimming, stand-up paddling, kayaking, fishing, kiteboarding, and sailboarding (page 154).

(Kahana Bay Beach Park: Where the valley opens to the ocean, there is a stream connecting as well, creating a perfectly moon-shaped beach of fine, soft sand. The water is shallow and calm, and towering trees shade the deep-set bay. Remnants of an ancient Hawaiian fishpond still stand on the south side of the bay (page 156).

(Hanauma Bay Nature Preserve: The first marine protected area in the state of Hawai'i, this unique, circular bay lies within an extinct volcanic cone, protected from wind and waves. Live coral reef, 400 species of fish, and endangered sea turtles call it home (page 159).

(Mokulua Islands: If you're planning on renting a kayak or booking a kayak tour, don't miss paddling out to the Mokulua Islands. Not only is the trip across the shallow inner waters invigorating, but beaching on an islet, turning around and looking back to the mainland, with the Ko'olau's rising up behind the beach, is a view you don't want to miss. Not to mention, you might see some nesting seabirds on the island as well (page 163).

(Koko Crater Botanical Garden: Nestled inside an extinct volcano, it's home to dryland species from around the world. With its succulents, cycads, a native Hawaiian *wiliwili* tree stand, and a plumeria grove, you can't miss this garden, especially when the plumeria are in bloom (page 176).

(Makapu'u Point State Wayside: Hike around the point to the lighthouse, whale-watch from November to March, swim and bodysurf at the beach, and explore the black lava tidepools (page 177).

(Ho'omaluhia Botanical Garden: Backed right up to the Ko'olau Mountains, this verdant botanical garden is known for its lake, canopy trees, and myriad species of palms from around the world. The bird-watching is phenomenal (page 178).

(La'ie Point State Wayside: A dramatic offshore, wave-battered sea arch sits just off a rugged point jutting sharply out into the Pacific. It's a great place to pull up and enjoy a quiet lunch or fish from the rocks. There's a cliff jumping spot on the south side—if you dare (page 180).

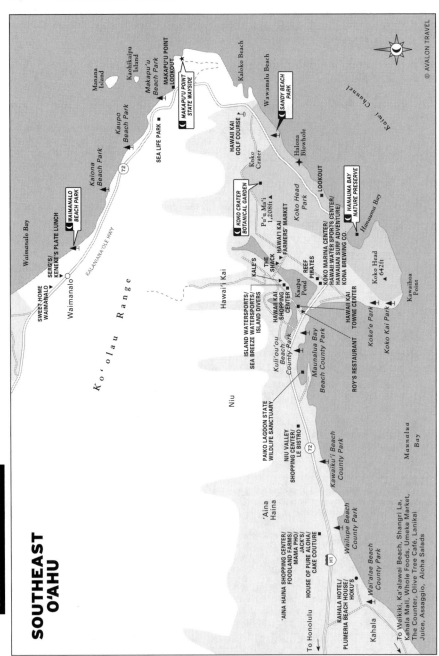

SOUTHEAST AND WINDWARD

SOUTHEAST O'AHU

© AVALON TRAVEL

seems to fall into the ocean while constantly battered by wind and chop. Koko Crater is home to a dryland botanical garden with a plumeria grove. Across the highway is Hanauma Bay Nature Preserve and Koko Head, which gives way to Maunalua Bay, known for its ample water sports activities, from surf and stand-up paddle lessons to Jet Ski rentals and wakeboarding.

PLANNING YOUR TIME

The southeast stretch of Oʻahu, from Kahala to Makapuʻu, and north to Laʻie near the island's northern tip on the windward coast, is a lot of coastline to cover, about 50 miles. With a 35 mph speed limit on both the Kalanianaole Highway and Kamehameha Highway, it's not a drive you want to rush. Not to mention, some of the attractions can easily become a full-day activity.

If you're heading to a windward locale and want to extend your scenic drive, taking the Kalanianaole Highway at least one way is a great option. There are numerous lookouts to see the rugged, dry, and wave-pummeled coastline. But it will add at least an hour to your day just to get from Kahala to Kailua. Otherwise, a full day can easily be spent enjoying the unique southeast coast. Hiking the Koko Crater stairs, snorkeling at Hanauma Bay, taking surf lessons or diving in Maunalua Bay are all halfday activities at least. Or there's bodysurfing at Sandy Beach or hiking and watching whales at Makapuʻu. Round it out with a meal in Hawaiʻi Kai and you're ready for bed.

On the windward side, other than the ranch tours at Kualoa Ranch and the Polynesian Cultural Center, everything is centered around the ocean. Whether you're snorkeling, fishing, stand-up paddling, or walking along a deserted stretch of sand, the beaches are the main attractions. If you see a nice spot along your drive and feel the need to pull over and swim, do it! The closer you look, the more you'll find the hidden gems. Don't forget, there are a few good hikes, if you don't mind mud and mosquitoes.

The weather changes fast on the windward side. A typical day might start out with sun in the morning, change clouds by midday, and bring heavy showers by the afternoon. Or, depending on the wind, it could be raining all morning, with the sun finally poking through in the late afternoon. Either way, on the windward side, you have to get out and explore or you'll never know. Don't trust the weather report.

The predominant trade winds blow out of the northeast and push air heavy with moisture evaporated from the ocean up against the Koʻolau Range. As the warm, humid air rises, it cools, condenses, and forms clouds, which become saturated and dump their payload, freshwater raindrops, down on the coast and the mountains. The windward side is wet to say the least, with the highest amounts of precipitation falling between Kaneʻohe and Laʻie. In times of extremely heavy rainfall, the Kamehameha Highway often floods and closes to through traffic.

Still, typical rain showers are often fleeting, localized events. Just because a shower is passing by doesn't mean you need to pack up the beach gear for the day. And the farther south along the Koʻolau Range past Kaneʻohe you go, the less rainfall hits the ground. On the dry, southeast tip of Oʻahu, Koko Crater receives 12-20 inches of rain annually, compared to the average 100 inches of rain that Hoʻomaluhia Botanical Garden in Kaneʻohe gets every year. The best thing to do if you're planning a beach day on the windward side is to hope for the best and prepare for the worst. At least it's still warm when it rains.

ORIENTATION
Southeast Oʻahu

Stretching from the upscale neighborhood of **Kahala** on the east side of Diamond Head to the easternmost tip of the island at Makapuʻu, the southeast coast has two distinct zones.

Beginning with Kahala and spanning along the Kalanianaole Highway east, there are **Aina Haina, Niu Valley, Kuliʻouʻou,** and **Hawaiʻi Kai.** The Portlock neighborhood lines the western flank of Koko Head and looks west over Maunalua Bay. As the highway rounds Koko

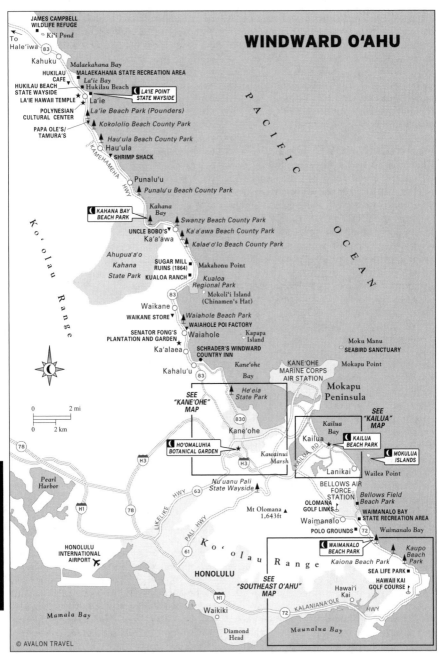

WINDWARD O'AHU

JAMES CAMPBELL WILDLIFE REFUGE
To Hale'iwa
Ki'i Pond
Kahuku
HUKILAU CAFE
HUKILAU BEACH STATE WAYSIDE
LA'IE HAWAII TEMPLE
POLYNESIAN CULTURAL CENTER
PAPA OLE'S/ TAMURA'S

Malaekahana Bay
MALAEKAHANA STATE RECREATION AREA
La'ie Bay
Hukilau Beach
La'ie
LA'IE POINT STATE WAYSIDE
La'ie Beach Park (Pounders)
Kokololio Beach County Park
Hau'ula Beach County Park
Hau'ula
SHRIMP SHACK

Punalu'u
Punalu'u Beach County Park

KAHANA BAY BEACH PARK
Kahana Bay
UNCLE BOBO'S
Ka'a'awa
Swanzy Beach County Park
Ka'a'awa Beach County Park
Kalae'o'io Beach County Park

Ahupua'a'o Kahana State Park
SUGAR MILL RUINS (1864)
KUALOA RANCH
Makahonu Point
Kualoa Regional Park
Mokoli'i Island (Chinamen's Hat)

Waikane
WAIKANE STORE
SENATOR FONG'S PLANTATION AND GARDEN
Waiahole
Waiahole Beach Park
WAIAHOLE POI FACTORY
Kapapa Island
Ka'alaea
SCHRADER'S WINDWARD COUNTRY INN
Kahalu'u

Moku Manu SEABIRD SANCTUARY

Kane'ohe Bay
KANE'OHE MARINE CORPS AIR STATION
Mokapu Point

SEE "KANE'OHE" MAP
He'eia State Park
Mokapu Peninsula

Kane'ohe
HO'OMALUHIA BOTANICAL GARDEN
Kawainui Marsh

Kailua Bay
SEE "KAILUA" MAP
Kailua
KAILUA BEACH PARK
MOKULUA ISLANDS
Lanikai
Wailea Point

Nu'uanu Pali State Wayside
BELLOWS AIR FORCE STATION
Bellows Field Beach Park
OLOMANA GOLF LINKS
Mt Olomana 1,643ft
Waimanalo
POLO GROUNDS
WAIMANALO BAY STATE RECREATION AREA
Waimanalo Bay
WAIMANALO BEACH PARK
Kaupo Beach Park
Kaiona Beach Park
SEA LIFE PARK
HAWAII KAI GOLF COURSE

Pearl Harbor
HONOLULU INTERNATIONAL AIRPORT
HONOLULU
SEE "SOUTHEAST O'AHU" MAP
Hawai'i Kai
Waikiki
Diamond Head
Mamala Bay
Maunalua Bay

PACIFIC OCEAN
Ko'olau Range
KAMEHAMEHA HWY
LIKELIKE HWY
PALI HWY
KALANIANA'OLE HWY
KAILUA RD

0   2 mi
0   2 km

© AVALON TRAVEL

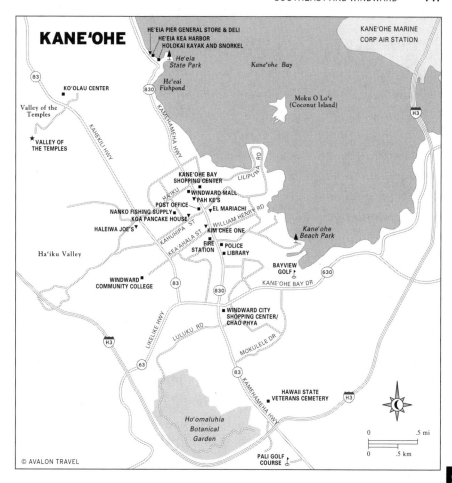

KANE'OHE

HE'EIA PIER GENERAL STORE & DELI
HE'EIA KEA HARBOR
HOLOKAI KAYAK AND SNORKEL

He'eia State Park

Kane'ohe Bay

KANE'OHE MARINE CORP AIR STATION

KO'OLAU CENTER

He'eai Fishpond

Moku O Lo'e (Coconut Island)

Valley of the Temples

★ VALLEY OF THE TEMPLES

KANE'OHE BAY SHOPPING CENTER

WINDWARD MALL
PAH KE'S
POST OFFICE
NANKO FISHING SUPPLY
KOA PANCAKE HOUSE
EL MARIACHI

HALEIWA JOE'S

KIM CHEE ONE
FIRE STATION
POLICE
LIBRARY

Kane'ohe Beach Park

Ha'iku Valley

WINDWARD COMMUNITY COLLEGE

BAYVIEW GOLF

KANE'OHE BAY DR

WINDWARD CITY SHOPPING CENTER/ CHAO PHYA

HAWAII STATE VETERANS CEMETERY

Ho'omaluhia Botanical Garden

PALI GOLF COURSE

© AVALON TRAVEL

0   .5 mi
0   .5 km

Head, the landscape changes drastically along one of the driest parts of the island from Koko Head to Makapu'u, the beginning of the windward coast. Along this windy stretch you'll find Koko Crater and Sandy Beach.

Makapu'u and Waimanalo

The Makapu'u headland is the easternmost tip of the island. It is known for its beautiful beaches, bodysurfing, and whale-watching. To the immediate north is Waimanalo town, a local village with a few food trucks, plate lunch eateries, and white sand beaches lined by tall whispy ironwood trees. Waimanalo is known for its local farms, ranches, and beach camping.

Kailua

To the north of Waimanalo is Kailua. Kailua offers boutique shopping and upscale restaurants, while the beaches are some of the prettiest on the island—fine white sand stretching for miles along the coast. The beaches are generally windy and known for kitesurfing and windsurfing. To the immediate south of Kailua is the quaint Lanikai neighborhood, where the Mokulua Islands sit right offshore.

SOUTHEAST AND WINDWARD

YOUR BEST DAY IN SOUTHEAST AND WINDWARD O'AHU

The Southeast and Windward regions are a mix of suburban and rural communities and cover a lot of coastline. Framed by the Pacific Ocean and the Ko'olau mountain range, these regions are strikingly diverse and beautiful. To experience the area to its fullest, a rental car is a must to cover the distance and have the flexibility for a change of plans if the weather dictates.

- Start the day by snorkeling one of the best reef habitats on O'ahu, **Hanauma Bay Nature Preserve** in Hawai'i Kai. With a beautiful beach set way back in the sheltered bay, an extinct volcano, spend a couple hours viewing the immense diversity found on a healthy reef ecosystem. Keep in mind that if you arrive after 9:30am, you could be turned away if the parking lot is full. If you'd rather start your morning with a hike, walk the Makapu'u trail to the lighthouse. From November to April, this vantage point is one of the prime locations to view Pacific humpback whales.

- For lunch, pick up a sandwich at **Kalapawai Market** and head to **Kailua Beach Park** or **Lanikai Beach** for a picnic lunch on the beach. Lanikai has beautiful views of the Mokulua Islands; Kailua Beach is one of the most beautiful white sand beaches on O'ahu.

- After taking in all that beauty from the beach, you'll want to get in the water and cruise around. The best way to do that is to rent a kayak. Kailua town is the hub for kayak rentals. Either stick around in Kailua and paddle to **Flat Island** and the **Mokulua Islands,** or put the kayak on the roof and go exploring. Other great areas for kayaking are **Kane'ohe Bay, Kualoa Beach Park,** and **Kahana Bay.**

- After all that outdoor activity, you'll be in the mood for a delicious meal. Try **Buzz's Lanikai,** just across the street from Kailua Beach Park, for a great steak. For a more relaxed atmosphere and pizza, fresh fish, and great local beers on tap, try **Kona Brewing Co.** in Hawai'i Kai.

Kane'ohe

Complete with a mall and ample fast food, Kane'ohe is one of the larger and more congested towns on the windward coast. Because of the bay there are no beaches, but the sheltered waters offer great potential for kayaking in the bay and out to the Kane'ohe Bay Sandbar. Fishing is also the draw here.

Kualoa to La'ie

Once you travel past the northern neighborhood of Kane'ohe, Kamehameha Highway hugs the coast from one beach town to the next. Most are quite small—maybe a food truck and convenience store—and others are strictly residential. But they all have beautiful beaches in common. Kualoa Regional Park and Kualoa Ranch are points of interest in the Kualoa area. To the north is Ka'a'awa, the last stop for fuel until La'ie, then the beautiful Kahana Bay with the remnants of an ancient Hawaiian fishpond and hiking in the valley. Farther north is Punalu'u, then Hau'ula, and finally La'ie, a town defined by its connection to the Church of Jesus Christ of Latter-day Saints and the home of the Polynesian Cultural Center, which is under the church's wing.

Beaches

Because of the natural geography of Maunalua Bay on the southeast shore, there are only a few beaches along this stretch of coast. Houses have been built to the water's edge along the peninsulas and what little beach is accessible at low tide is soon underwater as the tide rises. Fortunately, for those looking to escape the crowds of Honolulu and Waikiki beaches, Kahala is close by.

The beaches along Oʻahu's windward coast, from Makapuʻu to Laʻie, are raw, natural, and often windswept, thanks to the pervasive trade winds blowing from northwest to southeast. The different ribbons of sand tend to be bastions of solitude, where you can pull off the highway and find a quiet nook under *naupaka* and palm trees. A barrier reef stretching the length of the windward coast keeps waves at most beaches to a minimum. You'll find driftwood, rocks, fine white sand, shells, and spectacular views of the verdant Koʻolau Mountains from the water's edge. Beachgoers should be prepared for passing showers, as the trade winds also bring rain.

KAHALA
Kaʻalawai Beach

Tucked away in the affluent Kaʻalawai neighborhood, **Kaʻalawai Beach** is a narrow strip of sand that runs from the end of Kulamanu Place to the Diamond Head cliffs. Framed by lavish beachfront properties beyond the vegetation line, the secluded spot draws a younger crowd and is a favorite for topless sunbathers. The shoreline is predominately rock and reef, so getting in the water can involve finding a sandy nook to take a dip. The view to the east of Black Point is picturesque, and the clear water is often choppy from the trade winds.

To access the beach, park on Kulamanu Street and walk down Kulamanu Place to the access point. Follow the sand to the right, west, and find your own spot.

There are also some great tidepools at Kaʻalawai. Once through the access point, turn left instead of right and explore them. Be aware that the terrain is smooth and slippery in some spots as well as sharp and jagged others. There are no services in the vicinity.

DISAPPEARING SANDS

It's no secret: Oʻahu's beaches are its top attractions and best commodities, for recreational, social, and cultural reasons. But in some locales where urban development has marched right up to the high tide mark, the beaches are in serious danger of disappearing, if they're not gone already. There are natural processes in Hawaiʻi, like large swell events, seasonal currents, and storms with heavy rainfall, that move sand up and down the beach, offshore, and then back again. This natural and transient process is called coastal erosion and has been going on for centuries and will continue to shape the beaches until the island erodes back into the Pacific altogether.

In the meantime, recent human alteration of the shoreline has played a detrimental leading role in the disappearance of sand and entire beaches altogether. On Oʻahu, when the ocean shoreline encroaches within 20 feet of a structure, the property owner can be granted a variance that allows them to build a seawall to protect the property. Once the natural beach dune system is stripped away and replaced with a seawall, the beach has no way to store or replenish sand for periods of natural coastal erosion, leading to a permanent state of beach erosion. You'll find this phenomenon in Kahala, Lanikai, and on other stretches of beach along the windward coast where dwellings have been built right up to sand. Where the shoreline is armored, the beaches have washed away.

© KEVIN WHITTON

Waialae Beach

Waialae Beach Park

From Diamond Head Road, follow Kahala Avenue east toward the Kahala Hotel & Resort. Once you cross the Waialae Stream bridge, turn right into the **Waialae Beach Park** parking lot. Complete with free parking, showers, bathrooms, picnic benches, and a shaded arbor at the beach's edge, Waialae Beach Park is usually uncrowded and a favorite destination for kitesurfers and newlyweds taking wedding pictures. It's a fine place for a barbecue or picnic. The park is actually split in two by the steam, and a beautiful narrow beach unwinds to the west. This quiet stretch of sand, dotted with shells and bits of coral, is fringed by Oʻahu's most magnificent homes and mansions. The shallow waters, with a flat sand and rock bottom, are great for snorkeling and great for families looking to escape the Waikiki crowds, but are right in the path of the predominant trade winds, so be prepared to tie down umbrellas and keep your light and loose belongings secure. There are several access points along Kahala Avenue from the beach park to

Hunakai Street. Park along Kahala Avenue. The beach park is closed 10pm-5am daily.

AINA HAINA
Kawaikuʻi Beach Park

In Aina Haina you'll find that **Kawaikuʻi Beach Park** is more of a park than a beach. At low tide there is a small strip of coarse sand fronting the park, which has mature shade trees, an expansive lawn, and bathrooms and showers. The inner waters are usually murky and not exactly inviting, but this park is still favored by surfers, windsurfers, kiteboarders and stand-up paddlers for the surf spots that break along the barrier reef quite a ways out and by anglers taking advantage of the shallow bay.. From Kalanianaole Highway heading east, turn right at Puuikena Drive (there is a traffic signal here) to access the parking lot. Parking is free.

KULIʻOUʻOU
Kuliʻouʻou Beach Park

Nestled up against the Paiko Lagoon Wildlife Sanctuary in the Kuliʻouʻou neighborhood, **Kuliʻouʻou Beach Park** is one of the few areas along the Maunalua Bay coastline offering a shallow bay beside a well-maintained park. The sandy seafloor of Maunalua Bay is very shallow and dotted with bits of rock, reef, and seaweed. At low tide the water is literally ankle deep, while at high tide, it's waist deep at best. In fact, take a walk all the way out to the barrier reef, roughly a quarter-mile out to sea, keeping an eye out for sea cucumbers, crabs, and fish, all within knee-deep water. The park has facilities, picnic benches, and a free parking lot. From Kalanianaole Highway, Bay Street will take you straight there. Kuliʻouʻou Beach Park is closed 10pm-5am daily.

HAWAIʻI KAI
◖ Sandy Beach Park

A few minutes past the eastern side of Koko Head in Hawaiʻi Kai, along rugged and dramatic coastline, you'll find the infamous **Sandy Beach Park.** Sandy Beach is notorious for its high-impact shorebreak and draws bodysurfers,

SOUTHEAST AND WINDWARD

bodyboarders, and surfers to its challenging waves. The beach is rather wide by Hawai'i standards and draws a host of locals and visitors who come to watch the aqua blue waves slam onto the shore. The ocean currents here are dangerous, the sand is studded with rocks, and the surf can get big and extremely powerful, detonating onto dry sand. The shorebreak has caused injuries and even fatalities, so only expert swimmers should enter the water. However, when the waves are pumping, it is quite a spectacle to watch. Parking in the dirt lot can get somewhat haphazard and choked on the weekends. And while parking is free, theft is common so take precautions.

Sandy Beach Park is just off Kalanianaole Highway. The turn is visible from both directions. At the beach park, a road runs the length of the beach, and Wawamalu Beach Park sits at the north end. There's no sand here, just jagged lava running into the ocean, but it is a great place to stop and stretch or have a bite while watching waves break just off the rocks. There

are restrooms, and a long park frequented by kite-flying enthusiasts.

MAKAPU'U AND WAIMANALO
Makapu'u Beach Park

Makapu'u Point marks the arid southeast tip of O'ahu. Just to the north of the formidable headland, you'll find **Makapu'u Beach Park,** a beautiful crescent of white sand set against the deep blue ocean and dry, rugged cliffs. The scenery at Makapu'u is breathtaking, complete with Rabbit Island and Black Rock, two seabird sanctuaries, protruding from deep water just offshore. Makapu'u is also known for its pounding shorebreak, alluring to bodyboarders, bodysurfers, and locals and visitors alike. Because of the wave action, there are strong currents, and swimming should be done with caution. Check with the lifeguard for current ocean conditions. On days when the surf is flat and the wind is light, the water becomes very clear. Snorkeling is best at the south end of the beach, where the rocks and cliff begin. There

© KEVIN WHITTON

Sandy Beach

SOUTHEAST AND WINDWARD

© KEVIN WHITTON

Makapu'u Beach Park and Tidepools, as seen from the Makapu'u headland lookout

are restrooms and showers, but parking is very limited, so it's best to get there early. There is a small paved parking lot for the beach park, another dirt lot that is severely rutted and only safe for four-wheel-drive vehicles, or you can park up on the highway in the designated lookout area and walk down to the beach.

On the north side of the beach park are the **Makapu'u Tidepools.** The coast is fringed with black lava, creating some wonderful tidepools to explore. Be aware that the surf can wash up onto the tidepools, so its best explore the area when the surf is small to flat. To get to the tidepools, you can walk up the coast on dirt paths from Makapu'u Beach Park and meander across the lava as far as you'd like to go, or you can park right at the tidepools. Coming from Koko Head, turn just past Sea Life Park into the oceanside parking area.

Kaupo Beach Park

Just on the other side of the Makapu'u Tidepools you'll come to **Kaupo Beach Park**, a great beach for snorkeling, playing on the sand, fishing or learning to surf, with all the same great views as Makapu'u. Here, the lave opens up to offer sandy beaches among the rocks and coastal shrubs. It has character, is safe for kids, and is a favorite for local families on the weekends. It's the perfect spot to take a break from the road and have a dip or bite to eat while enjoying the scenery. As the beach arcs north toward the Makai Research Pier, there are small, gentle waves that break just off the shore. The parking lot for Kaupo Beach Park is at the same turn as the Makapu'u Tidepools, just stay to the left. There is also roadside parking for several vehicles right in front of where the waves break, or you can park down by the research pier. There are restroom and shower facilities in the beach park parking lot.

Kaiona Beach Park

About a mile north of the research pier on Kalanianaole Highway in Waimanalo is a small grassy park with restrooms and showers and a narrow but beautiful beach. **Kaiona Beach**

Park is a favorite area for local families with shallow, clean, and clear water great for swimming and snorkeling. The ocean floor, a combination or white sand and reef, gives the water a magnificent azure color. Just to the south of the beach access is Pahonu Pond, an ancient Hawaiian turtle pond. Today, it's perfect for the youngest of kids to get comfortable in a calm and sheltered setting. The beach is also called Shriners by the locals after the Shriners Beach Club at the water's edge. The free parking lot is small and fills up quick. Use caution if you park along the road. The restroom at the beach park closes 7pm-7am daily.

◖ Waimanalo Beach Park

Right in the heart of Waimanalo town, **Waimanalo Beach Park** offers the same fine white sand, great snorkeling, swimming, and azure water as all along the Waimanalo coast. The beach park has free parking, showers, restrooms, and a grassy camping area, which is predominantly used by the homeless. While lean-tos and laundry lines don't sound like paradise, the camping area is just a small portion of the three-mile beach, one of the longest on O'ahu. The beach is also lined with ironwood trees, so it's easy to duck into the shade if the sun becomes too intense. Mostly uncrowded during the week, the beach shows a different face during the weekends as families post up, fish, relax, and have a good time. It can get pretty rowdy. The beach park is closed 9:30pm-7am daily.

Bellows Beach Park

At the north end of Waimanalo town, Bellow Air Force Station harbors **Bellows Beach Park.** It's open to the public every Friday, Saturday, and Sunday. Here you'll find more of Waimanalo's signature white sand, ironwood-lined beaches. Camping complete with facilities is also available at Bellows by permit. Take the well-marked Bellows AFB turnoff from Kalanianaole Highway and follow the road to the beach, where parking is free.

© KEVIN WHITTON

Waimanalo Beach Park's white sand is fringed by tall ironwood trees.

SOUTHEAST AND WINDWARD

© KEVIN WHITTON

Kailua Beach is famous for its fine white sand.

KAILUA
Kailua Beach Park

This ocean activity hub of the windward coast offers everything—swimming, bodyboarding, kitesurfing, sailboarding, stand-up paddling, and kayaking. **Kailua Beach Park,** at the south end of Kailua, marks the start of the world-famous Kailua Beach, composed of fine grains of white sand and stretching 2.5 miles up the coast in a gentle arc. The water is shallow and often calm, perfect for families and swimming, but there can be small shore-breaking waves along parts of the beach.

Because the ocean floor is sand, ditch the snorkel mask and fins and get on top a kayak. There are outfitters within walking distance to the beach and along Kaʻelepulu Stream. Popoiʻa Island, better known as Flat Island, is a quick paddle offshore. There is also a boat ramp where residents launch their watercraft. Locals tend to gravitate to the small beach on the south side of the boat ramp, where they can park their trucks and anchor just off the beach.

Kailua Beach Park has restrooms, showers, and three free parking lots that fill to maximum capacity nearly every day. The park is clean with manicured landscaping, a walking path, and beautiful canopy trees. There is also a restaurant and market right across the street. Weekends are always more crowded than weekdays, but summer weekends see the crowds swell in both the park and along the beach. Police adamantly ticket illegally parked vehicles.

To get to Kailua Beach Park from Honolulu, the Pali Highway turns into Kalanianaole Highway, which becomes Kailua Road. From Waimanalo, turn right onto Kailua Road from Kalanianaole Highway. Continue straight on Kuulei Road as Kailua Road veers right and into Kailua's shopping district. Follow Kuulei Road until it dead-ends at South Kalaheo Avenue. Turn right, then make a left at Kailua Road to access the first parking lot, or continue on Kalaheo Avenue and over the bridge as the road turns into Kawailoa Road. The next parking lot is on the left, just on the south side of the stream. At the stop sign, take a left onto

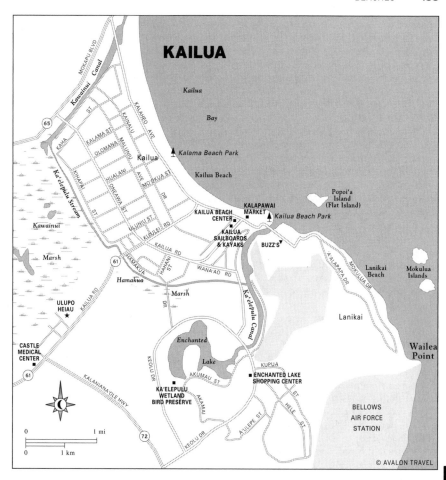

KAILUA

Kailua

Bay

🔺 *Kalama Beach Park*

Kailua

Kailua Beach

Kawainui

Marsh

Popoi'a
Island
(Flat Island)

**KALAPAWAI
MARKET**

**KAILUA BEACH
CENTER** ■

🔺 *Kailua Beach Park*

**KAILUA
SAILBOARDS
& KAYAKS** ■

BUZZ'S ▼

Lanikai
Beach

Mokulua
Islands

Hamakua

Marsh

**ULUPO
HEIAU** ★

Lanikai

Enchanted

Lake

**CASTLE
MEDICAL
CENTER** ■

KUPUA

■ **ENCHANTED LAKE
SHOPPING CENTER**

Wailea
Point

**KA'ELEPULU
WETLAND
BIRD PRESERVE**

BELLOWS
AIR FORCE
STATION

0 ___ 1 mi

0 ___ 1 km

72

© AVALON TRAVEL

Alala Road and the third parking lot is on the left side of the boat ramp. All three lots border Kailua Beach Park and are closed 10pm-5am daily. The restrooms are locked until 6am.

Lanikai Beach

Lanikai Beach fronts the affluent and quaint Lanikai neighborhood. The aesthetics of Lanikai Beach are the same as Kailua, except Lanikai Beach gets narrower as you head south, until it disappears altogether and a seawall and million-dollar homes take its place. The draw at Lanikai Beach, apart from the great swimming

and calm, turquoise water, is the Mokulua Islets. A trip to "The Moks," as they are locally referred to, is the quintessential kayak destination on O'ahu. You can take a tour or paddle the 0.75 mile solo to the islands. Most people land on Moku Nui, the larger and more northerly of the two islets. It has a small beach that offers a postcard perfect view of the mainland and the Ko'olau Mountains, a perspective most visitors will never attain. There is also a trail to the back of the island. It is against the law to deviate from the trail, as the island is also home to nesting seabirds. Parking for Lanikai

Beach is on the street through the neighborhood. There are no sidewalks, so be mindful of residents landscaping and driveways. There are several public beach access walkways in between the homes, which are obvious and well signed.

Mokulua Islands

On the western shore of **Moku Nui,** the larger and more northern of the **Mokulua Islands,** is a small beach, the perfect respite after making the kayak crossing from Kailua or Lanikai. Once here, you'll find an amazing view of the leeward coast from a unique vantage point. The water is clear and blue, and the vibe on the beach is often festive. You can spot the burrows of the island's nesting sea birds from the white sand beach. Moku Nui is a bird sanctuary, so public access is limited to the beach and a narrow footpath that circles the island. Paddling across via kayak, stand-up paddleboard, or other watercraft is the only way to access the beach. There are no facilities here.

Kalama Beach Park

At the north end of Kailua Beach is a wooded park has a soft, manicured lawn, showers, and restrooms: **Kalama Beach Park.** The beach here is slightly less crowded than at Kailua Beach Park, and at Kalama Beach Park you'll avoid many of the kitesurfers and kayakers. Walk either way up or down the beach from the beach park to nab your own swath of sand and surf. From Kuulei Road, turn left onto North Kalaheo Avenue. You'll see the small parking lot for the beach park on the right where parking is free. The gate gets locked 6pm-7am daily. If it's full or if you're planning on staying after hours, street parking in the neighborhoods is the next option.

KUALOA TO LA'IE
Kualoa Regional Park

After you pass through Kahalu'u, Waikane, and Waiahole on Kamehameha Highway, all set in Kane'ohe Bay with nearshore mudflats instead of beaches, the next beautiful sandy beach you come to is at **Kualoa Regional Park** (49-479

Kamehameha Hwy., 808/237-8525, www1.honolulu.gov/parks/programs/beach/kualoa.htm). The water is clear and calm, and the ocean bottom is a mix of sand, rock, and reef, a good place to swim and snorkel. Kualoa Regional Park is also a kayaker's destination because of the Mokoli'i Islet just offshore. Chinaman's Hat, as it's known, has a small beach on the north side. There are showers and restrooms, but no outfitters here, so you'll need to rent a kayak either in Kailua or in Honolulu. There is camping by permit in the park. The parking lot is free, and the entrance to the park is signed and visible from the highway. The park is closed and gated 8pm-7am daily.

Ka'a'awa Beaches

Just north of Kualoa you'll pass through Ka'a'awa. The Pacific Ocean pushes right up to Kamehameha Highway along much of Ka'a'awa, but there are a couple sandy nooks worth a stop. The first beach you'll come to is **Kalae'o'io Beach Park.** Simply pull off the highway under the trees. There's a grassy area, picnic tables, and a clean beach with light blue water. The beach is usually empty.

Ka'a'awa Beach Park is just a skip to the north up the highway. You'll see the restrooms and showers from the road, and notice there are only three parking spaces. If they're full, just pull off the highway and park on the shoulder. This narrow beach is a local favorite for fishing and camping and can be packed on the weekends. The restrooms are closed 9pm-6:30am daily.

Beyond the beach park, across from the U.S. post office and gas station is **Swanzy Beach Park,** where camping is allowed with a permit. The beach is small and a mix of sand and rock, but it's a great zone for snorkeling when the winds are calm. The beach park has restrooms, showers, and an expansive grassy area with no shade. The views of the Ko'olaus from Swanzy are quite extraordinary. The parking lot is closed 10pm-6am daily.

◀ Kahana Bay Beach Park
Kahana Bay Beach Park (52-222

© KEVIN WHITTON

Kahana Bay

Kamehameha Hwy., 808/237-7767, www.hawaiistateparks.org), found in dramatic Kahana Bay, offers camping by permit, a great area for a picnic, and calm, sheltered water for stand-up paddling. At the base of the bay, the Kahana Valley meets the sea and Kahana Stream spills into the Pacific, depositing fine silty sand along the beach and out into the bay. The water is often murky and a bit chilly, but remains shallow quite a ways out. The area is perfect for families with kids. Parking is right off Kamehameha Highway on the ocean side, and there are restrooms and showers. The remnants of the ancient Huilua fishpond are on the south side of the bay. The beach park and facilities are open during daylight hours.

Kokololio Beach Park

Kokololio Beach Park, at the north end of Hau'ula, offers a wide beach by Hawai'i standards with a shoreline fringed with tropical almond canopy trees and *naupaka*. The ocean floor is sandy and the water is clear when the winds are light. During the winter months when the surf is up, the shorebreak can get quite powerful, and a surf break appears on the outer reef. Swimming becomes dangerous during periods of high surf due to strong currents. There are restrooms and showers in the park, as well as a large grassy area with a large parking lot. Camping is allowed with a permit, and on the weekends, especially during the summer, the park is filled with local residents and families. The beach is also a favorite for fishing. The gated parking lot is locked 8pm-6:45am daily.

La'ie Beach Park

Just to the north, on the other side of an outcropping of limestone cliffs that marks the end of Kokololio Beach Park, is **La'ie Beach Park**. The beach park is also known as Pounders, named after the bodysurfing area near the cliffs, where the shorebreak can get big and powerful during the winter months. The beach is relatively small and often lined with organic debris, but the park is beautiful and dotted with picnic benches. Swimming here is better in the summer months. Stroll to the north to find another small beach on the other side of the point. There are no facilities at this beach park, but a paved parking lot is right off the highway.

Hukilau Beach

On the north end of La'ie town sits the lovely **Hukilau Beach,** a long, crescent-shaped sandy beach with dunes covered in *naupaka*. During the summer months the water is great for swimming, but the surf and currents make for poor conditions during the winter months. Throughout the year, this area has the propensity for strong trade winds, which can also create unfavorable beach and swimming conditions. The park itself is beautiful, with shade from ironwood trees, grass, and picnic benches—beachgoers are always welcome. There are showers, but no restrooms, and a dirt parking lot off Kamehameha Highway, which is closed on Sunday.

Malaekahana State Recreation Area

Continuing up the same crescent of sand from Hukilau Beach, you'll come to the **Malaekahana State Recreation Area**

(808/537-0800, www.hawaiistateparks.org), framed in by Kalanai Point and Goat Island to the north. When the wind is not whipping onshore from the northwest and the surf is flat, the sandy bottom makes for great swimming and crystal clear water. There is more rock and reef to the north end of the beach, which is better for snorkeling if all the other weather conditions are favorable. The beach is also a favorite for fishing. Malaekahana State Recreation Area has showers, restrooms, and picnic tables, and camping is allowed with a permit on the south side of Kalanai Point. On the north side, or Kahuku side of Kalanai Point is Malaekahana Park-Kahuku section, a private 37-acre camping area. The entrance to Malaekahana State Recreation Area is off Kamehameha Highway and well marked; the beach is not visible from the highway. Follow the road back to the parking lot, which is known as a high theft area. The entrance to the Malaekahana Park-Kahuku section is just north of the state recreation area. Look for a small faded blue sign on the side of the road. From Labor Day to March 31 the recreation area is open 7am-6:45pm daily. From April 1 to Labor Day it remains open till 7:45pm daily.

Snorkeling and Diving

This region has some great snorkeling locales, but it's up to you find the best spots during your stay. The windward side is heavily affected by the trade winds, which create chop on the ocean surface and wind waves can stir up sediment in the water. Beaches with an outer reef that blocks the surf and shallow, protected inner waters with a mix of rock, reef, and sand are best. And unless you're heading to Kailua, where the snorkeling is subpar, you'll need to have your own gear ready at hand because there are no shops to rent equipment along the windward coast. Scuba diving is centered in Maunalua Bay, with charters leaving from Hawai'i Kai Marina.

SNORKELING

Beyond Makapu'u Point, most of the windward coast is fringed by an outer reef, which creates calm and shallow nearshore waters. Add an ocean floor covered in rock and reef to that equation and you have the perfect conditions for snorkeling. **Waimanalo, Kualoa, Ka'a'awa, Hau'ula,** and **La'ie** all have great beaches to explore in mask and fins, as long as weather conditions are also cooperating. Wind is always a factor on the windward side, as the trade winds barrel straight into the coastline, creating chop on the water surface—the stronger the trades, the choppier the ocean. The northern windward beaches, like Hau'ula and La'ie are also prone to high surf in the winter months, which

© KEVIN WHITTON

The Hanauma Bay Nature Preserve is O'ahu's premier snorkeling area.

creates dangerous ocean currents and can stir up the usually crystal clear water. Because of the dips and bends in the coastline, ocean conditions can vary greatly from beach to beach, so it can be as much of an adventure to find the perfect spot to snorkel as it is to explore the water.

Most windward towns are small, residential communities without snorkeling or diving outfitters renting or selling gear, with the exception of a few options in Kailua. **Kailua Sailboards & Kayaks** (130 Kailua Rd., Ste. 101B, 808/262-2555 or 888/457-5737, www.kailuasailboards.com, 8:30am-5pm daily) rents mask, snorkel, and fins for $12 half day, $16 full day, and $48 per week. **Twogood Kayaks** (134B Hamakua Dr., 808/262-5656, www.twogoodkayaks.com, 9am-6pm Mon.-Fri., 8am-6pm Sat.-Sun.) has snorkel sets for $10 day, $35 per week. **Aaron's Dive Shop** (307 Hahani St., 808/262-2333 or 888/847-2822, www.hawaii-scuba.com, 7am-7pm Mon.-Fri., 7am-6pm Sat., 7am-5pm Sun.) also rents and sells snorkel gear.

◖ Hanauma Bay Nature Preserve

Hanauma Bay Nature Preserve (7455 Kalanianaole Hwy., 808/395-2211 or 808/396-4229, 6am-6:20pm Wed.-Mon., $7.50 admission, $1 parking) is the first Marine Life Conservation District in the state and the most popular snorkeling site on O'ahu. Located just to the east of Koko Head on the southeast shore, the bay lies within a volcanic cone with a semicircular beach and fingers of shallow reef that stretch from the edge of the bay all the way to the beach. After decades of preservation after rampant overuse, Hanauma Bay now boasts about 400 species of fish and an abundance of green sea turtles. Keep in mind that the water close to shore can get quite crowded with snorkelers and you'll have to swim a ways out to find some territory to yourself. If you're driving in, arrive as early as possible, as the parking lot usually fills to capacity by 10am and cars are turned away till others leave, usually around 2pm. You can bring your own snorkel gear, or snorkel sets are available to rent for $12 per day. There are also food concessions at the beach. Visitors are required to view a short film and presentation about the preserve and proper etiquette while snorkeling. Admission is free for children under 13 and Hawai'i residents.

DIVING

Island Divers (377 Keahole St., 808/423-8222 or 888/844-3483, www.oahuscubadiving.com, 6am-8pm daily) is a PADI 5-Star Dive Center that operates out of the Hawaii Ka'i Shopping Center. They cater to all levels of divers and offer PADI certification courses. They have pickup and drop-off services available from Waikiki hotels, or you can meet at their own private dock. Their two-tank boat charter dives start at $85. Island Divers is a complete dive center as well, with snorkel and scuba equipment available for rent and sale.

Reef Pirates Diving (7192 Kalanianaole Hwy., 808/348-2700, www.reefpirates.com, 7am-6pm daily) also operates in Hawai'i Kai, but is based in the Koko Marina Shopping Center. They are a complete dive center with sales and rentals and offer PADI certification as well as dive charters. Their two-tank charters start at $120.

A complete dive shop based in Kailua, with scuba and diving sales and rentals, **Aaron's Dive Shop** (307 Hahani St., 808/262-2333 or 888/847-2822, www.hawaii-scuba.com, 7am-7pm Mon.-Fri., 7am-6pm Sat., 7am-5pm

Sun.) offers certification and dive charters out of Hawai'i Kai Marina. They have pickup and drop-off service for Waikiki hotels, or you can meet at the shop or the dock. Two-tank charters start at $130.

China Walls

Maunalua Bay, which stretches from Kahala to Koko Head along the southeastern shore, has a wealth of dive sites and several operators that specifically service this region, with charters leaving from the Hawai'i Kai Marina. Special to the area is a dive site known as **China Walls.** This vertical wall dropping off the south side of Koko Head and reaching down to depths of 75 feet is made up of caves and ledges, and attracts sharks, turtles, jacks, rays, eels, and the endangered Hawaiian monk seal. Whale songs can be heard in the area during the winter months. China Walls is located at the southernmost tip of Koko Head, the headland that frames the eastern side of Maunalua Bay.

Maunalua Bay is home to airplane- and shipwrecks, like the WWII-era Corsair plane, a barge, and a marine landing craft known as an LST. There are also caves, reefs, and overhangs where you'll find turtles, Galapagos sharks, whitetip reef sharks, eels, countless tropical fish, and rare black coral.

Diving in the Maunalua Bay is dependent on ocean and weather conditions, and high winds or high surf can cause diving conditions to deteriorate.

Surfing, Stand-Up Paddling, and Kitesurfing

The windward side is typically just that, windy, a weather condition that can adversely affect surfing conditions unless the winds are blowing offshore. Unfortunately, the windward side usually sees onshore winds, leaving little in the way of consistent, good quality waves for surfing. On the other hand, sports like sailboarding and kitesurfing that flourish in the windy conditions are popular in this region, centered around Kailua where most of the outfitters are located.

HAWAI'I KAI

The outer reefs of **Maunalua Bay** hold a wealth of surf spots for expert surfers who are comfortable with very long paddles to the breaking waves and surfing over shallow and sharp coral reefs. Because the waves break so far offshore mixed with a lack of shoreline access, it's nearly impossible for the visiting surfer to distinguish between the different breaks and know which break is surfable and which waves are breaking over dry reef.

There are some options, however, for those who would like to learn to surf, or charter a boat to surf in Maunalua Bay. **Hawaiian Surf Adventure** (7192 Kalanianaole Hwy., 808/396-2324, http://hawaiiansurfadventure. com, 9am-5pm Mon.-Sat.) accesses a secluded wave in Maunalua Bay by boat, which is a gentle surf break perfect for beginner surfers. There are no crowds to contend with, just you and the instructor. Group lessons are $89; private lessons are $149. Hawaiian Surf Adventure also offers stand-up paddle lessons and tours of Maunalua Bay starting at $99 as well as outrigger canoe tours. **Island Watersports Hawaii** (377 Keahole St., 808/224-0076, www.island-watersportshawaii.com, 7am-7pm daily) also taps into the uncrowded waves of Maunalua Bay with two-hour group surf lessons for $99 and 1.5-hour private lessons starting at $125. If

you'd rather stand-up paddle the bay, two-hour group lessons are $99 and 1.5-hour private lessons start at $125.

Sandy Beach

To the east of Koko Head is the infamous **Sandy Beach,** known for its powerful shorebreak. As a favorite of local bodyboarders and bodysurfers, the water's edge fills with heads bobbing up and down, waiting to drop into a heaving barrel, right onto the sand. If this sounds dangerous, that's because it is. Every year people are seriously injured at Sandy Beach, with everything from broken limbs to broken necks, even death. The waves can get big, especially in the summer months. If you're not a strong swimmer or comfortable in the surf zone, take solace in the fact that it's quite amusing to watch people get slammed from the safety of the beach. Check with lifeguards for current conditions. There are also two surfing breaks over a sharp and shallow coral reef, Full Point and Half Point, at the north end of the beach.

MAKAPU'U AND WAIMANALO

Much like Sandy Beach, **Makapu'u Beach Park** is known for its powerful shorebreak which can get quite big with the right swell conditions. When the surf is smaller, the shorebreak is a bit more playful and forgiving than Sandy Beach, but you'll still leave with sand in your ears. Surfboards are prohibited in the water, but people will paddle out after the lifeguards have left for the day.

Just north of Makapu'u at **Kaupo Beach Park** there is a gentle little wave called Cockroach that breaks inside the rocky cove, perfect for beginners on big boards. During the winter months, when northeast swells sneak around Rabbit Island, the surf can get big and the currents quite strong.

KAILUA

All along Kailua beaches, from Lanikai to Kalama Beach Park, the ocean conditions are usually just right for stand-up paddling. With a soft, sandy bottom, little to no shorebreak, and generally calm water, the area around **Kalama Beach Park** is perfect for distance paddling up and down the coast. If you paddle out from **Kailua Beach,** there is **Flat Island** to explore. And if you're paddling from **Lanikai Beach,** there is a bit more rock and reef off the beach, so you can explore the near-shore waters or paddle out to the **Mokulua Islands.** During the winter months, there are two surf breaks that reveal themselves on either side of Moku Nui, the larger of the two islands. Keep in mind that if the surf is big enough for waves to be breaking on the outer reefs, the ocean currents will be much stronger. Stand-up paddle surfing should only be attempted by expert stand-up paddlers.

Stand-up paddling can become more of a chore than a pleasurable experience in extremely windy conditions. When the wind does pick up and the ocean surface becomes choppy and bumpy, sailboarders and kitesurfers take to the water in Kailua instead.

You can rent stand-up paddle boards at **Kailua Sailboards & Kayaks** (130 Kailua Rd., Ste. 101B, 808/262-2555 or 888/457-5737, www.kailuasailboards.com, 8:30am-5pm daily) for $49 half day and $59 full day, with multiday prices and free carts to walk the board to the beach. They rent beginner and advanced sailboard setups starting at $59 half day and $69 full day, and offer a Windsurf Tour for $99. They have kiteboards and gear for sale, but pre-ordering your gear is recommended. The retail outlet is within walking distance of Kailua Beach Park. **Windward Watersports** (33 Hoolai St., 808/261-7873, www.windwardwatersports.com, 9am-5pm daily) is a complete water sports shop selling new and used boards and gear for many activities. They rent stand-up paddle boards starting at $49 half day and $59 full day, with two-hour lessons for $99. They rent kiteboards starting at $30. Actual rental of the

Favorable trade winds make Kailua Beach a go-to spot for kitesurfing.

© KEVIN WHITTON

kite is contingent upon your skill level, or beginners can take a one-hour course with a certified instructor. Located in Kailua town, they'll help you put racks and watercraft on your vehicle for the short drive to the beach. **Hawaiian WaterSports** (167 Hamakua Dr., 808/262-5483, www.hawaiianwatersports. com, 9am-5pm daily) also located in Kailua, rents stand-up paddle boards starting at $69 for a full day with multiday rentals. They have a wide range of boards 7-14 feet and boards for all skill levels, and you can exchange your board at any time during your rental period. Sailboard rentals start at $59 half day, $69 full day, and they also offer two-hour lessons—group lessons start at $99, private for $179. Kiteboards are also available for rent starting at $29 per day. Different lessons are offered depending on your skill level. Private lessons start at $179 for 1.5 hours of instruction.

KUALOA TO LA'IE

Just after you pass the row of oceanfront homes across from Kualoa Ranch, the road bends and Kualoa Valley opens up to your left and the beach comes into view on your right. There's immediate roadside parking for a washy surf spot called **Rainbows.** Shallow patches of flat reef amid a sandy bottom create a few different zones where mushy waves break haphazardly. Usually windblown and choppy, this break is favored by beginner surfers and longboarders.

Kahana Bay is a great spot to stand-up paddle. The bay is somewhat protected from the pervasive trade winds, and the water is usually calm and flat, with only tiny waves lapping up onshore. The sandy bottom stays shallow all around the bay, and you can paddle up to the fishponds on its southern edge or explore around the point to the north.

On the southern edge of La'ie town, pull off Kamehameha Highway into the La'ie Beach Park parking lot and walk just to the south toward the jagged limestone cliff jutting out into the ocean. The shorebreak next to the cliff is known as **Pounders.** It gets big and powerful during the winter months when swells out of the north arrive on O'ahu shorelines. During the summer, it's usually flat and a great place to swim.

Kayaking

KAILUA
Kailua Beach Park

For all the same reasons that make **Kailua Beach Park** an attractive destination for swimming, stand-up paddling, and relaxing on the beach—white sand beaches, shallow and calm water, and beautiful views all around—it is also the hub for kayaking on O'ahu. You can launch from Kailua Beach Park and paddle out to Flat Island, or paddle up and down the coast. Another popular place to launch from is Lanikai.

For those not comfortable with a little swell or chop on the ocean surface, you can also kayak in Ka'elepulu Stream, which spills into the ocean at Kailua Beach Park. The stream opens up into Ka'elepulu Pond, a wetland area that was flooded to create the Enchanted Lake neighborhood. The water in the stream will contain urban runoff, and if the mouth of the stream has not opened in some time, it can be a bit stinky. On the other side of the coin, the water will be smooth, calm, and more protected from the wind. Just try not to get wet. For first-time kayakers, a group tour is a great way to get acquainted with the kayak and the water.

◖ Mokulua Islands

The **Mokulua Islands,** less than a mile offshore from Kailua Beach, are a popular draw. You can actually land on Moku Nui, the larger, more northern island. There's an inviting beach on the leeward side, just make sure to pull your kayak all the way up to the rocks to allow other people to land. Pack a lunch and put your camera in a dry sack because the view of mainland Oʻahu from the island is breathtaking. There is trail that circles the island, but make sure to remain on the trail because the island is a seabird nesting sanctuary.

Outfitters

In Kailua, you can rent kayaks at **Hawaiian WaterSports** (167 Hamakua Dr., 808/262-5483, www.hawaiianwatersports.com, 9am-5pm daily). Single kayaks start at $49 half day, and double kayaks start at $59 half day. All rentals include life vests, paddles, seats, backrests, and dry bags. Add a snorkel set to a kayak rental for an extra $15. They also offer two- and four-hour group and private tours of Kaneʻohe Bay and the Mokulua Islands. Rates start at $99 per person for the group tour and $179 for private tours.

Windward Watersports (33 Hoolai St., 808/261-7873, www.windwardwatersports.

com, 9am-5pm daily) rents single kayaks starting at $49 half day, double kayaks for $55 half day, and triple kayaks for $79 half day. Kayaks can be picked up at their retail store or dropped off and ready for you at the beach. They offer a three-hour guided excursion to Flat Island and Lanikai Beach for $95, a four-hour guided adventure that includes a trip to the Mokulua Islands and lunch for $125, and a six-hour guided fishing expedition starting at $175.

Twogood Kayaks (134B Hamakua Dr., 808/262-5656, www.twogoodkayaks.com, 9am-6pm Mon.-Fri., 8am-6pm Sat.-Sun.) rents single kayaks for $45 half day and tandem kayaks for $55 half day. Rentals come with a paddle, but there is an additional charge for a dry bag and backrest. They offer free delivery of kayaks to Kaʻelepulu Stream at Kailua Beach Park and basic instruction. They will deliver kayaks to other Kailua areas for $15. Twogood Kayaks has two packages that run 9am-3pm: an Adventure Package for $75 per person with kayak rental, life jacket, paddle, lunch, and round-trip transportation from Waikiki and a Guided Tour for $125 per person with extras like a guide, snorkel gear, dry bag, and backrest.

Just across the street from Kailua Beach Park you'll find **Kailua Sailboards & Kayaks** (130 Kailua Rd., Ste. 101B, 808/262-2555 or 888/457-5737, www.kailuasailboards.com, 8:30am-5pm daily). They rent single kayaks for $59 half day, and high-performance single kayaks and double kayaks for $69 half day. Dry bag, cooler, and backrest are an additional fee. For tours, they have a four-hour guided tour for beginners that includes snorkeling, transportation from your hotel, and lunch for $129 adults and $114 children 8-12; a two-hour guided kayak tour with a one-hour massage after your paddle for $229; a four-hour guided adventure of Kailua Bay, Flat Island. and the Mokulua Islands with snorkeling, lunch, and hotel transportation for $179; and a six-hour exploration tour for experienced kayakers with snorkeling, lunch, and hotel pickup for $249.

WHALE-WATCHING

Humpback whales make an annual migration of 3,500 miles from the Gulf of Alaska to the warm waters of the main Hawaiian Islands every winter. While the greatest congregation of whales is found off the windward coast of Maui, humpback whales routinely frequent Oʻahu waters during their Hawaiʻi stay from October to March. Once in the shallow waters, they engage in mating behaviors and give birth to massive calves.

On the windward coast, whales can be seen breaching, tail slapping, and spitting plumes of spray from their blowhole as they cruise along the coast. Fortunately for whale-watchers, humpback whales like to congregate in the waters from Makapuʻu to Koko Head, and swim very close to shore as they pass by. The lookouts at the Makapuʻu Point State Wayside are a great vantage point for watching their exhibitions, as well as the several lookouts along the winding Kalanianaole Highway toward Hanauma Bay.

Kane'ohe Bay offer kayakers much to explore.

© KEVIN WHITTON

KANE'OHE
Kane'ohe Bay

Kane'ohe Bay is a unique natural treasure in Hawai'i, the largest sheltered body of water in the islands, and has several worthwhile sights that make kayaking in the bay quite an extraordinary experience. Devoid of beautiful sandy beaches, the draw in Kane'ohe Bay is what's in the bay. Coconut Island is just a stone's throw from the Kane'ohe coast, but a world all its own. The entire island is a marine research facility, so the public cannot go onshore, but the reefs surrounding the island are protected and pristine, home to species of coral found only in Kane'ohe Bay. The water is crystal clear, and the reefs teem with fish. Farther to the north is the Kane'ohe Bay Sandbar, also known as Sunken Island. At low tide, the expansive sandbar, the size of a football field, is a favorite destination for locals and visitors. Sailboats pull right up on the sand, kayakers stop for rest, and people set up beach chairs in the sand and just relax. On the northern fringes of the bay, you'll also find the remains of several ancient fishponds.

Outfitters

In Kane'ohe, **Holokai Kayak and Snorkel Adventures** (46-465 Kamehameha Hwy., 808/235-6509, www.heeiastatepark.org, 8:30am-2pm Mon.-Sat.) rents tandem kayaks and offers a three-hour guided tour of the bay for $80 per adult, kayaking from Coconut Island to the He'eia fishpond. Otherwise, you'll need to have your kayak already in tow. Many of the outfitters in Kailua or Honolulu offer free racks for your vehicle.

KUALOA TO LA'IE
Kualoa Regional Park

You can put your kayak in the water and paddle out to Chinaman's Hat, a small island with a distinctive profile just off the shore, from **Kualoa Regional Park.** The ocean floor off the beach is a mix of sand, reef, and rock, so there is much to see in the water. It's also very shallow, which keeps the surface rather calm. There are no outfitters in the area, so you'll need to have your kayak already on top of the car. Aside from a nice kayak adventure, the park makes a comfortable setting for a picnic lunch.

Fishing

Shoreline fishing and spearfishing are popular activities on the windward coast, whether for hobby, sport, or sustenance. Between Sandy Beach and La'ie, there are miles of accessible coastline where you can pull out the rod and reel, or hold your breath, and fish. You can shoreline fish from the beaches of **Waimanalo, Kailua, Ka'a'awa, Kahana, Punalu'u, Hau'ula, La'ie Point State Wayside,** and **Malaekahana State Recreation Area.** In Kane'ohe Bay, people often fish from **He'eia Pier.** In some areas, especially from Kualoa to Kahana, where the ocean pushes right up again the highway, you can find a place to pull off on the shoulder, pop up a tent, and cast a line. Spearfishing is also popular along the shallow nearshore waters where rock and reef make up the ocean bottom. Waimanalo, Kualoa, Ka'a'awa, and Malaekahana State Recreation Area are all good spots to spearfish, and octopus, locally known as *tako,* is abundant in these areas—if you can find them.

If you're inclined to get out on the open water to fish, kayak fishing is the easiest way to go. Waimanalo, Kailua, and Kane'ohe Bay are more protected from the wind and better for fishing from a kayak. Ka'a'awa also has nice long stretches of nearshore water to troll as well, but is more prone to the trade winds.

The deep waters off the southeast and windward coast can be rough, so deep-sea fishing charters stick to the south and west shores. But the dark blue deep also holds the bigger fish like wahoo, yellowfin tuna, and marlin. **Island Watersports Hawaii** (377 Keahole St., 808/224-0076, www.islandwatersportshawaii. com, 7am-7pm daily) is the only fishing charter operating out of the Hawaii Ka'i Marina. Depending on ocean and weather conditions, they troll for big game fish or fish the ledges off of Maunalua Bay. The charter is $300 per hour, with a four-hour minimum and six-passenger maximum. Fishing gear and a captain are included in the price, and they will let you keep some of your catch, something a lot of charters don't offer. Call the office, located in the Hawaii Ka'i Shopping Center, to inquire about discounted rates.

If you're coming from Honolulu and forget your fishing gear, you'll need to stop at **Nanko Fishing Supply** (46-003 Alaloa St., 808/247-0938, 8am-6pm Mon., 8am-8pm Tues.-Sat., 9am-2pm Sun.), the hub of fishing gear for the windward side. Also, **Longs** (46-047 Kamehameha Hwy., 808/235-4511, 7am-midnight daily) in the Kaneohe Bay Shopping Center sells basic fishing supplies and three-prong spears.

FISHPONDS

© KEVIN WHITTON

Explore an ancient Hawaiian fishpond at Kahana Bay.

Ancient Hawaiians communities were organized by *ahupua'a,* land divisions that stretched in giant swaths from the mountains all the way into the sea. Fishing was just as important as farming, and pre-contact Hawaiians were expert at both. Fishponds were constructed in shallow, nearshore waters by the people of the *ahupua'a* to store fish for food, because high surf and adverse ocean conditions often kept them onshore. This way they could guarantee a catch. Even more important, the fishponds were constructed as spawning grounds to ensure sustainability of certain species. In fact, Hawaiian fishponds were the first marine protected areas in Hawai'i, and the people were not allowed to catch the fish that were spawning and considered *kapu,* off limits.

The fishponds were made by building a wall of stone on the reef that would enclose a body of water. The remnants of these fishponds are visible up and down the windward coast, and some are being restored and put into practice. There is the Moli'i fishpond at Kualoa Ranch, the Huilua fishpond in Kahana Bay, the Kahalu'u fishpond, the Pahonu Pond at Kaiona Beach Park in Waimanalo, which was also used to keep turtles, and He'eia fishpond on the north end of Kane'ohe Bay. Friends of He'eia Fishpond is a nonprofit organization dedicated to maintaining the working fishpond for the community.

Hiking, Biking, and Bird-Watching

HIKING
Kuli'ou'ou

Even though the southeast corner of O'ahu is one of the drier parts of the island, receiving less than 20 inches of rain annually, once you get off the coast and up into the southern reaches of the Ko'olau Range, the ecosystem changes dramatically. The **Kuli'ou'ou Ridge and Valley Trails** are a great example of this phenomenon. An excellent trek for any level of hiker, the mostly shaded Kuli'ou'ou Ridge trail follows Kuli'ou'ou Stream up Kuli'ou'ou Valley, traverses some switchbacks to the ridgeline, and terminates at a summit of 2,028 feet. With stunning views from Waimanalo and the windward coast all the way to Diamond Head, the five-mile round-trip hike passes through ironwood trees and Cook pines, and native *'ohi'a* and *lama* forests. At about the halfway point there are two covered picnic tables to rest if you've gone far enough. If you prefer, at a signed junction, stay on the Kuli'ou'ou Valley trail, which passes a small pool and waterfall and terminates at a second waterfall, about two miles round-trip.

To get there from Kalanianaole Highway, turn *mauka* onto Kuli'ou'ou Road and find your way to the very back of the neighborhood, at the back of the valley. There is neighborhood street parking in the cul-de-sac. Take the one-lane paved road down to the stream and the trailhead.

Hawai'i Kai

For a great cardio workout and 360-degree views of the southeast shore, the **Koko Crater Trail** is a daunting 1,048 steps up the south side of Koko Crater. The stairs, actually railroad ties, follow the track of an old World War II military tramway that took supplies to the top of Koko Crater more than 1,000 feet to the summit. At the top you'll find several cement military instillations and amazing views all around. From Kalanianaole Highway, turn *mauka* onto Koko Head Park Road and park in the Koko Head District Park parking lot. It's about a 0.25-mile walk to the base of the stairs.

Kailua

There is a popular walking trail along **Kawainui Marsh,** one of the few wetland ecosystems on O'ahu and home to several species of native waterbirds like the Hawaiian coot, Hawaiian moorhen, and the Hawaiian stilt along with a host of other feathered inhabitants. The mile-long path is a raised, paved trail that crosses the marsh from Kailua Road to Kaha Street, off Oneawa Street on the north end of the Kailua neighborhood known as Coconut Grove.

Maunawili Falls is a short hike in the shadow of Olomana that follows Maunawili Stream and terminates at the falls. From Kalanianaole Highway, turn into A'uola Road in the Maunawili neighborhood. Immediately fork left onto Maunawili Road and follow it

THE KO'OLAU RANGE

The drastic, verdant and corduroy cliffs of Ko'olau Range are not actually mountains in the traditional sense, but the remnants of the western half of the Ko'olau Volcano, which erupted nearly two million years ago. The caldera and eastern portion are thought to have slid cataclysmically into the ocean in prehistoric times. As erosion has chipped away at the peaks over hundreds of thousands of years, the tallest peak, Pu'u Konahuanui, now measures only 3,100 feet, but was once thought to be about three times that height. Spanning the entire windward coast, the smaller and more recent volcanoes we refer to today as Diamond Head, Punchbowl Crater, Hanauma Bay, Koko Crater, Koko Head, and Tantalus were all created by eruptions from the Ko'olau Volcano.

© KEVIN WHITTON

Follow 1,048 stairs to the top of Koko Crater.

through the subdivision and a forested area to the end at Kelewina Street. Park near the intersection and continue on foot on the one-lane private road. A sign indicates the way to the falls, which in part is on private land, so stay on the trail. Along the stream look for 'ape, a plant with huge, elephant-ear-shaped leaves. A ridgeline section offers views of Koʻolau Range, Olomana and Kaneʻohe Bay. Regain the stream and follow it to a large, deep pool and Maunawili Falls. On the hike you'll cross the stream several times and the trail can be quite muddy. It is also very popular and heavily used on the weekends. There is a second smaller pool at the top of the falls and the trail continues back from there if you wish to continue exploring the forest.

Kualoa to Laʻie

Just north of Kaʻaʻawa is the verdant and lush Kahana Valley, a state park designed to foster native Hawaiian culture. There are two trails that intermingle, loop, and wind through the valley, the **Kapaʻeleʻele Trail** and the **Nakoa Trail.** The Kapaʻeleʻele Trail is a one-mile loop passing cultural sites with views of Kahana Bay. And the Nakoa Trail is a 2.5-mile with *koa* and *hau* tree forests, pools along the stream, and a mountain apple grove. From Kamehameha Highway, turn *mauka* into the Ahupuaʻa O Kahana State Park. There is an Orientation Center, where you can find trail maps and other information, as well as restrooms. Be prepared for mud and mosquitoes on the hike.

BIKING
Kailua

Kailua is the most bike-friendly town on Oʻahu. The beaches and neighborhoods are in relatively close proximity to the town center, where all the dining, shopping, and services are located. The town is flat, the weather is exceptional, and the traffic is usually so congested that it's faster to get around on two wheels. In addition to riding around town, bikes are allowed on the trail that crosses the Kawainui Marsh.

Because of these factors, Kailua is home to the first bike share program in the state. There are two **Hawaii B-cycle** kiosks in the town center: 767 Hamakua Drive (near the intersection of Hamakua Dr. and Kailua Rd.), and 515 Kailua Road (near the intersection of Hahani St. and Kailua Rd.). Simply swipe your credit card at the kiosk, grab a bike, and go. When you park the bike at either location, your card is charged for the time you used it. The cruisers come equipped with a lock, comfy seat, and baskets.

Or you can rent a bike the traditional way, from an outfitter. **The Bike Shop** (270 Kuulei Rd., 808/261-1553, www.bikeshophawaii.com/kailua, 10am-7pm Mon.-Fri., 9am-5pm Sat., 10am-5pm Sun.) is a full-service bicycle shop. They rent 21-speed cruisers for $20 per day and road bikes for $40 per day. **Kailua Sailboards & Kayaks** (130 Kailua Rd., Ste. 101B, 808/262-2555 or 888/457-5737, www.kailuasailboards.com, 8:30am-5pm daily) rents bikes for $25 a full day and $85 for seven days.

BIRD-WATCHING
Kuli'ou'ou

Just to the west of Kuli'ou'ou Beach Park, the **Paiko Lagoon Wildlife Sanctuary** was established in 1981 to protect native Hawaiian waterbirds, migratory species, and their habitat. Hawaiian stilts, plovers, ducks, and other fowl grace the shallow lagoon, which is naturally separated from Maunalua Bay by a small strip of earth complete with plants and trees. It is illegal to remove anything from the area.

Kailua

There are several areas perfect for bird-watching in Kailua. The 800-acre **Kawainui Marsh** is the largest wetland area in the state. A paved trail traverses it from Kailua Road to Kaha Street, about a mile long. Look for native Hawaiian waterbirds, migrant waterfowl, and other curious residents, like the black-crowned night heron with its large black beak and piercing red eyes. Binoculars are a must for this area.

Hawaiian coots can be spotted at the Ka'elepulu Wetland Bird Preserve.

© KEVIN WHITTON

If you don't have binoculars and want to get an up-close look at a Hawaiian moorhen or a Hawaiian stilt, check out the **Hamakua Marsh,** which parallels Hamakua Drive. In the parking lot behind Down To Earth market is a viewing area with informative signs about the residents of the marsh. Though the parking lot leaves much to be desired for a natural setting for bird-watching, many of the native Hawaiian waterbirds congregate here in large numbers.

Another area close by to view waterbirds is in the Enchanted Lake neighborhood. The **Ka'elepulu Wetland Bird Preserve** is a small wetland area bordered by homes, and this little nook is a favorite for waterbirds. In addition to the Hawaiian duck, stilt, moorhen, and coot, look for red-footed boobies and great frigatebirds. From Keolu Drive, turn into Kiukee Place, a short dead-end road. Park and watch the birds from the sidewalk.

Kane'ohe

Ho'omaluhia Botanical Garden, nestled up against the base of the Ko'olau Mountains in Kane'ohe, is frequented by a wide range of urban and forest birds. Within several different areas corresponding to regional plantings, there are myriad trails and tropical foliage where you can search for birds. Bring binoculars as the gardens have canopy trees as well as interesting flowering plants and palm. Stop by the Visitor Center to speak with a docent about the birds that are around the garden during your stay and the best areas for sightings. You can get to the gardens, in a residential area on Luluku Road, from both Kamehameha Highway and the Likelike Highway.

Adventure Sports

HAWAI'I KAI

Hawaii Ka'i Marina and Maunalua Bay are home to all the aquatic thrill rides available in this region for adventure seekers. Wakeboard, water ski, and ride a Bumper Tube and Banana Boat at high speeds in the marina, or Jet Ski, parasail, and drive a sub scooter in the bay. New to the lineup is Jetlev flight, using a controlled, water-propelled jet pack that can send you soaring 30 feet into the air.

Sea Breeze Watersports (377 Keahole St., #E-103, 808/396-0100, www.seabreezewatersports.com, opens 8:30am daily), based in the Hawaii Ka'i Shopping Center, has a wide range of activities on offer. Bumper Tubes and Banana Boat rides are $49 per person, Jet Ski rentals are $49 per person for a two-seater and $69 for a single rider. Jet Ski rates are based on half-hour rides. Parasail flights are $49 per person for a 7- to 10-minute ride, with two people sailing at a time, and Sea Breeze is the only outfitter offering the Jetlev flight, starting at $169 for 15 minutes. They also offer snorkeling, scuba, speed sailing, and surfing lessons, and have discounts for multiple activity reservations.

Island Watersports Hawaii (377 Keahole St., 808/224-0076, www.islandwatersportshawaii.com, 7am-7pm daily), also based in the Hawaii Ka'i Shopping Center, has the sub scooter, an electric submersible scooters that allow you to explore underwater without diving or scuba gear; $99 for a 20-minute ride. They have kayak tours starting at $99 per person, two-hour whale-watching cruises from November to May for $99, two-hour turtle watching and sunset cruises also for $99 per person. In addition they offer snorkeling, scuba, fishing, and hiking adventure packages.

Based in the Koko Marina Shopping Center, behind Kona Brewing Company, **Hawaii Water Sports Center** (7192 Kalanianaole Hwy., 808/395-3773, http://hawaiiwatersportscenter.com, 8:30am-4pm daily) is another operator offering a slew of activities. Bumper tube and Banana Boat rides run $29 per person, wakeboarding and water skiing runs $49 per

RIDING THE THERMALS

The pervasive, fresh trade winds blowing up against the Ko'olau Range, combined with the splendid beauty of clear, tropical waters and verdant cliffs, creates the perfect amphitheater for hang gliding and paragliding. Makapu'u is the premier ridge-soaring site with five launch zones and one landing zone on the beach. Pilots also fly in the Kahana area. These are not recreational activities where you can merely rent a hang glider and jump off a cliff, but regulated endeavors for trained pilots who must register with one of the accredited associations on O'ahu to fly from specific sites.

Visiting paragliding pilots with their own gear should contact the **Hawaii Paragliding Association** (53-040 Pokiwai Pl., www. windlines.net). Contact any board member, their information is listed on the website, to become a member and get in the air. Visiting hang gliding pilots with gear need to contact the **Hawaiian Hang Gliding Association** (45-015 Likeke Pl., http://files.windlines.net/ hha/index.htm). Contact information is on the site about becoming a member and flying windward skies.

person, and parasailing is $59 per person and they flight side-by-side riders. Jet Skis are also available for $49 per person for two riders, and $69 for a single-person craft. They also offer scuba and snorkeling packages and multiple activity discounts.

Golf and Tennis

GOLF
Hawai'i Kai

With beautiful views of Koko Crater, the Makapu'u cliffs, and the Pacific Ocean, which can be seen from every hole, the **Hawaii Kai Golf Course** (8902 Kalanianaole Hwy., 808/395-2358, www.hawaiikaigolf. com/e) with two 18-courses is both enjoyable and challenging. The Championship Course has the largest greens in the state with deep bunkers, and the Executive Coarse, a much shorter layout with undulating, sloping greens, focuses on putting and chipping for the most advanced golfers. The wind is always a factor as well, blowing straight off the ocean and creating another factor to consider on these courses. Greens fees for the Championship Course are $110, $70 twilight (after 1pm) and for Executive Course are $38.50 weekday, $43.50 weekend. The entrance to the golf course is right off Kalanianaole Highway, between Sandy Beach Park and Makapu'u.

Makapu'u to Waimanalo

Just outside of Waimanalo town, on the Kailua side, is **Olomana Golf Links** (41-1801 Kalanianaole Hwy., 808/259-7926, www.olomanagolflinks.com), an 18-hole, par-72 course. The front nine has level fairways and water hazards at every hole, while the back nine features rolling hills and sand bunkers. The course also has stunning views of the Ko'olau Mountains. Play 18 holes with a cart for $95, $80 second visit, and $60 each additional visit. Twilight greens fees are $80 after 1:30pm.

Kane'ohe

Bay View Golf Park (45-285 Kaneohe Bay Dr., 808/247-0451, www.bayviewgolfcourse.com) is an affordable 18-hole course in Kane'ohe that has a double-decker range facility and is open for night play during the week. Visitor rates are $18 weekday, $26 weekend, $10 cart fee for 9 holes, and $26 weekday, $34 weekend, $14 cart fee for 18 holes.

For a more scenic and lush experience,

visit the 18-hole **Pali Golf Course** (45-050 Kamehameha Hwy., 808/233-7499). This challenging, hillside course has three sets of tees for different skill levels. Greens fees are $50 daily.

TENNIS

Public tennis courts can be found from Kahala to Kaneʻohe on the southeast and windward side of Oʻahu and are generally located in district parks with restrooms, drinking fountains, and ample parking. District parks close 10pm-6am daily. In Kahala, there are two courts at **Kahala Community Park** (4495 Pahoa Ave., 808/733-7371), but the area around the courts can get extremely crowded on weekdays when the elementary school nearby lets out and the park fills up with kids for baseball and football practice. **Koko Head District Park** (423 Kaumakani St., 808/395-3096) in Hawaiʻi Kai has six courts, **Waimanalo District Park** (41-415 Hihimanu St.) has four courts, **Kailua District Park** (21 S. Kainalu Dr.) has eight public courts, and **Kaneʻohe District Park** (45-660 Keaahala Rd.) has six courts.

Yoga and Fitness

KAHALA

Core Power Yoga (4211 Waialae Ave., 866/441-9642, www.corepoweryoga.com) opened a brand-new studio in 2012 in the Kahala Mall. Located in the lower level directly in front of the Hunakai Street entrance, the climate-controlled venue offers power yoga, hot yoga, power fusion yoga, and yoga sculpt. The studio's complete package includes changing rooms, showers, lockers, and a full apparel boutique. The drop-in rate is $20 per session. Check the website for a schedule.

HAWAIʻI KAI

In Hawaiʻi Kai, **Yoga Hawaii** (1152 Koko Head Ave., 808/739-9642, www.yoga-hawaii.com) has a real earthy and positive vibe. They have a wide range of yoga, like beginner yoga, vinyasa, hatha, ashtanga, pregnancy yoga, and yoga for stress. Visit the Om Lounge and pick up yoga apparel and local community-made products. They offer a three-class package for visitors for $45.

Bikram Yoga-Hawaii Kai (7192 Kalanianaole Hwy., 808/396-8838) is in the Koko Marina Shopping Center on the second floor across from the movie theater. This small, quiet, and intimate setting is heated by an infrared system.

KAILUA

The **Yoga School of Kailua** (326 Lala Pl., 808/292-9642, www.yogakailua.com) is a satellite school of the International Yoga College, a trauma healing center, and a teacher training facility. The nonprofit organization offers public group classes in asana/prananyama yoga four days a week, one class per day. Donations are requested. Check their website for classes and times.

Mindful Matters (407 Uluniu St., #412, 808/230-2476, www.mindfulmatterskailua.com) is right in the heart of Kailua town in the Kailua Medical Arts Building. This complete wellness center offers tai chi/qigong, massage, naturopathy, acupuncture, Pilates, and a host of different forms of yoga to suit every function or need. Ashtanga, core stability, hatha, power flow, restorative, vinyasa, and yoga for pregnancy are some of the disciplines they cover. The first-time drop-in rate is $10 followed by $15 each additional drop-in session.

Hot Yoga By The Sea (320 Uluniu St., Ste. 6, 808/469-1541, www.hotyogabythesea.com) is tucked away by the Kailua Wellness Center, in suite 6 down the alleyway. Look for Buddha statue outside the door. They practice hot ashtanga, power, vinyasa, and yoga basics. Drop-ins are welcome on a first-come, first-served basis, and the rates start at $18 with 3-, 5-, 10-, and 20-class packages.

Aloha Yoga Kula (38 Kaneohe Bay Dr. or 1300 Kailua Rd., 808/772-3520, www.

alohayogakula.com) has two studios in Kailua and offers nine forms of yoga to suit your needs, from kids/family yoga to vinyasa and ashtanga. There is no registration necessary, and they have mats and props available in the studios. The drop-in rate is $10 per class.

The Pali Studio, off Kailua Road near Castle Medical Center, has free parking at the Christ Church Uniting Disciples and Presbyterians, and the Aikahi Studio, across from the Aikahi Shopping Center, has parking at the Windward United Church of Christ.

Spas

KAHALA

Based in the ritzy Kahala Hotel & Resort, **Kahala Spa** (5000 Kahala Ave., 808/739-8938, www.kahalaresort.com/spa, 8am-9pm daily) has 10 lavish, tropically decorated treatment rooms with shower, deep-soak tub, changing area, and wardrobe closet. Known for their award-winning exceptional service, the staff combines the latest trends in spa therapy with organically grown, natural, and locally sourced ingredients from Hawai'i to produce the finest results in healing, relaxing, detoxifying, and rejuvenation. One-hour massages start at $170, with four different styles; 30-minute poolside massages and treatments start at $60; one-hour facials start at $160; and 75-minute signature massages begin at $230. They offer teeth whitening, waxing, and nail care service, as well as 90-minute massage and body treatment packages starting at $250.

KAILUA

Honu You Hawaiian Spa (122 Oneawa St., 808/261-1268, www.honuyou.com) focuses on balance and simplicity. They have treatments on par with the major hotel spas and, in addition, employ an educated staff focused on providing the individual with designer treatments. They offer three levels of service experience: Junior Therapists, Senior Therapists, and Master Therapists. Facials with a Master Therapist start at $48 for 30 minutes, lomi lomi and body treatments with a Master Therapist start at $35 for 30 minutes, and they have a two-hour couples package for $340. Honu You provides waxing services as well. There is also a location next to the Kailua Wellness Center on the other side of the Kailua town center (320 Ulumiu St., 808/261-5200, 9am-5pm Tues.-Sat.).

Located near many of the other wellness providers in downtown Kailua, **Maluhia Face & Body** (408 Uluniu St., 808/262-2100, www.maluhiafaceandbody.com, 9am-5pm Tues.-Fri., 9am-3pm Sat.) is a boutique day spa offering massage, skin care, and waxing. Facials start at $85 for 55 minutes, or they have an express facial, $45 for a 30-minute treatment. Massages start at $75 for 55 minutes, and they offer a signature massage, lomi lomi, and deep tissue massage.

Sights

KAHALA
Shangri La

A fitting estate for the upscale neighborhoods of Kahala, **Shangri La** (4055 Papu Cr., 808/734-1941 or 808/532-3853, www.shangrilahawaii. org) was the seasonal home of American heiress and philanthropist Doris Duke. Built in 1937, replete with amazing views from a small cliff above the water's edge, Shangri La was designed to hold Duke's vast collection of Islamic art, and today it serves as a center for Islamic art and culture. Portions of this home that blends Islamic architecture and Hawaiian landscaping are open to the public via guided tours led by the Honolulu Museum of Art. The 12-person group tour begins in the Arts of the Islamic World gallery at the Honolulu Museum of Art, followed by a short video about Duke and her estate, and then a minivan shuttles the group to the estate for a 1.5-hour tour featuring the public rooms of the main house and parts of the grounds. Tours are held 9am, 10:30am, and 1:30pm Wednesday through Saturday. General admission is $25, and reservations are strongly encouraged.

HAWAI'I KAI
Maunalua Bay Lookout

There are several lookouts beside Kalanianaole Highway in between Hawai'i Kai and Makapu'u. The coastline is rugged, the road winds precariously close to the edge of the sea cliff, and open ocean swells constantly batter rock outcroppings. The **Maunalua Bay Lookout** is an often forgotten lookout on the mountain side of the highway, just before you arrive at the Hanauma Bay turnoff if you're heading east with sweeping views of Koko Crater, Hawai'i

© KEVIN WHITTON

Maunalua Bay

SOUTHEAST AND WINDWARD

Kai Marina, and Maunalua Bay, which stretches all the way to Diamond Head.

Haunama Bay Nature Preserve Park

The first marine protected area in the state of Hawai'i, **Hanauma Bay Nature Preserve Park** (7455 Kalanianaole Hwy., 808/395-2211 or 808/396-4229, 6am-6:20pm Wed.-Mon.) is the most popular snorkeling site on O'ahu. Located just to the east of Koko Head on the southeast shore, the nearly circular bay lies within a volcanic cone with a semicircular beach and fingers of shallow reef that stretch from the edge of the bay all the way to the beach. If you're driving in, arrive as early as possible, as the parking lot usually fills to capacity by 10am and cars are turned away till others leave, usually around 2pm. There is a $1 parking fee per car and a $7.50 entry fee. Children under 13 are free. You can bring your own snorkel gear or rent snorkel sets for $12 per day. There are also food concessions at the beach. Visitors are required to view a short film and presentation about the preserve and proper etiquette while snorkeling.

Halona Blowhole

Formed by molten lava tubes meeting with the ocean, the **Halona Blowhole** funnels ocean surges through a narrow opening in the rock to create a geyser that can send a plume of spray 30 feet into the air. The blowhole isn't always active; it takes a windy day, a high tide, and high surf on the windward side to get the blast really shooting high. However, if you're there on an off day, the view toward Sandy Beach is still worth the stop.

The Halona Blowhole is located along the Kalanianaole Highway, in between Sandy Beach and Makapu'u. There is a good-sized parking lot located on the cliff side of Kalanianaole Highway, and several designated viewing areas along the cliff, right above the blowhole.

◖ Koko Crater Botanical Garden

Sited inside arid Koko Crater, **Koko Crater**

Koko Crater Botanical Garden is dedicated to dryland species.

© KEVIN WHITTON

Botanical Garden (end of Kokonani St., 808/522-7060, www1.honolulu.gov/parks/ hbg/kcbg.htm, closed Christmas Day and New Year's Day) takes advantage of the sheltered spot for plantings of rare and endangered dryland plant species from around the world. Koko Crater is actually two craters in one, an inner and outer crater, of which 60 acres of the basin have been cultivated. A two-mile loop trail takes you from the fragrant and magnificent hybrid plumeria grove in the inner crater, to a stand of native Hawaiian *wiliwili* trees in the back of the outer crater. In between are succulents, cycads, and over 200 species of trees. The plumeria grove is in full bloom April to June. There are no facilities on-site, except for a lone portable toilet, so it's best to use those at nearby Sandy Beach Park. To get here from Kalanianaole Highway, turn onto Kealahou Street, then turn left onto Kokonani Street. The paved road becomes a dirt road and ends at the garden parking lot. The gardens are open from sunrise to sunset, and there are trail maps at the entrance gate.

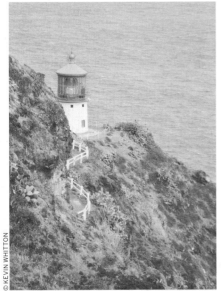

© KEVIN WHITTON

Makapu'u Point Lighthouse

MAKAPU'U TO WAIMANALO
◀ Makapu'u Point State Wayside

Makapu'u, which translates to "bulging eye" in Hawaiian, marks the rugged and dry eastern tip of O'ahu. The rough black rock is dotted with cacti and small flowering shrubs, like the native Hawaiian *'ilima* with its cute yellow and orange blossoms. The **Makapu'u Point State Wayside** holds several areas of interest. There are two parking lots at Makapu'u. Coming from Hawai'i Kai on Kalanianaole Highway, the first parking lot offers direct access to the trail that rounds Makapu'u Point and leads to the Makapu'u Point Lighthouse. Roughly a 3-mile round-trip walk, the wide, paved road gains elevation gradually as you circle the point from the south to face the Pacific Ocean. On a clear day you can see the islands of Moloka'i and Maui in the far distance. The hike has an added bonus of being one of the premier whale-watching venues while the humpback whales breed and rear their young in Hawaiian waters from November to March. It is also cooler during this period as well, as the shadeless hike can get rather hot in the midday, summer sun. There are informational signs along the trail about humpback whale activity and behavior.

At the end of the hike are a couple lookout platforms and the **Makapu'u Point Lighthouse,** a 46-foot-tall active lighthouse constructed in 1909. The lighthouse itself is off limits to the public, but you can get close enough to get a nice picture with the blue Pacific as the backdrop. Feel free to scamper around the rocks and explore the summit at 647 feet, but be careful as the area is scattered with sharp rocks, boulders, and cactus.

At the second parking lot, just to the north of the first, is a magnificent lookout area with views of the Waimanalo Coast, the rugged southern end of the Ko'olau Range, and two nearby offshore islands, **Manana Island and Koahikaipu Island State Seabird Sanctuary.** The islands are home to nesting wedge-tailed shearwaters, sooty terns, brown noodies, and several other species. It is illegal to set foot on the islands. Manana Island is commonly referred to as Rabbit Island, because a rancher actually tried to raise rabbits here prior to its designation as a seabird sanctuary.

If you consider yourself an avid hiker, from the lookout you can scramble up the back side of the point to the summit, regain the trail near the lighthouse, and follow the paved path back to the lookout for a nice loop.

Sea Life Park

Sea Life Park (41-202 Kalanianaole Hwy., 808/259-2500, www.sealifeparkhawaii.com, 10:30am-5pm daily) is an aquatic park just north of Makapu'u Point on the *mauka* side of the highway. Focused on education and interaction with exotic sealife and animals, the park is known for its dolphin adventure programs, where guests can literally swim with the dolphins. The Dolphin Royal Swim takes you on a dorsal fin ride with two dolphins and culminates with the foot push, where the dolphins push you around the pool by your feet, $235 and park admission is included. The Dolphin Swim Adventure lets you interact with dolphins and take a belly ride for $185. The Dolphin Encounter is designed for families with children to interact with dolphins in shallow water for $105. Guests can also swim with sharks, sea lions, or rays. Beyond getting in the water with the sea creatures, the park also offers a Hawaiian shark tank, dolphin shows, sea lion shows, penguins, a kids play area, turtle feeding, and an open-air aquatic theater. Adult general admission is $30, kids age 3-12 $20.

KAILUA
Ulupo Heiau State Historic Site
The massive stone platform of the **Ulupo Heiau State Historic Site** was supposedly built by the legendary *menehune* and shows remarkable skill with stone, measuring 140 feet wide by 180 feet long by 30 feet high at its tallest edge, although the stepped front wall has partially collapsed under a rockfall. The *heiau* overlooks Kawainui Marsh, and below the *heiau*, you can see traditional *kalo lo'i*, taro growing in small ponds. Ulupo Heiau was one of three *heiau* that once overlooked the former fishpond. The other two, located on the west side of the

marsh, are Pahukini and Holomakani Heiau. Some restoration has been done to Pahukini Heiau, but both remain largely untouched and inaccessible.

To get to Ulupo Heiau as you approach Kailua on the Pali Highway, turn left at the Castle Medical Center onto Uluoa Street, following it one block to Manu Aloha Street, where you turn right. Turn right again onto Manu O'o and park in the Windward YMCA parking lot. The *heiau* is directly behind the YMCA building.

KANE'OHE
◖ Ho'omaluhia Botanical Garden
Ho'omaluhia Botanical Garden (45-680 Luluku Rd., 808/233-7323, www1.honolulu.gov/parks/hbg/hmbg.htm, 9am-4pm daily, closed Christmas Day and New Year's Day) is a botanical gem nestled at the base of the verdant corduroy of the Ko'olau Range. With 400 acres of geographically organized gardens—covering the Philippines, Hawai'i, Africa, Sri Lanka, India, Polynesia, Melanesia, Malaysia, and Tropical America—and a network of trails interconnecting the plantings, one could spend an entire day in the garden. The Visitor Center is staffed with extremely knowledgeable docents who can help identify birds and interesting plants in flower during your visit. You can also grab a trail map there, too. A paved road links all the plantings and there are separate parking lots for each, so you can pick and choose where you'd like to spend your time. Drive slowly on the road, as the path is a lovely, popular walk for residents and garden guests. Ho'omaluhia also boasts its own lake, Lake Waimaluhia. Catch-and-release fishing is permitted on the weekends 10am-2pm. The garden is serene, quiet, lush, and often wet, so be prepared for the passing shower, mud, and mosquitoes. Rustic camping is also permitted from Friday afternoon till Monday morning. Check in at the Visitor Center for a pass. The garden is located in a residential area on Luluku Road, which you can access from both Kamehameha Highway and the Likelike Highway.

© KEVIN WHITTON

Ho'omaluhia Botanical Garden features palm trees, a lake, and a variety of trails.

Coconut Island

Coconut Island (808/235-9302, http://coconutislandnews.blogspot.com), tucked away deep in Kane'ohe Bay, literally had its 15 seconds of fame as part of the opening reel of scenic shots for the 1960s TV sitcom hit, *Gilligan's Island.* But the island has a much more eclectic and interesting history than just appearing on television. Once fertile fishing grounds belonging to Kamehameha I and Bernice Pauahi Bishop, the island was purchased in the 1930s and expanded by a young heir to the Fleischmann yeast company. He transformed it into a zoo and aquarium, as well as a tuna fish packing plant, the remnants of which are still visible on the island. The island changed hands several more times over the decades and today is the Hawai'i Institute of Marine Biology and one of the seminal locations for marine research on O'ahu. The education outreach arm of the institute offers tour once or twice a month, depending on docent availability, for a nominal fee based on the number of people in your party. Call

for a reservation or visit their blog for more information.

If you wish to simply view the island from shore, you can get a great view of the island from the elevated vantage of Lilipuna Road as it hugs the coastline. There is no public parking on Lilipuna for the institute, but you can find street parking a little ways south of the dock and walk back to the point to snap some pictures. Be careful walking along the road, as there is no shoulder or designated pedestrian area. Turn onto Lilipuna Road from Kamehameha Highway at the north end of Kane'ohe town, by the Windward Mall.

Valley of the Temples

Located along the Kahekili Highway just north of Kane'ohe town, **Valley of the Temples** (47-200 Kahekili Hwy., 808/239-8811, www.valley-of-the-temples.com) is a memorial park with lush landscaping and a wealth of gardens and temples to honor many faiths. The memorial park is open to the public, and the peaceful and serene setting is only

© KEVIN WHITTON

La'ie Point State Wayside is a beautiful spot to relax and eat lunch, go fishing, or cliff dive.

amplified by the natural amphitheater of cliffs of the Ko'olaus.

KUALOA TO LA'IE
Chinaman's Hat

Just offshore from Kualoa Regional Beach Park (49-479 Kamehameha Hwy.) is the curious islet known as **Chinaman's Hat.** Mokoli'i Island is its Hawaiian name. The island is a quick kayak trip from the beach and has a tiny little private alcove of sand on the back side. You can hike, or rather scramble, up to its 213-foot summit.

Kualoa Ranch

Kualoa Ranch (49-560 Kamehameha Hwy., 808/237-7321, www.kualoa.com) is both a 4,000-acre working cattle ranch, activity, and cultural center and the site for many of the Hollywood blockbuster movies filmed in Hawai'i. They offer historical and cultural tours like their Movie Sites and Ranch Tour, Jungle Expeditions Tour, Ancient Fishing Grounds and Tropical Garden Tour, or Kahiko Hula Lessons starting at $24 adult, $15 children. For adventure tours they provide one- and two-hour ATV or horseback

packages, starting at $69. They also have venues for weddings and corporate events, and even have tours that include lunch or dinner. Cultural/historic tour package tours start at $59, adventure tour packages start at $99.

◖ La'ie Point State Wayside

The **La'ie Point State Wayside** is a hidden marvel, the perfect place to pull up to the edge of the rugged point, relax, have a snack, and watch waves crash against a small seabird sanctuary just offshore, a little island noteworthy for its sea arch. There are trash cans, but no services in the area. It is also a popular spot for cliff jumping. On the south face of the cliff is a small area where jumpers plunge roughly 30 feet to the warm water below. There is a nook in the cliff to climb out of the water and up an extremely sharp and rocky gorge to the top of the cliff. It's best to watch a few others jump and get back up before you try. There are no lifeguards, and you're on your own, quite far from a sandy beach.

Tucked away at the back of a neighborhood and out of view from the highway, turn off of

Kamehameha Highway onto Anemoku Street, then hang a right onto Naupaka Street and follow it to the end of the point. Anemoku Street is across the highway from the Laie Village Center.

Laie Hawaii Temple

Built in 1919, the **Laie Hawaii Temple** (55-600 Naniloa Loop, 808/293-2427, www.ldschurch-temples.com/laie, 9am-8pm daily) was the first temple erected by the Church of Jesus Christ of Latter-day Saints outside the state of Utah, and also the first in Polynesia. You can tour the grounds and gardens of this stark white, grand edifice, and there's an accompanying visitors' center free to the public.

Shopping

KAHALA

Kahala Mall (4211 Waialae Ave., 808/732-7736, www.kahalamallcenter.com, 10am-9pm Mon.-Sat., 10am-5pm Sun.) is the nexus for shopping in Kahala. The small and airy, two-story mall is conveniently located right off the H-1 freeway. From Honolulu, take the Waialae Avenue exit and the mall is on your right. You'll find the mall basics like **Macy's** (808/737-5429), **Barnes & Noble** (808/737-3323), **Longs Drugstore** (808/732-0784), **Starbucks** (808/737-0283), **Jamba Juice** (808/734-7988), and even **Whole Foods** (808/738-0820). Kahala Mall also has some unique boutique stores that are worth a look.

Super Citizen (808/599-4333) is a boutique shop that specializes in all things sustainable living. They offer a new look and style that combines sensibility with modern fashion with their original jewelry, art, and clothing all sourced locally and made with earth-friendly materials. **In My Closet** (808/734-5999) is a small, hip boutique with eclectic and fashionable clothing and accessories. **Island Sole** (808/738-8430) is a one-stop shop for slippers, or what you might call flip-flops or sandals. If you'd like island-themed decorations for your living spaces, check out **SoHa Living** (808/591-9777). The store carries a plethora of shells and beachy knickknacks.

HAWAI'I KAI

For produce direct from local farmers and other locally made prepared foods, the **Hawaii Kai Farmers Market** (511 Lunalilo Home Rd., 808/388-9696, http://haleiwafarmersmarket.com/hawaii-kai.html, 9am-1pm Sat.) has you covered. At the Kaiser High School parking lot location, you'll find the freshest fruits and vegetables, prepared foods like honey and jelly, baked goods, and best of all, hot food from a handful of health-conscious establishments. From Kalanianaole Highway, turn north onto Lunalilo Home Road. The market is open rain or shine.

KAILUA

In downtown Kailua, park the car, get outside, and walk around the busy town center, where most of Kailua businesses are located. There are definitely some great finds in Kailua town.

Haute couture has made its mark on the seaside hamlet of Kailua thanks to **Mu'umu'u Heaven** (767 Kailua Rd., 808/263-3366, www.muumuuheaven.com, 10am-6pm Mon.-Sat., 11am-4pm Sun.), a fashionable and stylish boutique that sells island-style dresses made from vintage mu'umu'u and aloha wear. The store is warm and inviting, the staff is extremely friendly, and the outfits are in high demand. The one-of-a-kind pieces are handmade right in Hawai'i. They also sell art, handmade and unique jewelry and accessories, vintage home decor, recycled T-shirts, and collared shirts for the guys.

Get your fill of reading material at **Book Ends** (600 Kailua Rd., 808/261-1996, 9am-8pm Mon.-Sat., 9am-11pm Sun.), a great independent bookstore (one of the few left) with volumes stacked ceiling to floor. The knowledgeable staff can get you into the perfect book for your stay. For records, CDs, and other music paraphernalia, check out **Hungry Ear Records** (418 Kuulei Rd., 808/262-2175, http://hungryear.com, 10:30am-6pm Mon.-Sat.), a classic independent record store with a great selection of new and used music. Hungry Ear is a must for record collectors. If you'd rather play than listen to music, next door is Kailua's famous **Coconut Grove Music** (418 Kuulei Rd., 808/262-9977, www.coconutgrovemusic.com, 10am-6pm Mon.-Sat., 11am-4pm Sun.), a complete music store selling new, used, and vintage instruments. There's nothing like strumming a ukulele while you're relaxing on Kailua Beach. And if by chance you need a new swimsuit for said beach, **Pualani** (111 Hekili St., Ste. 102, 808/262-3830, http://pualanikailua.com, 10am-7pm Mon.-Sat., 10am-5pm Sun.) is a smart bikini boutique with functional mix-and-match suits and women's activewear.

For local farm-fresh produce and prepared foods, hit up the **Kailua at Night** farmers' market (609 Kailua Rd., 5pm-7:30pm Thurs.). The market sets up in the covered parking lot by Longs.

There is also a Sunday market featuring all local farmers and vendors: **Kailua Town Farmers' Market** (315 Kuulei Rd., 808/388-9696, http://haleiwafarmersmarket.com, 9am-1pm Sun.) sets up in the Kailua Elementary School parking lot. Just look for the rows of white tents.

KANE'OHE

On the corner of Kamehameha Highway and Haiku Road in Kane'ohe, the **Windward Mall** (46-056 Kamehameha Hwy., 808/235-1143, www.windwardmall.com, 10am-9pm Mon.-Sat., 10am-5pm Sun.) serves the windward side of the island with national brands and a few local retailers. **Macy's** and **Sears** are the big department stores and there is the **Regal Cinemas 10,** but the mall is more a hangout where local families congregate and grab a bite to eat, and not necessarily geared toward the visitor.

Entertainment and Events

NIGHTLIFE
Hawai'i Kai

The Shack (377 Keahole St., 808/396-1919, 11am-2am daily, $7-24) is the quintessential pub and sports bar in the Hawai'i Kai area. Dark, a bit musty, dark wood furniture, darts, pool, TVs all around, classic bar food including ribs, and interesting, even curious decorations make this bar come alive. Not to mention, it's located right on the water in the Hawaii Ka'i Shopping Center, with outside seating as well. And the happy hour and daily specials will make you extra happy.

Kailua

Located at the intersection of Hamakua Drive and Hahani Street, **Boardriders Bar & Grill** (201 Hamakua Dr., 808/261-4600, www.boardridersbarandgrill.com, noon-2am daily, $9-15) is better known as a bar than a grill, but they do serve pizza, salad, steak, stir-fry, and classic bar munchies. Boardriders has a couple pool tables and is the best venue for catching live music on the windward side. The bar sees local, national, and international artists and favors reggae and jawaiian music. *Pau hana* is 4pm-6pm daily.

Nestled next to the Hamakua Marsh is a small but friendly, blue-collar bar called **The Creekside Lounge** (153 Hamakua Dr., 808/262-6466, http://creeksidelounge.com, 8am-2am daily). Established in 1982, the Creekside is a biker bar with a cadre of friendly female bartenders. The bar shows live sporting events and is no frills, but they have a huge local following. Smoking is allowed on the patio overlooking the marsh, where most patrons regularly spill out to.

CULTURAL TOURS AND LU'AU

The windward side has two venues for cultural tours and lu'au. **Kualoa Ranch** (49-560 Kamehameha Hwy., 808/237-7321, www.kualoa.com) offers historical and cultural tours of the working ranch, bordering valleys, and coastline. Established in 1850 the ranch is steeped in tradition and has a unique perspective and story to tell about the area. There is an Ancient Fishing Grounds and Tropical Gardens Tour, Legends and Legacy Tour, Hakipu'u Hike, Kahiko Hula Lessons, Secret Island Beach Tour, and Jungle Expedition Tour. The tours are $24 adult and $15 child, the hike is $15 adult and includes one child. On the northern end of the windward side, in La'ie, the **Polynesian Cultural Center** (55-370 Kamehameha Hwy., www.polynesianculturalcenter.com, 800/367-7060, 11:30am-9pm Mon.-Sat.) introduces visitors to the people and cultures of Hawai'i, Samoa, Maori New Zealand, Fiji, Tahiti, Marquesas, and Tonga as you walk through and visit the different villages and interact with the people demonstrating their specific arts and crafts. There is also a canoe ride that explores the villages as well. Dining is paramount to the experience, and you can choose between the Island Buffet with a mix of local Hawaiian fare, Prime Dining with prime rib, crab legs, and sushi in a secluded setting, or the famous Ali'i Luau, with authentic Hawaiian food including traditional *imu* pork, a large pig cooked in an earthen oven. There is also an evening show called "Ha: Breath of Life," which is a culmination of story, dance, Polynesian music, and fire. General admission, which is for the day experience only, is $49.95 adult, $39.95 child. Admission, buffet, and evening show will run $69.95 adult, $54.95 child, and packages for admission, the lu'au, and show start at $91.95 adult, $67.95 child.

CINEMA

If you're keen to grab a movie and popcorn on the southeast and windward sides, there are three theaters. **Consolidated Theaters Kahala 8** (4211 Waialae Ave., Ste. 3080, 808/733-6243) is located inside Kahala Mall on the ground floor level. General admission is $10.50, matinee (before 4pm) $8.25, and 3-D films are an additional $4. They offer blockbusters as well as acclaimed art, independent, and foreign films. **Regal Cinemas 10** ((46-056 Kamehameha Hwy., 808/234-4006) is on the south side of the Windward Mall and shows major motion pictures, art films, digital presentations, and 3-D, RPX, and IMAX movies. General admission is $10, matinee (before 6pm) is $7.50. In La'ie you'll find **Laie Palms Cinemas** (55-510 Kamehameha Hwy., 808/232-0006, www.laiepalmscinemas.com) in the Laie Shopping Center strip mall. General admission $8.50, matinee (before 5pm) is $6.75. The theater does not show R-rated films and is closed on Sunday.

FESTIVALS AND EVENTS

Kailua

The **"I Love Kailua" Town Party** (last Sun. of Apr.) is a daytime festival in the heart of downtown Kailua. Kailua Road is closed to vehicular traffic, and people from all over the island come out to eat, shop, and celebrate Kailua. There are activities for the kids and local restaurants and retail outlets line the street with tents full of merchandise and delicious fare.

Kane'ohe

The Kaneohe Bay Marine Corps Base opens its gates to the public for **BayFest** (mid-July). The festival is a mix of live music from big-name rock-and-roll stars, carnival rides, military displays, and fireworks. The three-day event has been running for more than two decades and draws some big musical acts. Traffic can be extremely slow entering the base due to the security checkpoints.

Orchids are a big deal in Hawai'i and the **Windward Orchid Society** holds an annual spring show and plant sale in the King Intermediate School gym (46-155 Kamehameha Hwy., www.windwardorchidsociety.org). The two-day event showcases the best in orchid cultivars as well as other unusual plants.

Food

The gastronomic landscape of this vast region changes just as much as the climate as you make your way from Kahala to La'ie. In the more affluent areas, health food is king, while in others, fast food and Hawaiian food reign.

KAHALA
Quick Bites
The Counter (4211 Waialae Ave., E-1, 808/739-5100, www.thecounterburger.com/honolulu, 11am-9pm Sun.-Thurs., 11am-10pm Fri.-Sat., $7-15) is Kahala's premier burger joint. The menu, as well as the interior, is quite modern, and their take on the burger is welcoming and refreshing. With signature burgers and a build-your-own-menu, there are a wide variety of gourmet toppings and aiolis to choose from, as well as different size burgers, up to one-pound patties. Put all that on a bun or in a bowl, your choice, but either way, they stack it high. One caution to the brave: because everything is priced individually, you're custom burger can cost you a small fortune. Fortunately, they have happy hour (3pm-6pm Mon.-Fri.) with half-price everything on their starter menu and $2 off beer, wine, and select drinks.

Steak and Seafood
Plumeria Beach House (5000 Kahala Ave., 808/739-8760, www.kahalaresort.com, 6:30am-10pm daily, $26-45), an open-air sea-side restaurant inside The Kahala Hotel & Resort, serves breakfast, lunch, and dinner and has entrée and buffet options. The small menu selection for lunch and dinner means each dish is carefully crafted to capture the best of Hawai'i regional and Pacific Rim cuisine. This comfortable island home setting takes advantage of beautiful ocean views. The Plumeria Beach House is best known for its breakfast buffet, but they also have many other à la carte choices as well.

Also in The Kahala Hotel & Resort is **Hoku's** (5000 Kahala Ave., 808/739-8760,

www.kahalaresort.com, 5:30pm-10pm Wed.-Sun., $28-69), an award-winning fine dining restaurant. The food is a fusion of Hawaiian, Asian, and European cuisine with steak, duck, lamb, chicken, and fish entrées as well as a sushi menu. An artisan cheese menu makes for a delightful appetizer, and their Sunday brunch, 10am-2pm, features a wide variety of seafood and a prime rib and lamb cutting station.

Italian
Assaggio Bistro (4346 Waialae Ave., 808/732-1011, 11:30am-2:30pm and 5pm-9:30pm Sun.-Thurs., 5pm-10pm Fri.-Sat., $16-36) has a huge menu of classic Italian dishes. Their portions come in two sizes, small and large, with the small portion more than enough for a complete meal. Each main dish has the choice of pasta, potatoes, rice, or vegetables for the side. Reservations are recommended. To get to Assaggio from Hawai'i Kai, take the Waialae Avenue off-ramp and turn right into the parking lot from the ramp. From Waialae Avenue eastbound, turn left onto Kilauea Avenue and then make an immediate right into the parking lot.

Mediterranean
Located on the corner of Kilauea Avenue and Pahoa Avenue is a popular BYOB called the **Olive Tree Café** (4614 Kilauea Ave., Ste. 107, 808/737-0303, 5pm-10pm daily, $11-15). Offering Mediterranean and Greek fare, the menu has plenty of vegetarian, as well as meat, options. The environment is warm, friendly, and casual with both indoor and outdoor seating. The café has open seating and there is no waiter service. It is a popular joint, so it's best to arrive either early or late to avoid a long wait. Luckily, there is a wine shop just next door.

Health Food
Not only is **Whole Foods** (4211 Waialae Ave., 808/738-0820, www.wholefoodsmarket.com/

stores/honolulu, 7am-10pm daily, $3.50 and up) a market where you can pick up organic and locally grown produce and vegetables, but they also make to order sushi, Chinese food, burgers, Mexican food, sandwiches, pizza, and they have a hot food bar, salad bar, and dessert and coffee bar. Known to be on the high side of the price point, they do have $1 street tacos on Tuesday and $2 off per pound from the hot food bar on Wednesday. They are located in the Kahala Mall, ground level, right off Waialae Avenue.

Lanikai Juice (4346 Waialae Ave., 808/732/7200, www.lanikaijuice.com, 7am-8pm Mon.-Sat., 7am-7pm Sun., $5-8) is a locally owned and operated smoothie shop that uses organic and locally sourced products when available.

◖ Aloha Salads (4211 Waialae Ave., 808/735-8334, www.alohasalads.com, 10am-9pm daily, $6-10) is another locally owned and operated establishment dedicated to using locally sourced products and produce, and gourmet meats and cheese. Their menu is simple yet sophisticated, and they have a nice selection of island-inspired soups, sandwiches, and salads. With greens from the North Shore, tomatoes from the windward side, papayas from Moloka'i, and ahi tuna from Hawai'i waters, the food is fresh, delicious, and eco-conscious. The Aloha Passion with grilled steak and the Ono Island Ahi salads are the most popular. They are located inside Kahala Mall on the ground level right next to Whole Foods.

AINA HAINA
Quick Bites
The small community of Aina Haina has a small strip mall, the **Aina Haina Shopping Center** (820-850 W. Hind Dr.), along Kalanianaole Highway that has a complete sampling of services and a handful of eateries. **Jack's Restaurant** (808/373-4034, 6:30am-2pm daily, $1-13) serves biscuits and gravy, eggs, omelets, and other seafood breakfast and lunch dishes. Simple and good, the eggs with corned beef hash are a local favorite. You can pick up a big, handmade sandwich at **Foodland**

Farms (808/373-2222, 5am-11pm daily), or dig a spoon and chopsticks into some pho at **Mama Pho** (808/373-8887, 11am-9pm Sun.-Thurs., 11am-10pm Fri.-Sat., $4-10). Kid's pho bowls come with ice cream and a drink.

Sweets and Treats
If you're looking to satisfy your sweet tooth, the Aina Haina Shopping Center has two delicious options. **Cake Couture** (808/373-9750, http://cakecouture.com, 10:30am-6:30pm Mon.-Fri., 10:30am-5:30pm Sat., $3-4) has ridiculously delicious cupcakes in nearly 40 distinctive flavors that rotate throughout the week. Check their website for the flavor schedule.

◖ Uncle Clay's House of Pure Aloha (808/373-5111, www.houseofpurealoha.com, 11am-6pm Mon.-Thurs., 10:30am-8pm Fri.-Sun., $4-9) indulges in the local favorite shaved ice. Rising above the competition with handmade syrups actually produced from locally sourced ingredients and friendly, family-style service, Uncle Clay's takes shaved ice to a new culinary level. The small shop also has healthy grab-bag snacks for sale.

NIU VALLEY
Steak and Seafood
The Niu Valley Shopping Center in Niu Valley has one noteworthy tenant on the food front, **Le Bistro** (5730 Kalanianaole Hwy., 808/373-7990, 5:30pm-9pm Wed.-Mon., $25-40). This contemporary French restaurant, casual yet elegant, is a fixture in the Honolulu dining scene. The chef recommends his legendary short ribs, a staple on the menu since they opened a decade ago, and the beef quartet, a sampler entrée chosen by the chef himself. Robust soups, stews, and salads round out the menu.

HAWAI'I KAI
Steak and Seafood
At the water's edge in the Koko Marina Center in Hawai'i Kai is the **◖ Kona Brewing Co.** (7192 Kalanianaole Hwy., 808/396-5662, http://konabrewingco.com, 11am-10pm daily, $12-26), a local brewpub serving fresh steak and seafood, all with a twist—their signature

brew is incorporated in some way into most of the recipes. They have a huge signature pizza menu, specialty beers on tap you can't find in the stores, and brews to go. They also have a great weekday happy hour 3pm-6pm: half off draft beers and select appetizer specials.

For fine dining in Hawai'i Kai, **◖ Roy's** (6600 Kalanianaole Hwy., 808/396-7697, 5:30pm-9pm Mon.-Thurs., 5:30pm-9:30pm Fri., 5pm-9:30pm Sat., 5pm-9pm Sun., $15-45) is a must. They serve signature Hawaiian fusion cuisine with exemplary service and attention to detail, and their sushi creations pair wonderfully with the entrées. They also have indoor and lanai bar seating that is first-come, first-served, accompanied by soft, live music, a much more casual option than the main, second floor dining room with beautiful views of Maunalua Bay.

Health Food

In the Hawai'i Kai Shopping Center is **Kale's Natural Foods** (377 Keahole St., 808/396-6993, www.kalesnaturalfoods.com, 8am-8pm Mon.-Fri., 8am-5pm Fri.-Sat., $6-10), a market and deli serving natural products and organic produce. The small kitchen specializes in vegetarian, vegan, macrobiotic foods, and free-range meat options. The food is fresh, home-made, and surprisingly creative.

MAKAPU'U TO WAIMANALO
Quick Bites

Waimanalo has a few places to stop and grab a quick bite as you make your way along the Kalanianaole Highway. **Keneke's Plate Lunch & BBQ** (41-857 Kalanianaole Hwy., 808/259-9811, 9:30am-5:30pm daily, $2-7) serves up the typical Hawaiian plate lunch and is very popular. **Serg's** (41-865 Kalanianaole Hwy., 808/259-7374, 11am-8pm Mon.-Sat., opens at 8am Sun., $3-12) brings Mexican food to Waimanalo with carnitas, carne asada, carne al pastor, and their famous flauta. **Sweet Home Waimanalo** (41-1025 Kalanianaole Hwy., 808/259-5737, http://sweethomewaimanalo. com, 9:30am-7pm Thurs.-Mon., 9:30am-3pm Tues.-Wed., $6-10) mixes Hawaiian-style

cooking with the principles of sourcing their ingredients locally and using organic when possible.

KAILUA
Steak and Seafood

◖ Buzz's Lanikai (413 Kawailoa Rd., 808/261-4661, http://buzzssteakhouse.com/ lanikai.htm, 11am-9:30pm daily, $17-33) is famous for its kiawe charcoal broiled burgers and steaks as well as its salads. The small, popular restaurant is quirky and fun, complete with a tree right in the middle of the lanai seating. It's right across from Kailua Beach Park, so it's usually packed with a wait. Buzz's is also known for its signature mai tai, a mix of rum with a cherry on top. If you'd like a juice mixer with it, order the B.F.R.D. Don't forget to ask what that stands for.

Formaggio Grill (305 Hahani St., 808/263-2633, www.formaggio808.com, 11:30am-11pm Mon.-Thurs., 11:30am-1am Fri.-Sat., 11am-11pm Sun., $12-69) blends Italian dishes with favorites from the grill like prime rib, lamb chops, barbecued ribs, and filet mignon. Thin crust pizzas and rich lobster bisque complement the dishes, as does the wine-by-the-glass selection, over 50 bottles. Parking is extremely limited in front of the restaurant. Try the lot across the street by Macy's.

Quick Bites

Kalapawai Market (306 S. Kalaheo Ave., 808/262-4359, www.kalapawaimarket.com, 6am-9pm daily, $8-24) is right at Kailua Beach Park, with another location in downtown Kailua (750 Kailua Rd., 808/262-3354, 6am-9pm Mon.-Thurs., 6am-9:30pm Fri., 7am-9:30pm Sat., 7am-9pm Sun., $8-24). The beach park location has a small sandwich deli and a limited grocery store that also sells beer and wine. The downtown location is strictly a café and deli with a coffee and wine bar and bakery. Open for breakfast, lunch, and dinner with indoor and outdoor seating, they have made-to-order sandwiches and a selection of prepared gourmet foods.

Boots and Kimo's Homestyle Kitchen (151

Hekili St., 808/263-7929, 7:30am-2pm Mon.-Fri., 7am-2:30pm Sat.-Sun., $4-14) is all about pancakes, and people line up for them—macadamia nut pancakes to be exact. They also serve other traditional breakfast items and Hawaiian-style favorites all day long with a few lunch items as well. The restaurant is awash in sports memorabilia.

◖Morning Brew (600 Kailua Rd., 808/262-7770, http://morningbrewhawaii.com, 6am-9pm Sun.-Thurs., 6am-10pm Fri.-Sat., $1-9) is the go-to coffeehouse and bistro in Kailua. With good coffee, a great assortment of bakery goods, sandwiches, snacks, free Internet, and two-stories of seating, plus outdoor seating, it's an easy all-day hangout if you have some work to do.

Mexican

Cactus (767 Kailua Rd., 808/261-1000, http://cactusbistro.com, 11am-10pm daily, $6-24) offers a blend of locally sourced ingredients and Central and South American cuisine, including influences from Cuba, Puerto Rico, and Mexico. The restaurant has a modern style, complete with regional wines and premium rums, tequilas, and liquors. They serve lunch and dinner.

In the Kailua Shopping Center, **Mexico Lindo** (600 Kailua Rd., 808/263-0055, www.mexicolindohawaii.com, 11am-9pm Mon.-Thurs., 11am-10pm Fri., 10am-10pm Sat., 10am-9pm Sun., $7-20) has the standard bean and rice, tacos and tostadas, Corona and tequila menu. Large portions and the yellow, white, and red decor make the stop worthwhile.

Japanese

Noboru (201 Hamakua Dr., A-102, 808/261-3033, http://noborukailua.com, 11:30am-3pm Mon.-Sat., 5pm-9pm daily, $4-29) is the premier sushi restaurant in Kailua. They also serve teishoku, shabu-shabu, chanko nabe, and have a modern sake bar with over 25 different kinds of sake.

Thai

Check out **Champa Thai** (306 Kuulei Rd.,

808/263-8281, www.champathai.com, 11am-2pm and 5:30pm-9:30pm Mon.-Sat., 5pm-9pm Sun., $7-11). Once you pick from the nearly 100 options of sauce, noodle, meat, and vegetable combinations, all that's left is for you to decide is how spicy to make it.

Health Food

Down To Earth (201 Hamakua Dr., 808/262-3838, www.downtoearth.org, 7:30am-10pm daily) is an all-vegetarian organic and natural food store. In addition to groceries, vitamins, cosmetics, bulk items, and produce, they also have a hot food bar and bakery. There are a few tables in front of the store where you can enjoy your meal. Hamakua Marsh is just across the parking lot.

Whole Foods (629 Kailua Rd., #100, 808/263-6800, www.wholefoodsmarket.com/stores/kailua, 7am-10pm daily) has a hot food bar, sandwiches, cold prepared foods, fresh pizza, Chinese food, burgers, burritos, even a few beers on tap, and a comfortable outdoor lanai for sitting down and enjoying your grub.

KANE'OHE

Kane'ohe is a town that has not been largely altered by tourism, the proof being that you won't find any fine dining restaurants or chic clothing boutiques. Instead, Kane'ohe is littered with local and national fast-food chains and small and simple ethnic eateries.

Quick Bites

Once you pass through Kane'ohe, it's all about mom-and-pop places where you can grab a quick bite. And at the top of the list is the **Waiahole Poi Factory** (49-140 Kamehameha Hwy., 808/239-2222, http://waiaholepoifactory.com, 11am-6pm daily, $5-11). Serving up real Hawaiian food like squid and beef lu'au, kalua pig, lomi salmon, lau lau, and chicken long rice, they have mini plates that come with rice and lomi salmon and combo plates for a larger appetite. They also sell hand-pounded poi, which has a firmer texture and lighter flavor than milled poi.

Just past the Poi Factory, the **Waikane Store**

(48-377 Kamehameha Hwy., 808/239-8522, 8:30am-5pm daily) is a historical landmark on the Hawai'i Register of Historic Places. Established in 1898, they're still serving up many of the snacks and treats they've been selling for decades: boiled peanuts, fresh cooked chicken, local fruits, and homemade peanut butter cookies.

Breakfast

For a local-style diner breakfast, stop by **Koa Pancake House** (46-126 Kahuhipa St., 808/235-5772, 6:30am-2pm daily, $2-8). It's a popular breakfast spot on the weekends and is usually packed all morning, so expect a wait. The parking lot is very small, and if it's full, park on Kawa Street.

Korean

Kim Chee Restaurant (46-010 Kamehameha Hwy., 808/235-5560, 9am-9pm Mon.-Sat., 7am-9pm Sun., $8-27) is revered as the best local-style Korean food eatery on the windward side. The big potions come with different styles of kimchi. The menu is full of choices, but the kalbi is a must. One downside, there are only a couple parking spots in front of the restaurant.

Chinese

Pah Ke's (46-018 Kamehameha Hwy., 808/235-4505, http://pahke.com, 10:30am-9pm daily, $6-24) Chinese restaurant is just down the street from Kim Chee Restaurant and equally as popular. It's a big venue that can accommodate large parties quite easily, although it does fill up for dinner. The dishes tend to be simple combinations or a protein, vegetable, and sauce.

Thai

If you're in the mood for Thai, try **Chao Phya** (45-480 Kaneohe Bay Dr., 808/235-3555, 11am-9pm Mon.-Sat., opens at 5pm Sun., $8-10) in the Windward City Shopping Center next to Starbucks. It's a good option for takeout as well.

LA'IE TOWN

If you drive through La'ie town on a Sunday, it might take a few minutes to notice that there's something different here that you won't find anywhere else on O'ahu–or in Hawai'i, for that matter. Everything is closed. Everything, that is, except for the places of worship of the Church of Jesus Christ of Latter-day Saints. Mormons first came to La'ie in the mid-1800s and purchased a 6,000-acre parcel in 1865. By 1919, the first Mormon temple outside of Utah had been built, the Hawaii Temple.

The town of La'ie, O'ahu's only "dry" town, has developed in concert with the growth of the church in Hawai'i and reflects the values of the religious institution. The Latter-day Saints erected their signature, private Brigham Young University next door, and built the Polynesian Cultural Center, providing jobs for the students and capitalizing on tourism to spread their message to the masses.

Mexican

There is a very small Mexican restaurant in Kane'ohe called **El Mariachi** (45-1151 #B Kamehameha Hwy., 808/234-5893, 11am-9pm daily, $10-27) right behind the Aloha gas station on the *makai* side of Kamehameha Highway. With just a few tables available, they serve traditional Mexican food like burritos, enchiladas, and chile rellenos. They also have seafood selections.

Delis

◖ He'eia Pier General Store & Deli (46-499 Kamehameha Hwy., 808/235-2192, www.heeiapier.com, 7am-4pm Tues.-Sun., $9-13) is a breath of fresh air in terms of high-quality fresh local food. Whether you order guava chicken, fresh fish, burgers and fries, the deli is known for sourcing organic and local produce and meats. They also have a few old-time dishes on offer.

Steak and Seafood

For a sit-down, true steak and seafood dining experience, **⊆ Haleiwa Joes** (46-336 Haiku Rd., 808/247-6671, http://haleiwajoes.com, 4:30pm-9:30pm Mon.-Thurs., 4:30pm-10:30pm Fri., 4:30pm-10pm Sat., 7am-9pm Sun., $24-33) is Kaneʻohe's answer. Nestled in a lush garden setting, Joes serves up prime rib, fresh fish, and a handful of local favorites like poke, sashimi, sizzling mushrooms, and sticky ribs. They also have a Sunday brunch.

KUALOA TO LAʻIE
Quick Bites

In Hauʻula you'll find the **Shrimp Shack** (58-360 Kamehameha Hwy., 808/256-5589 http://shrimpshackoahu.com, 10am-5pm daily, $2-24), a big yellow food truck serving up garlic and coconut shrimp, mahi, crab, mussels, calamari, and even steak.

Papa Oleʻs Kitchen (54-316 Kamehameha Hwy., 808/293-2292, www.papaoles.com, 7am-9pm Thurs.-Mon., 7am-3pm Tues., $3-12) is a Hawaiian food family restaurant open for breakfast, lunch, and dinner with loco moco, plate lunches, and fresh baked desserts.

In Laʻie, stop by **Hukilau Cafe** (55-662 Wahinepee St., 808/293-8616, 6am-2pm Tues.-Fri., 6am-11:30am Sat., $5-13) for Hawaiian breakfast and lunch plates. Think burgers with egg, kalua pork with two scoops of white rice. The food is delicious, and the portions are ample. Cash only.

Markets

Tamuraʻs (54-316 Kamehameha Hwy., 808/232-2332, 8am-9pm daily) is a small, but fully stocked grocery store and the last place you'll be able to buy alcoholic beverages until you get to the North Shore.

You can also pick up groceries in Laʻie at **Foodland** (55-510 Kamehameha Hwy., 808/293-4443, 5am-midnight Mon.-Sat.). This location does not sell alcohol and is closed on Sundays.

Information and Services

LIBRARY

Internet access is available at the **Aina Haina Public Library** (5246 Kalanianaole Hwy., 808/377-2456, http://ainahainalibrary.org, 1pm-8pm Tues., 10am-5pm Wed.-Sat.), the **Hawaiʻi Kai Public Library** (249 Lunalilo Home Rd., 808/397-5833), the **Kailua Public Library** (239 Kuulei Rd., 808/266-9911), and the **Kaneʻohe Public Library** (45-829 Kamehameha Hwy., 808/233-5676). Visitors need a valid HSPLS library card to use an Internet computer. Three-month visitor cards are available for $10. You can reserve Internet computer time online or in person. You can also find printed bus schedules, too.

MAIL

Post offices on the southeast shore are located in Kahala (4354 Pahoa Ave., 808/737-8937) on the ocean side of Kahala Mall, in the Aina Haina Shopping Center (820 W. Hind Dr.), and in Hawaiʻi Kai (7040 Hawaii Kai Dr., 808/396-6431). On the windward side, find them in Kailua (335 Hahani St., 808/266-3996), Kaneʻohe (46-036 Kamehameha Hwy., 808/235-1055), Kaʻaʻawa (51-480 Kamehameha Hwy., 808/237-8372), and Hauʻula (54-316 Kamehameha Hwy., 808/293-5057).

SOUTHEAST AND WINDWARD

Getting There and Around

BY CAR

Getting around the southeast and windward coasts is very simple, because for the most part, the highway is hemmed in by the Pacific Ocean on one side and the Koʻolau Mountains on the other. On the southeast shore, the H-1 becomes Kalanianaole Highway (Highway 72) as it merges with Waialae Avenue. Kalanianaole Highway circles the southeastern tip of Oʻahu and runs through Waimanalo before pulling away from the coast and intersecting the Pali Highway (Highway 61) at the Kamehameha Highway (Highway 83) junction in the Maunawili area. Kamehameha Highway runs north/south through the town of Kaneʻohe, regaining the coast for the rest of the way to the North Shore. There is a parallel highway in Kaneʻohe, the Kahekili Highway (Highway 83), which mirrors Kamehameha Highway, but bypasses the town closer to the mountains and with much fewer traffic signals.

There are three basic ways to go to get to the windward side from Honolulu or Waikiki: the Kalanianaole Highway takes you along the southeast shore, from Kahala to Kailua; the Pali Highway puts you directly into Kailua; and the Likelike Highway puts you directly into Kaneʻohe. From Kaneʻohe to the North Shore, the Kamehameha Highway unfolds with the Pacific Ocean on one side and the dramatic Koʻolau Mountains on the other.

To get to Kailua directly from Honolulu without going around the southeastern tip of Oʻahu, simply take the H-1 to the Pali Highway. Once you are descending the Pali on the windward side, the Pali Highway becomes Kalanianaole Highway for a short way until you reach Castle Medical Center, where Kalanianaole Highway takes a right turn toward Waimanalo. Kailua-bound traffic continues straight ahead on Kailua Road and straight into Kailua town.

To get to Kaneʻohe directly from Honolulu, take the H-1 to Likelike Highway (Highway 63). Once you are descending on the Likelike, you can either take the Kahekili Highway turn off and continue heading north toward the North Shore, bypassing Kaneʻohe town, or continue to the Kamehameha Highway intersection. Turning left, or north, takes you toward the North Shore. Turning right, south, takes you to the Pali Highway and Kalanianaole Highway junction.

BY BUS

TheBus (808/848-5555, www.thebus.org) has several routes accessing southeast and windward locales. If you're traveling from Waikiki, get to Kahala, Hanauma Bay, and Sea Life Park by using Routes 22 or 23.

From Honolulu, get to Hawaiʻi Kai via Routes 80, 80A, or 82; travel onward to Kaneʻohe via Route 65, or to Kailua and Waimanalo via Route 89. Routes 56, 57, and 57A travel to Kailua, departing from the Ala Moana Shopping Center (1450 Ala Moana Blvd.), with Route 56 continuing to Kaneʻohe.

CENTRAL AND SUBURBAN

Central Oʻahu is defined by agriculture. Pineapples abound. With sugarcane production defunct, pineapples, coffee, and corn are the staple crops growing in the vast plateau between the Koʻolau and Waiʻanae Mountains. Having opened in 1950 as a fruit stand, the Dole Plantation is now the main attraction in the area. And as agriculture land has been rezoned residential to house Oʻahu's growing population, towns like Mililani and Waikele have transformed the central Oʻahu landscape, which now resembles the planned communities of Southern California. The Waikele Outlet Mall is a draw for both residents and visitors.

With the recent expansion of neighborhoods from central Oʻahu down through the ʻEwa Plain and into Kapolei, developers made sure to include recreation in their community models. The region has grassy parks and 12 golf courses, many designed by world-renowned golfers. There's even a water park in Kapolei.

Down on the south shore, Pearl Harbor, a placid, deep-water harbor still evokes a military presence and sense of reverence for the people who lost their lives during the attack on December 7, 1941. The World War II Valor in the Pacific National Monument is part of the National Park Service and comprised of the Pearl Harbor Visitor Center and four historic sites.

PLANNING YOUR TIME

The sights and activities in central and suburban Oʻahu are most likely attractions that you should take in on your way to somewhere else on the island, rather than as the focus of

© KEVIN WHITTON

HIGHLIGHTS

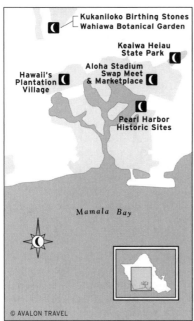

© AVALON TRAVEL

LOOK FOR ◖ TO FIND RECOMMENDED SIGHTS, ACTIVITIES, DINING, AND LODGING.

◖ **Pearl Harbor Historic Sites:** The most visited place in the state pays homage to the lives lost during the Pearl Harbor attack on December 7, 1941. The four historic monuments, the USS *Arizona* Memorial, USS *Bowfin* Submarine Museum and Park, USS *Oklahoma* Memorial, and the Battleship *Missouri* Memorial are part of the larger World War II Valor in the Pacific National Monument (page 200).

◖ **Keaiwa Heiau State Park:** The Keaiwa Heiau was once a sacred area used for treating and healing ailments and injuries with plants, fasting, and prayers (page 202).

◖ **Hawaii's Plantation Village:** This outdoor museum tells the story of sugar plantation life in Hawai'i from the mid-19th century to the mid-20th century by leading visitors through a replica historic village (page 202).

◖ **Wahiawa Botanical Garden:** This unique tropical rainforest botanical garden set on O'ahu's high elevation plateau features a variety of epiphytes like ferns, aroids, orchids, and bromeliads (page 202).

◖ **Kukaniloko Birthing Stones:** These 40 large boulders, seemingly haphazardly placed in a pineapple field, are where the royal wives would come to give birth to their exalted offspring: future nobles of the islands (page 203).

◖ **Aloha Stadium Swap Meet & Marketplace:** A mix of imported merchandise, handmade goods, produce, local snacks, and other souvenirs and treasures, the swap meet features hundreds of merchants (page 207).

an entire day, although Pearl Harbor could be planned that way. Consider stopping at the Wahiawa Botanical Garden, Dole Plantation, Hawaii's Plantation Village, or the Kukaniloko Birthing Stones on your way to or coming back from the North Shore. Likewise, if you see Pearl Harbor in the morning, spend the afternoon shopping at the Waikele Premium Outlets or head to Keaiwa Heiau State Park for a reflective afternoon celebrating nature and Hawaiian culture. The drier, secluded beaches in 'Ewa and Kalaeloa are best seen if the breeze is light, because heavy trade winds make the area much less inviting.

ORIENTATION
Pearl Harbor

Pearl Harbor dominates this region, both geographically and psychologically. Three lochs comprise the harbor—East Loch, Middle Loch, and West Loch—and most of the area, save for the West Loch Shoreline Park and the Pearl Harbor Historic Sites, is off limits to the public. The communities of Waipahu, Pearl

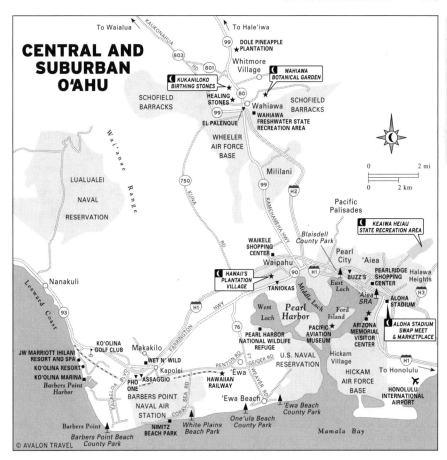

City, ʻAiea, and Halawa border the harbor from west to east. Waikele and Waipio are to the immediate north of Waipahu.

Mililani

Along the H-2 freeway, north of the Pearl Harbor district, is the master-planned community of Mililani. The residential enclave is known for tract homes, golf courses, and parks.

Wahiawa

Wahiawa is north of Mililani on Oʻahu's central plateau. It is surrounded by Lake Wilson, military installations, and agriculture.

ʻEwa

To the west of Pearl Harbor, on Oʻahu's arid southwestern plain, is the residential community of ʻEwa—miles and miles of apartment complexes, condominiums, and homes. ʻEwa Beach is immediately south of ʻEwa, an old local community right along the beach. ʻEwa Beach stretches out west to Kalaeloa and the Kalaeloa Airport, an old military operation now used for light, local air traffic. To the west of ʻEwa on the ʻEwa Plain is **Kapolei,** a brand-new planned community on the south side of the H-1 freeway.

YOUR BEST DAY IN CENTRAL AND SUBURBAN O'AHU

The Central and Suburban regions have two main things to offer: history and golf. Residential neighborhoods dominate the area. You'll probably want to plan for lunch or dinner in another region with a wider range of restaurant offerings.

- If golf is your game of choice, there are championship courses throughout the region, including courses in 'Ewa, 'Aiea, Waipahu, and Mililani. Eat at one of the restaurants at the course where you choose to play.

- If history interests you, wake up early and head directly to Pearl Harbor to visit the **Pearl Harbor Historic Sites.** There are memorials, museums, and tours. Some are free and others require a fee, but they are all first come, first served. Getting there early helps to cut down on the wait time for the tour package you choose. If visiting Pearl Harbor becomes an all-day affair, you'll want to plan for dinner back at your hotel.

- For those that only spend a half day at Pearl Harbor, head up to Wahiawa and grab lunch at **El Palenque,** a great little Mexican joint. While in Wahiawa, check out **Wahiawa Botanical Garden.** It's a high-elevation plateau garden featuring rainforest plants and trees with a lovely collection of palms.

- From there, check out **Dole Plantation** in Wahiawa or **Hawaii's Plantation Village** in Waipahu. Both offer insight into the agricultural history of O'ahu.

Beaches

In this region, all the beaches are on the west side of Pearl Harbor, from 'Ewa Beach to Barbers Point. They are very narrow, often bordered by a sharp, rocky shelf emerging from the sand and jutting out into the ocean, and usually swept by the pervasive trade winds. On the flip side, they are remote and uncrowded compared to the Honolulu and Waikiki beaches and predominately frequented by a curious mix of local residents, surfers, anglers, and military families.

'EWA
'Ewa Beach

'Ewa Beach is a long, narrow strip of sand fronting the 'Ewa Beach community. There are a few access points along Ewa Beach Road, but parking is scarce since the road runs through the old and weathered community. At the east end of Fort Weaver Road, which parallels Ewa Beach Road along the coast, is **'Ewa Beach Park.** The park has a basketball court, baseball field, basic amenities, no shade to speak of, and a sandy beach suitable for swimming. There are also soft rolling waves offshore. You can reach the beaches by taking Fort Weaver Road from the H-1. The beach park is closed 10pm-5am.

Oneula Beach Park

On the west end of 'Ewa Beach you'll find **Oneula Beach Park,** one of the few beaches on O'ahu where you can drive your car right up to the sand. The beach is a small strip of sand that quickly gives way to a sharp limestone shelf before it meets the ocean. It's dry and dusty with little vegetation, but you can find a nice little sandy cove if you walk about a quarter mile to the east, where big hau trees line the shore. A word of caution, the hau trees sometimes shelter the homeless. There are basic amenities and a surf break off the east end of the beach. The view of Diamond Head and Honolulu from this vantage is part of the draw for making the long trek to this secluded spot.

© KEVIN WHITTON

Oneula Beach, with Diamond Head in the distance

To find Oneula, turn right onto Papipi Road from Fort Weaver Road before it bends east.

Nimitz Beach Park

From Roosevelt Avenue, which mirrors Kapolei Parkway to the south, turn onto Coral Sea Road to get to **Nimitz Beach Park** in Kalaeloa, more of the same narrow strip of sand and intermittent limestone rock shelf that fronts 'Ewa Beach. The remote strip of beach is backed by the Kalaeloa Airport and lined with *hale koa* and mesquite trees. You'll really feel like you're out in the sticks. Surfers paddle out to the gentle waves that roll onto the reef all the way down to the end of the road, where there's a beach park with amenities and several more

dangerous, powerful waves quite far out to sea. There is no coastal road connecting 'Ewa Beach to the Kalaeloa beaches. The only way to access them is through Kapolei

White Plains Beach Park

Where Coral Sea Road meets the coast, you can also turn left and head south on Eisenhower Road along the beach, which is called **White Plains Beach Park.** It is a favorite for local surfers and does draw a crowd on summer weekends despite its remoteness. The beach is sandy and suitable for swimming. The surf is gentle, and there are picnic areas, restrooms, and a snack shop that is open during the summer. Weekend camping is also available.

Water Sports

SURFING
'Ewa

All the best surfing spots in the region are located along 'Ewa and Kalaeloa beaches. At 'Ewa Beach you'll find the surfing spots **Empty Lots** and **Shark Country**. These surf breaks tend to be heavily localized and are easily blown out by the pervasive trade winds. Parking here can be risky, since beach access is through a local neighborhood, and there's a possibility that your rental car may get broken into.

At the east end of Oneula Beach Park, right in front of the mass of hau trees, is a surf break named **Hau Bush.** The nice thing about Hau Bush is that you can see your vehicle from the water.

White Plains Beach Park has gentle waves great for beginners. When it's small, the slow rollers break up and down the beach, so you don't have to worry about crowds and territorialism. You'll need to have your surf equipment before you get to the beach, as there are no services where you can rent or buy surfboards or other beach gear.

FISHING

The beaches from 'Ewa Beach Park to Barbers Point Beach Park are a favorite stretch for shoreline fishing. Barbers Point Beach Park, off Olai Street, requires a drive through Campbell Industrial Park and the backdrop is anything but "tropical." Many anglers post up at the west end of Oneula Beach Park, but anywhere along this bit of coast is fair game. For fishing supplies in 'Ewa there are two good options: **Fishing Rods of Hawaii** (91-769 Makule Rd., #A, 808/373-4400) and **Ewa Beach Buy & Sell** (91-775 Papipi Rd., #C, 808/689-6368, 9am-5pm Mon.-Sat.). Ewa Beach Buy & Sell stocks a full line of new and used fishing gear and also buys used fishing supplies.

Hiking, Biking, and Bird-Watching

HIKING

The Ko'olau Range above Pearl City and 'Aiea is full of trails that explore the ridges and valleys of its leeward foothills. Most of the hikes are suitable for novices and offer waterfalls, pools, and great views. A sampling of the trails is listed below.

Pearl City

Waimano Pool is a three-mile round-trip hike that takes you to a couple deep swimming pools and a waterfall in the 'Ewa Forest Reserve. Walk through lush Waimano Valley to a native *'ohi'a* forest and the Waimano Stream. At the end, there are two pools separated by a cascade and a waterfall. The hike is most rewarding in the winter, when there is more average precipitation and the stream, pools, and waterfall are swollen with water. In the summer, unless you're out following a heavy rain, expect just a trickle of water in the stream.

If you'd rather do a ridge hike than walk through the valley, take the left fork in the Waimano Pool Trail at a metal stake onto the **Manana Trail** and follow the ridge as far as you'd like. To get to the trailhead, take Waimano Home Road to the Pacific Palisades subdivision. Turn left onto Komo Mai Drive and follow it to the end of the road. Park on the street just before the cul-de-sac. Walk through the opening in the fence at the back of the circle and up the dirt road to the trailhead.

'Aiea

The **'Aiea Loop Trail** is a popular introductory hike to the region. This 5-mile loop begins

© KEVIN WHITTON

The highest peak on O'ahu, Mount Ka'ala can be seen from the 'Aiea Loop Trail.

in the **Keaiwa Heiau State Recreation Area** (808/483-2511, www.hawaiistateparks.org) and winds through the foothills of the Ko'olau Range. There are great views of the Wai'anae Range, including Mount Ka'ala, the highest peak on O'ahu. On the trail you'll encounter several species of native Hawaiian trees like *'ohi'a; koa,* with its distinctive sickle-shaped leaves; *alahe'e,* a short tree with dark green leaves; and *'iliahi,* the native sandalwood tree. The mostly shaded hike also has views of beautiful North Halawa Valley. The entrance to the recreation area is at the end of Aiea Heights Drive. Once you are inside the park, drive past the *heiau* (native Hawaiian temple made of rock walls) to the upper parking lot, where you'll find restrooms and the trailhead.

For a valley hike to a swimming pool and waterfall in the same area, begin on the 'Aiea Loop Trail, but after you pass a power line tower at the beginning of the hike, take the left fork to access the **Kalauao Trail.** The path descends through mountain apple trees, down to the Kalauao Stream. Follow the stream up

to the waterfall. During dry periods, the stream can run dry, so it's best to hike this trail in the winter or after heavy rains.

BIKING

While mountain biking is not permitted on most hiking trails on O'ahu, the **Manana Trail** in the 'Ewa Forest Reserve above Pacific Palisades in Pearl City is an exception. The trail follows paved road, Jeep road, and single-track, with grades, roots, and climbs. At the fork in the trail, stay left and bike along the ridgeline offering spectacular views.

For touring, the **Pearl Harbor Bike Path** weaves along the Pearl Harbor shoreline from the 'Aiea Bay State Recreation Area, through Neal S. Blaisdell Park, past the Pearl Harbor National Wildlife Refuge, to Waipi'o Point Access Road near the Makalena Golf Course in 'Ewa. The 10-mile, two-lane asphalt trail crosses wooden bridges, major roads, has pedestrian traffic, and passes through some industrial areas. The best scenery is around the East Loch.

In 'Aiea, **The Bike Shop** (98-019 Kamehameha Hwy., 808/487-3615, www. bikeshophawaii.com, 10am-8pm Mon.-Fri., 9am-5pm Sat., 10am-5pm Sun.) is a full-service rental, retail, and repair shop. They rent mountain bikes for $85 per day, road bikes starting at $40 per day, and seven-speed city bikes for $20 day. If you need racks for your rental car, they charge $5 per day.

BIRD-WATCHING

To see O'ahu's forest birds, start looking in the **Keaiwa Heiau State Recreation Area** (808/483-2511, www.hawaiistateparks.org) in 'Aiea. This natural area is at the end of Aiea Heights Drive. You can also find forest birds on the hikes along the foothills of the Ko'olaus in this region. The **Pearl Harbor National Wildlife Refuge** (808/637-6330, www.fws.gov/pearlharbor) is a sanctuary for native Hawaiian waterbirds and migratory waterfowl. There are two small conservation areas, which are not open to the public, but you can view the refuge from the Pearl Harbor Bike Path as it rounds Middle Loch. Since you can't physically enter the refuge, bring binoculars.

Golf

In the master-planned communities of central and suburban Oʻahu, golf courses take center stage, and there are a plethora of public courses, especially on the ʻEwa Plain.

PEARL HARBOR

Overlooking Pearl Harbor, the USS *Arizona* Memorial, and the USS *Missouri*, the **Pearl County Club** (98-535 Kaonohi St., 808/487-3802, www.pearlcc.com) combines scenery and engaging golf with challenging course conditions and speedy downhill putts. The mature course also has a driving range, practice putting green, and a short game area. Rates for 18 holes are $130, twilight (after 3:30pm) $50.

With views of Pearl Harbor, downtown Honolulu, and Diamond Head, the **Royal Kunia Country Club** (94-1509 Anonui St., 808/688-9222, www.royalkuniacc.com) in Waipahu is a Robin Nelson-designed course situated across an undulating landscape with abundant water features and 101 bunkers. Greens fees for 18 holes are $150, twilight rates (after 2pm) are $80.

Also in Waipahu, the **Ted Makalena Golf Course** (93-059 Waipio Access Rd., 808/675-6052, www1.honolulu.gov/des/golf/makalena.htm), an 18-hole par-71 course, has a level layout and is great for beginners. The greens fees for 18 holes are $52, twilight or nine holes $26; cart rental is $20 for 18 holes and $10 for nine holes.

Situated in a planned residential development, the 18-hole golf course at **Waikele Country Club** (94-200 Paioa Pl., 808/676-9000, www.golfwaikele.com) is full of water features like ponds and waterfalls, along with strategically placed bunkers for a challenging Ted Robinson-designed course. Greens fees are $130; twilight $80 after 1pm.

MILILANI

Wooded with Cook pine, eucalyptus, and red African tulip trees, **Mililani Golf Course** (95-176 Kuahelani Ave., 808/623-2222, www.mililanigolf.com) is an 18-hole, par-72 course offering a sense of remoteness and tranquility situated between the Koʻolau and Waiʻanae Ranges with amazing views. Visitor greens fees are $99 and $75 for twilight, after 11am.

WAHIAWA

Hawaii Country Club (92-1211 Kunia Rd., 808/621-5654, www.hawaiicc.com) is designed into the natural landscape of the area, utilizing the hills, valleys and nearly 200 wide-spreading monkeypod trees. The course favors accuracy over long-range driving. Greens fees for U.S. residents are $70 weekdays and $80 weekends for 18 holes; rates for international visitors are $85 weekdays and $90 weekends for 18 holes. Check online for discounted rates. Carts are included. There is also a driving range and practice green.

ʻEWA

Designed by Robin Nelson, the **West Loch Golf Club** (91-1126 Okupe St., 808/675-6076, www1.honolulu.gov/des/golf/westloch.htm) is a par 72 with a short but challenging layout. It has a variety of water features including lakes, streams, and the West Loch of Pearl Harbor. The greens fees for 18 holes are $52, twilight or nine holes $26; cart rental is $20 for 18 holes and $10 for nine holes.

The **Ewa Villages Golf Course** (91-1801 Park Row St., 808/681-0220, www1.honolulu.gov/des/golf/ewa.htm) is rated as Oʻahu's toughest 18-hole course among the five most difficult courses. With the tight fairways, wind plays a major factor on this links-style course. The greens fees for 18 holes are $52, twilight or nine holes $26; cart rental is $20 for 18 holes and $10 for nine holes.

Coral Creek Golf Course (91-1111 Geiger Rd., 808/441-1112, www.coralcreekgolfhawaii.com) is another Nelson designed course. Water features are prevalent, found on more than 13

© KEVIN WHITTON

Golf courses like Hawaii Prince Golf Club are central Oʻahu's main draw.

holes, and the wind also factors into the course and your game. Elevated greens are protected by strategic bunkers incorporating sloping conditions. Rates are $180 for 18 holes, $80 for twilight (after noon), $70 nine-hole play after 11am. Carts are included with greens fees, and they offer a golf and transportation package for $170, club rental for an extra $20.

The **Hawaii Prince Golf Club** (91-1200 Fort Weaver Rd., 808/944-4567, www.princeresortshawaii.com/hawaii-golf-courses.php) is a 27-hole, par-72 championship course designed by Arnold Palmer and Ed Seay. Water is a major design feature throughout the three nines that were initially carved from coral rock. Don't be surprised to see Hawaiʻi's native waterbirds taking advantage of the lush, verdant setting. The non-hotel guest rate is $160 for 18 holes, $60 for twilight (after 2:30pm), and

an additional nine holes the same day is $26. There are discounted rates for Hawaii Prince Hotel guests. They also have transportation and golf packages.

At the end of Fort Weaver Road you'll find the 18-hole **Ewa Beach Golf Club** (91-050 Fort Weaver Rd., 808/689-6565, www.ewabeachgc. com). Great for all abilities, the creative course is relatively level with rolling greens set amid a kiawe forest. Housing and water features border the course. Greens fees are $140; twilight $95 after 1pm.

A former site of the LPGA Hawaiian Ladies Open, the **Kapolei Golf Course** (91-701 Farrington Hwy., 808/674-2227, www.kapoleigolfcourse.com) has over 70 sand bunkers, three lakes, wide landing areas, and greenside chipping areas to accommodate all levels of golfers. Greens fees are $160.

Tennis, Yoga, and Spas

TENNIS

Free public tennis courts in the central and suburban neighborhoods of Oʻahu can be found from Mililani to Kapolei. The **Central Oahu Regional Park Tennis Complex** (94-801 Kamehameha Hwy., 808/676-6982) in Waipahu has 20 lighted tennis courts, while **Waipahu District Park** (94-230 Paiwa St., no phone) has 4 lighted courts. **Mililani District Park** (94-1150 Lanikuhana Ave.) and **Salt Lake District Park** (1159 Ala Lilikoi Pl.) also have four courts apiece. **Pearlridge Community Park** (98-960 Moanalua Rd.) in ʻAiea has six courts, while the **Ihilani Tennis Garden** (92-1001 Olani St., 808/679-3197), a private club in Kapolei, accepts nonmembers at its six courts.

YOGA

In Waipahu you'll find **Yoga Loft Hawaiʻi** (94-547 Ukee St., #205, 808/677-5154, http://yogalofthawaii.com). This boutique studio recently opened in 2012 to serve the central Oʻahu community and is focused on meeting individual needs. It specializes in vinyasa flow, yoga of the heart, and hatha. The drop-in rate is $15, a five-class pass is $70, and a 10-class pass is $130. They have yoga mat rentals for $2.

In Kapolei, check out **Kapolei Yoga and Dance Studio** (2106 Lauwiliwili St., 808/674-9642, http://kapoleiyogaanddancestudio.com). From Zumba to yoga, you can find balance, wellness, and exercise at this studio for a $6 drop-in rate, $25 for five classes, and $50 for 10 classes. There is a $25 onetime registration fee.

SPAS

If you find yourself in central Oʻahu in need of a spa treatment, your best bet is to head to Kapolei, where you can go to **Gialuchi Full Service Salon and Day Spa** (91-590 Farrington Hwy., 808/674-4424, www.gialuchidayspa.com, 10am-7pm Mon.-Sat., noon-5pm Sun.). They offer manicures and pedicure, facials, massage therapy, full body waxing, and even a permanent makeup service. Their massage service features seven types of massage starting at $50 for 30 minutes, facials start at $75 for one hour, and body treatments start at $75.

Also in Kapolei, **Beautiville Salon, Spa & Boutique** (525 Farrington Hwy., 808/674-9999, www.beautiville.com, 10am-5pm Mon., 9am-8pm Tues.-Sat.) has massages starting at $75 for 60 minutes, facials starting at $70 for 60 minutes, and offers nail, hair, and waxing services.

Sights

PEARL HARBOR

◖ Pearl Harbor Historic Sites

The USS *Arizona* Memorial, USS *Bowfin* Submarine Museum and Park, USS *Oklahoma* Memorial, and the Battleship *Missouri* Memorial comprise the **Pearl Harbor Historic Sites.** Over 1.7 million people visit the USS *Arizona* Memorial and the historic sites each year, making this one of the most heavily toured areas in the state. The four sites together tell the story of Hawaiʻi's and the Unites States's involvement in World War II, from the surprise attack on Pearl Harbor to the surrender of the Japanese. Pearl Harbor also serves as the central point of the **World War II Valor in the Pacific National Monument.**

Once you arrive and find free parking in one of several designated lots, enter the 17-acre park where you'll first see the **visitor center** (808/454-1434, www.pearlharborhistoricsites.

org, 7am-5pm daily) and the USS *Bowfin* Submarine Museum. If you're planning on touring any of the historic sites, especially the USS *Arizona,* arrive as early as possible and head directly to the Visitor Center to get in line to receive a stamped ticket for a tour time. Admission to the monument is free and the 1.25-hour program includes a 23-minute documentary and a short boat ride to the memorial. Tickets are issued on a first-come, first-served basis. On a busy day, be prepared to wait several hours for your tour.

A better option is to reserve tickets online at www.recreation.gov. You can select the date, time, tour, or tour package you'd like to take. When you arrive at the Visitor Center, a separate line awaits for those who have reserved tickets.

If you do have a long wait ahead of you, check out the other historical sites, like the USS *Bowfin* Museum, or take the shuttle bus, which departs every 15 minutes, to the Battleship *Missouri* Memorial and the **Pacific**

Aviation Museum. Other than the USS *Arizona* Memorial, which is free, all sites charge admission for adults and children ages 4-12. There are also package tours, half-day tours, and one- or two-day passes available. Alleviate the wait time by taking advantage of the online ticket reservations to streamline your visit to Pearl Harbor.

The Pearl Harbor Historic Sites park is located off Kamehameha Highway, Route 99, just south of Aloha Stadium. There is ample signage coming from both directions. If you're on the H-1 freeway west, take exit 15A and follow the signs. You can also take TheBus, nos. 20 or 42 from Kuhio Avenue in Waikiki, or nos. 20, 42, or 52 from Ala Moana Center or downtown and be dropped off within a minute's walk of the entrance. Depending on stops and traffic, this ride could take over an hour. Also, The Arizona Memorial Bus Shuttle (808/839-0911), a private operation from Waikiki run by VIP Transportation, takes about half an hour

© KEVIN WHITTON

The Pearl Harbor Historic Sites see over 1.7 million visitors a year.

MILITARY ON O'AHU

O'ahu differs from the other main Hawaiian Islands in that there is a strong military presence here. All four branches of the military have installations on the island, and men and women in uniform are a common sight from the windward to the leeward side.

A few military strategists realized the importance of Hawai'i early in the 19th century, but most didn't recognize the advantages until the Spanish-American War. It was clearly an unsinkable platform in the middle of the Pacific from which the United States could launch military operations. General Schofield first surveyed Pearl Harbor in 1872, and this world-class anchorage was given to the U.S. Navy for its use in 1887 as part of the Sugar Reciprocity Treaty. In August 1898, four days after the United States annexed Hawai'i, U.S. Army troops created Camp McKinley at the foot of Diamond Head, and American troops were stationed there until

it became obsolete in 1907. Named in General Schofield's honor, Schofield Barracks in central O'ahu became (and remains) the largest military installation in the state. It first housed the U.S. 5th Cavalry in 1909 and was heavily bombed by the Japanese at the outset of World War II. Pearl Harbor, first dredged in 1908, was officially opened on December 11, 1911. The first warship to enter was the cruiser *California*.

The Japanese navy attacked Pearl Harbor and other military installations on December 7, 1941. The flames of Pearl Harbor ignited World War II's Pacific theater operations, and there has been no looking back. Ever since that war, the military has been a mainstay of the island economy. Following the war, the number of men, women, and installations decreased; today there is a force of more than 55,000 active duty personnel, with all branches of the military represented.

and will pick you up at any Waikiki hotel. It charges $11 round-trip; reservations are necessary, so call a day in advance. Because the park is on an active military base, there are no bags allowed inside the area. There is a $3 bag storage fee.

◖ Keaiwa Heiau State Park

In 'Aiea, the **Keaiwa Heiau State Park** (808/483-2511, www.hawaiistateparks.org/parks/oahu/keaiwa.cfm) is home to a healing *heiau* located in a forested state recreation area. Four-foot stacked rock walls enclose a sacred area once used for treating and healing ailments and injuries with plants, fasting, and prayers. The *heiau* is at the entrance to the park. The 384-acre park itself is a reforestation project from the 1920s. Groves of Cook pines and lemon eucalyptus scent the air and give an alpine feel to the area. There are picnic tables and four large tent camping sites available Friday through Wednesday by permit only. There are also exceptional views of Pearl Harbor. At the back of the park is the trailhead for the 'Aiea

Loop Trail. To park is located at the end of Aiea Heights Drive.

◖ Hawaii's Plantation Village

Hawaii's Plantation Village (94-695 Waipahu St., 808/677-0110, www.hawaiiplantationvillage.org, 10am-2pm Mon.-Sat., $13 adult, $10 out-of-state senior, $7 children ages 4-11), in Waipahu, is an outdoor museum telling the story of sugar plantation life in Hawai'i from the mid-nineteenth century to the mid-twentieth century. Almost 30 original structures featuring personal artifacts, clothing, furniture, and art have been assembled to create a village that speaks to the hard work of the hundreds of thousands of immigrants of many different ethnicities during this time period. Guided tours by local docents take about 90 minutes and start every hour. There are also demonstrations and hands-on activities throughout the village.

WAHIAWA
◖ Wahiawa Botanical Garden

Because of its high elevation plateau, at

© KEVIN WHITTON

At Wahiawa Botanical Garden, it's all about what's growing in the trees.

Wahiawa Botanical Garden (1396 California Ave., 808/621-7321, www1.honolulu.gov/parks/hbg/wbg.htm, 9am-4pm daily, free) you'll find tropical flora in a rainforest setting and a collection of native Hawaiian plants. The 875 and 1,000 feet in elevation, the cool temperatures, and the ample rainfall at the garden create unique conditions to find plants that thrive in cooler, tropical climates. Initially an experimental arboretum, today the 27-acre mature garden has tall canopy trees that are home to a variety of epiphytes, plants that grow on or attached to other plants like aroids, ferns, bromeliads, and orchids. There is also a ravine to explore filled with native Hawaiian plants, a palm selection, and hibiscus varieties. From Route 80 (the main drag through Wahiawa), turn onto California Street.

◖ Kukaniloko Birthing Stones

Just north of Wahiawa town, on Route 80, you'll come to a traffic signal at Whitmore Avenue. Turn onto the dirt road and park at the gate. Follow the track to the eucalyptus grove in the midst of fallow pineapple fields where you'll find the **Kukaniloko Birthing Stones.** About 40 large boulders are clustered on the plateau between the Ko'olau and Wai'anae Ranges. Kukaniloko was of extreme cultural and spiritual importance to pre-contact Hawaiians and some say the site has been used for at least 800 years; the royal wives would come here, assisted by both men and women of the ruling *ali'i* class, to give birth to their exalted offspring and future nobles of the islands. On the edge of this group of stones is one special stone that is fluted all the way around with a dip in the middle. It, along with other stones nearby, seems perfectly fitted to accept the torso of a reclining woman. Nearby was the *heiau* Ho'olono-pahu, where the newborns were consecrated and the baby's umbilical cord, a sacred talisman, was cut.

Dole Plantation

North of Wahiawa, as central O'ahu's pineapple fields unfold toward the Wai'anae Mountains and down to the Pacific, is **Dole**

CENTRAL AND SUBURBAN

© KEVIN WHITTON

The Dole Plantation was originally opened as a fruit stand in 1950.

Plantation (64-1550 Kamehameha Hwy., 808/621-8408, www.dole-plantation.com, free). Originally a fruit stand in 1950, the Dole Plantation opened in 1989 and is a popular visitor attraction centered on the pineapple. The Dole stop is a monument to retailing with its huge gift shop (open 9am-5:30pm), full of packaged and ready-to-eat pineapples and other food items, logowear, and souvenirs made in Hawai'i. While at the Dole Plantation, visit the "World's Largest Maze." Certified by the *Guinness Book of World Records,* the maze is nearly two acres in area and formed by more than 11,000 native Hawaiian bushes and flowering plants. The **maze** (9am-5pm daily, $6 adults and $4 children 4-12) will take 20-30 minutes to find your way through. The **Pineapple Express Train Tour** (9am-5pm daily, $8 adults, $6 kids) is a miniature train that rides a two-mile narrow-gauge rail line for a 20-minute tour through plantation fields. While not a great attraction, this narrated tour is a pleasant ride for the kids. There is also a **Plantation Garden Tour** (9am-5pm daily, $5 adults and $4.25 for kids), a narrated walk through eight small gardens with commentary on life in the communities that served this plantation.

EXPRESSLY PINEAPPLE

Ananas comosus of the family Bromeliaceae is a tropical fruit that originated in southern South America. During the 1500s and 1600s, voyaging ships' captains took this unusual and intriguingly sweet fruit around the world on their journeys. Pineapples seem to have been brought to Hawai'i from somewhere in the Caribbean in the early 1800s, but it wasn't until the mid-1880s that any agricultural experimentation was done with them. James Dole planted the first commercial pineapple plots for production on the Leilehua Plateau at Wahiawa just after the turn of the 20th century. To preserve the fruit, he built an on-site cannery in 1903 and later a second in Iwilei in Honolulu. Expanding his operation, Dole bought the island of Lana'i in 1922 and proceeded to turn the Palawai Basin into one huge pineapple plantation—some 18,000 acres at its greatest extent. The Lana'i plantation produced a million pineapples a day during peak harvest. Relying heavily on canning, Dole made the "king of fruits" a well-known and ordinary food to the American public.

Pineapple production is a lengthy process. First the ground must be tilled and harrowed to ready the soil for planting. The crowns of the pineapple fruit (which themselves look like miniature pineapple plants) or slips from the stem are planted by hand into long rows—some 30,000 plants per acre. A drip-irrigation system is then installed and the soil covered with ground cloth to help control pests and weeds. Fertilizers and pesticides are sprayed as needed, and the plants grow in the warm tropical sun. After 11-13 months these plants fruit. Generally each plant yields one fruit, which grows on a center stalk surrounded by sharp and spiky curved leaves. The plant sprouts again and, about 13 months later, a second crop is taken. Sometimes a third crop is also harvested from these same plants, before the remainders are tilled into the soil and the process begins again. Pineapples are picked by hand—a hot, dusty, and prickly job—and then placed on a boom conveyor that dumps them into trucks for transportation to the cannery. There, all are pressure-washed and sorted by size and quality before being canned or fresh-packed into boxes and shipped to market. Generally about two-thirds are sold as fresh fruit; the remainder is canned. All aspects of production are rotated to keep pineapples available for market throughout the year. There are no longer any pineapple canneries on O'ahu.

Shopping

While there is a major shopping center and premium outlets in this region, a draw for international visitors with shuttles going back and forth between the outlet mall and Waikiki, the stores in the mall are geared toward area residents, with national clothing, jewelry, and department store brands. Most likely, you won't find anything unique that you couldn't pick up somewhere across the continental United States.

PEARL HARBOR

In Pearl Ridge, the **Pearlridge Center** (98-1005 Moanalua Rd., 808/488-0981, www.

pearlridgeonline.com, 10am-9pm) has a curious layout with two separate shopping malls connected by an elevated tram system and caters to local residents. With **Sears** (808/487-4211) and **Macy's** (808/486-6701) as its big department stores, the mall is peppered with national brands in addition to local retailers and full of fast-food and big chain restaurants. Local popular urban streetwear brand **In4mation** (808/488-0411, www.in4mants.com) has a space, as well as local surf brand **Hawaiian Island Creations** (808/483-6700, www.hicsurf.com).

Just off the H-1 freeway, 15 miles west of

Honolulu in Waikele are the **Waikele Premium Outlets** (94-790 Lumiaina St., 808/676-5656, www.premiumoutlets.com, 9am-9pm Mon.-Sat., 10am-6pm Sun.). With 50 outlet stores from top national and international brands like **Coach** (808/678-6991), **Tommy Bahama** (808/686-9030), and **Vans** (808/676-7169), the center has a wide variety of name-brand clothing and apparel at discount prices. Don't get discouraged if you can't find parking in the front area because the lot continues all the way to the back of the property on both sides of the main mall area. If you prefer not to drive, **P.G. Plover** (808/922-0055) operates a Waikele Premium Outlets shuttle service from Waikiki that departs twice a day with three Waikele departures; round-trip transfer is $10. Reservations are recommended. There is also an open-air **Waikele Trolley** (808/591-2561) that includes a narrated tour and other historical points of interest along the way.

Entertainment and Events

LU'AU

Set on a secluded beach at Barbers Point is **Germaine's Luau** (91-119 Olai St., 808/367-5655, www.germainesluau.com, 6pm-8:45pm daily, $72 adult, $62 junior ages 14-20, $52 children ages 6-13, free for children 5 and under). The multicourse Hawaiian American buffet is a combination of traditional island dishes and American favorites for those less adventurous. They also have a full premium bar and serve up tropical cocktails to liven the party. The dinner and show include three free alcoholic drinks for those of age, an *imu* ceremony, a Polynesian show, and complimentary round-trip transportation to Waikiki locations. Advanced reservations are required, which can be done online.

If you plan on driving in, from the H-1 freeway take exit 1, Campbell Industrial Park, which puts you onto Kalaeloa Boulevard. Follow that street through the industrial park. Turn right at the dead end, which is Olai Street. A short drive down that road will lead to the Germaine's Luau parking lot at the end.

CINEMA

If you're looking to catch a movie, Pearlridge Center has the **Pearlridge West 16** (98-1005 Moanalua Rd., 808/483-5339), Mililani has the **Mililani Stadium 14** (95-1249 Meheula Pkwy., 808/627-0200), and in Kapolei you'll find the **Kapolei 16** (890 Kamokila Blvd., 808/674-8031). These three theaters are operated by Consolidated theaters, and general admission is $10, Friday and Saturday after 4pm $10.50, matinee (before 4pm) $7.50.

BOWLING

If bowling is your game, check out **Aiea Bowl** (99-115 Aiea Heights Dr., #310, 808/488-6854, www.aieabowl.com, 9am-2am Thurs.-Tues., 9am-1am Wed.). The bowling alley has standard open bowling during the day and cosmic bowling at night with a DJ, light show, and rotating party theme. There is a restaurant called The Alley that serves gourmet pizza, steak, and seafood, and The Bar Lounge is open 11am-2am. Open bowling is $3.50 per game on Monday, Tuesday, and Thursday, $2 per game on Wednesday, and $4.50 a game on Wednesday night and all day Friday through Sunday. Cosmic bowling is $5 per game on Monday and Thursday, and $25 per lane, per hour Friday through Sunday. Check the website for the current bowling schedule as times do vary per day. Shoe rental is $3.

WATER PARKS

Head west to Kapolei and in the dry southern foothills of the Wai'anae Mountains visit O'ahu's only water park, **Wet 'n' Wild** (400 Farrington Hwy., 808/674-9283, www.wetnwildhawaii.com). With 25 rides and attractions for all ages and thrill seekers there are exciting slides for adults including the Flow Rider, where you can surf a constant flow of water, and for the kids a lazy river, wave pool, and interactive water playground. General admission is $44.99, juniors under 42 inches are $34.99, children 2 years and under are free. Parking is $7 per vehicle. The park is just off the H-1 freeway. Take the 1E exit. June through August the park opens daily at 10:30am; September through May the park is open Thursday through Monday with various closing times.

FESTIVALS AND EVENTS
Aloha Stadium
Located in 'Aiea and visible from all around, **Aloha Stadium** (99-500 Salt Lake Blvd., 808/480-2750, http://alohastadium.hawaii. gov) is the home of the University of Hawai'i Warriors football team and the state's largest outdoor arena. It's also the venue for the NFL Pro Bowl and arena concerts by the biggest internationally acclaimed artists. Check the website for the schedule of events and ticketing.

◖ Aloha Stadium Swap Meet & Marketplace
Every Wednesday, Saturday, and Sunday, the parking lot surrounding Aloha Stadium transforms into the **Aloha Stadium Swap Meet & Marketplace** (808/486-6704, www.alohastadiumswapmeet.net, 8am-3pm Wed. and Sat.-Sun.). Offering a mix of imported merchandise, handmade goods, produce, local snacks, and other souvenirs and treasures, the swap meet features hundreds of merchants surrounding the stadium. There is a $1 entrance fee for guests 12 and older.

Kam Swap Meet
For a more nitty-gritty exploratory swap meet experience, check out the **Kam Swap Meet** (98-850 Moanalua Rd., 808/483-5933, www.kamswapmeet.com, 5am-1pm Wed. and Sat.-Sun.) in 'Aiea. The blacktop is like a giant yard sale featuring home sellers. It is a favorite for treasure hunters and collectors.

Food

PEARL HARBOR
Overlooking Pearl Harbor, **Buzz's Pearl City** (98-751 Kuahao Pl., 808/487-6465, 5pm-9pm daily, $17-33) is Buzz's original steak house, the sister location is in Lanikai. Famous for their kiawe broiled steaks, seafood, and no-nonsense cocktails, Buzz's is the perfect finish to a day at Pearl Harbor. Call at 4pm and make reservations.

For a local favorite specializing in Hawaiian food, bentos, and *poke*, check out **Taniokas** (94-903 Farrington Hwy., 808/671-3779, www.taniokas.com, 8am-5pm Mon.-Fri., 9am-5pm Sat., 9am-3pm Sun., $5-15). The extensive menu covers the wide range of flavors found in local food from teriyaki and musubi to stews and kimchi, but seafood, in many preparations, is definitely the cornerstone of the menu.

WAHIAWA
El Palenque (177 S. Kamehameha Hwy., 808/622-5829, 10am-2pm and 5pm-9pm Tues.-Fri., 11am-9pm Sat., 10am-3pm Sun., $3-14) is a tiny hole-in-the-wall Mexican food joint in Wahiawa, a corner of home cooking among a town full of fast-food and plate lunch options. Many say it's the best Mexican food on the island. Either way, it's a great place to stop for a quick meal coming from or going to the North Shore.

'EWA
In Kapolei, if you're looking for organic, vegan, and vegetarian food or groceries, stop in at **Down To Earth** (4460 Kapolei Pkwy., 808/675-2300, www.downtoearth.org, 7:30am-10pm daily). In addition to natural and organic foods, produce, and dairy products, they have a bakery, deli, hot food bar, and bulk food station.

If you're in the mood for Italian, **Assaggio** (777 Kamokila Blvd., Ste. A, 808/674-8801, http://assaggiohi.com/kapolei.asp, 11:30am-2:30pm and 5pm-9:30pm Sun.-Thurs., 5pm-10pm Fri.-Sat., 5pm-9:30pm Sun., $16-36) serves up fresh southern Italian cuisine. Their extensive menu features small and large portion plates, and they have takeaway deli items like marinara sauce, meat sauce, meatballs, and homemade Italian bread.

Pho One (777 Kamokila Blvd., 808/674-8189, 10am-9:30pm, $7-13) has a great selection of Vietnamese food and is a community favorite. It's clean, has friendly service, and fresh ingredients.

Information and Services

LIBRARY

Internet access is available at the **Aiea Public Library** (99-143 Moanalua Rd., 808/483-7333, www.librarieshawaii.org), the **Pearl City Public Library** (1138 Waimano Home Rd., 808/453-6566), the **Waipahu Public Library** (94-275 Mokuola St., 808/675-0358), the **Mililani Public Library** (95-450 Makaimoimo St., 808/627-7470), the **Wahiawa Public Library** (820 California Ave., 808/622-6345), and the **Kapolei Public Library** (1020 Manawai St., 808/693-7050). Visitors need a valid HSPLS library card to use an Internet-wired computer. Three-month visitor cards are available for $10. You can reserve Internet computer time online or in person. You can also find printed bus schedules, too.

MAIL

Post offices in central and suburban O'ahu are located in Pearl City (950 Kamehameha Hwy., 808/453-0111), 'Aiea (99-040 Kauhale St., 808/483-0010), Waipahu (94-245 Leoku St., 808/671-0369), Mililani (95-1030 Mehelua Pkwy., 808/625-0320), Wahiawa (115 Lehua St., 808/622-1182), 'Ewa (91-1202 Renton Rd., 808/681-4451), and Kapolei (1001 Kamokila Blvd., 808/671-0369).

Getting There and Around

BY CAR

Central and suburban O'ahu cover a big portion of the island, spreading from the central plateau, down to Pearl Harbor, and west across the 'Ewa Plain. While that's a lot of distance to cover, getting around is fairly easy. In Moanalua, the H-1 freeway splits and takes a southern track by the airport while the H-201 spans to the north, around the Salt Lake community. The freeways rejoin near Aloha Stadium, where the H-1 continues west crossing 'Aiea, Pearl Ridge, and Pearl City. After Pearl City the H-2 breaks away from the H-1, heading to the North Shore. En route you'll pass through Mililani and end up in Wahiawa. From there, the H-2 diverges into Route 80, Kamehameha Highway, which takes you through Wahiawa, and Route 99, Wilikina Drive, which takes you through Schofield Barracks.

If you continue west on the H-1 past the H-2 exit, you'll travel through Waipahu before reaching the 'Ewa Plain. Use the Fort Weaver Road exit to access 'Ewa Beach and exit 2 or exit 1B to find your way into Kapolei.

To access the business district of Pearl Ridge and Pearl City, take the Kamehameha Highway, Route 99, which parallels the H-1 and follows the contour of the Pearl Harbor shoreline. Also, Farrington Highway parallels the H-1 to the west of Pearl City, running through Waipahu and then connecting 'Ewa to Kapolei.

Once again, rush hour traffic plays a major role in the ease of getting in and out of the region, especially 'Ewa. While the heaviest traffic in the morning is coming from 'Ewa to

Honolulu, the traffic on the H-1 freeway heading west can be just as heavy. If you're going to 'Ewa to play golf or visiting Pearl Harbor early, give yourself some extra time for possible traffic delays.

Conversely, when it's time for Honolulu traffic to return home at the end of the day, the buildup on the H-1 happens again, predominantly heading west. Also be prepared for heavy traffic heading east starting where the H-201 and H-1 merge and continuing through Honolulu, a problematic bottleneck.

CENTRAL AND SUBURBAN

LEEWARD

The leeward side of O'ahu, also known as the Wai'anae Coast, is arid and rugged, receiving only sporadic rainfall throughout the year. The dry, red dirt ridgelines extend to the coast, where reef, rocks, and cliffs often take the place of sandy beaches. Undesirable land in other communities becomes home to the most economically depressed segment of society; the leeward coast is no different and has historically been a refuge for O'ahu's displaced native Hawaiian population. At times, generally after dark, the vibe can be unwelcoming, if not unfavorable for outsiders, and theft is common in beach parks and roadside parking areas.

Warnings aside, the leeward coast also has some of the most beautiful beaches on the island and an unobstructed view for every day's precious sunset, where green flashes occur on a regular basis. The deep waters off the coast are prime fishing grounds for sportfishing, and there are a few surf spots that break year-round, the most famed being Makaha, home to the first world championship professional surfing event. Spinner dolphins, humpback whales, and sea turtles frequent the waters, and the conditions are usually perfect for diving. Don't forget to look inland, where the verdant valleys of the Wai'anae Range lie in stark contrast to the parched land along the coast.

If luxury, pampering, golf, and fine dining better suit your taste, then Ko Olina, at the southwestern tip of the island, is a prime destination. A sprawling community of condos, timeshares, hotels, dining, golf, and four artificial lagoons on private land, Ko Olina is an oasis in the dessert. Geared to be the next

© KEVIN WHITTON

HIGHLIGHTS

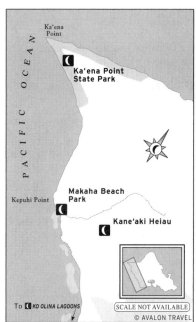

◖ Makaha Beach Park: Steeped in surfing history, this dramatic point offers one of the best waves on O'ahu, which breaks nearly year-round. The arcing wide sandy beach forms a small bay where trees provide shade for picnicking and surf-gazing (page 215).

◖ Ko Olina Lagoons: Four ocean-fed lagoons with sandy beaches, swaying palms, grassy parks, and clean facilities offer a safe and beautiful environment for a family day at the beach (page 216).

◖ Kane'aki Heiau: One of the best preserved *heiau* on O'ahu, this restored stone structure is a historic and spiritual window into the world of Hawaiian culture and perseverance on the leeward coast (page 225).

◖ Ka'ena Point State Park: Stretching from breathtaking Yokohama Bay to the western tip of O'ahu, Ka'ena Point State Park provides wildlife viewing, native plantlife, verdant valleys, a secluded white sand beach with turquoise water, and a dramatic volcanic coast (page 226).

LOOK FOR ◖ TO FIND RECOMMENDED SIGHTS, ACTIVITIES, DINING, AND LODGING.

Waikiki, the area offers full-service amenities, but the price is definitely on the high side.

PLANNING YOUR TIME

If you're planning on any activity in the Ka'ena Point State Park, whether it be hiking to the natural reserve at the tip of the point, mountain biking the dirt road to the point, or kayaking in Yokohama Bay, then head there first, as early as possible, to beat the heat of the midday sun. After a half day in the state park, head back south and take in the sights and snap some pictures along the way. The beaches and valleys will be perfectly lit by the afternoon sun. Finish up with dinner in Ko Olina at one of their premier restaurants.

For a beach day on the west side, it is absolutely essential to bring an umbrella, plenty of water, and sunscreen. Shade is sparse in the region. If you're heading west just for the sunset, don't wait too late in the afternoon, as rush hour traffic heading west could spoil your sunset plans. Check out Pearl Harbor in the morning, then make your way to the west side. Lounge in one of the Ko Olina Lagoons all afternoon or post up at one of the leeward beaches, where you'll be in a prime sunset-viewing location. Keep in mind that Ko Olina is a busy resort, so there will be many people with the same sunset ideas. You'll need to keep heading west if you're in the market for your own piece of private

LEEWARD

beach real estate to watch the sun go down on another day.

If golfing is your main reason for heading to the leeward side, there are two courses to choose from. The course in Wai'anae Valley is very affordable, or for a shorter drive, stop in Ko Olina for a world-class golf experience in the resort community.

ORIENTATION
Leeward Coast

The leeward coast stretches about 20 miles from Barbers Point to Yokohama Bay in Ka'ena Point State Park, and is connected by one thoroughfare, Farrington Highway. The majority of the commercial property is along the highway, as the neighborhoods snake back into the dry valleys between the massive ridges that extend to the coast. The main communities from south to north are **Nanakuli, Ma'ili, Wai'anae,** and **Makaha.** The highway dead-ends at Ka'ena Point State Park, the westernmost tip of the island.

Ko Olina

Ko Olina is a private resort and lifestyle community located on the coast in between Barbers Point and Nanakuli, right where the highway meets the coast after crossing the 'Ewa Plain. Ko Olina has its own exit off Farrington Highway and a gated entrance manned by resort staff. This high-end community is home to three major resort hotels and four artificial lagoons for both resort guests and the public.

YOUR BEST DAY IN LEEWARD OʻAHU

The Leeward Coast is rough, rugged, and beautiful in its own right. In the lee of wind, this side of Oʻahu tends to be hot and dry, so for any excursion to the Leeward Coast, be prepared with sunscreen, hats, and plenty of water.

- For an awe-inspiring natural experience, hiking to **Kaʻena Point** is a must. Plan to mitigate the heat and arrive at **Kaʻena Point State Park** as early as possible, preferably as the sun is coming up. Walk out to the point and spend the morning exploring the **Kaʻena Point Natural Area Reserve,** where you'll most likely see Hawaiian monk seals and nesting seabirds. The coastline is dramatic and the views are breathtaking.

- On your return to your vehicle, take a refreshing dip in the ocean at **Yokohama Bay,** with its beautiful turquoise water.

- Head south down the Leeward Coast. Grab a quick snack at **Ohana Market** in Makaha. Continue south until you get Ko Olina. Have a sit-down lunch at one of the poolside restaurants at the three resort properties.

- For families, visit one of the four sheltered lagoons in Ko Olina for a playful afternoon in the water. For couples, try a spa treatment at **Ihilani Spa.**

- Ko Olina has many fine-dining restaurants. Try **Roy's** for Hawaiian fusion cuisine, **Ushio-Tei** for traditional Japanese fare, or **Azul,** an award-winning Italian restaurant.

LEEWARD

Beaches

If you're feeling adventurous and don't mind an hour's drive across the island, the beaches of leeward Oʻahu offer uncrowded, wide swaths of white sand under clear, sunny skies. As the trade winds blow across the island from east to west, the leeward coast's waters remain calm and protected, offering beautiful conditions for swimming, surfing, fishing, snorkeling, diving, or just soaking up the sun. Waves are common along leeward beaches all year long, but generally get the biggest in the winter, from October to March. Make sure to exercise caution and assess the ocean conditions before entering the water. Check with a lifeguard for the safest place to swim.

NANAKULI
Kahe Point Beach Park

Kahe Point Beach Park is right across the highway from the smokestacks and industrial buildings of the Waimanalo Gulch Sanitary Landfill and Waste Management Facility, just north of Ko Olina but before Nanakuli. Amenities include restrooms, picnic tables, a small pavilion, and only a small beach called Electric Beach, where scuba divers often access the water. The beach park is closed 10pm-5am daily.

Just to the north is a much nicer beach, although still overshadowed by the power plant, called **Tracks.** It gets its name from the train tracks that run along the shore. As it is the first sandy beach you come to on the west side, it is often the most crowded, a favorite for surfers, bodyboarders, and beachgoers. It has a nice sandy beach favorable for swimming, clear water, and trees and bushes along the vegetation line that offer shade. The dirt parking lot is rocky and rutted, so drive slowly to avoid a flat and don't leave any valuables in plain sight in your car or on the beach. From Farrington Highway heading north, there is a left turn lane to safely cross the highway into the designated parking area. Tracks is also closed 10pm-5am daily.

Nanakuli and Ulehawa Beach Parks

Just up the road is **Nanakuli Beach Park,** a

LEEWARD

© KEVIN WHITTON

Ma'ili Beach Park offers camping, snorkeling, swimming, fishing, and great surf.

community-oriented park with a baseball diamond, basketball courts, and other recreational facilities. The beach on the southern end is fronted by a cliff and favored by anglers, while the sandy beach to the north is better for swimming. Past that and on the other side of the Ulehawa Stream is **Ulehawa Beach Park,** with a long stretch of cliffs and a sandy beach. There are restrooms and picnic tables here, but not much else. The best area for swimming is a sandy pocket near the south end of the beach by the lifeguard tower. The trees and palms at the vegetation line offer shade, which is lacking along Nanakuli Beach. During the winter months, a strong shorebreak and currents affect these two beaches and make swimming dangerous. There are more scenic and safer swimming beaches and parks up the coast. Both beach parks are closed 10pm-5am daily.

MA'ILI
Ma'ili Beach Park
Marking the beginning of Ma'ili town and its long stretch of beach, **Ma'ili Point** is one of the more dynamic and picturesque settings along the leeward coast. There is a small park with picnic tables and grass on the southern side of the point. The shoreline rocks extend out into the water and meet up with the shallow reef here, creating a lot of whitewater and surf action to watch while relaxing or having a snack. On the north side of the point **Ma'ili Beach Park** runs the length of Ma'ili town. Situated between two streams that run down from the mountains, the sandy beach is widest during the summer when the waves are smaller, and the gently arcing beach is great for swimming and snorkeling. During the winter, however, the sand tends to migrate elsewhere with the more frequent high surf, revealing a rock shelf along the shore. There are restrooms, picnic areas, and camping on the weekends by permit only. Ma'ili Beach Park is closed 10pm-5am daily.

WAI'ANAE
Poka'i Bay Beach Park
Between the small boat harbor and Kane'ilio

Point sits a beautiful sheltered bay and wide sandy beach called **Poka'i Bay Beach Park.** There is a breakwater offshore and a reef in the middle of the bay that keep the water calm along the shoreline year-round, making this a perfect spot for swimming and families. Small waves break over the reef during the winter, which attracts novice surfers. In addition to the beautiful beach, the **Ku'ilioloa Heiau** is also out on the point and has three terraced platforms. The *heiau* is thought to have been a place for learning the arts of fishing, navigation, and ocean-related skills. The beach park is closed 10pm-5am daily.

MAKAHA
◖ Makaha Beach Park

A world-class surf break with a recent history entwined with the birth of international professional surfing, **Makaha Beach Park** is the hub of surfing on the leeward coast. The beautiful beach is framed at both ends by rocky headlands, the north end being the site of the surf break and the sharp reef that absorbs the ocean's energy. The surf here breaks all year, but is biggest in the winter months, when waves can reach 40 to 50 feet high on the face during the biggest swell episodes. In the summer, swimming is best in the middle of the beach, or if the waves are completely flat, you can snorkel over the reef shelf. There are restrooms, showers, and a few shade trees and hau bushes along the road where everyone parks. If there is surf during your stop at Makaha, check with the lifeguards for the best place to enjoy the water.

Kea'au Beach Park

North of Makaha, the last hamlet on the leeward coast, the road narrows and civilization falls off the radar. Here you'll find a shady, grassy beach park called **Kea'au Beach Park,** which has restrooms, picnic facilities, and a number of camping sites on the coast. There is a small beach in front of the park area, but lava and coral front the rest of the area. When the ocean is calm, it's a great place to snorkel or fish.

Makua Beach

At the north end of Makua Valley, the only valley in the area fenced off and privately held by the U.S. Army, is a small parking area on the ocean side of the road under some trees with access to **Makua Beach.** This undeveloped, secluded white sand beach is a great place to find solitude. When the waves are flat, it's also fine for swimming and snorkeling, but during high surf the ocean is dangerous at Makua Beach.

Yokohama Bay

Referred to on maps and by many as **Yokohama Bay,** Keawa'ula Bay is by far the most picturesque beach on the leeward coast. Part of **Ka'ena Point State Park,** the white sand beach curves to the northwest and points the way toward the western tip of the island, Ka'ena Point. The turquoise water sees waves throughout the year and is extremely dangerous for swimming during times of high surf. The surf breaks in the area are for expert surfers only. When the water is calm, the ocean is ideal for swimming. There is no shade on the beach, so be prepared with an umbrella or tent to mitigate the piercing sun. To complete the stunning views, behind the bay are several valleys that change from a dry, reddish hue to verdant green the farther back your eye takes you. There are public restrooms and lifeguards on duty.

KO OLINA
Paradise Cove

Just past the entrance gate to Ko Olina and next to Paradise Cove Luau is a small, yet beautiful sandy cove and lagoon called **Paradise Cove.** In the past it has been called Lanikauka'a and then Lanikuhonua Beach. Paradise Cove is one of three sacred lagoons in the immediate area where Queen Ka'ahumanu was said to have bathed and performed religious ceremonies. The shallow lagoon is protected from ocean swells by a raised reef rock shelf on its ocean side. There are trees on the beach for shade and tidepools. All in all, it's a great out-of-the-way nook to take the kids and explore. Parking is a little tricky. Take a right into the third driveway past the entrance gate. On the right is a small,

© KEVIN WHITTON

Paradise Cove, Ko Olina

free public parking area for about 10 cars. The sidewalk leads to a sandy pathway between two tall fences down to the beach.

Ko Olina Lagoons

Ko Olina has four lagoons open to the public from sunrise to sunset. The **Ko Olina Lagoons** are numbered one through four, heading from west to east, and also have the Hawaiian names, Kohola, Honu, Napa, and Ulua, respectively. They are more widely known and referred to by their number. The lagoons are artificially constructed semicircles cut from the sharp and rugged reef rock shelf that creates the shoreline. Channels were cut into the shelf to allow ocean water to flow in and out of the lagoons while blocking any surf from entering. With sandy beaches, grassy parks, a fair bit of shade from palms and trees, and a meandering pathway connecting all four lagoons, this oasis provide a sheltered, manufactured, resort-style of beach experience, completely opposite to the rest of the leeward beaches. Each lagoon has its own access road from Aliinui Drive, the main road through Ko Olina. Turn right on Kamoana Place to reach Lagoon 1. The next three consecutive streets will lead to a lagoon and its parking area. There are no lifeguards on duty, but there is plenty of security known as the Aloha Patrol monitoring the lagoons from golf carts. Ever vigilant, they will be sure to let you know if you're breaking any rules from the long list of prohibited actions and items. Parking is free, but very limited at each lagoon, with Lagoon 4 having the most.

© KEVIN WHITTON

LEEWARD

Ko Olina has four seaside lagoons.

Surfing

Much of the surf on the leeward side breaks over sharp and shallow reef, making it best suited for expert surfers. Scaling rocks and reef to enter and exit the water can be a challenge for newcomers, and the locals are quite territorial when it comes to their surf breaks. Still, with the right attitude, there's definitely a wave to be had on the leeward coast.

The leeward coast basically faces west, so it is prone to waves all year long. Southerly summer swells and the northwesterly winter swells both offer opportunities for great quality surf. Winter swells can get quite big—scary big actually. When a high surf advisory is called for the coast and waves are above the 20-foot mark, it's best to leave the surfboard at home and watch the locals who are familiar with the challenging breaks.

NANAKULI
Tracks

The first break you'll come to on the leeward coast is **Tracks,** just past the power plant and across the train tracks as the name implies. Tracks usually has small waves that break close to shore over sand and flat reef. Good for bodyboarding and surfing, the break can get quite crowded as many of the surfers coming from central O'ahu stop and surf here. The nice thing, though, is that the waves are spread out over the length of the beach. The dirt parking lot is rocky and rutted, so take it easy to avoid a flat tire.

MA'ILI
Ma'ili Point

Ma'ili Point is one of the best waves on this

stretch of coastline. A predominantly left breaking pointbreak, the wave breaks over a shallow coral shelf, which can be a nearly dry reef at low tide. On south swells, the wave is a bit slopey and sometimes rights will break off the main peak. On northwesterly swells, Ma'ili Point is a freight train wave, with fast breaking and barreling lefts suited for experts only. Park in the parking lot on the north side of the point. Getting in and out of the water can be tricky because of the rocky shelf along the beach, so watch or ask one of the local surfers the best way to get in without getting hurt.

WAI'ANAE
Poka'i Bay

Inside the breakwater in Poka'i Bay in Wai'anae is a rolling wave perfect for beginners. Longboarders, stand-up paddlers, and first-time surfers can get the feel of a board under their feet at this soft break. The wave

MASTER-PLANNED PARADISE

If you notice that there's something too good to be true about Ko Olina's four clam-shell-shaped lagoons on the southwest tip of O'ahu, that's because the coastline has been severely altered to created Lagoons 1-4, part of the master-planned resort and lifestyle community. Before Ko Olina and the lagoons were developed, the rugged shoreline was quite inhospitable. Four- to six-foot cliffs of extremely sharp fossil reef rock protruded from the land into the sea, dropping straight into the surging waves. The area was devoid of sandy beaches. To create safe and desirable shoreline access for resort guests, they cut channels in the reef rock shelf to allow the flow of natural ocean water into half-moon lagoons, while keeping the surf and ocean currents at bay. Add sand, grass, and a few tall palm trees, and you have an artificial tropical paradise in a safe and controlled setting—not for everyone, but the ideal vacation for many.

breaks over a wide reef and is small and calm, even when the surf is larger elsewhere.

MAKAHA
Makaha Beach Park

Makaha is a righthand pointbreak steeped in surf history. The site of the Makaha International Surfing Championships from 1954 to 1971, the waves at Makaha can range from fun and playful to massive and life threatening. Makaha breaks in summer and winter, with the largest waves occurring during the wintertime high surf advisories. The wave breaks over shallow reef at the top of the point and runs into deeper water with a sandy bottom near the beach, famous for its backwash. Makaha gets crowded and has a well-established pack of locals of all ages. If you paddle out at Makaha, smile, say hello, and don't hassle anyone for a wave, or you'll be on the beach before you know it. At Makaha, you'll find people pursuing ocean sports of all kinds: surfing, bodyboarding, stand-up paddling, and bodysurfing. Parking along the road is the safest so you can keep an eye on your car.

Yokohama Bay

About eight miles past Makaha, in the Ka'ena Point State Park at the end of the road, are several challenging, barreling surf breaks. Nestled in the beautiful and secluded Keawa'ula Bay, better known as **Yokohama Bay,** swells approach out of deep water from the north and the south and detonate along the bay's shallow reefs. The waves are very dangerous as they break on extremely shallow reef shelves close to shore. This is a favorite spot for expert surfers and bodyboarders.

Outfitters

Hale Nalu (85-876 Farrington Hwy., #A2, 808/696-5897, http://halenalu.com, 10am-5pm daily) has new and used boards and rents bodyboards starting at $14 per day, shortboards starting at $20 per day, longboards starting at $30 per day, and stand-up paddle boards starting at $50 per day. They also have discounts for three-day and week rentals.

© KEVIN WHITTON

Makaha Beach is a legendary surf break.

West Oahu SUP (84-1170 Farrington Hwy., 808/954-2091, http://westoahusup.com, 9am-5pm daily) rents bodyboards for $20 per day, $60 per five-day week; shortboards $25 per day, $85 per week; longboards $15 hourly, $25 full day, and $95 per week; and stand-up paddle boards with paddle for $25 hourly, $60 full day, and $215 per week.

Snorkeling and Diving

SNORKELING

When the surf is flat and the ocean is calm, generally during the summer, the leeward coast is a snorkeler's dream come true. Crystal clear turquoise water, ample rock outcroppings and patches of reef beside white sandy beaches, and calm nearshore waters protected from the trade winds make for excellent snorkeling all along the coast. Look for areas where a sandy beach connects to rock and reef for the best opportunities to see marine life with safe and easy passage in and out of the water. While there are many places to just pull off the road and jump in the water, it's always safer to swim or snorkel by lifeguards and first check with them about the current ocean conditions. And remember that strong currents accompany high surf, even if there are no waves breaking in your immediate aquatic locale. Green sea turtles and spinner dolphins are common sights on the leeward side.

The best bet is to bring your snorkel gear with you from your point of origin, because if you find yourself on the west side in need of snorkel gear, you'll have to drive to Waiʻanae or Makaha to rent or purchase equipment. **Hale Nalu** (85-876 Farrington Hwy., #A2, 808/696-5897, http://halenalu.com, 10am-5pm daily) is a sporting goods store located in Waiʻanae across from Pokaʻi Bay renting snorkel gear for

© KEVIN WHITTON

The leeward coast offers the best ocean conditions for snorkeling and diving.

$10 per day, $20 for three days, and $35 per week. In Makaha, **West Oahu SUP** (84-1170 Farrington Hwy., 808/954-2091, http://westoahusup.com, 9pm-5am daily) rents snorkel sets for $15 full day and $50 five days. Inside the same retail space you'll also find **Paradise Isle** (84-1170 Farrington Hwy., #AE, 808/695-8866), a fish and dive shop where you can purchase new gear.

DIVING
West Side Wrecks

Nestled in the lee of the trade winds, the west side has some of the best conditions for diving on a consistent basis. The underwater world has shallow reef diving with lava tubes and arches, the Makaha caverns and rock formations—a favorite for turtles and monk seals—and several wrecks including a plane fuselage, a landing craft unit, an airplane, and a minesweeping vessel. Look for octopus, whitemouth morays, porcupine puffer fish, whitetip reef sharks, Hawaiian stingrays, and spinner dolphins.

Outfitters

Captain Bruce's (86-222 Moeha St., 808/373-3590, www.captainbruce.com) operates a Pro-42 Jet Boat built for 28 passengers, yet only takes a maximum of 16 divers with one guide per six divers. They dive all the wrecks and reefs along the leeward coast and can accommodate all skill levels. The boat is decked out for ultra comfort with hot water showers, complimentary snacks and beverages, restrooms, and they even set up all your gear for you. A two-tank certified dive is $150; two-tank introductory dive, $135. They have snorkel ride-alongs for $79 adult and $59 child. They also offer a three-day open water certification course for $550 and PADI and NAUI two-day referral dive courses for $325.

Ocean Concepts (85-371 Farrington Hwy., 808/696-7200, www.oceanconcepts.com) is based in Pearl Harbor yet operates primarily out of the Wai'anae Small Boat Harbor. They offer daily two-tank boat dives for $115. They also have multiday rates: two two-tank dives for $210 and three two-tank dives for $300. All equipment can be rented as a set for $25 or by the piece. Ocean Concepts has photo options and will burn you a CD of your scuba trip or they can use your SD card when taking pictures.

Pearl Harbor Divers (725 Auahi St., 808/589-2177, http://pearlharbordivers.com), also based in Honolulu, dives the west side in addition to the south and southern coasts. Their two-tank boat dives from the Wai'anae Small Boat Harbor are $99 per person. They also offer a special three-tank Ka'ena Point drift dive once or twice a month for $109.

Kayaking and Sailing

KAYAKING

From the water, the leeward coast is nothing less than spectacularly beautiful. Its rugged coastline, a combination of white sand beaches, rock and reef outcroppings, and jagged cliffs, is only complemented by the deep valleys lying in succession all the way up the coast. Sea kayaking affords a perspective unmatched and unobtainable by land, far from the spiderweb power of power lines over the neighborhoods and the bustle of Farrington Highway. In addition, the crystal clear water runs from turquoise to deep blue, and humpback whale-watching is at its best on this side of the island during their annual stay from November to March.

As the trade winds rise over the Wai'anae Range, they create pristine conditions for ocean activities. Calm nearshore waters afford easy paddling and more abundant ocean life. You can enter the water from Tracks, at the south end of the leeward coast, but be prepared to deal with small waves along the shore. From here, you can explore the jagged cliffs and find small pockets of sand only accessible from the water. Sheltered Poka'i Bay in Wai'anae is perfect for launching the kayaks. For the best views of the valleys, put in at Makaha, Makua Beach, or Yokohama Bay, but only if the surf is flat, which is more likely to occur in summer.

West Oahu SUP (84-1170 Farrington Hwy., 808/954-2091, http://westoahusup.com, 9am-5pm daily) rents single-rider kayaks for $25 hourly, $50 full day, and $175 per five-day week. They rent two-person kayaks for $25 hourly, $60 full day, and $215 per week. They also rent roof racks or tie-downs for $10.

SAILING

If you prefer to charter a catamaran and let someone else do the navigating for you so you can focus on taking in the sights, **Wild Side Hawaii** (87-1286 Farrington Hwy., 808/306-7273, http://sailhawaii.com) has three tours that leave from Wai'anae Small Boat Harbor: Morning Wildlife Cruise is a three-hour nearshore cruise with snorkeling, spinner dolphin swims, and seasonal whale-watching for $115; Best of the West is a 3.5-hour tour with dolphin swims, whale-watching, turtle and tropical reef snorkeling with a maximum of six guests for $195 per person; the Deluxe Family Charter is a mid-morning three-hour cruise focusing on hands-on learning about Hawai'i's marine creatures with dolphin swims, snorkeling instruction, and whale-watching for $175 adult, $145 child. They also have a full-day cruise departing from Honolulu to the leeward coast for $335.

Eo Waianae Tours (2101 Nuuanu Ave., 808/538-9091, www.eowaianaetours.com) has morning and afternoon west side catamaran tours with snorkeling and kayaking. Adults $115, children ages 5-12 $95, children ages 4 or younger $45. They also offer transportation from Waikiki.

LEEWARD

Fishing

While shoreline fishing is common from the cliffs and beaches in the region—papio, kumu, and moana being the sought-after take—fishing charters also run out of the area and take advantage of the frequently calm ocean conditions and the steep ledges offshore attracting pelagic fish. There is a 3,000-foot ledge just three miles from Wai'anae Harbor and another 6,000-foot ledge just seven miles out. It's also not uncommon to see people fishing from kayaks just offshore along the coast.

In the Ko Olina Marina, **Kahuna Sportfishing Hawaii** (92-100 Waipahe Pl., 808/227-3305, http://hawaiioffshoresportfishing.com) offers deep-sea excursion off Ko Olina and the west coast on their 43-foot fishing yacht. Their private charters are for a maximum of six passengers: the four-hour charter is $550, six hours go for $700, and eight hours will run you $800. Shared charters for two people start at $275 for the four-hour charter. The rate drops per additional passenger up to four passengers on the shared charter.

In the Wai'anae Small Boat Harbor you'll find **Boom Boom Sportfishing** (85-371 Farrington Hwy., Pier A, 808/306-4162, www.boomboomsportfishing.com). They offer private and shared charters for a maximum of six passengers with two departure times daily. Four-hour private charters are $595, six hours $695, 8-10 hours $875, and 12 hours $1,250. They offer shared charters starting at $150 for four hours and free round-trip transportation or a 10 percent discount for Ko Olina Resort guests.

Live Bait Sportfishing (808/696-1604, www.live-bait.com) also operates out of the Wai'anae Harbor from slip B-2 and provides all equipment and tackle. You are responsible for bringing food and drinks. They primarily fish for marlin, wahoo, tuna, and mahimahi, and give a meal-sized portion of the catch to passengers. They offer half-day trips for $550 and full-day trips for $750 with a four-passenger maximum.

For fishing gear and tackle retailers, check out **Westside Tackle and Sports Shop** (87-701 Manuaihue St., 808/696-7229) in Wai'anae or **Paradise Isle** (84-1170 Farrington Hwy., #AE, 808/695-8866) in Makaha.

Hiking, Biking, and Bird-Watching

HIKING

The leeward side is notoriously dry, sunny, and hot, so hiking is best done early in the morning or late in the day. No matter when you go, bring plenty of water, a hat, and sunscreen.

In **Ka'ena Point State Park** (www.hawaiistateparks.org), hiking out to **Ka'ena Point** is a special experience. The rough and rocky trail, a little over five miles round-trip, follows a well-worn dirt road along the cliff out to the point. The volcanic coast is breathtaking, with tidepools, natural stone arches, and surf surging onto rock outcroppings. The road has washed away not far from the point, so follow the narrow side trail around the cliff. You'll reach a formidable fence designed to keep out invasive species; enter through the double doors. Once you are inside the **Ka'ena Point Natural Area Reserve** (www.state.hi.us/dlnr/dofaw/kaena/index.htm), an ecosystem restoration project, it is of the utmost importance to stay on the marked trails as not to disturb the seabird nesting grounds. The dunes are covered with native Hawaiian plants and home a handful of Hawaiian and migratory seabirds. Continue down to the shoreline past some old cement installments and look for Hawaiian monk seals basking in the sun. There are no

© KEVIN WHITTON

Ka'ena Point's rugged volcanic coast

facilities along the hike and no water, so bring plenty of fluids. To get to the trail, follow Farrington Highway to Yokohama Bay. Drive along the beach till the paved road ends. Park in the dirt parking area and proceed down the dirt road on foot. The state park is open from sunup to sundown.

Explore the deep valley behind Wai'anae, in the shadow of O'ahu's tallest peak, Mount Ka'ala. The six-mile **Wai'anae Kai** loop trail is full of ups and downs with a final climb to an overlook. It then follows an ancient Hawaiian trail back to the main route. You'll find native Hawaiian trees, shrubs, and herbs along the hike and the likes of the Japanese bush warbler. There are views of Wai'anae, Lualualei, and Makaha Valleys. The trail is unimproved and rough, so proper footwear is essential. To get there, follow Waianae Valley Road to the back of the valley. Continue on it after it turns into a one-lane dirt road. Park in the dirt lot across from the last house at the locked gate. Continue past the locked gate and followed the dirt road on foot.

BIKING

The leeward coast does have a gem of a mountain biking trail, the road to **Ka'ena Point.** Part of **Ka'ena Point State Park** (www.hawaiistateparks.org), the trail is flat, so there's no climbing or downhill involved, but the rocky, rutted, and curving cliffside dirt road is a challenging ride none the less. At 2.7 miles one way from the parking area to the point, the ride is extremely scenic, passing rocky coves, sea arches, and crashing waves. Once at the fence to keep out invasive species from the natural reserve portion of the park, you can bike around the point along the perimeter of the fence to the Mokule'ia side and continue up the North Shore, or you can walk your bike through the double doors in the fence. However, the trails inside the reserve are narrow and sandy. The sun is intense, and there is no shade in the area, so bring plenty of water and wear sunscreen.

To get to the trail, follow Farrington Highway to Yokohama Bay. Drive along the beach until the paved road ends. Park in the dirt parking area and proceed down the dirt road on foot. The state park is open from sunup to sundown.

Hale Nalu (85-876 Farrington Hwy., #A2, 808/696-5897, http://halenalu.com, 10am-5pm daily), in Wai'anae, rents mountain bikes for $30 per day, $60 for three days, or $90 for one week.

BIRD-WATCHING

The **Ka'ena Point Natural Area Reserve** (www.state.hi.us/dlnr/dofaw/kaena/index.htm) inside the Ka'ena Point State Park is the premier bird-watching area on the leeward coast. The 59-acre reserve is an active ecosystem restoration project designed to restore the native ecosystem on the point and bolster the number of endangered species, both flora and fauna, that call the area home. Look for Laysan albatross, wedge-tailed shearwater, and white-tailed tropicbird that nest in dunes. Nesting begins in November, with the adults departing in late spring and juveniles leaving the nests by late June. The area is also home to several species of

LEEWARD

PREDATOR-PROOF FENCE

Ka'ena Point has long been home to a variety of Hawai'i's wildlife, a chorus of flora and fauna on land and in the sea. In years past, human impact took a devastating toll on the fragile ecosystem: off-road vehicles tore up the dunes destroying native vegetation and disturbing seabird nesting sites, and feral cats, dogs, rats, and mongooses decimated seabird populations, namely the wedge-tailed shearwater and Laysan albatross that nest in the dunes, by eating eggs and killing juvenile birds.

Today, because of the Ka'ena Point Natural Area Reserve Ecosystem Restoration Project, Ka'ena Point is a natural restoration success story. Integral to the return of native plant species, native insects, and nesting seabirds is the predator-proof fence. Completed in 2011, the 6.5-foot-high fence uses a fine mesh technology to protect the 59-acre reserve from predation by invasive species. Spanning 700 yards and following an old railroad track roadbed around the point, the fence is also buried underground with the ability to keep two-day-old mice from entering. A double-gated entry system ensures unwanted pests cannot sneak in, as only one door can open at a time. The fence is unobtrusive and colored to blend in with the natural vegetation and geography. Since its completion, native vegetation has returned and nesting seabird populations are steadily increasing.

native Hawaiian birds including the great frigatebird, red-footed, brown, and masked boobies, sooty and white terns, and the Hawaiian short-eared owl. Other migratory birds like the wandering tattler and the Pacific golden plover also frequent the area.

Golf and Tennis

GOLF
Makaha

In Makaha you'll find the **Makaha Valley Country Club** (84-627 Makaha Valley Rd., 808/695-9578, www.makahavalleycc.com) surrounded by the ridges of the Wai'anae Mountains in the expansive Makaha Valley. Opening out to the Pacific Ocean, the 18-hole, par-71 course has a rolling topography known for its challenging par-3 holes. Greens fees start at $65 weekdays and $75 weekends.

Ko Olina

In manicured Ko Olina, the **Ko Olina Golf Club** (92-1220 Aliinui Dr., 808/676-5300, www.koolina.com) is the regions premier golf destination. The beautiful, Ted Robinson layout features views of the Wai'anae Mountains and the Pacific Ocean. The 18-hole course has expansive landing areas and multitiered greens for golfers of all skill levels. They also have an internationally recognized golf shop and offer private, group, and corporate classes at the Ko Olina Golf Academy, with a PGA Professional teaching staff. Greens fees start at $189 with discounted rates for Ko Olina Resort guests.

TENNIS
Ko Olina

The hot and dry climate of the leeward coast is probably not the best weather for a tennis match, but if the court is calling, the **JW Marriott Ihilani Resort** (92-1001 Olani St., 808/679-0079, www.ihilani.com, 7am-8pm daily, $23/court or $14 pp) has a professional outdoor tennis complex with three hard courts and two synthetic sand courts. The weekly rate is $45 per person. They rent rackets and shoes for $5 apiece and ball machines for $28 per hour. They also offer clinics and lessons. Book the courts through the spa department.

Spas and Fitness

KO OLINA
Inside the **JW Marriott Ihilani Resort** (92-1001 Olani St.) in Ko Olina you'll find the **Ihilani Spa** (808/679-3321, www.ihilanispa.com). In addition to standard spa services like massage, facials, and body treatments, they offer full salon and nail services, as well as spa fitness. The spa is situated by the ocean, and the ocean theme is represented throughout. Fifty-minute massages start at $130, 50-minute facials start at $140, and 50-minute body treatments start at $65 for a cool *ti* leaf wrap. For men, the spa offers a 25-minute salt scrub and water massage for $65. Couples can get side-by-side massages by choosing from any of the services offered. Prices are per person.

Ihilani Spa also has several complimentary fitness group classes like a guided lagoon walk, aqua job, beach workout, and Zumba. They offer 60-minute yoga sessions for $15. Contact the spa for the current schedule of classes.

Sights

MAKAHA
◀ Kane'aki Heiau
Located deep in Makaha Valley is one of the best preserved *heiau* on O'ahu, the **Kane'aki Heiau.** Begun in 1545, the final structure was only completed by 1812, during the reign of King Kamehameha. Two restoration phases of construction occurred to preserve the physical, spiritual, and historic aspects of the *heiau.* Originally dedicated to Lono, the Hawaiian god of harvest and fertility, it was later converted to a *luakini heiau* for human sacrifice. The thatched huts used as prayer and meditation chambers, along with a spirit tower and carved images, have all been replicated. Because the *heiau* is within a private gated community, access is limited to 10am-2pm Tuesday through Sunday. It may be closed even during those times when it's too rainy or muddy. Stop at the guardhouse and let them know where you're heading. They will ask to see your identification and car registration or car rental agreement before they sign you in.

Kaneana Cave
Spelunkers rejoice, just off Farrington Highway on the edge of Makua Valley is the **Kaneana Cave,** a sacred ancient Hawaiian site. At 100 feet high and about 450 feet deep, this cave, *ana,* is spoken of in Hawaiian legend as the womb of the earth, where mankind emerged and spread throughout the Wai'anae coast. It is named after Kane, the god of creation. In Hawaiian lore it is also thought to be the home of Nanaue, the shark man. The cave is dark and often slippery, so bring a flashlight. It is also

SOUL'S LEAP
Ka'ena Point is a sacred place, and not just for its natural beauty. Ancient Hawaiians thought Ka'ena Point to be a jumping-off point for the spirits of the dead to enter the afterlife. Legend has it that humankind emerged from the depths of Kaneana Cave, the womb of the Earth goddess, and spread across the Wai'anae coast. The souls of the deceased would find their way to Ka'ena Point by following the sun past the sunset, to the eternal night. Their leap would take them to Po, the realm of ancestral spirits, a spiritual place akin to heaven and described as being a sea of eternity. Once in Po, the soul is thought to have completed the cycle of life.

© KEVIN WHITTON

Ka'ena Point

unmaintained, and there are several side tunnels off the main cavern that should be avoided for your own safety. Look for the painted cement road barrier that marks the entrance.

【 Ka'ena Point State Park

Ka'ena Point State Park (www.hawaiistateparks.org) is the most scenic, raw, and naturally breathtaking area on the leeward side. It is also an embodiment of all things found on the leeward coast. Located at the end of Farrington Highway and stretching all the way out to the western tip of O'ahu, Ka'ena Point State Park provides outdoor and ocean recreational activities, wildlife viewing, native plantlife, verdant valleys, a secluded white sand beach with turquoise water, and a dramatic volcanic coast all under the hot west side sun. It is truly about as far removed from Honolulu and Waikiki as you can get on O'ahu.

As you round the last bend in the road with a slight elevation, the gentle arcing white sand of Yokohama Bay, also known as Keawa'ula Bay, stretches out in front of you to the west. Pristine and uncrowded, it begs for you to pull the car over and take in the serenity. Look back into the valley to catch a glimpse of the unspoiled, verdant mountains of the Wai'anae Range. As you come to the end of the paved road, a rutted, rocky dirt track completes the way to Ka'ena Point. You can walk or mountain bike out to the western tip of the island, where you'll find the Ka'ena Point Natural Area Reserve. This is prime territory for wildlife viewing. Look for spinner dolphins and green sea turtles in the water; on the beach you'll probably see Hawaiian monk seals basking in the sun; and the sand dunes are a protected site for nesting seabirds.

Shopping

MAKAHA

In the Makaha Marketplace, on the corner of Farrington Highway and Makaha Valley Road, is **Makaha Art Gallery** (84-1170 Farrington Hwy., 808/3434916, www.makahaartgallery.com, 10am-6pm Sat.-Sun.). The gallery is packed full of surf art and memorabilia, as well as Hawaiiana collectibles like ukulele, hula dolls, and wooden bowls and gourds. Their collection of ocean- and surf-themed prints, posters, and photographs by well-known artists is exceptional. If you're on the west side during the week and you'd like to stop in, call for an appointment.

Entertainment

KO OLINA

Paradise Cove Luau (92-1089 Aliinui Dr., 808/842-5911 or 800/775-2683, www.paradisecovehawaii.com) is located just inside the Ko Olina main entry gate. Set on 12 oceanfront acres, the luʻau probably has one of the best sunset views on Oʻahu. An evening at Paradise Cove actually begins before sunset. For about two hours, guests can explore the beautiful property, trying traditional arts and crafts, playing traditional Hawaiian games, shopping, or sipping mai tais. Guests can even partake in a *hukilau,* pulling fishing nets up onto the shore. After a sunset ceremony, the feast starts with traditional luʻau favorites, then begins the Paradise Cove Hawaiian Revue. Packages start at $88 adult, $78 youth, and $68 children. For better seats during the revue, there are two more packages available with higher rates. Reservations are available online.

Food

NANAKULI
Markets

In Nanakuli you're complete grocery store will be **Sack N Save** (87-2070 Farrington Hwy., 808/668-1277, www.foodland.com/stores/sack-n-save-nanakuli, 5am-11pm daily), encompassing a bank, Western Union, and full-service bakery, deli, meat, and seafood departments.

MAʻILI
Steak and Seafood

For a sit-down meal in Maʻili town overlooking the ocean, check out **Maili Sunset Bar & Grill** (87-064 Farrington Hwy., 808/679-9080, www.mailisunsetbarandgrill.com, 4pm-2am daily, $8-24). Open for dinner and late-night shenanigans, it's just about the only restaurant on the west side with a great location, modern decor, full bar, and a sit-down menu. The cuisine is a combination of steak, seafood, and bar food prepared local-style. They also have live music and entertainment on occasion.

WAIʻANAE
Markets

Tamura Super Market (86-032 Farrington Hwy., 808/696-3321, www.tamurasupermarket.com, 7am-8pm daily) in Waiʻanae has a deli featuring daily hot specials like roast beef, Filipino food, and Hawaiian plates.

MAKAHA
Markets

In the Makaha Marketplace on the corner

LEEWARD

of Farrington Highway and Makaha Valley Road, you'll come to **Ohana Market** (84-1170 Farrington Hwy.), your last chance for snacks, local sundries, and beverages if you're headed to Ka'ena Point.

KO OLINA

If you're looking for a traditional sit-down, white tablecloth meal on the west side, then drop into Ko Olina, where top chefs have set up shop to cater to the resort guests.

Quick Bites

Off the Hook (92-1185 Aliinui Dr., 808/674-6200, http://resorts.disney.go.com/aulani-hawaii-resort, 9am-11pm daily, $9-15) is an open-air, beachside lounge in the Aulani Resort, resembling a seaside fishing shack with Hawaiiana-inspired decor. The appetizer menu features Asian-influenced fare with the option to build your own seafood platter priced per piece. The full bar specializes in tropical cocktails.

Island Country Market (92-1048 Olani St., 808/671-2231, 6:30am-11pm daily) and **Two Scoops Ice Cream** (92-1048 Olani St., 808/680-9888, www.twoscoopsicp.com, 11am-9pm daily, $3-9) are both located in the Ko Olina Center & Station, near the Ko Olina entrance on the mountain side of the golf course and train tracks. The market has a full deli with hot and cold prepared foods, groceries, produce, raw foods, and alcohol. They also have tourist garb like towels, shirts, and souvenirs. Two Scoops is a locally owned ice cream parlor with sundaes, frozen drinks, smoothies, and coffee drinks. In addition to supreme ice cream, they also have a jumbo hot dog and Philly cheesesteak on the menu.

Steak and Seafood

Inside the Marriott Beach Club **Chuck's Steak & Seafood** (92-161 Waipahe Pl., 808/678-8822, www.chuckshawaii.com/steakseafood.html, 4:45pm-9:30pm Mon.-Thurs., 4:45pm-10pm Fri.-Sun., $20-45) serves classic, no frills steak and seafood dishes. They have indoor and outdoor seating and a full bar with two nightly happy hours.

A Hawai'i staple, **Roy's** (92-1220 Aliinui Dr., 808/676-7697, www.roysrestaurant.com, 11am-2pm and 5:30pm-9:30pm Mon.-Fri., 11am-2pm and 5pm-9pm Sat.-Sun., $15-45) offers lunch and dinner in the Ko Olina Golf Club. Known for its signature Hawaiian fusion cuisine, Roy's blends fresh ingredients with European sauces and Asian spices. The desserts are made fresh to order and are exceptional as well. They also have a prix fixe menu with wine pairing and indoor or outdoor seating overlooking the golf course.

Japanese

Located in the JW Marriott Ihilani, **Ushio-Tei** (92-1001 Olani St., 808/679-0079, www.ihilani.com, 5:30pm-9pm daily, $5-52) brings traditional Japanese fare to Hawai'i along with sushi and sashimi selections in an authentic Japanese garden setting. They have steak and seafood complete dinners, as well their Tabehodai all-you-can-eat buffet (Fri.-Sun., $43 adult, $21.50 children 5-12) featuring cold items, hot fare, and maki sushi.

Italian

Azul (92-1001 Olani St., 808/679-0079, www.ihilani.com, 6pm-9pm daily, $20-42) is also located in the JW Marriott Ihilani. This award-winning, fine dining Italian restaurant blends Italian cuisine with island ingredients. Reservations are recommended, and resort evening attire is required.

Information and Services

Internet access is available at the **Waianae Public Library** (85-625 Farrington Hwy., 808/697-7868, www.librarieshawaii.org). Visitors need a valid HSPLS library card to use an Internet computer. Three-month visitor cards are available for $10. You can reserve Internet computer time online or in person. You can also find printed bus schedules, too.

There is also a full service **post office** (86-014 Farrington Hwy., 808/696-0161) in Wai'anae between the First Hawaiian Bank and Lualualei Homestead Road.

Getting There and Around

GETTING THERE

To get to the leeward coast from Waikiki or Honolulu, take the H-1 freeway west. Right before Ko Olina the H-1 turns into Farrington Highway, Route 93. Farrington Highway runs the entire length of the leeward coast. The drive from Honolulu to Ko Olina takes about 45 minutes if traffic is flowing. If Ko Olina is your destination, take the Ko Olina exit, which puts you right onto Aliinui Drive, Ko Olina's main road. If you have questions about where to go once inside the community, ask the attendant at the gate as you enter Ko Olina.

GETTING AROUND

Getting around the leeward side is simple; there is only one major road running north and south along the coast—Farrington Highway. Farrington Highway loops past Ko Olina and shoots up the west side, parallel to the coast, all the way to the Ka'ena Point State Park where it ends. Farrington Highway has two lanes in each direction. From Nanakuli to Makaha, there are a lot of traffic signals, so the short distance drive can take upwards of 45 minutes. Road construction, which is quite common, will bring the highway down to one lane in each direction and cause immediate traffic delays. Even though the west side is still rugged and underdeveloped compared to most other communities on O'ahu, there are still frequent gas stations, several groceries stores, and places to stop and eat if you don't mind fast food.

TheBus (808/848-4500, www.thebus.org) routes C, 40, 401, 402, and 403 service the leeward side, and there is a transfer station in Wai'anae. Route C is an express route from Ala Moana Center in Honolulu to Makaha. Route 40 runs from Ala Moana Center to Makua, while routes 401, 402, and 403 service the leeward valleys and neighborhoods.

ACCOMMODATIONS

While O'ahu does have its share of bed-and-breakfasts and vacation rentals in choice seaside locales, the majority of the hotels and big-name resorts are in Waikiki. First-time visitors will find everything they need in Waikiki: tropical scenery, myriad ocean activities, family-friendly sights and attractions, an international range of cuisine, and accommodations for any budget. Once you've explored O'ahu from Waikiki as a home base and become more familiar with the regions, you'll know if lodging outside of the Waikiki bubble better suites your tastes.

For those who are looking to escape the hustle and bustle of Waikiki, there are two other small resort areas on O'ahu. For a modern, high-end resort experience, visit the condos, vacation rentals, hotels, and resorts in Ko Olina, a gated resort community on the southwest corner of the island where golf and protected seaside lagoons are the draw. Turtle Bay Resort, on the North Shore, is the only high-occupancy hotel in the region and has beautiful ocean views and championship golf courses. There is a small pocket of vacation rentals in sleepy Makaha on the west side. Kailua, on the windward side, is known for its bed-and-breakfasts and vacation rentals just steps away from one of the most beautiful beaches on O'ahu.

© JW MARRIOTT IHILANI RESORT AND SPA

FINDING A VACATION RENTAL

A vacation rental is like a home away from home. They offer the comfort of separate bedrooms with linens, full kitchens complete with cookware and dinnerware, laundry, and an element of uniqueness to your holiday. On O'ahu, they can be found in the form of high-rise condominiums in Waikiki and Makaha, golf course condominiums of Turtle Bay, neighborhood houses in Kailua and Lanikai, and oceanfront homes all along the coast.

When researching vacation rentals, start with a locale in mind and then search the properties in that area. In addition to the rate, most rentals will have a cleaning fee and possibly other booking fees. Also take into consideration whether tax is included in the rate. You'll want to note the minimum night requirement of the rental as well.

A huge selection of O'ahu vacation rentals can be had at www.vrbo.com, organized by region and by town to help narrow down your selections. Another major website with a substantial amount of listings is www.vacationrentals.com. Vacation rentals, luxury rentals, and condos are listed on www.hawaiianbeachrentals.com, and www.hawaii-beachhomes.com specializes in vacation rental homes on the beach.

For Waikiki vacation rental listings, check out www.aliibeachrentals.com and www.waikiki-oceanfrontrentals.com. The local Inga's Realty specializes in Makaha vacation rentals, check out the site at www.skrrentals.com. If you're looking for timeshare and vacation rentals in Ko Olina, its best to use a major vacation rental site like Vrbo.

On the windward shore, you'll find all sorts of studios, bed-and-breakfasts, vacation rentals, and oceanfront homes. Possible sources are www.lanikaibb.com, having a handful of vacation rentals; www.kailuabeachhomes.com with luxurious beachfront homes in Kailua, Lanikai, and Waimanalo for extended stays, and www.lanikailuabeachrentals.com, specializing in Kailua and Lanikai studios, bed-and-breakfasts, cottages, and homes at very reasonable rates.

The North Shore has vacation rental condos at Turtle Bay and studios and homes in the North Shore neighborhoods. Shark's Cove Rentals, www.sharkscoverentals.com, a local operation with an office right across from Sharks Cove, specializes in vacation homes. For condo rentals at Turtle Bay, www.turtlebay-rentals.com has accommodations on one of the championship golf courses in The Estates at Turtle Bay development, or check out www.turtlebaycondos.com for condo rentals at the Kuilima Estates development.

Once you've found your match, the only thing left to do is stock the fridge for the week.

Waikiki

With over sixty hotels and resorts packed in between the Ala Wai Canal and the Pacific Ocean, Waikiki's options for accommodations to suit your needs, and your budget, can seem daunting. Selecting a hotel here is all about setting your priorities during your stay. Are you after a beachfront hotel with sand and ocean activities just steps from your room, or is location not a factor because you plan on spending little time in Waikiki? Are you on a romantic getaway where ocean views are a must, or are you traveling with the family and looking for an affordable two-bedroom suite. For business or leisure, Waikiki has it all, including the beautiful beaches, weather, and water it's famous for.

UNDER $100

Pacific Ohana Hostel (2552 Lemon Rd., 808/921-8111, www.hawaiihostelwaikiki.com, $28-85) has female dorms, coed dorms, semiprivate single and double rooms, and private rooms. They have private rooms available with air-conditioning for an additional $10

WAIKIKI ACCOMMODATIONS

Name	Type	Rates	Best Feature(s)
Aqua Bamboo	boutique hotel	$219	studios and multi-room suites with kitchens
Aqua Waikiki Pearl	condo hotel	$177	award-winning service, full kitchens, private lanai
Aston at the Waikiki Banyan	condo resort	$191-207	free Wi-Fi, full kitchen, private lanai, pool, jet spa
Aston Pacific Monarch	condo resort	$196-229	studios and suites with kitchens, rooftop pool
Aston Waikiki Beach Tower	hotel	$607-707	all-suites hotel, gourmet kitchens
Courtyard by Marriott	hotel	$269-316	high-speed Internet, business center
Diamond Head Beach Hotel	vacation rental	$95-99	studio and multi-room condos, private beach access
DoubleTree Alana	hotel	$209-229	heated outdoor pool and 24-hour fitness center
Embassy Suites	hotel	$399	all-suites hotel, mini-kitchens, fitness center
The Equus	hotel	$149-169	equestrian theme, in-room wireless Internet
Hawaii Prince Hotel Waikiki	hotel	$219-279	all oceanfront hotel, day spa and fitness center
Hilton Hawaiian Village	resort	$339-369	22-acre oceanfront property, pools, saltwater lagoon
Holiday Inn Waikiki Beachcomber	hotel	$217-235	sundeck and swimming pool
Hotel Renew	boutique hotel	$229-239	"sophisticated interior," wireless Internet
Hyatt Regency Waikiki Beach	hotel	$345-395	spa, ground-level mall, classy decor
Halekulani	historic hotel	$490-675	marble vanities, deep soaking tubs, spa, fine dining
Ilikai	hotel	$299-319	30 stories of ocean views

per night. All rooms have private bathrooms and some units have full kitchens. There is a community kitchen open 8am-8pm. There is a small charge for linens and towels, and there's coin-operated laundry on-site.

Also on Lemon Road on the east end of Waikiki, **Waikiki Beachside Hostel** (2556 Lemon Rd., 808/923-9566, www.waikiki-beachsidehostel.com, $22-218) is the largest hostel on O'ahu. They offer small and large

coed and female dorms. Their semiprivate rooms have two beds, air-conditioning, lockers, private lanai, and a shared kitchen, while the small and large private suites sleep from two to four people and include full kitchen, bathroom, lockers, closet, and electronic door locks. The facility has free wireless Internet access, coffee and toast in the morning, and free local calls from every room. They also have a storage room for $5 per day if you need

Why Stay Here	Best Fit For
luxury suites have outdoor lanai with gas grill and furniture	couples, honeymooners
affordable multi-bedrooms suites	families
family focus on recreation	families, large groups
great location and affordable for extended stay	families, couples
spacious suites centrally located by Kuhio Beach	luxury-loving families, groups
flexible open spaces for business purposes	business travelers
oceanfront property near Diamond Head	couples, budget travelers
modern rooms with latest in available technology	business travelers, couples
condo-like experience in the heart of Waikiki	luxury lovers, couples, families
location on outskirts of Waikiki	business travelers, budget travelers
luxury suites, caters to golfers	golfers, luxury lovers
self-contained resort with malls, restaurants, beaches, and luxury tower	couples, families, honeymooners
central Waikiki location	families, couples
small boutique hotel emphasizing natural harmony	couples
central Waikiki location for ocean enthusiasts	beach lovers, couples, families
elegant and sophisticated oceanfront hotel	luxury lovers, couples, honeymooners
affordable ocean-view rooms with full kitchens, close to Ala Moana	couples, families

ACCOMMODATIONS

to leave personal items for an extended period of time.

The **Waikiki Sand Villa** (2375 Ala Wai Blvd., 808/922-4744, www.sandvillahotel.com, $98) is a traditional high-rise hotel for budget travelers. Located on Ala Wai Boulevard, the tower has city views and premium rooms have golf course views for a slightly higher rate. Their suites have kitchenettes.

On the beautiful stretch of coast closer to Diamond Head and away from the bustle of Waikiki, **Diamond Head Beach Hotel** (2947 Kalakaua Ave., 808/922-1928, www.obrhi. com/hawaii/diamond-head-beach-hotel, $95-99) offers discount vacation rentals in a 15-floor pyramid-shaped tower. The studio, one- and two-bedroom condos are fully furnished with the best views being toward the top of the building. There is also a private oceanfront lounge and private beach access from the property.

WAIKIKI ACCOMMODATIONS (CONTINUED)

Name	Type	Rates	Best Feature(s)
Miramar	hotel	$149-179	refurbished and modern rooms
Moana Surfrider	historic hotel	$415-515	oceanfront pool, spa, dining
The Modern Honolulu	boutique hotel	$329-379	sophisticated interior, pool, sundeck, plush furnishings
New Otani Kaimana Beach Hotel	hotel	$164-256	ocean and park views, free Wi-Fi, private lanai
Outrigger Luana	hotel	$159-169	swimming pool, sundeck, fitness center
Outrigger Reef on the Beach	hotel	$265-279	free high-speed Internet, restaurants, shops, pool
Outrigger Waikiki on the Beach	hotel	$319-389	pool, oceanfront location
Pacific Beach Hotel	hotel	$205-220	almost 1,000 rooms in two towers
Pacific Ohana Hostel	hostel	$28-85	private bathrooms, full kitchens
Queen Kapiolani Hotel	hotel	$199-239	views of ocean and park
Royal Hawaiian	historic hotel	$455-580	authentic Hawaiian decor, tropical gardens, spa, fine dining
Sheraton Princess Kaiulani	hotel	$250-285	three wings, private lanai, central pool
Sheraton Waikiki	hotel	$375-465	pool, infinity pool, bars and restaurants
Trump Hotel	hotel	$509	studios and suites, marble bathrooms, business service
Waikiki Beach Marriott	hotel	$279-319	swimming pool, spa, private lanai
Waikiki Beachside Hostel	hostel	$22-218	lockers, free wireless Internet
Waikiki Gateway Hotel	hotel	$118	views of ocean, city, park; extended stay studios
Waikiki Parc	hotel	$238-269	contemporary urban style luxury
Waikiki Sand Villa	hotel	$98	suites with kitchenettes, golf course views

$100-250

For families or large parties looking for multiple-room accommodations, the **Aston at the Waikiki Banyan** (201 Ohua Ave., 808/922-0555, www.astonwaikikibanyan.com, $191-207) is a condo resort where every suite has separate bedrooms, full kitchens, private lanai, and free wireless Internet. There is also a focus on recreation with a swimming pool, jet spas, sauna, tennis, basketball court, putting green, and playground.

The **Waikiki Gateway Hotel** (2070 Kalakaua Ave., 808/942-6006, www.waikikigateway.com, $118), located in Gateway Park, has stylish and modern standard rooms, while premium rooms have a private lanai. Most of the rooms in the tower offer unobstructed views of the ocean, city, and Fort DeRussy Beach Park.

Why Stay Here	Best Fit For
great central Waikiki location	families, budget travelers
historic beachfront hotel in the heart of Waikiki	luxury lovers, couples, honeymooners
located on the outskirts of Waikiki for a more luxurious experience	luxury lovers, couples, honeymooners
oceanfront property near Diamond Head and Kapi'olani Park	families, couples
affordable suites with full kitchens	families, budget travelers
beachfront hotel in the heart of Waikiki	groups, families, couples
central Waikiki location right on the beach, restaurants	beach lovers, couples, families
across from Kuhio Beach and reasonable rates for ocean-view rooms	families, couples
affordability with a near-beach location	students, budget travelers, backpackers
excellent location near beaches, park, and sights	families, couples
classic elegance, privacy, historic beachfront hotel in the heart of Waikiki	luxury lovers, couples, honeymooners
central Waikiki location	families, couples
oceanfront hotel with central Waikiki location	couples, families, honeymooners
luxury- and service-oriented hotel with large suites	luxury lovers, couples, honeymooners
located in the heart of Waikiki, mall	couples, families
affordability with a near-beach location	students, budget travelers, backpackers
affordability with easy access in and out of Waikiki	business travelers, budget travelers
plush rooms and access to services at the Halekulani	couples, honeymooners
affordability with privacy and views	budget travelers

The hotel also has larger rooms with kitchenettes designed for extended stay.

The Equus (1696 Ala Moana Blvd., 808/949-0061, www.equushotel.com, $149-169) is on the western outskirts of Waikiki, near the Ala Wai Harbor and Ala Moana Center. The contemporary, equestrian-themed decor is a departure from most hotel island-style furnishings. All 67 rooms have a midsize refrigerator and wireless Internet access. There is a small plunge pool as well.

The **Miramar** (2345 Kuhio Ave., 808/922-2077, www.miramarwaikiki.com, $149-179), conveniently located behind the International Marketplace in the center of Waikiki, has refurbished and modern rooms with partial and ocean views for a great bargain rate, like $219 for the ocean view rooms. There is also a popular Korean restaurant on the property.

Boasting beautiful views of Fort DeRussy Beach Park, **Outrigger Luana** (2045 Kalakaua Ave., 808/955-6000, www.outriggerluanawaikikihotel.com, $159-169) is decorated in contemporary island style with standard rooms, studios with kitchenettes, and suites with full kitchens starting at $219. There is a swimming pool, sundeck, and fitness center at the hotel.

For accommodations closer to Diamond Head and outside the pulse of Waikiki in this price range, check out the **New Otani Kaimana Beach Hotel** (2863 Kalakaua Ave., 808/923-1555, www.kaimana.com, $164-256). With beachfront at Kaimana Beach and right across from Kapi'olani Park, the well-appointed modern rooms have ocean or park views, free Wi-Fi or broadband Internet, private lanai, and refrigerators. Rooms in the Diamond Head Wing also have a microwave and kitchen sink. With Kaimana Beach right out front and the zoo nearby, it's the perfect family location.

The **Aqua Waikiki Pearl** (415 Nahua St., 866/970-4162, www.aquawaikikipearl.com, $177) may not have the best location, but for families looking for affordable multi-bedroom accommodations, Waikiki Pearl is a good choice. Known for their award-winning service, the one-, two-, and three-bedroom suites are simply decorated with an island theme and have full kitchens complete with dinnerware and cookware and a private lanai with city views. Two-bedroom suites are 986 square-feet for $407 a night, and three-bedroom suites are 1,157 square-feet for $477 a night.

The **Aston Pacific Monarch** (2427 Kuhio Ave., 808/923-9805, www.astonpacificmonarch.com, $196-229) is a small condominium resort just a couple blocks from famous Kuhio Beach Park. They have studios with kitchenettes and one-bedroom suites with full kitchens. One-bedroom suites start at $252 with partial ocean views. Their suites have floor to ceiling glass doors that open up to the trades. There is also a rooftop pool.

Queen Kapiolani Hotel (150 Kapahulu Ave., 808/954-7418, www.queenkapiolani.

com, $199-239) is all about location. With great views of Kapi'olani Park and the ocean looking toward Diamond Head, the beach is right across the street, as is the park and the Honolulu Zoo.

Across from Kuhio Beach is the **Pacific Beach Hotel** (2490 Kalakaua Ave., 808/922-1233, www.pacificbeachhotel.com, $205-220). With 839 rooms in two towers, they are able to offer very reasonable rates for ocean view rooms, starting at $228.

On the west end of Waikiki with mountain, ocean, and park views is the contemporary **DoubleTree Alana** (1956 Ala Moana Blvd., 808/941-7275, http://doubletree3.hilton.com, $209-229). The smart design with Hawaiian accents complements the chic and modern rooms with the latest in technology and amenities. There is a small heated outdoor pool and 24-hour fitness center. They offer smoking and nonsmoking rooms, and their high-end suites have private outdoor decks.

The **Holiday Inn Waikiki Beachcomber** (2300 Kalakaua Ave., 808/922-4646, www.waikikibeachcomberresort.com, $217-235) has a central location, and the rooms are bright with light tropical accents. There is a swimming pool on the sundeck and a large workout center. Oceanview one-bedroom suites start around $700.

Decked out in cool, tropical, and Asian-influenced decor from the pool and lobby to the guest rooms, **Aqua Bamboo** (2425 Kuhio Ave., 808/922-7777, www.aquabamboo.com, $219) has standard rooms, studio kitchenettes, and one- and two-bedroom suites. The boutique hotel's sky-high luxury bedroom has an outdoor lanai with a gas grill and patio furniture.

The **Hawaii Prince Hotel Waikiki** (100 Holomoana St., 888/977-4623, www.princeresortshawaii.com/hawaii-prince-hotel-waikiki, $219-279) is an all-oceanfront accommodation, meaning that its design affords every room a floor-to-ceiling ocean view, overlooking Ala Moana Harbor and Ala Moana Beach and Park. Located on the western edge of Waikiki near Ala Moana Center, the sophisticated hotel has 57 luxury suites, restaurants, day spa, and fitness center, and caters to golfers with packages for play at the Hawaii Prince Golf Club in 'Ewa. One-bedroom suites start at $379, and two-bedroom suites start at $599.

Hotel Renew (129 Paoakalani Ave., 808/687-7700, www.hotelrenew.com, $229-239) is a small, modern boutique hotel with a sophisticated interior focused on balance and harmony. Wireless Internet, use of beach gear, and morning coffee or tea are complimentary in all 72 rooms, themed to echo the natural environment. Their oceanview rooms start at $289 a night.

The **Waikiki Parc** (2233 Helumoa Rd., 808/921-7272, www.waikikiparc.com, $238-269) offers contemporary urban style and luxury. It's modern, the guest rooms are plush, and it's billed as the chicest boutique hotel in Waikiki. Guests have access to services at their sister hotel, Halekulani, right across the street as well.

$250-400

Located on one of the busiest corners in Waikiki, Kalakaua and Kaiulani Avenues, the **Sheraton Princess Kaiulani** (120 Kaiulani Ave., 808/922-5811, www.princess-kaiulani. com, $250-285) has three distinct buildings that comprise the hotel. All rooms in the Kaiulani Wing and Ainahau Tower have a private lanai. There is a pool in the center courtyard, and the hotel has suites and family rooms. The rooms have a simple and clean feel with light colors and wood furnishings.

A beachfront hotel on the western end of Waikiki, the **Outrigger Reef on the Beach** (2169 Kalia Rd., 808/923-3111, www.outriggerreef-onthebeach.com, $265-279) offers restaurants, shops, and renewed accommodations in an elegant modern style. Their moderate-rate rooms have no view, but there is free high-speed Internet access throughout the hotel. For families and large groups, the hotel has one-bedroom ocean and city-view suites, and two-, three-, and four-bedroom oceanview suites.

The **Courtyard by Marriott** (400 Royal Hawaiian Ave., 808/954-4000, www.marriott. com/hotels/travel/hnlow-courtyard-waikiki-beach, $269-316), just behind the Duty Free Shopping Galleria on Kuhio Avenue, has comfortable rooms with soft colors and wood decor. With high-speed Internet throughout the hotel, business center, and flexible open spaces in the lobby, the hotel is geared toward business travel.

The **Waikiki Beach Marriott** (2552 Kalakaua Ave., 808/922-6611, www.marriott. com/hotels/travel/hnlmc-waikiki-beach-marriott-resort-and-spa, $279-319) is a resort right across the street from Kuhio Beach Park. There are shops and restaurants on the 5.2-acre property, swimming pool and spa, and the rooms are stylish with wood accents and private lanai.

Located on the west side of the Hilton Hawaiian Village, fronting the Ala Wai Boat Harbor, the **Ilikai** (1777 Ala Moana Blvd., 808/949-0892, www.ilikaihotel.com, $299-319) has 30 stories of ocean views. They also have mountain-view and oceanview full kitchen rooms starting at $339, as well as mountain- and oceanview two-bedroom suites starting at $399.

For accommodations right in the heart of Waikiki on Waikiki Beach, check out the **Outrigger Waikiki on the Beach** (2335 Kalakaua Ave., 808/923-0711, www.outrigger.com/hotels-resorts/hawaiian-islands, $319-389). Perfect for visitors interested in taking advantage of all of Waikiki's ocean activities, the hotel also has one of the best, and most famous, restaurants in Waikiki, Duke's Waikiki. The guest rooms are Hawaiian themed with dark wood furnishings.

Overlooking the Ala Moana Small Boat Harbor, **The Modern Honolulu** (1775 Ala Moana Blvd., 808/954-7427, www.themodernhonolulu.com, $329-379) mixes sophistication and smart modern design with a laid-back surf culture vibe. The Sunrise Pool has a warm, wood deck with potted shade trees, and the Sunset Pool, an adults-only blue-tiled pool, is surrounded by sand imported from neighboring islands. The luxurious rooms have innovative design features and plush furnishings. One-bedroom suites are available.

The **Hilton Hawaiian Village** (2005 Kalia Rd., 808/949-4321, www.hiltonhawaiianvillage.com, $339-369), a 22-acre oceanfront mega-resort on the west end of Waikiki, is practically its own town. Nestled right up to the sand on Duke Kahanamoku Beach, the widest beach in Waikiki with calm water perfect for the family, the resort has swimming pools, waterslides, and waterfalls, a saltwater lagoon, its own luʻau, 18 restaurants, retail shops, and a Friday night fireworks show. For accommodations, there are five towers: the Rainbow Tower is right on the beach with amazing views, the Aliʻi Tower focuses on luxury, with separate check-in, a private pool, whirlpool, and fitness center, and three Village Towers offer lower-rate rooms.

The **Hyatt Regency Waikiki Beach** (2424 Kalakaua Ave., 808/923-1234, http://waikiki.hyatt.com, $345-395) holds prime real estate across from Waikiki Beach and is the perfect hub for travelers looking to take advantage of all the beach activities Waikiki has to offer. Within its central location, it also has a spa, a mall on ground level, and several well-known restaurants. The rooms are simple but classy with a light tropical feel. The suites are modern and sophisticated.

Another beachfront resort that towers over the Pacific, the **Sheraton Waikiki** (2255 Kalakaua Ave., 808/922-4422, www.sheraton-waikiki.com, $375-465) has stylish and comfortable accommodations, two pools, and on-site dining and shopping. The Infinity Edge pool is a treat for guests 16 and older. There is no beach in front of the hotel, but there is a pathway that runs along the edge of the water and offers beach access in both directions.

Situated in the Waikiki Beach Walk outdoor mall, a hub for Waikiki shopping and dining, **Embassy Suites** (201 Beach Walk St., 808/921-2345, http://embassysuiteswaikiki.com, $399) is an all-suite hotel that offers a condo-like experience. One- and two-bedroom suites have complimentary high-speed Internet, made-to-order breakfasts, and mini-kitchens. There is also a fitness center.

$400-650

The **Halekulani** (2199 Kalia Rd., 808/923-2311, www.halekulani.com, $490-675) has a long history of hospitality in Waikiki going back nearly 100 years. Today, the Halekulani is a mark of elegance and sophistication. The rooms and suites are light and bright with marble vanities, deep soaking tubs, and glassed-in showers. The oceanfront hotel has a full-service spa and several fine dining restaurants.

Just steps from Kuhio Beach, the **Aston Waikiki Beach Tower** (2470 Kalakaua Ave., 808/926-6400, www.astonwaikikibeachtower.com, $607-707) is an all-suites hotel specializing in spacious two-bedroom suites with fully equipped gourmet kitchens and in-room washer and dryer. Perfect for families that want to be close to the beach for ocean activities.

The first hotel in Waikiki, opening in 1901, the **Moana Surfrider** (2365 Kalakaua Ave., 808/922-3111, www.moana-surfrider.com, $415-515) is a historic icon along the Waikiki shoreline. Situated in the heart of Waikiki on Waikiki Beach, the original, stately building remains with additional wings and towers to offer over 800 rooms. The hotel also offers an oceanfront spa, pool, and dining on the veranda under the historic banyan tree. The room decor is modern, yet captures the legacy of the hotel.

Opening in 1927, the **Royal Hawaiian** (2259 Kalakaua Ave., 808/923-7311, www.royal-hawaiian.com, $455-580) is a landmark hotel also known as "The Pink Palace of the Pacific." The classic elegance of the guest rooms have been preserved, down to the hand-carved wooded doors of those in the main building. There is also a tower in addition to the historic original hotel. There are garden-view rooms of the tropical gardens and coconut grove, and a range of oceanview rooms and suites on the beachfront on hopping Waikiki Beach. Spa, fine dining, shopping, and a pool and hot tub round out the services.

The **Trump Hotel** (223 Saratoga Rd., 877/683-7401, www.trumphotelcollection.com/waikiki, $509) is all about luxury and service. They offer large studios to three-bedroom suites with fully equipped kitchens with brand-name appliances, Italian marble bathrooms with deep soaking tubs, and sophisticated furnishings. Studios range from 400 to 500 square feet, while the three-bedrooms have over 2,000 square feet of living space. They also offer business services, beach gear, nanny services, a 24-hour fitness center, a spa, and complimentary wireless Internet access.

Honolulu

Even though it is the biggest metropolis in the middle of the Pacific, there aren't many places to stay in Honolulu, most likely because Waikiki is practically next door. There are a few hotels near the airport for those who have an overnight layover and don't wish to take a taxi into Waikiki, one hotel downtown serving a strictly business clientele, and a two more hotels near Ala Moana Center.

ALA MOANA
Under $100
The **YMCA Central Branch** (401 Atkinson Dr., 808/941-3344, www.ymcahonolulu.org, $45-75), next to the Hawai'i Convention Center and across from Ala Moana Center, is the largest YMCA facility on O'ahu. They have partially furnished single and double rooms for men, women, and couples. They also offer rooms with a private shower and bathroom for an additional $10 a day. The double rooms with private baths have a minifridge and microwave, and all guests can use the laundry and fitness facilities. There is no smoking or alcohol permitted on the premises. Weekly and monthly rates are available.

The **YMCA Nu'uanu Branch** (1441 Pali Hwy., 808/536-3556, www.ymcahonolulu.org, $42) is a male-only facility just north of downtown and Chinatown and has 70 single rooms for $42 per night. For women, the **YWCA Fernhurst** (1566 Wilder Ave., 808/941-2231, www.ywca.org, $45) offers a secure residence with 24-hour electronic access located in the downtown Historic District. Double occupancy rooms are $45 per night and singles are $65 per night. The rooms are equipped with telephones and free Internet access. They also have a free computer lab.

$100-250
The **Pagoda Hotel** (1525 Rycroft St., 808/948-8356, www.pagodahotel.com, $128-192), near the Ala Moana Center, is a great option for travelers on a budget who won't be spending a lot of time at their hotel and don't feel the necessity to stay in Waikiki. The Asian-influenced design and decor is complete with Japanese gardens, koi ponds, and waterfalls. The 359-room hotel has standard guest rooms in the main tower and studios, one-, and two-bedroom units with kitchenettes in the five-story terrace wing.

Just on the outskirts of Waikiki and situated between the Ala Moana Center and the Hawai'i Convention Center is the **Ala Moana Hotel** (410 Atkinson Dr., 808/955-4811, www.alamoanahotelhonolulu.com, $169-219). A bargain compared to some of the beachfront hotels in Waikiki, the location lends itself to those attending a convention or visitors wanting the flexibility of getting out the door and on the road without worrying about the congestion of Waikiki. The two towers offer ocean and city skyline views, and the rooms have free Internet access. They also have one-bedroom suites. And with Ala Moana Center next door, there are plenty of dining options a quick walk from the hotel.

GREATER HONOLULU
$100-250
Built in 1912 in lush Manoa Valley and listed in the National Register of Historic Places, the **Manoa Valley Inn** (2001 Vancouver Dr., 808/947-6019, www.manoavalleyinn.com, $125-195) is a bed-and-breakfast set in a luxurious Victorian inn filled with European

HONOLULU ACCOMMODATIONS

Name	Type	Rates	Best Feature(s)
Airport Honolulu Hotel	budget hotel	$169	free Wi-Fi, microwave, 24-hour airport shuttle service
Ala Moana Hotel	hotel	$169-219	free Internet access, city skyline views, bargain rates
Best Western the Plaza Hotel	budget hotel	$199-209	free Wi-Fi, microwave, 24-hour airport shuttle service, pool
Manoa Valley Inn	bed and breakfast	$125-195	heated saltwater pool, six rooms, country cottage
Pagoda Hotel	hotel	$128-192	Japanese gardens, studios, and multi-room suites
Sand Island State Recreation Area	camping	$18	weekend shoreline camping, basic facilities
YMCA Central Branch	hostel	$45-75	rooms for men, women, and couples; monthly rates
YMCA Nu'uanu Branch	hostel	$42	male-only facility
YWCA Fernhurst	hostel	$45	female-only facility, in-room free Internet access, computer lab

ACCOMMODATIONS

antiques. Nestled in verdant Manoa Valley, the intimate retreat is peaceful and unique, with six rooms and a country cottage available. The residence is surrounded by a tropical garden and has a heated saltwater swimming pool with a meandering waterfall. There are four friendly dogs and a cat on the premises.

The **Airport Honolulu Hotel** (3401 N. Nimitz Hwy., 808/836-0661, www.outrigger.com/hotels-resorts/hawaiian-islands/oahu-waikiki/airport-honolulu-hotel, $169) has basic 300-square-foot rooms with free wireless high-speed Internet, microwave, refrigerator, and free 24-hour airport shuttle service to the hotel.

Clean and scenic for a hotel near the airport, the **Best Western the Plaza Hotel** (3253 N. Nimitz Hwy., 808/836-3636, http://bestwesternhawaii.com/hotels/best-western-the-plaza-hotel, $199-209) offers 274 rooms with

microwaves, refrigerator, and free high-speed Internet. They also have free airport shuttle service. There's even a pool if you need to take a quick dip and can't make it to the beach.

CAMPING

Sand Island State Recreation Area (end of Sand Island Access Rd., 808/832-3781, www.hawaiistateparks.org/parks/oahu/sand-island.cfm, $18) offers weekend-only shoreline camping along 14 arid acres fronting an industrial area of Honolulu Harbor. There is a small beach and a surf break just offshore. The campground is a favorite for local families. From April 1 to Labor Day the area is gated 7:45pm-7am, and from Labor Day to March 31 it's gated 6:45pm-7am. The fee is $18 per campsite per night. Facilities include outdoor showers and restrooms.

Why Stay Here	Best Fit For
proximity to Honolulu International Airport, overnight layovers	business and budget travelers
located next to Ala Moana Center and Convention Center	business and budget travelers
proximity to Honolulu International Airport, overnight layovers	business and budget travelers
Victorian inn, peaceful and unique, tropical gardens	couples, honeymooners
great location for people expecting to spend little time at their hotel	families, budget travelers
only camping area in Honolulu	budget travelers, backpackers
opportunity for extended stay, no alcohol, no smoking	students, budget travelers, backpackers
Chinatown location	students, budget travelers, backpackers
downtown location	students, budget travelers, backpackers

North Shore

Keeping true to the North Shore's rural and relaxed atmosphere, you won't find the high-rise hotels that identify Waikiki, though many visitors would love to spend their entire vacation in this beautiful region. Turtle Bay Resort has the distinction of being the only high-occupancy accommodation on the North Shore, a designation reflected in its room rates. Luckily for travelers enamored by the North Shore, the community is full of vacation rentals. The North Shore is more family-friendly in the summer when the surf is flat and the conditions for swimming and snorkeling are perfect.

NORTH SHORE BEACHES
Under $100
Hawaii Backpackers (59-788 Kamehameha Hwy., 808/638-7838, http://backpackers-hawaii.com, $27-62) is the North Shore's only hostel and is a collection of several properties around the Three Tables area. They have three

location choices for hostel beds and four locations for private rooms and studios as well. Their hostel beds start at $27 per night; they have private rooms with shared kitchen and bath starting at $62 per night; their private studio apartments have ocean views and a patio overlooking the beach with a full bath and start at $120 per night; and their private cabins sleep four to eight people and have full kitchens starting at $160 per night. They also offer a 10 percent discount off weekly rates.

$100-250
Ke Iki Beach Bungalows (59-579 Ke Iki Rd., 808/638-8829, http://keikibeach.com, $160-230) is located on Ke Iki Beach, just to the north of Sharks Cove and not far from Pipeline. The studio, one-, and two-bedroom bungalows are clean, stylishly appointed in tropical decor and could not be in a more beautiful location, fronted by the Pacific Ocean and surrounded

NORTH SHORE ACCOMMODATIONS

Name	Type	Rates	Best Feature(s)
Hawaii Backpackers	hostel	$27-62	private rooms, private studios with ocean views
Kaiaka Bay Beach Park	camping	$50	seven-site beach camping
Ke Iki Beach Bungalows	cottages	$160-230	studio and multi-bedroom bungalows, five beachfront
Turtle Bay Resort	resort	$251-315	suites, beach cottages, villas, surf break, beach, snorkeling

by tropical foliage. The five beachfront bungalows sleep between three and five people and start at $195 per night. Six garden-view bungalows sleep between two and eight people and start at $160 per night. Extra cleaning fees apply.

TURTLE BAY
$250-400

Turtle Bay Resort (57-091 Kamehameha Hwy., 808/293-6000, www.turtlebayresort.com, $251-315) is the North Shore's premier hotel and resort. The property is spread across almost five miles of beachfront and the family-friendly, surf-friendly, and golf-friendly resort has a wide range of accommodations including 375 guest rooms and 25 suites ($330-660) in their six-story main hotel, 42 beach cottages ($500), and luxury ocean villas with beachfront locations along Kuilima Cove. The pool and waterslide will keep the kids busy all day. There is a surf break right off Kuilima Point where the hotel sits, and the resort is home to two championship golf courses. Package rates for golf and accommodations are also available.

CAMPING

Just west of Hale'iwa in Waialua, camping is available Friday through Wednesday at **Kaiaka Bay Beach Park** (66-449 Hale'iwa Rd., 808/768-3440, https://camping.honolulu.gov, $50). There are seven campsites right on the rocky point at the mouth of the Waialua River, and not much shelter from the elements. The beach is good for fishing off the rocks, but not for swimming. You can walk up the beach to the east to reach a sandy beach safer for swimming. The camping area has outdoor showers and restrooms and is gated 6:45pm-7am. Permits are $50 for five nights plus fees.

Why Stay Here	Best Fit For
only hostel on the North Shore, can accommodate large groups	backpackers, budget travelers
natural environment close to Hale'iwa Town	nature lovers, budget travelers
very affordable beachfront cottages, beautiful natural location	nature lovers, couples, honeymooners
the only resort on the North Shore, ample ocean and nature opportunities	nature lovers, couples, honeymooners, families

Southeast and Windward

On the southeast shore you'll find the only resort in this region, the high-class Kahala Hotel & Resort, and vacation rentals in Hawai'i Kai. On the windward coast, camping is prevalent in the beach parks, just be prepared for rain and wind, common weather conditions on this side of the island. Kailua boasts an array of bed-and-breakfast accommodations and vacation rentals to service the seaside hamlet, a great option for escaping from the Waikiki scene to one of the prettiest white sand beaches on the island.

SOUTHEAST O'AHU
$400-650
At the end of Kahala Avenue in the affluent Kahala neighborhood is the luxurious **Kahala Hotel & Resort** (5000 Kahala Ave., 808/739-8888, www.kahalaresort.com, $495-675). The rooms and suites are decorated in a light tropical palette with island accents, and guests can enjoy the secluded white sand beach just steps away. The hotel has its own private lagoon where guests can interact with dolphins and other sea creatures. A swimming pool, high-end spa with 10 private treatment suites, and a beachfront fitness center are a few of the amenities.

KAILUA
Under $100
Set on the Ka'elepulu Stream, four blocks from Kailua Beach, **Sharon's Kailua Serenity Bed & Breakfast** (127 Kakahiaka St., 808/262-5621, www.sharonsserenity.com, $80-95) has two rooms and one suite available with a continental breakfast. Casual and homey, the Blue Room has one queen-size bed, and the Poolside Room has a king and a twin bed. The suite is designed for a family of three to four. There is wireless Internet and no cleaning fees. There is also a dog on the premises.

$100-250
Just a few blocks away from Kailua Beach, **Pillows in Paradise** (336 Awakea Rd., 808/262-8540, www.pillowsinparadise.com, $99-119) offers two units: a private one-bedroom unit and a spacious studio suite with king- and queen-size beds, perfect for families. Both units have private bathrooms and entrances, coffeemaker, refrigerator, microwave, and other kitchen items. A swimming pool graces the tropical garden.

The **Sheffield House Bed & Breakfast** (131 Kuulei Rd., 808/262-0721, www.hawaiisheffieldhouse.com, $129-169) is just steps away from Kailua Beach and has two suites with private entrances, Mexican tile floors, wireless Internet, kitchenettes, and off-street parking. The Ginger Studio with Secret Garden sleeps two to three and has a tropical garden

ACCOMMODATIONS

SOUTHEAST AND WINDWARD ACCOMMODATIONS

Name	Type	Rates	Best Feature(s)
Ahupua'a O Kahana	camping	$18	beachfront camping on sheltered bay
Bellow Field Beach Park	camping	$30	three-day camping, lifeguards, gated campground
Hau'ula Beach Park	camping	$50	basic amenities, pavilion, convenient store nearby
Hawaii's Hidden Hideaway Bed and Breakfast	B&B	$145-195	private bathrooms, kitchenettes, laundry facilities
Ho'omaluhia Botanical Garden	camping	$30	forest camping, basic facilities, three campgrounds
Kahala Hotel and Resort	resort	$495-675	beachfront, secluded beach, private lagoon, spa
Kokololio Beach Park	camping	$50	beachfront sheltered campsite under tall trees
Kualoa Regional Park	camping	$30-50	two campgrounds, basic services
Lanikai Bed and Breakfast	B&B	$160-175	two stylish suites, king-size bed, kitchenettes
Malaekahana State Recreation Area	camping	$18	37 sites in two areas, picnic areas, basic facilities
Malaekahana Campgrounds	camping	$12-350	private campground, cabins, yurts
Papaya Paradise	bed and breakfast	$100	swimming pool, mountain views, Wi-Fi Internet
Pillows in Paradise	bed and breakfast	$99-119	private bathrooms, pool, kitchen appliances
Sharon's Kailua Serenity Bed & Breakfast	B&B	$80-95	pool, wireless Internet, no cleaning fee
Sheffield House Bed & Breakfast	bed and breakfast	$129-169	wireless Internet, private entrances, kitchenettes
Waimanalo Bay Beach Park	camping	$50	tree-covered beach camping, basic facilities

and fountain outside the entrance. The Garden Suite sleeps two to four and can be combined with the Ginger Studio to form a two-bedroom, two-bath rental. There are cleaning fees in addition to the rate and a complimentary breakfast on the first morning of the stay.

Located a half-mile from the beach, **Papaya Paradise** (395 Auwinala Rd., 808/261-0316, www.kailuaoahuhawaii.com/papaya.htm, $100) has a large swimming pool, great views of the Ko'olau Mountains, and a covered lanai

for relaxing, reading, and enjoying the daily complimentary continental breakfast on. The rooms have wireless Internet, private entrances, private baths, two beds, and tropical furnishings. They also have beach accessories on hand to borrow.

Just south of Kailua in the Lanikai enclave, **Hawaii's Hidden Hideaway Bed and Breakfast** (1369 Mokolea Dr., 808/262-6560, www.ahawaiibnb.com, $145-195) has several suites surrounded by tropical foliage with

Why Stay Here	Best Fit For
ocean activities and hiking in the valley	couples, nature lovers, budget travelers
safe campsite on active military base, beautiful beach	families, budget travelers, couples
fishing, central location on Windward Coast	budget travelers
located in upscale Lanikai neighborhood	couples, honeymooners
forest camping with catch-and-release fishing, bird-watching	groups, families, nature lovers
beach property, luxury resort outside of Waikiki	luxury lovers, couples, honeymooners
close to La'ie town, fishing	budget travelers
fishing and ocean recreational activities	couples, families, nature lovers
beautiful location with mature trees, very close to beach	couples, honeymooners
ocean activities, beautiful beach	couples, nature lovers, budget travelers
coastal camping or sheltered camping, proximity to the North Shore	couples, families, budget travelers
family-oriented locale near Kailua Beach	couples, families
few blocks from Kailua Beach, privacy	couples, families
casual and homey for families	families
steps from the beach, privacy	couples, families
ample shade, beautiful beach	budget travelers, nature lovers, couples

ACCOMMODATIONS

private entrances, private bathrooms, kitchenettes, dining areas, lanai, wireless Internet, and laundry facilities. The Deluxe Studios each sleep two and offer a choice of king, queen, or twin beds. The Peacock Suite sleeps two to three and has a large lanai with an outdoor spa. The units can be interconnected, and there are additional cleaning fees of $55 per unit.

Lanikai Bed and Breakfast (1277 Mokulua Dr., 808/261-7895, http://lanikaibedandbreakfast.com, $160-175) is 100 yards from Lanikai Beach. The Garden Studio has teak and bamboo furnishings, an outdoor dining area, and a king-size bed. The Tree House is a spacious upstairs two-bedroom suite surrounded by mature trees. Both units have high-speed Internet, kitchenettes, and are stylishly appointed with a tropical theme.

CAMPING
Makapu'u and Waimanalo
Waimanalo Bay Beach Park (41-043 Aloiloi

CAMPING ON O'AHU

With the exception of Malaekahana Campground, the only privately operated campground on O'ahu, all camping facilities are managed by either the City and County of Honolulu or the state of Hawai'i, and campers must obtain a permit from them. The fees differ between state and county campgrounds, but many of the rules are the same.

CITY AND COUNTY CAMPGROUNDS

- 17 campgrounds around O'ahu and 225 campsites
- Permits can be applied for no more than two weeks in advance
- Campgrounds offer either 3-day camping or 5-day camping
- Permits for 3-day camping are $30; permits for 5-day camping are $50; no refunds or discounts for campers that do not stay in the campground for the entire length of the permit
- 10 people and 2 family-size tents maximum per campsite
- Acquire permits and reserve a campsite online at https://camping.honolulu.gov

- Department of Parks and Recreation Camping Permit Office: 808/768-2267

STATE CAMPGROUNDS

- 4 campgrounds
- Permits can be applied for no more than 30 days in advance
- Campgrounds offer 5-day camping, except Sand Island State Recreation Area has 3-day camping
- Permits are $18 per campsite per night
- Permits are for up to six people; an additional fee of $3 per night is assessed for each additional person; maximum fee is $30 per night
- Aquire permits and reserve a campsite online at www.hawaiistateparks.org/camping/oahu.cfm
- DLNR Division of State Parks: 808/587-0300

RULES AND REGULATIONS

- Tent camping only, no sleeping in vehicles
- No campfires or bonfires in state parks
- No camping Wednesday and Thursday nights

St., 808/768-3440, https://camping.honolulu.gov, $50) has 10 campsites with five-day camping. Sharing the same beautiful beach as Bellows Beach Park, the area is gated 7:45pm-7am. The campsites are under tall ironwood trees for ample shade. There are outdoor showers and restrooms.

Bellow Field Beach Park (41-043 Kalanianaole Hwy., 808/768-3440, https://camping.honolulu.gov, $30) has 50 campsites for three-day camping. With campsites set under the ironwood trees, the beautiful and long stretch of white sand beach is just steps away. As part of an active military base, the campgrounds are not available before noon on Friday, and the park is closed between 8pm and 6am. No one is allowed to enter during this time, and campers must remain in their designated camping area. There are restrooms, outdoor showers, two lifeguard towers, barbecue cooking stands, and picnic tables.

Kane'ohe

Ho'omaluhia Botanical Garden (45-680 Luluku Rd., 808/768-3440, https://camping.honolulu.gov, $30) has rustic camping in a forest setting at the base of the Ko'olau Mountains. There are three separate camping areas on the property, all available for three-day camping. The **Kahua Kuou** campground has eight campsites and is set among plants from India and Sri Lanka. The **Kahua Lehua** campground has six campsites in the Native Hawai'i section of the garden, and the **Kahua Nui-Makai** campground is the largest in the park, with 15 sites and a recreational pavilion. There are restrooms, outdoor showers, picnic tables, and fire circles at all three camping areas.

Kualoa to La'ie

Kualoa Regional Park (49-479 Kamehameha Hwy., 808/768-3440, https://camping.honolulu.gov, $30-50) has two camping areas. The **Kualoa A Beach Park** section has seven campsites open to three-day camping, but is closed in the summer. **Kualoa B Beach Park** faces the coastline's iconic islet Chinaman's Hat, and has 14 campsites available for five-day camping. Adjacent to the fishponds, the area is known for fishing and recreational activities like snorkeling and kayaking.

At Kahana Bay, **Ahupua'a O Kahana** (52-222 Kamehameha Hwy., 808/237-7767, www.hawaiistateparks.org/parks/oahu/ahupuaa.cfm, $18), managed by the state, has 10 beach campsites on a beautiful and calm bay under tall trees offering five-day camping. The calm ocean conditions make the area great for families or ocean enthusiasts interested in stand-up paddling and kayaking. There are also several hiking trails in the valley across the highway. The area reports an average annual rainfall of 75 inches along the coast, so be prepared for precipitation. There are restrooms and outdoor showers. The beach area parking lot is gated 7:45pm-7am on April 1 to Labor Day, and from Labor Day to March 31 it's gated 6:45pm-7am.

Hau'ula Beach Park (54-135 Kamehameha Hwy., 808/768-3440, https://camping.honolulu.gov, $50) has eight campsites with five-day camping set on windswept, rocky coastline. There are restrooms, outdoor showers, and a pavilion. There is also a convenient store across the highway. Campers should be prepared for rain.

Just to the north is **Kokololio Beach Park** (55-017 Kamehameha Hwy., 808/768-3440, https://camping.honolulu.gov, $50), which borders quiet La'ie town. The five-day campground has five sites that are always in demand. The beach is sandy and beautiful, and the camping area is protected from the wind and rain by tall trees and coastal shrubs. There are outdoor showers and restrooms.

To the north of La'ie town are two adjacent campgrounds set back in the trees along the beautiful sandy beaches of La'ie and Malaekahana Bays. **Malaekahana State Recreation Area** (808/587-0300, www.hawaiistateparks.org/parks/oahu/malaekahana.cfm, $18) is managed by the state and has 37 sites in two camping areas along the coast. Camping is on the La'ie Bay side of Kalanai Point, but there is access to Malaekahana Bay north of the point as well. The campground has restrooms, outdoor showers, and picnic areas, and beach-related activities are the draw. The state park is gated 7:45pm-7am on April 1 to Labor Day, and from Labor Day to March 31 it's gated 6:45pm-7am.

Malaekahana Campgrounds (56-335 Kamehameha Hwy., 808/293-1736, www.malaekahana.net, $12-350) is just to the north of the state park along Malaekahana Bay. The privately managed campground has tent camping sites, cabins, and rental units like yurts and thatched huts nestled in the trees. The one-bedroom Eco-cabins have private bathrooms, beds, and kitchenettes. The other rental units have beds and other furniture and amenities. Guests must bring all cooking supplies and utensils, as well as linens and household supplies like trash bags and toilet paper. The rental units start at $60 per night and tent campsites are $12 per person per night.

CENTRAL AND SUBURBAN ACCOMMODATIONS

Name	Type	Rates	Best Feature(s)
Harbor Arms	apartment hotel	$113-125	one- and two-bedroom suites, swimming pool, Wi-Fi, cable
Harbor Shores	apartment hotel	$120	two-bedroom units, full-sized kitchen, private lanai
Kalaeloa Beach Park	camping	$30	shaded campsites, basic services
Keaiwa Heiau State Park	camping	$18	forested mountain camping, picnic areas

Central and Suburban

Predominantly residential neighborhoods mark this region, although you'll find several camping sites, both mountain and ocean, two hotels to service the Pearl Harbor area, and beachfront vacation rentals in 'Ewa Beach.

PEARL HARBOR
$100-250

The **Harbor Shores** (98-145 Lipoa Pl., 808/488-5742, www.harborshoreshi.com, $120) is an apartment hotel located on the shore of Pearl Harbor. They have basic, no frills two-bedroom units with full-size kitchens, private lanai, microwave, refrigerator, toaster oven, wireless Internet access, and a swimming pool. They cater to military families, budget travelers, and business travelers. Rates depend on the number of guests per room, and they offer weekly rates as well.

In similar fashion, the **Harbor Arms** (98-145 Lipoa Pl., 808/488-5556, www.harborarms. com, $113-125) apartment hotel has one- and two-bedroom suites with partial or full kitchens, private lanai, and free cable TV and wireless Internet. They also have a swimming pool, sundeck, and offer weekly rates.

CAMPING

In Aiea Heights, the **Keaiwa Heiau State Park** (end of Aiea Heights Dr., 808/483-2511, www.hawaiistateparks.org/parks/oahu/keaiwa.cfm, $18) offers a break from beach camping. The forested mountain setting has hiking trails and cultural sites. There are 10 campsites available for five-day camping at $18 per night. There are also restrooms, showers, drinking water, and picnic areas. From April 1 to Labor Day the area is gated 7:45pm-7am, and from Labor Day to March 31 it's gated 6:45pm-7am.

County-managed **Kalaeloa Beach Park** (Eisenhower Rd., 808/768-3440, https://camping.honolulu.gov, $30) on the 'Ewa Plain has 13 campsites for three-day camping. With outdoor showers and restrooms, this popular summertime beach and surf spot has a beautiful sandy beach and campsites under the trees. It is remote and secluded and there are no nearby services like restaurants or retail outlets, so come prepared with food and gear. The camping area is located just to the east of the intersection of Coral Sea Road and Eisenhower Road.

Why Stay Here	Best Fit For
proximity to Pearl Harbor, military installations, long-term stay	military families, business travelers
proximity to Pearl Harbor, military installations, long term stay	military families, business travelers
popular summertime beach and surf locale	outdoor lovers, budget travelers
hiking trails and cultural sites	outdoor lovers, couples

Leeward

Ko Olina is a great family destination for those seeking a controlled and manicured resort atmosphere without the crowds and nightlife of Waikiki. Inside Ko Olina you'll find the amenities of luxury resorts, hotels, and vacation rentals, but you'll also sacrifice Waikiki's selection of restaurants, ocean activities, and nearby sights, as Ko Olina is very isolated on the southwestern tip of the island. There is camping at west side beach parks, and Makaha has vacation rentals in condominium towers right on the beach.

LEEWARD COAST
$100-250

Unless you plan on camping, you'll only find visitor accommodations at Makaha. The **Hawaiian Princess** (84-1021 Lahilahi St., 800/776-2541, www.hawaiianprincessmakaha.com, $149-209) is one of the more stylish and well-maintained condominium buildings along Makaha Beach. Their one- and two-bedroom units have 180-degree views of the Pacific, full kitchens, washer/dryer, and private lanai. There is also a pool, hot tub, barbecue area, tennis court, and recreation room. One-bedroom units start at $149, and two-bedrooms rent for $209.

Makaha Shores (84-265 Farrington Hwy., 808/696-4186, www.makahashores.com) rents simple studio apartments with full-size kitchens and private lanai. There is a barbecue area by the swimming pool, and beautiful Makaha Beach is steps away. Other than ocean activities, there's not much to do in the area, or places to eat out, so guests should be comfortable with being self-sufficient on this quiet nook of coastline. Rates start at $525 per week and discounts are offered for longer stays.

KO OLINA
$250-400

Three swimming pools, seven whirlpool spas, and a beautiful seaside lagoon make the **Marriott's Ko Olina Beach Club** (92-161 Waipahe Pl., 808/679-4700, www.marriott.com/hotels/travel/hnlko-marriotts-ko-olina-beach-club, $295-600) the ultimate kid-friendly resort. Their one-, two-, and three-bedroom villas with fully equipped kitchens and tableware provide for a family vacation that is much more comfortable, and their master suites with oversize soaking tubs and king-size beds are the ultimate in relaxation for couples. The villas also have private lanai, washer/dryer, and wireless high-speed Internet.

LEEWARD ACCOMMODATIONS

Name	Type	Rates	Best Feature(s)
Hawaiian Princess	condominium	$149-209	full kitchens, washer/dryer, private lanai, ocean views
Makaha Shores	apartments	$525/week	studios with full-sized kitchens, swimming pool
Nanakuli Beach Park	camping	$50	five-day camping, shaded sites
Ma'ili Beach Park	camping	$30	12 sites, basic services
Kea'au Beach Park	camping	$50	25 sites for five-day camping, grassy sites
JW Marriott Ihilani	hotel	$369-419	marble bathrooms, spacious suites, spa, fine dining, pools
Aulani	resort	$505-650	aquatic adventure park, spa, fine and casual dining, suites
Ko Olina Beach Villas Resort	luxury villas	$832	elegant interiors, two- and three-bedroom villas, ocean views

$400-650

The **JW Marriott Ihilani** (92-1001 Olani St., 808/679-0079, www.ihilani.com, $369-419) is a bastion of luxury with marble bathrooms, dual vanities, and balconies for all their 640-square-foot rooms and spacious suites. The resort is complete with award-winning Ihilani Spa, two pools, tennis, golf, fine dining, and informal all-day restaurants and lounges. The resort also has direct access to one of Ko Olina's seaside lagoons.

Aulani (92-1185 Aliinui Dr., 808/674-6200 or 714/520-7001, http://resorts.disney.go.com/aulani-hawaii-resort, $505-650), A Disney Resort & Spa, is set on one of the trademark Ko Olina lagoons, and its Hawaiian theme is everything you'd expect from Disney. At the center of this family-oriented resort is Waikolohe Valley. The aquatic adventure park has a winding river with two tubing adventures, one with rapids and caverns, an enormous swimming pool with waterslides, a private snorkeling lagoon with tropical fish, and an interactive play area for the littlest ones. There are also a separate pool and spas away from the main pool

for parents wanting to enjoy some peace and quiet. During the day, Disney characters make appearances, and after the sun goes down there are age-specific theme parties for the kids. The rooms are modern and luxurious, and there are several types of views that dictate the room rate. The suites are designed for large families. They also have a spa, fine dining, and casual dining at the resort.

For families or couples after a romantic getaway, the **Ko Olina Beach Villas Resort** (92-106 Waialii Pl., 808/679-4088 or 877/333-3808, http://koolinabeachvillasresort.com, $832) features private villa suites, each with a unique floor plan and an elegant and sophisticated interior design. The two- and three-bedroom villas feature separate living and dining areas, private lanai, and partial to full ocean views. One-bedroom villas are only available during the low season for $405 per night. All rooms have a seven-night minimum stay.

CAMPING

Many of the county beach parks on the west side have camping available. **Nanakuli Beach**

Why Stay Here	Best Fit For
Makaha location, ample ocean activities, slow pace	couples, families
Makaha location has ample ocean activities, slow pace	couples, families
fishing	budget travelers
fishing, sandy beach, ocean recreation	budget travelers
proximity to Makaha and Ka'ena Point State Park	budget travelers
luxury hotel far removed from Waikiki, golf and ocean activities	luxury lovers, couples, honeymooners, families
family-oriented Disney resort, self-contained themed oasis	families
private and secluded, access to saltwater lagoon, long term stay	luxury-loving families, couples, honeymooners

Park (89-269 Farrington Hwy., 808/768-3440, https://camping.honolulu.gov, $50) has 11 campsites for five-day camping along a stretch of wide sandy beach. A popular fishing spot, it has sites nestled among trees, and there are restrooms and outdoor showers.

Ma'ili Beach Park (87-021 Farrington Hwy., 808/768-3440, https://camping.honolulu.gov, $30) has 12 campsites for three-day camping and fills up quick in the summer, since it is a favorite of local residents. There are restrooms and outdoor showers, very little shade, but a nice sandy beach.

Kea'au Beach Park (83-431 Farrington Hwy., 808/768-3440, https://camping.honolulu.gov, $50), north of Makaha, has 25 campsites for five-day camping. The spaces are grassy, but there is little shade and only a rocky beach. There are restrooms and outdoor showers.

ACCOMMODATIONS

BACKGROUND

The Land

When Papa, the Hawaiian earth mother, returned from vacationing in Tahiti, she was less than pleased on learning through a gossiping messenger that her husband, Wakea, had been playing around. Besides simple philandering, he'd been foolish enough to impregnate Hina, a lovely young goddess who bore him island children. Papa, scorned and furious, showed Wakea that two could play the same game by taking a handsome young lover, Lua. Their brief interlude yielded the man-child O'ahu, sixth of the great island children.

Geologically, O'ahu is the second oldest main island after Kaua'i. It emerged from beneath the waves as hissing lava a few million years after Kaua'i and cooled to form Hawai'i's third largest island. With four distinct shores—north, south, windward, and leeward—O'ahu is 44 miles long and 30 miles wide. There are 227 miles of shoreline, a mix of sandy beaches, armored shoreline, harbors, a major port, rocks, and cliffs. O'ahu is 72 miles southeast of Kaua'i across the Kaua'i Channel, and only 26 miles west of Moloka'i, separated by the treacherous Ka'iwi Channel.

GEOGRAPHY

Ancient Hawaiians worshipped Madame Pele, the fire goddess whose name translates

© KEVIN WHITTON

equally well as Volcano, Fire Pit, or Eruption of Lava. When she was angry, she complained by spitting fire, basaltic lava actually, which cooled and formed land. Two separate and extremely large shield volcanoes were behind the development of Oʻahu. The Waiʻanae Volcano is about 2.2-3.8 million years old, and the Koʻolau Volcano is roughly 1.8-2.6 million years old. The Waiʻanae and Koʻolau Mountain Ranges are the constantly eroding remnants of the two extinct volcanoes. Over the centuries, wind and rain have sculpted the dramatic *pali,* or cliffs, on the windward side, while streams cut the deep valleys along the leeward coast.

The island is also dotted by smaller tuft cone volcanoes—Diamond Head, Punchbowl, Koko Crater, Koko Head, and Hanauma Bay—which are believed to have erupted from 500,000 to just 20,000 years ago.

There are two distinct types of lava on Oʻahu for which the Hawaiian names have become universal geological terms: ʻaʻa and pahoehoe. They're easily distinguished by appearance, but chemically they're the same. ʻAʻa is extremely sharp, rough, and spiny. Conversely, pahoehoe, is billowy, ropelike lava that can mold into fantastic shapes. While Oʻahu has had no recent lava flows, examples of both are still visible across the island.

Oʻahu has no navigable rivers, but there are hundreds of streams. Oʻahu has the state's longest stream, **Kaukonahua,** which begins atop Puʻu Kaʻaumakua at 2,681 feet in the central Koʻolau Range and runs westward 33 miles through the Leilehua Plateau, emptying at the North Shore. En route, it runs through the Wahiawa Reservoir, which, at 302 acres, forms the second largest body of freshwater in Hawaiʻi. Two of Oʻahu's taller, accessible waterfalls are Manoa Falls, at the back of Manoa Valley, and **Waiheʻe Falls** in Waimea Valley on the North Shore, which has a drop of more than 40 feet. The only sizable and natural freshwater bodies of water on Oʻahu, both altered by man, are Salt Lake in Honolulu and Enchanted Lake in Kailua.

CLIMATE
Temperature
Oʻahu has comfortable weather year-round. The average daytime high temperature in winter is about 82°F, and the average summer day high raises the thermometer only a few degrees to 87.5°F. Nighttime temperatures drop about 10 degrees. Elevation, however, does reduce temperatures about three degrees for every 1,000 feet you climb.

Temperatures are both constant and moderate because of the trade winds, prevailing northeast breezes that blow at about 10-20 miles per hour. You can count on the trades to be blowing on an average of 300 days per year, hardly missing a day during summer and occurring half the time in winter. Although usually calm in the morning, they pick up during the heat of the afternoon, then weaken at night.

The tropic of Cancer runs through the center of Hawaiʻi, yet the latitude's usually oppressively hot and muggy weather is most often absent in the islands. Honolulu, on the same latitude as sweaty Hong Kong and Havana, has an acceptable 60-75 percent daily humidity factor.

Winds blowing from the south and southwest are known as kona winds. *Kona* means leeward in Hawaiian. Kona winds bring hot, humid air and unstable weather. If they persist for more than a couple days, they also bring vog, a thick haze caused by the Kilauea Volcano on the Big Island. Kona winds are most common October to April.

Rainfall
Precipitation is the biggest differentiating factor in Oʻahu's climate. Rainfall is most often localized and comes in waves of passing showers. Precipitation also occurs mostly at and below the 3,000-foot level with Oʻahu's mountains acting as rain magnets. As the trade winds push warm, moist air up against the mountains, the air rises, cools, and drops a payload of rain to the ground. Generally, the heaviest rainfall occurs on the windward side of Oʻahu and over both mountain ranges, and dry conditions prevail on the leeward side and south shore. Waiʻanae, Honolulu International Airport, and Waikiki average only

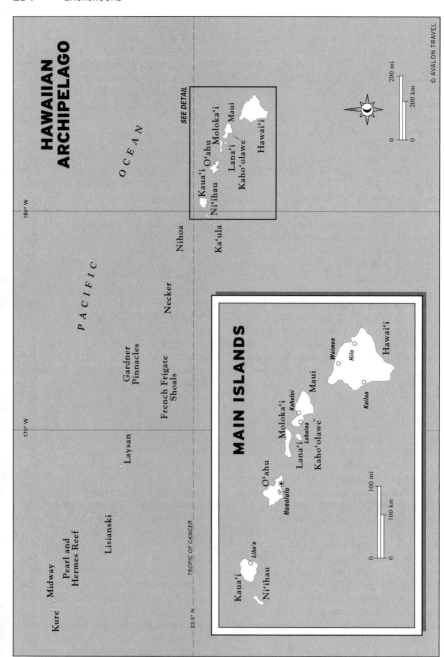

HAWAIIAN ARCHIPELAGO

PACIFIC

OCEAN

Kure
Midway
Pearl and
Hermes Reef

Lisianski

Laysan

Gardner
Pinnacles

French Frigate
Shoals

Necker

Nihoa

Ka'ula

Kaua'i O'ahu
Ni'ihau Moloka'i
Lana'i Maui
Kaho'olawe
Hawai'i

SEE DETAIL

160° W

170° W

23.5° N

TROPIC OF CANCER

0   200 mi
0   200 km

© AVALON TRAVEL

MAIN ISLANDS

Kaua'i
Ni'ihau
Lihu'e

O'ahu
Honolulu

Moloka'i
Kahului
Lana'i   Lahaina
Kaho'olawe   Maui

Waimea
Hilo
Kailua
Hawai'i

0   100 mi
0   100 km

THE NORTHWEST HAWAIIAN ISLANDS

Like tiny gems of a necklace, the Northwest Hawaiian Islands stretch across the vast Pacific. Popularly called the Leewards, most were discovered in the 19th century. The Leewards are the oldest islands of the Hawaiian chain, believed to have emerged from the sea 25-30 million years ago. Slowly they floated west-northwest past the suboceanic hot spot as the other islands were built. Measured from **Nihoa Island,** about 100 miles off the northwestern tip of Kaua'i, they span just under 1,100 miles to **Kure Atoll.** There are islets, shoals, and half-submerged reefs in this chain: Kure, Midway, Pearl, and Hermes Atolls and Lisianski, Maro Reef, Gardner Pinnacles, French Frigate Shoals, Necker, and Nihoa. Most have been eroded flat by the sea and wind, but a few tough volcanic cores endure. Together they make up a landmass of approximately 3,500 acres, the largest being the three Midway islands, taken together at 1,580 acres, and the smallest is **Gardner Pinnacles** at six acres.

Politically, the Leewards are administered by the City and County of Honolulu, except for Midway, which is under federal jurisdiction. None, except Midway, are permanently inhabited, but there are some lonely wildlife field stations on Kure and the French Frigate Shoals. All, except for Midway Atoll, are part of the **Hawaiian Islands National Wildlife Refuge,** established at the turn of the 20th century by Theodore Roosevelt. In 1996, following the closure of the Naval Air Base on Midway Island, Midway Atoll was turned over to the Department of the Interior and is now administered as the **Midway Atoll National Wildlife Refuge.** In June 2006, this 140,000-square-mile string of 10 islands and atolls and their surrounding waters, roughly 1,400 miles long and 100 mile wide, were officially designated a **Marine National Monument** (www.hawaiireef.noaa. gov), effectively creating the nation's largest wilderness preserve and the world's largest marine preserve.

20-25 inches of rain per year. The Leilehua Plateau in the center of the island averages 40 inches per year. Rain falls much more frequently and heavily in the Ko'olau Mountains and along the windward coast. The bay town of Kane'ohe sees 75-90 inches per year, while the Nu'uanu Reservoir in the mountains above Honolulu gets a whopping 120-130 inches yearly.

Localized weather means that weather patterns are very specific. If it's raining where you are, simply relocate to another part of the island or just wait a few minutes for the precipitation to pass. You can usually depend on the beaches of Waikiki and the leeward side to be sunny and bright. Ocean temperatures run 75-80°F year-round.

Severe Weather

Tsunami is the Japanese word for tidal wave. O'ahu's location in the middle of the Pacific Ocean puts it in the path of tsunamis as they travel from their point of origin and spread across the Pacific. A Hawaiian tsunami is actually a seismic sea wave that has been generated by an earthquake or landslide that could easily have originated thousands of miles away in Japan, South America, or Alaska. Not actual waves that break like the ones seen along O'ahu's reefs, tsunamis show up as a series of three to five tidal surges that affect coastal waters and shorelines over several hours, with about 30 minutes between each surge. Tsunamis can range from simply a larger than usual fluctuation in sea level over the duration of the event to a devastating tidal surge that can floor and damage shoreline property, especially the harbors, and cause loss of life. For visitors staying in shoreline hotels with six or more stories, the safest place to be during a tsunami event is on the third floor or higher. Otherwise, shoreline areas should be evacuated.

Hurricanes are also a threat in Hawai'i. They are rare, but destructive. Most hurricanes originate far to the southeast off the

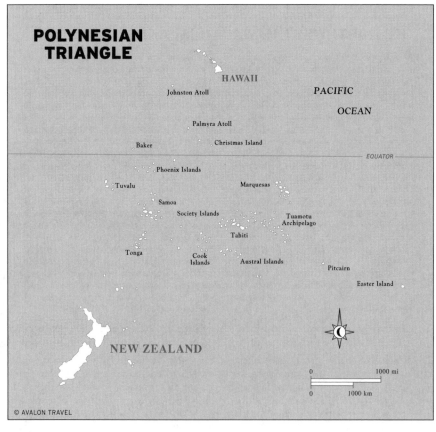

POLYNESIAN TRIANGLE

HAWAII

Johnston Atoll

PACIFIC

OCEAN

Palmyra Atoll

Baker   Christmas Island

EQUATOR

Phoenix Islands

Tuvalu   Marquesas

Samoa

Society Islands   Tuamotu Archipelago

Tahiti

Tonga   Cook Islands   Austral Islands

Pitcairn

Easter Island

NEW ZEALAND

0   1000 mi

0   1000 km

© AVALON TRAVEL

Pacific coast of Mexico and Latin America; some, particularly later in the season, start in the midst of the Pacific Ocean near the equator south of Hawai'i. Hurricane season is generally considered June through November. Most hurricanes pass harmlessly south of Hawai'i, but some, swept along by kona winds, do strike the islands. The most recent and destructive was Hurricane 'Iniki, which battered the islands in 1992, killing eight people and causing an estimated $2 billion in damage. It had its greatest effect on Ni'ihau, the Po'ipu Beach area of Kaua'i, and the leeward coast of O'ahu.

Kona storms are another matter. These subtropical low-pressure storms develop west of the Hawaiian Islands, and as they move east, they draw winds up from the south. Common only in winter, they can cause considerable damage to crops and real estate. There is no real pattern to kona storms. Some years they come every few weeks, whereas in other years they don't appear at all.

O'ahu is equipped islandwide with severe weather warning sirens, which indicate tsunamis, hurricanes, and earthquakes. They are tested at 11am on the first working day of each month. All island telephone books contain a civil defense warning and procedures section with which you should acquaint yourself. Note the maps showing which areas traditionally have been inundated by tsunamis and what procedures to follow in case an emergency occurs.

During tsunami events, boats leave the harbor for safer waters offshore.

Flora and Fauna

The Hawaiian Islands, about 2,500 miles from any continental landfall, are the most isolated landmass on the planet. Spawned from volcanic activity in the middle of the Pacific, the islands were originally devoid of plant or animal life. Over time, as plants, animals, and insects found their way to the islands, they slowly evolved into highly specialized organisms occupying the gamut of each island's microclimates. In Hawai'i, it is not uncommon for a particular plant species only to be found in a single valley across the entire island chain.

The unique plants and animals found only in Hawai'i are known as endemic, those species naturally occurring in Hawai'i but found elsewhere in the world are known as native, and those brought to the islands by people are called introduced species. Introduced species that are fast growing, rapidly increase in number, and easily spread over a region are referred to as invasive species. Invasive species and loss of habitat have been detrimental to the survival of Hawai'i's highly specialized native and endemic flora and fauna. Hawai'i is also known as the endangered species capital of the world, with most of its endemic plants and animals listed as rare and endangered, with many species having already gone extinct. The majority of the remaining pockets of native Hawaiian flora on O'ahu have been relegated to inaccessible valleys and steep mountain cliffs.

INTRODUCED PLANTS

Before settlement, Hawai'i had no fruits, vegetables, coconut palms, edible land animals, conifers, mangroves, or banyans. The early Polynesians brought in 27 varieties of plants that they needed for food and other purposes, like banana, sweet potato, breadfruit, sugarcane, and taro. They also carried along gourds

HURRICANES IN HAWAI'I

A **tropical depression** is a low-pressure system or cyclone with winds below 39 mph. A **tropical storm** is a cyclone with winds 39-73 mph. A **hurricane** is a cyclone with winds over 74 mph. These winds are often accompanied by torrential rains, destructive waves, high water, and storm surges.

The National Weather Service issues a **Hurricane Watch** if hurricane conditions are expected in the area within 36 hours. A **Hurricane Warning** is issued when a hurricane is expected to strike within 24 hours. The state of Hawai'i has an elaborate warning system against natural disasters using sirens high atop poles along many beaches and coastal areas to alert the public of potential or imminent natural disasters, like tsunamis and hurricanes. Over the decades, hurricanes have caused a great deal of property damage, but, thankfully, the loss of life has been minimal.

MAJOR HURRICANES SINCE 1950

- Hurricane Hiki: Occurred in August 1950, on Kaua'i. Resulted in one death.
- Hurricane Nina: Occurred in December 1957, on Kaua'i. No reported damages.
- Hurricane Dot: Occurred in August 1959, on Kaua'i. Resulted in damages of $5.5 million.
- Hurricane Fico: Occurred in July 1978, on the Big Island. No direct damage, since it didn't make landfall.
- Hurricane Iwa: Occurred in November 1982, on Kaua'i and O'ahu. Resulted in one death and $234 million of damage.
- Hurricane Estelle: Occurred in July 1986, on Maui and the Big Island. Resulted in $2 million of damage.
- Hurricane 'Iniki: Occurred in September 1992, on Kaua'i and O'ahu. Resulted in eight deaths and caused $1.9 billion of damage.

to use as containers, 'awa to make a basic intoxicant, and the *ti* plant to use for offerings or to string into hula skirts. About 90 percent of plants on the Hawaiian Islands today were introduced after Captain Cook first set foot here. Non-Hawaiian settlers over the years have brought mangoes, papayas, passion fruit, pineapples, and the other tropical fruits and vegetables associated with the islands. Also, most of the flowers, including protea, plumeria, anthuriums, orchids, heliconia, ginger, and most hibiscus, have come from every continent on earth. Tropical America, Asia, Java, India, and China have contributed their most beautiful and delicate blooms.

TREES

Koa and *'ohi'a* are two endemic Hawaiian trees still seen on O'ahu. Both have been greatly reduced by the foraging of introduced cattle and goats, and through logging and forest fires. The *koa* (*Acacia koa*) is Hawai'i's finest native tree. It can grow to more than 70 feet high and has a strong, straight trunk, which can measure more than 10 feet in circumference. The Hawaiians used *koa* as the main log for their dugout canoes, and elaborate ceremonies were performed when a log was cut and dragged to a canoe shed. *Koa* wood was also preferred for paddles, spears, and even surfboards. Today it is still considered an excellent furniture wood. To protect fine specimens found in reserves, *koa* is now being grown on plantations for future harvesting for commercial purposes.

The *'ohi'a* (*Metrosideros polymorpha*) is a survivor and a pioneer plant, one of the first types of plants to colonize lava flows. It is the most abundant of all the native Hawaiian trees. Coming in a variety of shapes and sizes, it grows as miniature trees in wet bogs or as 100-foot giants on cool slopes at higher elevations. The *'ohi'a* produces a tuft-like flower—usually red, but occasionally orange, yellow, or white, the latter being very rare and elusive—that resembles a bottlebrush. The flower was considered sacred to Pele; it was said that she would cause a rainstorm if 'ohi'a blossoms were picked without the proper prayers. The flowers

© KEVIN WHITTON

Ti was one of the 28 plants Polynesian settlers brought to Hawai'i in their canoes.

were fashioned into lei that resembled feather boas. The strong, hard wood was used to make canoes, poi bowls, and especially for temple images. *'Ohi'a* logs were also used as railroad ties and shipped to the mainland from the Big Island. It's believed that the "golden spike" linking rail lines between the U.S. East and West Coasts was driven into an *'ohi'a* log from the Big Island when the two railroads came together in Ogden, Utah.

MARINE LIFE

Although decades of overfishing have taken their toll on the marine life along O'ahu's reefs, entire populations of reef dwellers are bouncing back in specific locations thanks to managed Marine Protected Areas. **Hanauma Bay,** the **Waikiki Marine Life Conservation District,** and the **Pupukea-Waimea Marine Life Conservation District** are protected and managed no-take zones designed to give all types of marine species an environment and promote reef health and bolster populations

of reef-dwelling species. In turn, these healthy areas allow populations of fish to grow rapidly and reproduce in exponentially larger numbers, spilling over into unprotected waters and benefiting species higher up the food chain. Hawai'i has over 200 species of native fish.

Whales and dolphins are also common in Hawaiian waters. The most famous whale, and commonly seen, is the North Pacific humpback, but others include the sperm, killer, false killer, pilot, Cuvier's, Blainsville, and pygmy killer. There are technically no porpoises, but dolphins include the common, bottlenose, white-sided, broad- and slender-beaked, and rough-toothed. Small and sleek spinner dolphins are the ones you'll often see near the shore. The mahimahi, a favorite food fish found on many menus, is commonly referred to as dolphin fish but is unrelated and is a true fish, not a cetacean.

The **Hawaiian monk seal** is one of only two mammals native to Hawai'i (the Hawaiian hoary bat is the other). These curious seals are critically endangered and protected by law. Monk seals frequently relax on the beach and have a nap in the sun. If you see a monk seal, give it ample space and do not disturb or touch the seal in any way. Green sea turtles are also common along O'ahu's shorelines and share the endangered designation. Also protected, they should be given the same respect as the seals.

BIRDS

Due to the lack of native mammals and reptiles in pre-contact Hawai'i, native birds flourished, becoming widespread and highly specialized. Not to mention, they were able to feast on over 10,000 species of native insects. However, one of the great tragedies of natural history is the continuing demise of Hawaiian birdlife. Perhaps only 15 original species of birds remain of the more than 70 native families that thrived before the coming of humans. Since the arrival of Captain Cook in 1778, 23 species have become extinct, with 31 more in danger. And what's not known is how many species were wiped out before white explorers arrived. Experts believe that the Hawaiians annihilated about 40 species, including seven species of geese, a rare one-legged owl, ibis, lovebirds, sea eagles, and honeycreepers— all gone before Captain Cook showed up. Hawai'i's endangered birds account for 40 percent of the birds officially listed as endangered or threatened by the U.S. Fish and Wildlife Service. Almost all of O'ahu's native birds are gone, and few indigenous Hawaiian birds can be found on any island below the 3,000-foot level.

The shores around O'ahu, especially those off Koko Head, Ka'ena Point, and on the tiny islets of Moku Manu, Manana, and others on the windward side are home to thriving colonies of marine birds. On these diminutive islands it's quite easy to spot several birds from the tern family, including the white, gray, and sooty tern. Along with the terns are shearwaters and enormous Laysan albatross with its seven-foot wingspan. Tropicbirds, with their lovely streamer-like tails, are often seen along the windward coast.

THE ALL-PURPOSE KUKUI TREE

Reaching heights of 80 feet, the *kukui* (candlenut) tree was a veritable department store to the Hawaiians, who made use of almost every part of this utilitarian giant. Its nuts, bark, or flowers were ground into potions and salves to be taken as a general tonic, applied to ulcers and cuts as an effective antibiotic, or administered internally as a cure for constipation or asthma attacks. The bark was mixed with water, and the resulting juice was used as a dye in tattooing, tapa-cloth making, and canoe painting, and as a preservative for fishnets. The oily nuts were burned in stone holders as a light source, and they were ground and eaten as a condiment called *'inamona*. Polished nuts took on a beautiful sheen and were strung as lei. Finally, the wood was hollowed into canoes and used as fishnet floats.

If you're lucky, you can also catch a glimpse of the **pueo** (Hawaiian owl) in the mountainous areas of Wai'anae and the Ko'olau Range. Also, along trails and deep in the forest from Tantalus to the Wai'anae Range you can sometimes see elusive birds like the *'elepaio, 'amakihi,* and the fiery red *'i'iwi.* The *'amakihi* and *'i'iwi* are endemic birds not endangered at the moment. The **'amakihi** is one of the most common native birds; yellowish-green, it frequents the high branches of the *'ohi'a, koa,* and sandalwood trees looking for insects, nectar, or fruit. It is less specialized than most other Hawaiian birds, the main reason for its continued existence. The *'i'iwi,* a bright red bird with a salmon-colored, hooked bill, is found in the forests above 2,000 feet. **'apapane** is abundant in Hawai'i, and being the most common native bird, is the easiest to see. It's a chubby, red-bodied bird about five inches long with a black bill, legs, wingtips, and tail feathers.

O'ahu's exotic birds are the most common in the beach parks and in urban areas: black myna birds with their sassy yellow eyes are common mimics around town; sparrows, introduced to Hawai'i through O'ahu in the 1870s, are everywhere; and munia, first introduced as caged birds from Southeast Asia, have escaped and can be found almost anywhere around the island.

O'ahu is also home to several game birds found mostly in the dry upland forests. These include three varieties of dove, the Japanese quail, both the green and ring-necked pheasant, and Erckel's francolin.

INTRODUCED ANIMALS

Almost all of the mammals on O'ahu are introduced, and many have had severe and detrimental consequences for Hawai'i's natural environment and native species. Rats, mice, and mongooses thrive on O'ahu and are responsible for disease and the decline of ground nesting bird populations. Feral ungulates like pigs and goats destroy native forests as they root up and eat vegetation, creating fetid pools of water where mosquitoes thrive, contributing to

© KEVIN WHITTON

Hawaiian monk seal

the decline of forest bird populations through disease. In years past, grazing cattle was responsible for the deforestation of watersheds that led to landslides. Geckos, anoles, and chameleons are a few of the introduced reptiles that are common on O'ahu.

History

HAWAI'I'S SETTLERS

The great "deliberate migrations" from the southern Pacific islands seem to have taken place AD 500-800, though the exact date is highly contested by experts. It's generally agreed that the first planned migrations were from the violent cannibalistic islands called the Marquesas, 11 islands in extreme eastern Polynesia. The islands themselves are harsh and inhospitable, breeding toughness into the people that enabled them to withstand the hardships of long, unsure ocean voyages and years of resettlement. They were masters at building great double-hulled canoes with the two hulls fastened together to form a catamaran, and a hut in the center provided shelter in bad weather. The average voyaging canoe was 60-80 feet long and could comfortably hold an extended family of about 30 people. These small family bands carried all the staples they would need in the new lands.

For five centuries the Marquesans settled here and lived peacefully on the new land. The tribes coexisted in relative harmony, especially because there was no competition for land. Cannibalism died out. There was much coming and going between Hawai'i and Polynesia as new people came to the settlement over the course of hundreds of years. Then, it appears that in the 12th century a deliberate exodus of warlike Tahitians arrived and subjugated the islanders. This incursion had a terrific significance on the Hawaiian religious and social system. The warlike god Ku and the rigid *kapu* system were introduced, through which the new rulers became dominant. Voyages between Tahiti and Hawai'i continued for about 100 years, and Tahitian customs, legends, and language became the Hawaiian way of life. Then suddenly, for no recorded or apparent reason, the voyages discontinued and Hawai'i returned to total isolation.

CAPTAIN COOK

The islands remained forgotten for almost 500 years until the indomitable English seafarer, Captain James Cook, sighted O'ahu on January 18, 1778, and stepped ashore at Waimea on Kaua'i two days later. At that time Hawai'i's isolation was so complete that even the Polynesians had forgotten about it. The Englishmen had arrived aboard the 100-foot flagship HMS *Resolution* and its 90-foot companion HMS *Discovery*. The first trade was some brass medals for a mackerel. Cook provisioned his ships by exchanging chisels for hogs, while common sailors gleefully traded nails for sex. Landing parties were sent inland to fill casks with freshwater. After a brief stop on Ni'ihau, the ships sailed away, but both groups were indelibly impressed with the memory of each other.

Almost a year later, when winter weather forced Cook to return from the coast of Alaska, the *Discovery* and *Resolution* found safe anchorage at Kealakekua Bay on the kona coast of the Big Island on January 16, 1779. By the coincidence of his second arrival with religious festivities, the Hawaiians mistook Cook to be the return of the god Lono. After an uproarious welcome and generous hospitality for over a month, it became obvious that the newcomers were beginning to overstay their welcome. During the interim a sailor named William Watman died, convincing the Hawaiians that the *haole* were indeed mortals, not gods. Inadvertently, many *kapu* were broken by the English, and once-friendly relations became strained. Finally, the ships sailed away on February 4, 1779.

After plying terrible seas for only a week, *Resolution*'s foremast was badly damaged. Cook sailed back into Kealakekua Bay, dragging the mast ashore on February 13. The natives, now totally hostile, hurled rocks at the sailors. Confrontations increased when some Hawaiians stole a small boat and Cook's men set after them, capturing the fleeing canoe, which held an *ali'i* named Palea. The Englishmen treated him roughly, so the Hawaiians furiously attacked the mariners, who abandoned the small boat.

Next, the Hawaiians stole a small cutter from the *Discovery* that had been moored to a buoy and partially sunk to protect it from the sun. For the first time, Captain Cook became furious. He ordered Captain Clerk of the *Discovery* to sail to the southeast end of the bay and stop any canoe trying to leave Kealakekua. Cook then made a fatal error in judgment. He decided to take nine armed mariners ashore in an attempt to convince the venerable King Kalani'opu'u to accompany him back aboard ship, where he would hold him for ransom in exchange for the cutter. The old king agreed, but his wife prevailed upon him not to trust the *haole*. Kalani'opu'u sat down on the beach to think while the tension steadily grew.

Meanwhile, a group of mariners fired on a canoe trying to leave the bay, and a lesser chief, No'okemai, was killed. The crowd around Cook and his men reached an estimated 20,000, and warriors outraged by the killing of the chief armed themselves with clubs and protective straw-mat armor. One bold warrior advanced on Cook and struck him with his *pahoa* (dagger). In retaliation Cook drew a tiny pistol lightly loaded with shot and fired at the warrior. His bullets spent themselves on the straw armor and fell harmlessly to the ground. The Hawaiians went wild. Lieutenant Molesworth Phillips, in charge of the nine mariners, began a withering fire; Cook killed two natives.

Overpowered by sheer numbers, the sailors headed for boats standing offshore, while Lieutenant Phillips lay wounded. It is believed that Captain Cook stood helplessly in knee-deep water instead of making for the boats because he could not swim. Hopelessly surrounded, he was knocked on the head, then countless warriors passed a knife around and hacked and mutilated his lifeless body. A sad Lieutenant King lamented in his diary, "Thus fell our great and excellent commander."

UNIFICATION OF THE HAWAIIAN ISLANDS

In the 1780s the islands were roughly divided into three kingdoms: Kalani'opu'u ruled Hawai'i and the Hana district of Maui; wily and ruthless warrior-king Kahekili ruled Maui, Kaho'olawe, Lana'i, and later O'ahu; and Kaeo, Kahekili's brother, ruled Kaua'i. War ravaged the land until a remarkable chief, Kamehameha, rose and subjugated all the islands under one rule. Kamehameha initiated a dynasty that would last for about 100 years, until the independent monarchy of Hawai'i forever ceased to be.

Hawai'i under Kamehameha was ready to enter its "golden age." The social order was medieval, with the *ali'i* as knights, owing their military allegiance to the king, and the serf-like *maka'ainana* paying tribute and working the lands. The priesthood of *kahuna* filled the posts of advisors, sorcerers, navigators, doctors, and historians. This was Polynesian Hawai'i at its apex. But like the uniquely Hawaiian silversword plant, the old culture blossomed, and as soon as it did, it began to wither. Ever since, all that was purely Hawaiian has been supplanted by the relentless foreign influences that began bearing down upon it.

MISSIONARIES AND WHALERS

Kamehameha was as gentle in victory as he was ferocious in battle. Under his rule, which lasted until his death on May 8, 1819, Hawai'i enjoyed a peace unlike any the warring islands had ever known. However, the year 1819 was of the utmost significance in Hawaiian history. With the death of Kamehameha came the overthrow of the ancient *kapu* system, the arrival of the first whalers in Lahaina, and the departure of Calvinist missionaries from New England

determined to convert the heathen islanders. Great changes began to rattle the old order to its foundations. With the *kapu* system and all of the ancient gods abandoned (except for the fire goddess Pele of Kilauea), a great void opened the souls of the Hawaiians. In the coming decades Hawai'i, also coveted by Russia, France, and England, was finally consumed by America. The islands had the first American school, printing press, and newspaper west of the Mississippi. Lahaina, in its heyday, became the world's greatest whaling port, accommodating more than 500 ships of all types during its peak years.

In 1823, the first mission was established in Lahaina, Maui, under the pastorate of Reverend Richards and his wife. Within a few years, many of the notable *ali'i* had been, at least in appearance, converted to Christianity. By 1828 the cornerstones for Waine'e Church, the first stone church on the island, were laid just behind the palace of Kamehameha III.

THE GREAT MAHELE

In 1840, after moving the royal court to Honolulu, the new center of commerce in the islands, Kamehameha III ended his autocratic rule and instituted a constitutional monarchy. This brought about the Hawaiian Bill of Rights, but the most far-reaching change was the transition to private ownership of land, known as The Great Mahele. Formerly, all land belonged to the ruling chief, who gave wedge-shaped parcels called *ahupua'a* to lesser chiefs to be worked for him. The commoners did all the real labor, their produce heavily taxed by the *ali'i*. The fortunes of war, the death of a chief, or the mere whim of a superior could force a commoner off the land.

The Hawaiians, however, could not think in terms of owning land. No one could *possess* land, one could only *use* land, and its ownership was a foreign concept. As a result, naive Hawaiians gave up their lands for a song to unscrupulous traders, and land ownership issues remain a basic and unrectified problem to this day. In 1847 Kamehameha III and his advisors separated the lands of Hawai'i into three groupings: crown land (belonging to the king), government land (belonging to the chiefs), and the people's land (the largest parcels). In 1848, 245 *ali'i* entered their land claims in the *Mahele Book,* assuring them ownership. In 1850 the commoners were given title in fee simple to the lands they cultivated and lived on as tenants, not including house lots in towns. Commoners without land could buy small *kuleana* (farms) from the government at 50 cents per acre. In 1850, foreigners were also allowed to purchase land in fee simple, and the ownership of Hawai'i from that day forward slipped steadily from the hands of its indigenous people.

THE END OF A KINGDOM

Like the Hawaiian people themselves, the Kamehameha dynasty in the mid-1800s was dying from within. King Kamehameha IV (Alexander Liholiho) ruled 1854-1863; his only child died in 1862. He was succeeded by his older brother Kamehameha V (Lot Kamehameha), who ruled until 1872. With his passing the Kamehameha line ended. William Lunalilo, elected king in 1873 by popular vote, was of royal lineage, but not of the Kamehameha bloodline. He died after only a year in office, and being a bachelor, he left no heirs. He was succeeded by David Kalakaua, known far and wide as the "Merrie Monarch," who made a world tour and was well received wherever he went. He built 'Iolani Palace in Honolulu and was personally in favor of closer ties with the United States, helping to push through the Reciprocity Act. Kalakaua died in 1891 and was replaced by his sister, Lydia Lili'uokalani, last of the Hawaiian monarchs.

REVOLUTION AND ANNEXATION

When Lili'uokalani took office in 1891, the native population was at a low of 40,000, and she felt that the United States had too much influence over her homeland. She was known to personally favor the English over the Americans. She attempted to replace the liberal constitution of 1887 (adopted by her pro-American brother) with an autocratic mandate in which she would have had much more political and economic control of the islands.

When the McKinley Tariff of 1890 brought a decline in sugar profits, she made no attempt to improve the situation. Thus, the planters saw her as a political obstacle to their economic growth; most of Hawai'i's American planters and merchants were in favor of a rebellion. A central spokesperson and firebrand was Lorrin Thurston, a Honolulu publisher who, with a core of about 30 men, challenged the Hawaiian monarchy. Although Lili'uokalani rallied some support and had a small military potential in her personal guard, the coup was relatively bloodless—it took only one casualty. Naturally, the conspirators could not have succeeded without some solid assurances from a secret contingent in the U.S. Congress as well as outgoing President Benjamin Harrison, who favored Hawai'i's annexation. Marines from the *Boston* went ashore to "protect American lives," and on January 17, 1893, the Hawaiian monarchy came to an end.

Sanford B. Dole, who became president of the Hawaiian Republic, headed the provisional government. Lili'uokalani surrendered not to the conspirators, but to U.S. Ambassador John Stevens. She believed that the U.S. government, which had assured her of Hawaiian independence, would be outraged by the overthrow and would come to her aid. Incoming President Grover Cleveland *was* outraged, and Hawai'i wasn't immediately annexed as expected.

In January 1895, a small, ill-fated counterrevolution headed by Lili'uokalani failed, and she was placed under house arrest in 'Iolani Palace. Officials of the Republic insisted that she use her married name (Mrs. John Dominis) to sign the documents forcing her to abdicate her throne. She was also forced to swear allegiance to the new Republic. Lili'uokalani went on to write *Hawaii's Story* and the lyric ballad "Aloha O'e." She never forgave the conspirators and remained queen in the minds of Hawaiians until her death in 1917.

On July 7, 1898, President McKinley signed

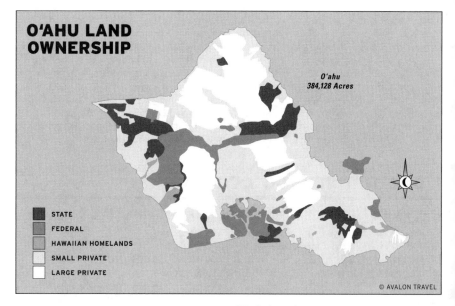

O'AHU LAND OWNERSHIP

O'ahu 384,128 Acres

- STATE
- FEDERAL
- HAWAIIAN HOMELANDS
- SMALL PRIVATE
- LARGE PRIVATE

© AVALON TRAVEL

the annexation agreement, arguing that the U.S. military must have Hawai'i in order to be a viable force in the Pacific.

PEARL HARBOR ATTACK

On the morning of December 7, 1941, the Japanese carrier *Akagi,* flying the battle flag of Admiral Togo of Russo-Japanese War fame, received and broadcast over its public address system island music from Honolulu station KGMB. Deep in the bowels of the ship a radio operator listened for a much different message, coming thousands of miles from the Japanese mainland. When the ironically poetic message "east wind rain" was received, the attack was launched. At the end of the day, 2,325 U.S. soldiers and 57 civilians were dead; 188 planes were destroyed; 18 major warships were sunk or heavily damaged; and the United States was engaged in World War II. Japanese casualties were ludicrously light. The ignited conflict would rage for four years until Japan, through the atomic bombing of Nagasaki and Hiroshima, was brought into total submission. By the end of hostilities, Hawai'i would never again be considered separate from America.

Statehood

Several economic and political motivations explain why the ruling elite of Hawai'i desired statehood, but put simply, the vast majority of people who lived there, especially after World War II, considered themselves Americans. The first serious mention of making the Hawaiian Islands a state was in the 1850s under President Franklin Pierce, but the idea wasn't taken seriously until the monarchy was overthrown in the 1890s. For the next 50 years statehood proposals were made repeatedly to Congress, but there was stiff opposition, especially from the southern states. With Hawai'i a territory, an import quota system beneficial to mainland producers could be enacted on produce, especially sugar. Also, there was prejudice against creating a state in a place where the majority of the populace was not white.

During World War II, Hawai'i was placed under martial law, but no serious attempt to confine the Japanese population was made, as it was in California. There were simply too many Japanese, and many went on to gain the respect of the American people through their outstanding fighting record during the war. Hawai'i's own 100th Battalion became the famous 442nd Regimental Combat Team, which gained notoriety by saving the Lost Texas Battalion during the Battle of the Bulge and went on to be *the* most decorated battalion in all of World War II. When these GIs returned home, *no one* was going to tell them that they were not loyal Americans. Many of these Americans of Japanese Ancestry (AJAs) took advantage of the GI Bill and received higher education. They were from the common people, not the elite, and they rallied grassroots support for statehood. When the vote finally occurred, approximately 132,900 voted in favor of statehood with only 7,800 votes against. Congress passed the Hawaii State Bill on March 12, 1959, and on August 21, 1959, President Eisenhower announced that Hawai'i was officially the 50th state.

Government and Economy

GOVERNMENT

There are only two levels of government in the state of Hawai'i: the state and the county. With no town or city governments to deal with, considerable bureaucracy is eliminated. Hawai'i, in anticipation of becoming a state, drafted a constitution in 1950 and was ready to go when statehood came. Politics and government are taken seriously in the Aloha State, which at one time consistently turned in the best national voting record per capita. These days, residents give greater importance to and show greater turnout for state elections. In the election to ratify statehood, hardly a ballot went uncast, with 95 percent of the voters opting for statehood. The bill carried every island of Hawai'i except Ni'ihau, where most of the people (total population 250 or so) are of relatively pure Hawaiian blood.

When Hawai'i became a state, Honolulu became its capital. Since statehood, the Democratic Party has dominated the legislative and executive branches of state government. Breaking a 40-year Democratic hold on power in the state and becoming the first woman to hold the position, former Maui mayor and Republican Linda Lingle was elected as governor in 2002 and reelected in 2006. Governor Neil Abercrombie (D) holds the office in 2013. Two senators, currently Mazie Hirono (D) and Brian Schatz (D), and two representatives, currently Colleen Hanabusa (D) and Tulsi Gabbard (D), represent Hawai'i in the U.S Congress.

City and County of Honolulu

O'ahu has been the center of government for about 160 years, since King Kamehameha III permanently established the royal court here in the 1840s. In 1879-1882, King David Kalakaua built 'Iolani Palace as the central showpiece of the island kingdom. Lili'uokalani, the last Hawaiian monarch, lived in the nearby residence Washington Place after her dethronement. While Hawai'i was a territory, and for a few years after it became a state, the palace was used as the capitol building, with the governor residing in Washington Place. Modern O'ahu, besides being the center of state government, governs itself as the City and County of Honolulu. The county covers not only the entire island of O'ahu, but also all the far-flung Northwestern Islands except for Midway, which is under federal jurisdiction.

The island of O'ahu houses three times as many people as the other islands combined. Nowhere is this more evident than in the representation of O'ahu in the bicameral state legislature. O'ahu claims 18 of the 25 state senators and 35 of the 51 state representatives. These lopsided figures make it obvious that O'ahu has plenty of clout, especially the Honolulu urban districts, which elect more than 50 percent of O'ahu's representatives. Frequent political battles ensue because what's good for the City and

County of Honolulu isn't always good for the rest of the state. More often than not, the political moguls of Oʻahu, backed by huge business interests, prevail.

Like the rest of the state, the voters on the island of Oʻahu are principally Democratic in orientation, but not in as great a percentage as on the other islands. The mayor in 2013 is Peter Carlisle (D). An elected county council consisting of nine members, one from each council district around the island, assists him. The Oʻahu state senators are overwhelmingly Democrats. Democratic state representatives also outnumber Republicans, but not by quite as huge a margin. For more information about the City and County of Honolulu, visit www.honolulu.gov.

ECONOMY

Hawaiʻi's mid-Pacific location makes it perfect for two primary sources of income: tourism and the military. Tourists come in anticipation of endless golden days on soothing beaches, while the military is provided with a strategic global position. Each economic sector nets Hawaiʻi billions annually. Also contributing to the state revenue are manufacturing, construction, and agriculture.

Economically, Oʻahu dwarfs the rest of the islands combined. A huge military presence, an international airport that receives the lion's share of visitors, and, unbelievably, half of the state's best arable land keep Oʻahu the leader in revenue. The famous "Big Five" and other major businesses all maintain their corporate offices in downtown Honolulu, from which they oversee vast holdings throughout Hawaiʻi and the mainland. The Big Five—C. Brewer and Co., Theo. H. Davies & Co., Amfac Inc., Castle and Cooke Inc. (Dole), and Alexander and Baldwin Inc., historically Hawaiʻi's major economic powerhouses—controlled the economic lifeblood of the islands through their web of subsidiary corporations and holding companies and for all practical purposes controlled politics on the islands through their influence in government until World War II. Based in about the same spots as when their founders helped overthrow the monarchy, they're still going strong, whereas the old royalty of Hawaiʻi has vanished.

Tourism

The flow of visitors to Oʻahu has gone on unabated ever since tourism outstripped sugar and pineapples in the early 1960s as Hawaiʻi's top moneymaker. Visitor expenditures bring in over 11 billion a year, and this is only the amount that can be directly related to the hotel and restaurant trades. Of the more than seven million people who visit the state yearly, more than half stay on Oʻahu. On any given day, Oʻahu plays host to about 90,000 visitors. And nearly all of the state's visitors at least pass through Oʻahu. While many travel to Hawaiʻi with a group or on a package tour, independent travelers make up the majority of the state's visitors. Hotels directly employ more than 16,000 workers, nearly half the state's total, not including all the shop assistants, food servers, taxi drivers, and everyone else needed to ensure a carefree vacation. Of the state's 77,000 accommodation units, Oʻahu claims 35,000; of those, about 29,000 are in Waikiki. The Oʻahu hotels consistently have some of the highest occupancy rates in the state, hovering around 81 percent. In contrast, the average daily room rate is the lowest in the state, making accommodations on Oʻahu slightly more of a bargain than on the other islands. The visitor industry generates more than $11 billion in annual revenue.

The Military

Hawaiʻi is the most militarized state in the United States, and all five services are represented on Oʻahu. Based in Honolulu, USPACOM (U.S. Pacific Command) is one of six U.S. Unified Combat Commands of the armed forces, which is responsible for more than 50 percent of the earth's surface, from California to the east coast of Africa and to both poles. The U.S. military presence dates back to 1887, when Pearl Harbor was given to the navy as part of the Sugar Reciprocity Treaty.

About 325,000 military and civilian

personnel are assigned to USPACOM. The U.S. Marine Corps has about 85,000 personnel, the U.S. Air Force has roughly 40,000, the Army has 60,000, and the Coast Guard has 27,000. The combined services are one of the largest landholders, with more than 238,000 acres, accounting for 6 percent of Hawaiian land. The two major holdings are the 100,000-acre Pohakuloa Training Area on Hawai'i and 81,000 acres on O'ahu, which is a full 21 percent of the island. The Army controls 63 percent of the military lands, followed by the Navy at 22 percent, the Marines with 11 percent, and the remainder goes to the Air Force and a few small installations to the Coast Guard.

Agriculture

You'd think that with all the people living on O'ahu, coupled with the constant land development, there'd hardly be any room left for things to grow, but that's not the case. The land is productive, although definitely stressed.

Although O'ahu has the smallest average size of farm in the state, it still manages to produce a considerable amount of pineapples and the many products of diversified agriculture and floriculture. Pineapples cover 9,100 acres, with the biggest holdings in the Leilehua Plateau belonging to Dole, a subsidiary of Castle and Cooke. As a result of demand and diversification, O'ahu now also raises a variety of organic greens, freshwater shrimp, coffee, and flowers. Only about 100 acres have been put into coffee, the smallest acreage of any of the islands—on land between Wahiawa and Hale'iwa—but this land produces a respectable 50,000 pounds per year. In the hills, entrepreneurs raise *pakalolo,* or marijuana, which has become one of the state's most productive cash crops. O'ahu is also a huge agricultural consumer, demanding more than four times more vegetables, fruits, meats, and poultry to feed its citizens and visitors than the remainder of the state combined.

People and Culture

POPULATION

Of the nearly 1.4 million people that reside in Hawai'i, 963,607 live on O'ahu, with slightly less than half of these living in the Honolulu metropolitan area. Statewide, city dwellers outnumber those living in the country by nine to one. For the island of O'ahu, 96 percent of the population is urban, whereas only 4 percent live rurally. O'ahu's population accounts for 70 percent of the state's population, yet the island comprises only 9 percent of the state's land total. Sections of Waikiki can have a combined population of permanent residents and visitors as high as 90,000 per square mile, making cities like Tokyo, Hong Kong, and New York seem roomy by comparison. The good news is that O'ahu *expects* all these people and knows how to accommodate them comfortably.

About 400,000 people live in greater Honolulu, the built-up area from 'Aiea to Koko Head. The next most populous urban centers after Honolulu are the Kailua/Kane'ohe area on the windward side with about 100,000 residents, Mililani and Wahiawa on the Leilehua Plateau with about the same number, followed by Pearl City and Waipahu with a combined total of about 70,000 or so. The strip of towns on the leeward coast, including Wai'anae, totals about 40,000 inhabitants. Since 2000, Mililani and 'Ewa have had the greatest increase in population.

PEOPLE

Nowhere else on Earth can you find such a kaleidoscopic mixture of people as in Hawai'i. Every major race is accounted for, and more than 50 ethnic groups are represented throughout the islands, making Hawai'i the most racially integrated state in the country. Ethnic breakdowns for the state include 25.3 percent Hawaiian/part Hawaiian, 20.5 percent Caucasian, 18.4 percent Japanese, 10 percent

Filipino, 8.9 percent Hispanic/Latino, and 4.2 percent Chinese. These statistics mirror the population demographics on O'ahu very closely.

Of the major ethnic groups you'll find the Hawaiians clustered around Wai'anae and on the windward coast in Waimanalo and near Waiahole; Caucasians tend to be in Wahiawa, the North Shore, around Koko Head, in Waikiki, and in Kailua/Kane'ohe; those of Japanese ancestry prefer the valleys heading toward the *pali,* including Kalihi, Nu'uanu, and Tantalus; Filipinos live just east of the airport, in downtown Honolulu, and in Wahiawa; the Chinese are in Chinatown and around the Diamond Head area. Of the minor ethnic groups, the highest concentration of African Americans is around Schofield Barracks; Samoans live with the Hawaiians in Wai'anae and the windward coastal towns, although they are most concentrated in downtown Honolulu; Koreans and Vietnamese are scattered here and there, but mostly in Honolulu.

Ni'ihau, a privately owned island, is home to about 160 pure-blooded Hawaiians, representing the largest concentration of Hawaiians, per capita, in the islands. The Robinson family, which owns the island, restricts visitors to invited guests only. The second largest concentration is on Moloka'i, where 2,700 Hawaiians, living mostly on a 40-acre *kuleana* of Hawaiian Home Lands, make up 40 percent of that island's population. The majority of mixed-blood Hawaiians, 240,000 or so, live on O'ahu, where they are particularly strong in the hotel and entertainment fields.

Native Hawaiians

When Captain Cook first sighted Hawai'i in 1778, there were an estimated 300,000 natives living in relative harmony with their ecological surroundings; within 100 years a scant 50,000 Hawaiians remained. Today, although more than 240,000 people claim varying degrees of Hawaiian blood, experts say that fewer than 1,000 are pure Hawaiian.

Ancient Hawaiian society was divided into rankings by a strict caste system determined by birth, and from which there was no chance of escaping. The highest rank was the *ali'i,* the chiefs and royalty. The impeccable genealogies of the *ali'i* were traced back to the gods themselves, and the chants (*mo'o ali'i*) were memorized and sung by a rank of a *ali'i* called *ku'auhau.* Ranking passed from both father and mother, and custom dictated that the first mating of an *ali'i* be with a person of equal status.

A *kahuna* was a highly skilled person whose advice was sought before any major project was undertaken, such as building a house, hollowing a canoe log, or even offering a prayer. The *mo'o kahuna* were the priests of Ku and Lono, and they were in charge of praying and following rituals. They were very powerful *ali'i* and kept strict secrets and laws concerning their various functions.

Besides this priesthood of *kahuna,* there were other *kahuna* who were not *ali'i,* but commoners. The two most important were the healers (*kahuna lapa'au*) and the sorcerers (*kahuna 'ana'ana*) who could pray a person to death. The *kahuna lapa'au* had a marvelous pharmacopoeia of herbs and spices that could cure over 250 diseases common to the Hawaiians.

The common people were called the *maka'ainana,* "the people of land"—the farmers, craftspeople, and fishers. The land they lived on was controlled by the *ali'i,* but they were not bound to it. If the local *ali'i* was cruel or unfair, the *maka'ainana* had the right to leave and reside on another's lands. The *maka'ainana* mostly loved their local *ali'i,* much like a child loves a parent, and the feeling was reciprocated. *Maka'ainana* who lived close to the *ali'i* and could be counted on as warriors in times of trouble were called *kanaka no lua kaua* (a man for the heat of battle). They were treated with greater favor than those who lived in the backcountry, *kanaka no hi'i kua,* whose lesser standing opened them up to discrimination and cruelty. All *maka'ainana* formed extended families called *'ohana* who usually lived on the same section of land, called *ahupua'a.* Those farmers who lived inland would barter their produce with the fishers who lived on the shore, and thus all shared equally in the bounty of land and sea.

A special group called *kauwa* was an untouchable caste confined to living on reservations. Their origins were obviously Polynesian, but they appeared to be descendants of castaways who had survived and became perhaps the aboriginals of Hawai'i before the main migrations. It was *kapu* for anyone to go onto *kauwa* lands; doing so meant instant death. If a human sacrifice was needed, the *kahuna* would simply summon a *kauwa* who had no recourse but to mutely comply. To this day, to call someone *kauwa,* which now supposedly only means servant, is still considered a fight-provoking insult.

Occasionally there were horrible wars, but mostly the people lived quiet and ordered lives based on the strict caste society and the *kapu* system of rigidly observed cultural taboos and laws. Famine was known, but only on a regional level, and the population was kept in check by birth control, crude abortions, and the distasteful practice of infanticide, especially of baby girls. The Hawaiians were absolutely loving and nurturing parents under most circumstances and would even take in *hanai* (an adopted child or oldster), a lovely practice that lingers to this day.

A strict division of labor existed among men and women. Men were the only ones permitted to have anything to do with taro. This crop was so sacred that there were a greater number of *kapu* concerning taro than concerning a man himself. Men pounded poi and served it to the women. Men were also the fishers and the builders of houses, canoes, irrigation ditches, and walls. Women tended to other gardens and shoreline fishing and were responsible for making tapa cloth. The entire family lived in the common house called the *hale noa.*

Certain things were *kapu* between the sexes. Primarily, women could not enter the *mua* (men's eating house), nor could they eat with men. Certain foods, such as pork, coconut, red fish, and bananas were forbidden to women, and it was *kapu* for a man to have intercourse before going fishing, engaging in battle, or attending a religious ceremony. Young boys lived with the women until they underwent a circumcision rite called *pule ipu.* After this was performed, they were required to keep the *kapu* of men. A true Hawaiian settlement required a minimum of five huts: the men's eating hut, women's menstruation hut, women's eating hut, communal sleeping hut, and prayer hut. Without these five separate structures, Hawaiian society could not happen because the *i'a kapu* (forbidden eating between men and women) rules could not be observed.

Ali'i could also declare a *kapu* and often did so. Certain lands or fishing areas were temporarily made *kapu* so that they could be revitalized. Even today, it is *kapu* for anyone to remove all the *'opihi* (a type of limpet) from a rock. The greatest *kapu, kapu moe,* was afforded to the highest-ranking *ali'i:* anyone coming into their presence had to prostrate themselves. Lesser-ranking *ali'i* were afforded the *kapu noho:* lessers had to sit or kneel in their presence. Commoners could not let their shadows fall on an *ali'i,* nor enter the house of an *ali'i* except through a special door. Breaking a *kapu* meant immediate death.

RELIGION

The Polynesian Hawaiians worshipped nature. They saw its forces manifested in a multiplicity of forms to which they ascribed godlike powers, and they based daily life on this animistic philosophy. Handpicked and specially trained storytellers chanted the exploits of the gods. These ancient tales, kept alive in a special oral tradition called *mo'olelo,* were recited only by day. Entranced listeners encircled the chanter; in respect for the gods and in fear of their wrath, they were forbidden to move once the tale was begun.

Any object, animate or inanimate, could be a god. All could be infused with *mana,* especially a dead body or a respected ancestor. *'Ohana* had personal family gods called *'aumakua* on whom they called in times of danger or strife. There were children of gods called *kupua* who were thought to live among humans and were distinguished either for their beauty and strength or for their ugliness and terror. It was told that processions of dead *aliʻi,* called "Marchers of the Night," wandered through the land of the living, and unless you were properly protected, it could mean death if they looked upon you. There were simple ghosts known as *akua lapu* who merely frightened people. Forests, waterfalls, trees, springs, and a thousand forms of nature were the manifestations of *akua liʻi,* "little spirits" who could be invoked at any time for help or protection. It made no difference who or what you were in old Hawaiʻi; the gods were ever present, and they took a direct and active role in your life.

Behind all of these beliefs was an innate sense of natural balance and order. It could be interpreted as positive-negative, yin-yang, life-death, or light-dark, the main idea being that everything had its opposite. The time of darkness when only the gods lived was *po.* When the great gods descended to the earth and created light, this was *ao,* and humanity was born. All of these *moʻolelo* are part of *The Kumulipo,* the great chant that records the Hawaiian version of creation. From the time the gods descended and touched the earth at Ku Moku on Lanaʻi, the genealogies were kept. Unlike in the Bible, these included the noble families of female as well as male *aliʻi.*

Ancient Hawaiians performed religious ceremonies at *heiau,* temples. The basic *heiau* was a masterfully built and fitted rectangular stone wall that varied in size from about as big as a basketball court to as big as a football field. Once the restraining outer walls were built, the interior was backfilled with smaller stones, and the top dressing was expertly laid and then rolled, perhaps with a log, to form a pavement-like surface. All that remains of Hawaiʻi's many *heiau* are the stone platforms or walls. The buildings on them, constructed in perishable wood, leaves, and grass, have long since disappeared.

The Hawaiian people worshiped gods who took the form of idols fashioned from wood, feathers, or stone. The eyes were made from shells, and until these were inlaid, the idol was dormant. The hair used was often human hair, and the arms and legs were usually flexed. The mouth was either gaping or formed a wide figure-eight lying on its side, and more likely than not was lined with glistening dog teeth. Small figures made of woven basketry were expertly covered with feathers. Red and yellow feathers were favorites, taken from specific birds by men whose only work was to roam the forests in search of them.

In the 1820s, missionaries brought Congregational Christianity and the "true path" to heaven to Hawaiʻi, setting out to convert the pagan Hawaiians and "civilize" them. Catholics, Mormons, Adventists, Episcopalians, Unitarians, Christian Scientists, Lutherans, Baptists, Jehovah's Witnesses, the Salvation Army, and every other major and minor denomination of Christianity that followed in their wake brought their own brand of enlightenment. Chinese and Japanese immigrants established major sects of Buddhism, Confucianism, Taoism, and Shintoism. Today, Allah is praised, the Torah is chanted in Jewish synagogues, and nirvana is available at a variety of Hindu temples, even the Church of Scientology is selling books and salvation.

LANGUAGE

In Hawaiʻi, English is the primary language spoken, yet the beat and melody of the local dialect is noticeably different. Hawaiʻi has its own unmistakable linguistic regionalism. The many ethnic people who make up Hawaiʻi have enriched the English spoken with words, expressions, and subtle shades of meaning that are commonly used and understood throughout the islands. The greatest influence on the English spoken here comes from the Hawaiian language, and words such as *aloha, hula, luʻau,* and *lei* are familiarly used and understood by all.

Pidgin

Other migrant peoples, especially the Chinese, Japanese, and Portuguese, influenced the local dialect to such an extent that the simplified plantation lingo they spoke has become known as "pidgin." English is the official language of the state, business, and education, but pidgin is the language of the people. Hawaiian words make up most of pidgin's non-English vocabulary, but it includes a good smattering of Chinese, Japanese, and Samoan as well. The distinctive rising inflection is provided by the melodious Mediterranean lilt of the Portuguese. Pidgin is not a stagnant language. It's kept alive by new slang words introduced by younger generations of speakers. *Maka'ainana* of all socioethnic backgrounds can at least understand pidgin. Most islanders are proud of it, but some consider it a low-class jargon.

Hawaiian

The Hawaiian language sways like a palm tree in a gentle wind. Its words are as melodious as a love song. With its many Polynesian root words easily traced to Indonesian and Malay, Hawaiian is obviously from this same stock. The Hawaiian spoken today is very different from old Hawaiian. Its greatest metamorphosis occurred when the missionaries began to write it down in the 1820s. Still, it nearly vanished. There has been a movement to reestablish the Hawaiian language over the last couple of decades. Not only are courses offered at the University of Hawai'i, but there is also a successful elementary school immersion program in the state, some books are being printed in it, and more and more musicians are performing in Hawaiian.

Hawaiian is, by and large, no longer spoken as a language except on Ni'ihau and in Hawaiian-language immersion classes and family settings; the closest tourists will come to it is in place-names, street names, and words that have become part of common usage, such as *aloha* and *mahalo*. There are sermons in Hawaiian at some local churches. Kawaiaha'o Church in downtown Honolulu is the most famous of these, but each island has its own.

Thanks to the missionaries, the Hawaiian language is rendered phonetically using only 12 letters. They are the five vowels, a-e-i-o-u, sounded as they are in Spanish, and seven consonants, h-k-l-m-n-p-w, sounded exactly as they are in English. Sometimes "w" is pronounced as "v," but this only occurs in the middle of a word and always follows a vowel. A consonant is always followed by a vowel, forming two-letter syllables, but vowels are often found in pairs or even triplets. A slight oddity about Hawaiian is the glottal stop called *'okina*. This is an abrupt break in sound in the middle of a word, such as "oh-oh" in English, and is denoted with a reverse apostrophe ('). A good example is the one in *ali'i* or, even better, the O'ahu town of Ha'iku, which actually means Abrupt Break.

Pronunciation Key

For those unfamiliar with the sounds of Spanish or other Romance languages, the vowels are sounded as follows:

A—pronounced as in "ah" (that feels good!). For example, *tapa* is "tah-pah."

E—short "e" is "eh," as in "pen" or "dent" (thus *hale* is "hah-leh"). Long "e" sounds like "ay" as in "sway" or "day." For example, the Hawaiian goose (*nene*) is a "nay-nay," not a "nee-nee."

I—pronounced "ee" as in "see" or "we" (thus *pali* is pronounced "pah-lee").

O—pronounced as in "no" or "oh," such as "oh-noh" (*ono*).

U—pronounced "oo" as in "do" or "stew." For example, "kah-poo" (*kapu*).

Diphthongs and Stresses

Eight vowel pairs are known as "diphthongs" (ae-ai-ao-au-ei-eu-oi-ou). These are the sounds made by gliding from one vowel to another within a syllable. The stress is placed on the first vowel. In English, examples would be **soil** and **bail**. Common examples in Hawaiian are *lei* and *heiau*.

The best way to learn which syllables are stressed in Hawaiian is by listening closely. It becomes obvious after a while. There are also some vowel sounds that are held longer than others; these can occur at the beginning of a word, such as the first "a" in *"'aina,"* or in the middle of a word, like the first "a" in *lanai*. Again, it's a matter of tuning your ear and paying attention. When written, these stressed vowels, called *kahako*, are noted with a macron, or short line, over them. Such stressed vowels are not indicated in this book.

Many Hawaiian words are commonly used in English, appear in English dictionaries, and therefore would ordinarily be subject to the rules of English grammar. The Hawaiian language, however, does not pluralize nouns by adding an "s"; the singular and plural are differentiated in context. For purposes of this book, and to highlight the Hawaiian culture, the Hawaiian style of pluralization will be followed for common Hawaiian words. The following are some examples of plural Hawaiian nouns treated this way in this book: *haole* (not *haoles*), *kahuna,* lei, and lu'au.

No one is going to give you a hard time if you mispronounce a word. It's good, however, to pay close attention to the pronunciation of street and place-names because many Hawaiian words sound alike; a misplaced vowel here or there could be the difference between getting where you want to go and getting lost.

FOOD

Thanks to Hawai'i's plantation past, immigrants from around the world also brought their cuisine to the islands, and many of the dishes remain local favorites to this day. You'll find Chinese dim sum and bao, char siu stuffed steamed buns called manapua, Korean kimchi, Vietnamese pho, Puerto Rican pasteles, Portuguese malasadas, tonkatsu from Japan, and SPAM, biscuits, and gravy from World War II Americans in ethnic eateries and on menus across O'ahu.

While local Hawaiian food is rooted in Polynesian techniques and flavors, it is also an amalgam of the cuisine from the immigrants who became an integral part of Hawaiian culture. Plate lunches, found mainly at O'ahu's drive-in restaurants (island-style fast food) are served with two scoops of rice, macaroni salad, and a protein including chicken katsu, kalbi, or kalua pork. This affordable and filling meal incorporates Japanese, Korean, American, and Hawaiian cooking. Loco moco is another favorite plate for lunch as well as breakfast: two fried eggs, a hamburger patty

over rice smothered in gravy—talk about East meets West.

The food served at lu'au is very similar to what you'll find at a Hawaiian food restaurant, and there are several staple dishes no matter where you go. Kalua pig is a favorite, a smoky-flavored pulled pork tossed with cabbage. Traditionally, it is cooked in an *imu,* an underground earthen oven. Chicken long rice has bits of thigh meat cooked with ginger, green onions, and long rice noodles in a chicken broth. Lau lau is fish, pork, or chicken wrapped in taro leaves and steamed in *ti* leaves, lomi salmon is raw cubed salmon tossed with tomatoes, onion, and chile peppers, and squid luau is young taro leaves and squid cooked in coconut milk, the end product a tasty dish resembling creamed spinach. *Poke* (pronounced like okay with a p), is a raw fish salad made with ahi tuna, soy sauce (called shoyu in Hawai'i), and sesame oil. There are all different kinds of *poke,* some have onions and seaweed, some are spicy, some are mayonnaise based, and sometimes the fish is replaced with *tako* (octopus). No Hawaiian lu'au is complete without poi, a staple starch made from pounded taro root, and haupia, a coconut milk-based dessert usually served as a congealed pudding.

THE ARTS
Music

Ancient Hawaiians past along stories through chants, in which the emphasis was placed on historical accuracy, not melody. The missionaries were the first to introduce the Hawaiians to melody through Christian hymns, and soon singing became both an individual and group pastime. Early in the 1800s, Spanish vaqueros from California were imported to teach the Hawaiians how to be cowboys. With them came guitars and moody ballads. Immigrants who came along a little later in the 19th century, especially from Portugal, helped create Hawaiian-style music. Their biggest influence was a small, four-stringed instrument called a *braga* or *cavaquinho,* the prototype of the homegrown Hawaiian instrument that became known as the ukulele. Jumping flea, the

O'AHU ARTS AND CULTURE

- **Bishop Museum** (1525 Bernice St., Honolulu, 808/847-3511, www.bishopmuseum.org), the world's *best* museum covering Hawai'i and Polynesia. The displays include exhibits, galleries, archives, demonstrations of Hawaiian crafts, and a planetarium.

- **Hawai'i Craftsmen** (P.O. Box 22145, Honolulu, 808/596-8128, www.hawaiicraftsmen.org). This organization increases awareness of Hawaiian crafts through programs, exhibitions, workshops, lectures, and demonstrations.

- **Honolulu Museum of Art** (900 S. Beretania St., Honolulu, 808/532-8700, www.honoluluacademy.org). This institution collects, preserves, and exhibits works of fine art and offers public art education programs related to its collections as well as tours, classes, lectures, films, and publications.

- **Mayor's Office of Culture and the Arts** (530 S. King St., Rm. 404, Honolulu, 808/523-4674, www1.honolulu.gov/moca), the City and County of Honolulu's official organ for visual and performing arts information islandwide.

- **Pacific Handcrafters Guild** (P.O. Box 29389, Honolulu, 808/254-6788, www.alternative-hawaii.com/profiles/crafters/phg.htm) focuses on developing and preserving handicrafts and fine arts of all mediums. The guild sponsors four major crafts fairs annually.

- **State Foundation on Culture and the Arts** (250 Hotel St., 2nd fl., Honolulu, 808/586-0300, www.hawaii.gov/sfca). Begun by state legislature in 1965 to preserve and promote Hawai'i's diverse cultural, artistic, and historical heritage, the foundation manages grants, maintains programs in folk arts and art in public places, and runs the Hawai'i State Art Museum.

translation of ukulele, is an appropriate name devised by the Hawaiians when they saw how nimble the fingers were as they jumped over the strings. Over many decades, Hawaiian music has evolved through techniques like slack key tuning, the twang and easy slide of the steel guitar, and the smooth falsetto singing that accompanies the relaxed melodies. Today, popular Hawaiian music has fused with the beat of reggae, creating a style of music locally known as jawaiian.

Hula

The hula is more than an ethnic dance; it is the soul of Hawai'i expressed in motion. It began as a form of worship during religious ceremonies and was danced only by highly trained men. It gradually evolved into a form of entertainment, but in no regard was it sexual. It was history portrayed in the performing arts. In the beginning an androgynous deity named Laka descended to earth and taught men how to dance the hula. In time the male aspect of Laka departed for the heavens, but the female aspect remained. The female Laka set up her own special hula *heiau* at Ha'ena on the Na Pali coast of Kaua'i, where it still exists. As time went on women were allowed to learn the hula. Scholars surmise that men became too busy wresting a living from the land to maintain the art form.

Men did retain one type of hula for themselves called *lua*. This was a form of martial art employed in hand-to-hand combat that evolved into a ritualized warfare dance called *hula ku'i*. During the 19th century, the hula almost vanished because the missionaries considered it vile and heathen. King Kalakaua is generally regarded as having saved it during the late 1800s, when he formed his own troupe and encouraged the dancers to learn the old hula. Many of the original dances had been forgotten, but some were retained and are performed to this day.

Today, hula *halau* (schools) are active on every island, teaching hula and keeping the old ways and culture alive. Hula combines the

HAWAIIAN LU'AU

The lu'au is an island institution. Local families have big lu'au for a baby's first birthday, anniversaries, graduations, and family reunions. Commercial operators have packaged the lu'au as nightly dinner and entertainment so visitors can get a glimpse of the tradition and traditional Hawaiian fare—kalua pig, lau lau, chicken long rice, lomi salmon, white rice, and poi. For a fixed price, you can gorge yourself on a tremendous variety of island foods, sample a few island drinks, and have an evening of entertainment as well. Generally, lu'au run from about 5pm to 8:30pm. On your lu'au day, eat a light breakfast and skip lunch.

All commercial lu'au have pretty much the same format, though the types of food and entertainment differ somewhat. The tourist variety of lu'au is a lot of food, a lot of fun, but definitely a show. To have fun at a lu'au you have to get into the swing of things, like the Polynesian Revue. Local performers dance and lead the tourist's hula—the fast version with swaying hips and dramatic lighting—a few wandering troubadours sing Hawaiian standards, and a muscular, sweaty man will swing flaming torches. Some offer an *imu* ceremony where the pig is taken from the covered oven, as well as traditional games, arts, and crafts. Food is usually served buffet-style, although a few do it family-style. Most tourist lu'au have American and Asian dishes for those less adventurous souls.

To cook the pig, the lu'au master starts the *imu* on the morning of the gathering. He lays the hot stones and banana stalks to create an underground oven, which must maintain a perfect 400°F. In one glance, the lu'au master can gauge the weight and fat content of a succulent porker and decide just how long it should be cooked. The water in the leaves covering the pig steams and roasts the meat so that it falls off the bone. Local wisdom has it that "All you can't eat in the *imu* are the hot stones."

---

chanting of the *mele* (story) and is accompanied by traditional instruments like the *ipu* (gourd). Performers spend years perfecting their techniques telling stories through dance. They show off their accomplishments during the fierce competition of the Merrie Monarch Festival in Hilo every April. The winning *halau* is praised and recognized throughout the islands.

Almost every major resort offering entertainment or a lu'au also offers a hula revue. Most times, young island beauties accompanied by proficient local musicians put on a floor show for the tourists. It's entertaining, but it's not traditional hula.

Weaving and Carving

Hawaiians became the best basket makers and mat weavers in all of Polynesia. *Ulana* (woven mats) were made from *lau hala* (pandanus) leaves. Once split, the spine was removed and the leaves stored in large rolls. When needed they were soaked, pounded, and then fashioned into various floor coverings and sleeping mats. Intricate geometrical patterns were woven in, and the edges were rolled and well fashioned. A wide variety of basketry was made from the aerial root *'ie'ie*, and the shapes varied according to use. Some baskets were tall and narrow, some were cones, others were flat like trays, and many were woven around gourds and calabashes.

Wood was a primary material used by Hawaiian artisans. They almost exclusively used *koa* because of its density, strength, and natural luster. It was turned into canoes, woodware, calabashes, and furniture for the *ali'i*. Temple idols were another major product of woodcarving. A variety of stone artifacts were also turned out, including poi pounders, fish sinkers, and small idols.

The most respected artisans in old Hawai'i were the canoe makers. With little more than a stone adze and a pump drill, they built canoes that could carry 200 people and last for generations—sleek, well-proportioned, and infinitely but special lei are highly prized by those who know what to look for. Of the different stringing styles, the most common is *kui*—stringing the flower through the middle or side. Most "airport-quality" lei are of this type. The *humuhumu* style, reserved for making flat lei, is made by sewing flowers and ferns to a *ti,* banana, or sometimes *hala* leaf. A *humuhumu* lei makes an excellent hatband. *Wili* is the winding together of greenery, ferns, and flowers into short, bouquet-type lengths. The most traditional form is *hili,* which requires no stringing at all but involves braiding fragrant ferns and leaves such as *maile.* If flowers are interwoven, the *hili* becomes the *haku* style, the most difficult and most beautiful type of lei.

Every major island is symbolized by its own lei made from a distinctive flower, shell, or fern. Each island has its own official color as well, although it doesn't necessarily correspond to the color of the island's lei. O'ahu, "The Gathering Place," is symbolized by yellow, the color of the tropical sun. Its flower is the delicate *'ilima,* which ranges in color from pastel yellow to a burnt orange. The blooms are about as large as a silver dollar, and lei made from *'ilima* were at one time reserved only for the *ali'i,* designating them as a royal flower.

The highly refined art of featherwork was practiced only on the islands of Tahiti, New Zealand, and Hawai'i, but the fashioning of feather helmets and idols was unique to Hawai'i. Favorite colors were red and yellow, which came only in a very limited supply from a small number of birds such as the *'o'o, 'i'iwi, mamo,* and *'apapane.* Professional bird hunters in old Hawai'i paid their taxes to *ali'i* in prized feathers. The feathers were fastened to a woven net of *olona* cord and made into helmets, idols, and beautiful flowing capes and cloaks. These resplendent garments were made and worn only by men, especially during battle, when a fine cloak became a great trophy of war. Featherwork was also employed in the making of *kahili* and lei, which were highly prized by the noble *ali'i* women.

© KEVIN WHITTON

The delicate yellow *'ilima* blossom is a cultural symbol for O'ahu.

seaworthy. The main hull was usually a gigantic *koa* log, and the gunwale planks were minutely drilled and sewn to the sides with sennit rope. Apprenticeships lasted for years, and a young man knew that he had graduated when one day he was nonchalantly asked to sit down and eat with the master builders. Small family-sized canoes with outriggers were used for fishing and perhaps carried a spear rack; large ocean-going double-hulled canoes were used for migration and warfare. On these, the giant logs had been adzed to about two inches thick. A mainsail woven from pandanus was mounted on a central platform, and the boat was steered by two long paddles. The hull was dyed with plant juices and charcoal, and the entire village helped launch the canoe in a ceremony called "drinking the sea."

Lei Making and Featherwork

Any flower or blossom can be strung into lei, but the most common are orchids or the lovely-smelling plumeria. Lei are all beautiful,

Tapa Cloth

Tapa, cloth made from tree bark, was common throughout Polynesia and was a woman's art. A few trees such as the *wauke* and *mamaki* produced the best cloth, but a variety of other types of bark could be utilized. First the raw bark was pounded into a felt-like pulp and beaten together to form strips (the beaters had distinctive patterns that helped make the cloth supple). The cloth was then decorated by stamping (a form of block printing) and dyed with natural colors from plants and sea animals in shades of gray, purple, pink, and red. They were even painted with natural brushes made from pandanus fruit, with an overall gray color made from charcoal. The tapa cloth was sewn together to make bed coverings, and fragrant flowers and herbs were either sewn or pounded in to produce a permanent fragrance. Tapa cloth is still available today, but the Hawaiian methods have been lost, and most tapa comes from other areas of Polynesia.

ESSENTIALS

Getting There and Around

BY AIR

All commercial flights to Oʻahu are routed to the **Honolulu International Airport** (300 Rodgers Blvd., 808/836-6411, http://hawaii.gov/hnl), as are most other flights with neighbor islands as final destinations. The Honolulu International Airport has three terminals: the Overseas Terminal accommodates international and mainland flights, the Interisland Terminal handles Hawaiian Airlines flights, and the Commuter Terminal handles the small interisland carriers. There is a free intra-airport shuttle service for getting around the airport and ground transportation is available just outside the baggage claim areas on the lower level, along the center median. The airport is a mere 10 miles from Waikiki, and six miles from downtown Honolulu.

Everyone visiting Hawaiʻi must fill out a *Plants and Animals Declaration Form* and present it to an airline flight attendant or the appropriate official upon arrival in the state. Anyone carrying any of the listed items must have those items inspected by an agricultural inspection agent at the airport. These items include but are not limited to fruits, vegetables, plants, seeds, and soil, as well as live insects, seafood, snakes, and amphibians. For additional information

© KEVIN WHITTON

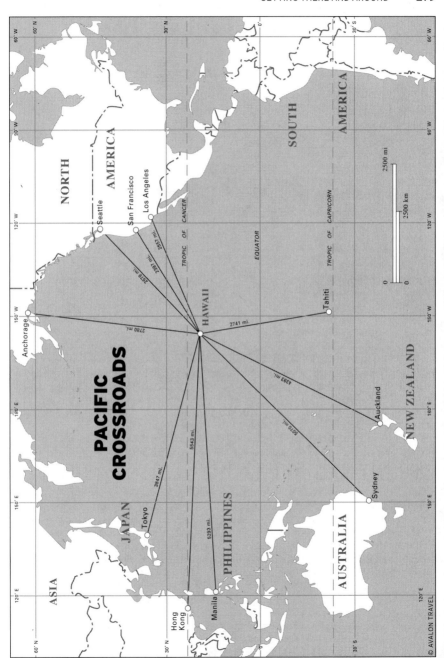

PACIFIC CROSSROADS

HONOLULU INTERNATIONAL AIRPORT

To Pearl Harbor

To Honolulu and Waikiki

NIMITZ HWY

COMMUTER TERMINAL

POST OFFICE

ROGERS BLVD

HONOLULU AIRPORT HOTEL

THE PLAZA HOTEL

KOAPAKA ST

PAIEA ST

UALENA ST

AOLELE ST

ARRIVALS GROUND LEVEL

LEI

INTERISLAND TERMINAL

GATES

DEPARTURES TOP LEVEL

BANK

OUT

IN

IN

CAR RENTALS

PARKING

MAINLAND AND INTERNATIONAL TERMINAL

SCALE NOT AVAILABLE

© AVALON TRAVEL

GATES

GATES

GATES

GATES

GATES

on just what is prohibited, contact any U.S. Customs Office or check with an embassy or consulate in foreign countries.

Also remember that before you leave Hawai'i for the mainland, all of your bags are subject to an agricultural inspection before you enter the ticketing line to check luggage and get your boarding pass. There are no restrictions on beach sand from below the high-water line, coconuts, cooked foods, dried flower arrangements, fresh flower lei, pineapples, certified pest-free plants and cuttings, and seashells. However, papaya must be treated before departure. Some other restricted items are berries, fresh gardenias, jade vines, live insects and snails, cotton, plants in soil, soil itself, and sugarcane. Raw sugarcane is acceptable, however, if it is cut between the nodes, has the outer covering peeled off, is split into fourths, and is commercially prepackaged. For any questions pertaining to plants that you want to take to the mainland, call the Agricultural Quarantine Inspection office (808/861-8490) in Honolulu.

BY CAR

The easiest way for independent travelers to get around O'ahu is by car, and there are plenty of rental car companies. There are six on-airport car rental agencies and several off-airport

companies. If you haven't booked a rental car online prior to your arrival, the registration counters are located in the baggage claim area. All car rental shuttles stop in the designated area along the center median on the ground level of the airport, just outside the baggage claim areas. Offices for the on-airport companies are located on the ground level opposite Baggage Claim G. Keep in mind that if you're staying at a hotel in Waikiki, there will most likely be an additional daily parking fee for your rental car.

Once you've acquired your ride, there is an H-1 freeway on-ramp at the east end of the airport. From the freeway you can head east to Honolulu and Waikiki or west to the windward side via the H-3, the North Shore via the H-2, or out to the leeward side of the island. If you're leaving from a car rental agency located on Nimitz Highway, head east under the freeway until you come to a junction where you can continue to Waikiki via Nimitz Highway, enter the H-1 freeway east to Honolulu or Waikiki, or access Dillingham Boulevard for Honolulu. Driving west on Nimitz will take you to an on-ramp for the H-1 freeway. From there you can access the H-3 to the windward side, the H-2 to the North Shore, or continue on the H-1 to the leeward side.

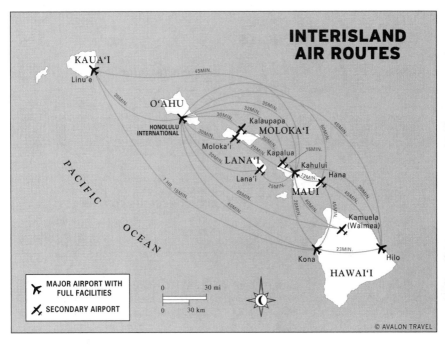

INTERISLAND AIR ROUTES

KAUA'I
Linu'e

O'AHU
HONOLULU
INTERNATIONAL

Kalaupapa
MOLOKA'I
Moloka'i   Kapalua
LANA'I
Kahului
Lana'i   Hana
MAUI

Kamuela
(Waimea)

Kona   Hilo
HAWAI'I

PACIFIC OCEAN

✈ MAJOR AIRPORT WITH
   FULL FACILITIES
✈ SECONDARY AIRPORT

0   30 mi
0   30 km

© AVALON TRAVEL

On O'ahu, there are several local courtesies to follow on the road. Drivers don't generally honk their horns except to say hello or in an emergency. It's considered rude to honk to hurry someone along. Hawaiian drivers reflect the climate: They're relaxed and polite. Often on small roads, they'll brake to let you turn left when they're coming at you. They may assume you'll do the same, so be ready, after a perfunctory turn signal from another driver, for him or her to turn across your lane. The more rural the area, the more apt this is to happen. On all roadways, it is customary to let a signaling motorist change lanes in front of you, and if you need to change lanes and someone lets you in, always give a thank-you wave. When merging, people generally allow every other car into the lane.

O'ahu has a seat belt law as well as a ban on cell phones while driving. Speed limits change periodically along the highways, particularly when they pass through small towns. Police routinely check the speed of traffic with radar

equipment, often hiding in a blind spot to radar and ticket speeding motorists.

BY BUS

From the airport, there are several shuttle services to hotels and resorts in the Waikiki area and beyond. Pick up shuttles along the center median on the ground level in front of the baggage claim areas. There is a complete list of shuttle service providers at the Honolulu International Airport website. **Roberts Hawaii** (808/539-9400 or 800/831-5541, www.robertshawaii.com) Express Shuttle has round-trip service from the airport to Waikiki hotels. **SpeediShuttle** (877/242-5777, www.speedishuttle.com) provides on-demand door-to-door service from the airport to Waikiki hotels, Kahala Resort, Ko Olina, Turtle Bay Resort on the North Shore, and residences around the island. Passengers are allowed two bags and a carry-on for free. Rates are based on the destination, and there are additional fees for bicycles, surfboards, golf bags, and extra baggage.

CAR RENTAL AGENCIES

AIRPORT

- Avis (808/834-5536 or 800/321-3712, www.avis.com)
- Budget (808/836-1700 or 800/527-0700, www.budget.com)
- Dollar (808/944-1544 or 800/800-4000, www.dollar.com)
- Enterprise (808/836-2213 or 800/736-8222, www.enterprise.com)
- Hertz (808/831-3500 or 800/654-3011, www.hertz.com)
- National (808/834-6350 or 800/227-7368, www.nationalcar.com)

BEYOND THE AIRPORT

- A-1 (808/833-7575, http://a1rentacarhawaii.com)
- Advantage (808/834-0461, www.advantage.com)
- Alamo (808/833-4585 or 800/327-9633, www.alamo.com)
- Thrifty (808/952-4238 or 800/367-5238, www.thrifty.com)

ECO-CONSCIOUS COMPANIES

- Green Car (877/664-2748, www.greencar-hawaii.com)

TheBus (808/848-4500, www.thebus.org) provides islandwide transportation, including from the airport. If you're planning on riding the bus from the airport to your hotel, keep in mind that your bags have to be able to fit under the seat or on your lap without protruding into the aisle. There are several bus stops on the second level of the airport on the center median. Route Nos. 19, 20, and 31 access the airport, and Route No. 19 eastbound will take you to Waikiki. Fares are $2.50 for adults, $1.25 children ages 6-17, children 5 and under are free if they sit on an adult's lap. The Visitors Pass, a four consecutive day pass, is $25 with unlimited use. Call 808/848-5555 for route information.

BY TAXI

Taxi service is available at the Honolulu International Airport from the center median fronting the baggage claim areas. Look for attendants in green shirts that say, "Taxi Dispatch." From the terminal to Waikiki costs about $35-40 during non-rush hour periods with a maximum of four passengers. The fare is by meter only, and there is a charge of 35 cents per bag.

To get around by taxi, it's best to call and make arrangements directly from a company or driver, rather than trying to hail one from the curb, as it is technically illegal for taxi drivers to cruise around looking for a fare. For taxi service call **Charley's Taxi** (808/233-3333 or 877/531-1333, http://charleystaxi.com), **City Taxi** (808/524-2121, www.citytaxihonolulu.com), and **The Cab** (808/422-2222, www.thecabhawaii.com). For earth-conscious travelers, try **Eco Cab** (808/979-1010, www.ecocabhawaii.com). If you need some special attention like a limousine service, try **Cloud 9 Limousines** (808/524-7999, www.cloudninelimos.com). It is one of about 50 limo services on the island.

Recreation

Outdoor activities are at the heart of the Hawai'i lifestyle, and a major draw to most visitors in the islands. With comfortable weather year round, warm ocean water and ample nature from mountain to sea, O'ahu holds the opportunity for outdoor enthusiasts to pursue their activity of choice in a beautiful, tropical setting.

SURFING

The art of riding waves for pleasure and athletic challenge was born in Hawai'i and legendary beach boy, waterman, and Olympic gold-medalist swimmer Duke Kahanamoku shared it with the world in the early 20th century, putting on expos in California and Australia. Today, surfing is enjoyed by people around the globe. Whether you're an expert surfer, a weekend warrior, or a beginner, O'ahu has surf breaks suited for surfers of all experience levels around the island.

For beginners and novice surfers, Waikiki is the perfect place to learn how to get on your feet or catch a few fun waves. While summer sees the most consistent surf, there's usually something rolling into Canoes that you can paddle into. Beginners usually stick to Canoes, the gentle surf break directly in front of the Moana Surfrider hotel. Talk to the beachboys who work at the beach services stands along Waikiki for lessons and rentals. Longboards are generally the surfboard of choice in Waikiki. Seasoned surfers who are looking for quality waves should paddle out to Publics, the break to the west of Canoes, or Queen's, which is the peak right in front of Kuhio Beach Park.

In the winter months, the North Shore sees nearly continual wave action with powerful breakers reaching up to 50 feet at top surf breaks like Waimea Bay. North Shore surf breaks are for experts only, and draw surfers from around the world riding all types of boards. There are several surfboard rental outfitters in Hale'iwa town and at Shark's Cove,

but if you're experienced enough to surf the big waves on the North Shore, you'll most likely have your own equipment in tow.

STAND-UP PADDLING

Stand-up paddling was invented by the Waikiki beachboys, who would paddle around the Waikiki lineups using canoe paddles on top their longboards. Stand-up paddling is very similar today, with the paddles being more refined, lighter, and easier to use. The boards are long, thick, and wide, making them very stable on top of the ocean surface. Stand-up paddling is done with the feet parallel, like skiing, whereas surfers stand one front in front of the other. Stand-up paddle surfing is when paddlers use specifically designed stand-up paddleboards to surf waves, as opposed to just paddling around the ocean, going from one place to another.

Stand-up paddling is most enjoyable in favorable ocean conditions: light winds, smooth ocean surface, and little to no surf. The sport is very popular in Waikiki year-round, and on the North Shore during the summer months when the surf is flat. You can also paddle up the 'Anahulu River in Hale'iwa town. Stand-up paddling is also popular in Kailua, but the predominant trade winds make choppy wave conditions a common occurrence.

All the beach services in Waikiki rent stand-up paddleboards and paddles, as well as give lessons. You can find the same rental and lesson services in Kailua and Hale'iwa as well, but you won't find boards to rent along the North Shore beaches, so you'll need to rent a board and some racks in Hale'iwa town and keep driving north to the beach of your choice.

KAYAKING

Kayaking is a great activity to get out in the water, exercise, and cover some distance over the reefs. The majority of recreational kayaking on O'ahu is done on the North Shore in the summer, and on the Windward Coast, where you'll find several islets to explore that offer a remarkable retreat and perspective of Oʻahu.

Kailua Beach Park and Lanikai are the most popular destinations for kayaking. There are outfitters right by the beach park that offer single and double kayaks for rent, as well as tour packages. If you're comfortable in the ocean and with your physical abilities, rent a kayak and trek out on your own. Explore the Mokulua Islands, Flat Island, or drive to Kaneʻohe Bay and paddle out to the sandbar, a unique natural phenomenon in the middle of the bay. Drive north even farther on the Windward side to Kualoa Ranch and paddle around Chinaman's Hat, a small islet just offshore. Kahana Bay, just north of Kualoa, also has great kayaking potential in the deep sheltered bay. If you like the idea and safety of kayaking with a guide, or are new to the sport altogether, take a tour and enjoy the added information about the area that you won't get on a solo adventure. (Not to mention, most tours offer lunch.)

On the North Shore, kayaking is a summer activity. Haleʻiwa town has outfitters that rent kayaks right on the beach at Haleʻiwa Beach Park, a great place to kayak. You can also paddle up the ʻAnahulu River. If you're feeling adventurous, rent some racks, put the kayak on top of the car and drive north to the North Shore beaches and explore the coast.

SNORKELING

While you can snorkel just about anywhere around Oʻahu, the best opportunity to see lots of marine life like fish and coral is over the island's healthiest reefs. You'll find these reefs in marine protected areas, where fishing is illegal. Like all ocean activities, the most pleasurable snorkeling experience requires certain conditions, namely light winds, calm seas, and a smooth ocean surface. Sunny days help bring out the colors in the reef and the fish.

Along the south shore, you'll find a small marine protected area in Waikiki, along Queen's Surf Beach, and the ever-popular Hanauma Bay in Hawaiʻi Kai. Hanauma Bay boasts hundreds of species of fish in the waters

and, apart from the crowds in the water and on the beach, you won't be disappointed by the bounty of life in the ocean. You can rent snorkel gear in Waikiki or at Hanauma Bay.

On the North Shore, Waimea Bay, Three Tables, and Sharks Cove make up the Pupukea-Waimea Marine Life Conservation District. A less structured experience than Hanauma Bay, the three consecutive beaches along the coast offer unique underwater topography and viewing possibilities. You'll find the best conditions to snorkel these areas in the summer. If you plan on snorkeling here, it's best to have your snorkel gear with you. There are outfitters in Haleʻiwa and one outfitter at Sharks Cove.

DIVING

Oʻahu is a great place to scuba dive. There are a host of reefs, interesting underwater geography, and wrecks to dive. There are boat dives, drift dives, shore dives, and night dives. Dive charters operate primarily out of Kewalo Basin in Honolulu, the Hawaiʻi Kai Marina in Hawaiʻi Kai, Haleʻiwa Harbor in Haleʻiwa on the North Shore, and on the Leeward side out of Waiʻanae Harbor in Waiʻanae.

The wreck dives are on the South and West Shores, and shore dives at Sharks Cove, in addition to boat dives, are common on the North Shore. The North Shore is known for its lava tubes, caves, and other interesting underwater geography. Hawaiʻi Kai is famous for the vertical walls off Koko Head crater that fall 70 feet into the blue Pacific. The South Shore has plane- and shipwrecks, and the Windward side has the opportunity for a drift dive from Kaʻena Point down the coast.

Dive operators offer dives for all levels of divers and instruction for many different types of certification. Many also offer transportation from and to Waikiki hotels. All dive operators will offer packaged rates including gear rental and some have retail outlets if you have your own gear.

HIKING

For all the ocean lovers that flock to Oʻahu, there are equal opportunities for hikers to

O'AHU SNORKELING

TURTLE BAY

SHARKS COVE

THREE TABLES

83

Kahuku

930

Hale'iwa

99

PACIFIC

OCEAN

Wahiawa

H2

83

99

Wai'anae

93

H3

Kane'ohe

Kailua

72

H1

H1

Waimanalo

HONOLULU

72

MAGIC ISLAND

QUEEN'S SURF BEACH

SANS SOUCI BEACH

HANAUMA BAY

Kaua'i Channel

0   5 mi

0   5 km

© AVALON TRAVEL

explore Oʻahu's mountains, valleys, forests, and waterfalls. There are two main mountain ranges on Oʻahu. The Koʻolau Mountains run the length of the windward coast, with valleys and rises spread along the South Shore and inland urban Honolulu neighborhoods. The mountains are verdant, with many native Hawaiian species of shrubs, ferns, and trees in the upper elevation reaches of the range. The Koʻolaus are best known for the dramatic cliffs stretching from Waimanalo to Kualoa. The Waiʻanae Range spans the Leeward Coast and is home to the highest peak on the island. The mountains are also green and lush in the upper portions, with many native Hawaiian species as well, but dry out significantly as the ridges push into the hot and dry Leeward Coast.

If you plan on doing some serious hiking, it's best to stop by a bookstore and pick up one of the several hiking trail guides for Oʻahu.

There are also many resources online that provide specific route descriptions and topographical maps.

Many of the shorter, more accessible hikes are located in the valleys above Honolulu. They are easy to get to and offer great opportunities ranging from a short walk in the wilderness to an all-out day hike with waterfalls and summits. Hiking in the Koʻolaus on the Windward side is more apt to be a muddy, slippery experience with mosquitoes and possible showers at any time, especially the higher up you venture. Hiking in the Waiʻanae Mountains is a rockier, drier experience. Hikers should set out early to beat the midday sun and heat. The North Shore also has a few trails on the Pupukea bluff and on the north-facing side of the Waiʻanae Range, which receives more rainfall than the leeward side of the mountains.

Not many trails are managed, so it's best to

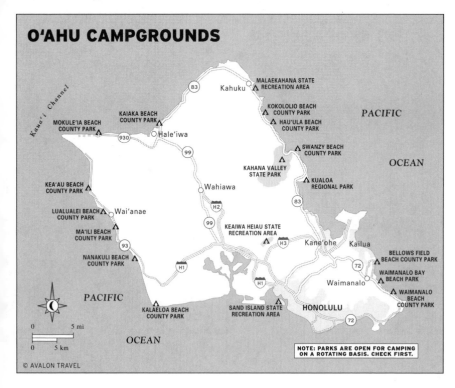

hike with others for safety. Be prepared for rain and wind, and let someone else know where you set out to hike before you begin. Bring ample water and sunscreen, and stay on marked trails. Don't leave valuables in your car when parking at trailheads.

GOLF

With 38 (and counting) public, private, municipal, and military golf courses scattered around such a relatively small island, golf is a main draw for residents and visitors alike. The courses range from modest nine-holers to world-class courses whose tournaments attract the biggest names in golf today. Prices range from $10 per round up to $175. An added attraction of playing O'ahu's courses is that you get to walk around on some of the most spectacular and manicured pieces of real estate on the island. Some afford sweeping views of the

coast, whereas others have a lovely mountain backdrop. Tough or easy, flat or full of definition, O'ahu's courses provide ample opportunity and variety for any golfer.

Municipal and public courses are open to everyone. Resort courses cater to the public as well as to resort guests. Semi-private courses set aside most of their time for members, but do have specified days and times when they are open to the public. Private courses are strictly for members only and their guests. Military personnel and dependents, Department of Defense personnel, and those who have access to military bases are welcome to golf at the military courses. Some are also open to the public. If you wish to golf at courses other than municipal or public courses, be sure to call ahead to verify accessibility.

Most golf courses offer lessons. Many have driving ranges, some lighted. Virtually

all have pro shops and clubhouses with restaurants and lounges or snack shops. Many courses offer reduced special time rates, twilight hour rates, and summer specials. Be sure to ask about these rates because they often afford substantial savings. On the other hand, some courses charge higher fees for non-U.S. residents. Military courses charge different greens fees for civilians than for military personnel, and the military fees might differ depending on rank.

For ease of use of municipal golf courses, the City and County of Honolulu has an automated tee time reservation and information system (808/296-2000) to make or check your reservation or to have your inquiry answered.

Tips for Travelers

WHAT TO TAKE

While O'ahu might be isolated in the middle of the Pacific Ocean, it still has all the products, services, and conveniences of a big city. When filling your suitcase, pack light: lightweight clothing and footwear. Leave the jeans at home and choose comfortable, casual wear. Even if you're planning on a fancy night out or two, guys can get away with an aloha shirt and slacks, while the ladies can wear a nice sundress. If you don't have any flip-flops, you can always pick them up when you arrive, as well as anything else you might find yourself in need of, like that colorful aloha shirt. Just make sure at the top of your clothing list is boardshorts or bikini.

For sports enthusiasts, bringing the necessary equipment is usually a matter of preference. Expert and professional surfers bring their own boards to the islands, but most visitors just rent boards. The airlines charge high fees for checking in surfboards. If you golf and don't want to lug your clubs around the airport, all the courses rent clubs. Hikers should bring their own boots, which will most likely get muddy. For convenience, tennis players should bring their own rackets.

Sunscreen is a must and mosquito repellent quite a good idea, just make sure you put them in your check-in baggage. A hat will protect your dome from the sun, and binoculars are key if you plan on whale- or bird-watching. And please don't forget your camera.

TRAVELING WITH CHILDREN

For those traveling with young children, consider leaving all the gear at home to make your luggage lighter and less cumbersome. Car rental companies rent car seats for a small fee, and you can rent all kinds of other products for your stay on O'ahu, like a crib, pack-n-play, stroller, and high chair, even beach gear. **Paradise Baby** (808/561-1061, www.paradisebabyco.com) rents luxury baby equipment with free islandwide delivery and pickup. **Baby Aboard** (808/393-7612, www.babyaboard.com) serves the entire island, and **Baby's Away** (808/640-6734 or 800/496-6386, https://babysaway.com) rents equipment for Honolulu and Waikiki area visitors.

For family beach days with the little ones just getting their feet wet for the first time, choose beaches with little to no shorebreak, like **Kaimana Beach** in Waikiki or the **Ko Olina Lagoons.** And don't forget to pick up an umbrella for respite from the sun.

TRAVELERS WITH DISABILITIES

For a smooth trip, travelers with disabilities should make as many arrangements ahead of time as possible. Tell the transportation

---

TRAVELING WITH PETS

Hawai'i has a very rigid pet quarantine policy designed to keep rabies and other mainland diseases from reaching the state. All domestic pets are subject to **120 days quarantine** (a 30-day quarantine and five-day-or-less quarantine are allowed by meeting certain pre-arrival and post-arrival requirements). The process is expensive and time-consuming, and there are additional airline fees as well. Unless you are contemplating a move to Hawai'i, it is not feasible to bring pets. Exceptions to the quarantine are made for animals originating in other rabies-free locales like Guam, Australia, New Zealand, and the British Isles. For complete information, contact the Department of Agriculture, Animal Quarantine Division (99-951 Halawa Valley St., 'Aiea, HI 96701, 808/483-7151, http://hawaii.gov/hdoa/ai/aqs) in Honolulu.

companies and hotels you'll be dealing with the nature of your restrictions in advance so they can make arrangements to accommodate you. Bring your medical records and notify medical establishments of your arrival if you'll need their services. Travel with a friend or make arrangements for an aide on arrival. Bring your own wheelchair if possible and let airlines know if it is battery-powered. Boarding interisland carriers sometimes requires steps. They'll board wheelchairs early on special lifts, but they must know you're coming. Most hotels and restaurants accommodate persons with disabilities, but always call ahead just to make sure.

The state Commission on Persons with Disabilities was designed with the express purpose of aiding disabled people. It is a source of invaluable information and distributes self-help booklets, which are published jointly by the Disability and Communication Access Board and the Hawaii Centers for Independent Living. Any person with disabilities heading to Hawai'i should write first or visit the office of the **Hawaii Centers for Independent Living** (414 Kuwili St., #102, Honolulu, HI 96817, 808/522-5400, www.hcil.org). Additional information is available on the Disability and Communication Access Board website: www.hawaii.gov/health/dcab/home.

O'ahu Services

At Honolulu International Airport, parking spaces are on the fourth floor of the parking garage near each pedestrian bridge and on each level near the elevators at the Interisland Terminal. Several of the airport shuttles have lifts for wheelchairs, and there is an on-demand van shuttle service for transportation between locations within the airport facility. O'ahu's public transit system, TheBus, operates most buses with lift capability, but most van transportation and taxis have steps.

For getting around, the City of Honolulu offers a curb-to-curb service for disabled persons; call **Handi-Van** (808/456-5555). You must make arrangements at least a day in advance or up to seven days in advance. A private special

taxi company operating all over the island is **Handi-Cabs of the Pacific** (808/848-4500); **The Cab** (808/422-2222) taxi service also has wheelchair accessible vans. Most of the large rental car companies can put hand controls (right or left) on their cars, but some restrict these controls to a certain size or type of vehicle. They generally require prior arrangements, one or two days at least, preferably when making your advance reservation. Rates are comparable with standard rental cars.

Access Aloha Travel (414 Kuwili St., #101, Honolulu, 808/545-1143 or 800/480-1143, www.accessalohatravel.com) rents wheelchair lift-equipped vans on O'ahu for $200 per day or $723 per week; monthly rentals are also possible. This is a full-service travel agency and a good source of information on traveling with disabilities.

Valid out-of-state **handicapped parking placards** may be used throughout the state of Hawai'i. Passes for disabled but ambulatory persons using **TheBus** cost $10. Check at TheBus Pass Office (811 Middle St., Honolulu, 808/848-4500; 7:30am-3:30pm Mon.-Fri.)

For **medical equipment rental,** see the following establishments for all kinds of apparatus: **Apria Healthcare** (98-720 Kuahao Pl., Pearl City, 808/485-0178, www.apria.com), **C. R. Newton Co.** (1575 S. Beretania St., Ste. 101, Honolulu, 808/949-8389 or 800/545-2078, www.crnewton.com), and **Hawaiian Islands Medical** (841 Pohukaina St., Ste. 8, Honolulu, 808/597-8087 or 866/246-4633, www.himed.cc).

LGBT TRAVELERS

The overall mind-set in Hawai'i, and on O'ahu, has long been acceptance of the LGBT community. In 2011, the state legalized civil unions for same-sex couples. O'ahu has gay and lesbian bars, nightclubs, accommodations, and beaches. **Hula's Bar & Lei Stand** in Waikiki is a well-known hangout, as is **Queen's Beach** and the surrounding area of Kapi'olani Park, just a short walk from Hula's.

The **Travel Alternative Group** (www.tagapproved.com), a resource for accommodations and attractions, has approved **Aqua Hotels & Resorts** (www.aquagaytravel.com), which offers discounts on reservations for LGBT travelers, and **Aston Hotels & Resorts** (www.AstonHotels.com). Another resource for finding accommodations and tours is the **International Gay and Lesbian Travel Association** (954/630-1637, www.iglta.org). They have tapped **Hotel Renew** (www.hotelrenew.com), **Discover Hawaii Tours** (808/690-9050, www.discoverhawaiitours.com), and **Waikiki Beach Marriott Resort & Spa** (www.marriott.com), among many other establishments, as gay and lesbian friendly.

Health and Safety

With the perfect weather, a multitude of fresh-air activities, soothing negative ionization from the sea, and a generally relaxed and carefree lifestyle, everyone seems to feel better in the islands. There are no cases of malaria, cholera, or yellow fever. Because of a strict quarantine law, rabies is also nonexistent. There is no need for vaccinations when traveling to O'ahu, the water is safe and the air quality is the best in the country.

The most common health risks come from heatstroke, sunburn, intoxication, dehydration, and drowning. If you cut yourself on the reef, make sure to clean the wound periodically and treat it with an antibiotic ointment to avoid infection, as cuts tend to heal slower in the tropical climate.

SUN

The warming, yet harmful rays of the sun come through more easily in Hawai'i because of the sun's angle, and you don't feel them as much because there's always a cool breeze. The worst part of the day to be in direct sun is 11am-3pm. O'ahu lies about 21.5 degrees north latitude, not even close to the equator, but it's still more than 1,000 miles south of sunny southern California beaches. Use sunscreen on your face and exposed skin every day, even if you're not at the beach. Hats, sunglasses, beach umbrellas, plenty of water, and a dose of common sense will keep you active outdoors without a sunburn souvenir. And just because it's cloudy doesn't mean you can skip the sunscreen.

Whether out on the beach, hiking in the mountains, or just strolling around town, be very aware of dehydration. The sun and wind tend to sap your energy and your store of liquid. Carry bottled water with you at all times. For those choosing to imbibe, make sure to drink even more water than normal to account for the stress on your body under the strong Hawai'i sun.

MOSQUITOES AND COCKROACHES

Mosquitoes were unknown in the Hawaiian Islands until their larvae stowed away in the water barrels of the *Wellington* in 1826 and were introduced at Lahaina. They bred in the tropical climate and rapidly spread to all the islands. They are a particular nuisance in the rainforests, watersheds, and periodically damp areas like the windward coast and mountains. Be prepared, and bring a natural repellent like citronella oil, available in most health stores on the islands, or a commercial product available in grocery and drugstores. Campers will be happy to have mosquito coils to burn at night as well.

Cockroaches are common in Hawai'i, and there are several different kinds you'll come across. There are the small roaches that live in leaf litter and the larger flying roaches that seek out light at night. One comforting thought is that in Hawai'i they aren't a sign of filth or dirty housekeeping. They love the climate like everyone else, and it's a real problem keeping them under control. Just do your best to handle it, they won't hurt you.

LEPTOSPIROSIS

Present in streams, ponds, and muddy soil, leptospirosis is a freshwater-borne bacteria deposited by the urine of infected animals. From 2 to 20 days after the bacteria enter the body, there will be a sudden onset of fever accompanied by chills, sweats, headache, and sometimes vomiting and diarrhea. Preventive measures include staying out of freshwater sources and mud where cattle and other animals wade and drink, not swimming in freshwater if you have an open cut, and not drinking stream water. Although not always the case, leptospirosis may be fatal if left untreated.

OCEAN SAFETY

More people drown in Hawai'i than anywhere else in the world. In addition, powerful shorebreaks are also the cause of severe injuries like broken backs and necks. But don't let these statistics deter you from enjoying the ocean. Instead, educate yourself on the day and area's ocean conditions and enjoy the water responsibly. Ask lifeguards or beach attendants about conditions and follow their advice. Common sense, good judgment, and respect for the ocean go a long way. And never turn your back on the ocean while enjoying the shoreline. Rouge waves can wash over reef, rock, and beach and pull you out into the water. Obey all warning signs posted on the beach, and if you're swimming, surfing, or snorkeling, return to shore before you get tired. If you engage in an ocean activity by yourself, make sure you tell others in your party your planned whereabouts in the event of an emergency. If you find yourself on the beach psyching yourself up to get in the water, it's probably better to heed the warning, "If in doubt, stay out."

Sharks, Urchins, and Coral

Sharks live in all the oceans of the world. Most mind their own business and stay away from shore. Hawaiian sharks are well fed—on fish—and don't usually bother with unsavory humans. If you encounter a shark, don't panic! Never thrash around because this will trigger their attack instinct.

Portuguese man-of-wars and other jellyfish put out long, floating tentacles that sting if they touch you. Jellyfish are blown into shore by winds on the 8th, 9th, and 10th days after the full moon. Don't wash the sting off with freshwater because this will only aggravate it. Locals will use hot saltwater to take away the sting, as well as alcohol (the drinking or rubbing kind), aftershave lotion, or meat tenderizer (MSG), but lifeguards use common household vinegar. After rinsing, soak with a wet towel. An antihistamine may also bring relief. Expect to start to feel better in about a half hour.

Coral can give you a nasty cut, and it's known for causing infections because it's a living organism. Wash the cut immediately and apply an antiseptic. Keep it clean and covered, and watch for infection. With coral cuts, it's best to have a professional look at it to clean it out. Most infection comes from tiny bits of coral that are left deep in the cut. Never stand on or grab coral. It damages the fragile lifeform and can send you to the hospital.

Poisonous sea urchins, like the lacquer-black *wana,* are found in shallow tidepools and reefs and will hurt you if you step on them. Their spines will break off, enter your foot, and severely burn. There are cures. Soaking a couple of times in vinegar for half an hour or so should stop the burning. If vinegar is not available, the local cure-all is urine.

Leave the fish, turtles, and seals alone. Fish should never be encouraged to feed from humans. Green sea turtles and seals are endangered species, and stiff fines can be levied on those who knowingly disturb them. Have a great time looking and taking pictures, but give them respect and space.

MEDICAL SERVICES

Full-service hospitals include **The Queen's Medical Center** (1301 Punchbowl St., Honolulu, 808/538-9011, www.queensmedical-center.net), **St. Francis Medical Center** (2230 Liliha St., Honolulu, 808/547-6011, www.stfrancishawaii.org), and **Straub Clinic and Hospital** (888 S. King St., Honolulu, 808/522-4000, www.straubhealth.org) in Honolulu; **Castle Medical Center** (640 Ulukahiki St., 808/263-5500, http://castlemed.org) in Kailua;

Wahiawa General Hospital (128 Lehua St., 808/621-8411, www.wahiawageneral.org) in Wahiawa; and **Kahuku Medical Center** (56-117 Pualalea St., 808/293-9221, www.hhsc.org/oahu/kahuku/index.html) in Kahuku on the North Shore.

Information and Services

TOURIST INFORMATION

The **Hawaii Visitors and Convention Bureau** (HVCB, 2270 Kalakaua Ave., Ste. 801, 808/524-0722 or 800/464-2924, www.gohawaii.com) is the state of Hawai'i's official tourism agency and website. The great thing about the HVCB is that everything they offer is free. The staff is extremely knowledgeable, and the office is packed with excellent brochures on virtually every facet of living in, visiting, or simply enjoying Hawai'i. The website features travel tips, quick facts, regional information, and service providers to help inform your vacation.

There is plenty of free tourist literature available at all major hotels, shopping malls, the airport, and stands along Waikiki's streets. They all contain up-to-the-minute information on what's happening and a treasure trove of free or reduced-price coupons for various attractions and services. Always featured are events, shopping tips, dining and entertainment, and sightseeing. The main ones are *This Week Oahu,* the best and most complete; *Spotlight Oahu Gold,* with good sections on dining and sightseeing; and the smaller *Activities and Attractions Oahu.* Heavy on sightseeing attractions and activities, *101 Things To Do: Oahu* also has maps, advertising, and some coupons. *Oahu Drive Guide,* handed out by all the major rental car agencies, has some excellent tips and orientation maps. It is especially useful to get you started from the airport. The major shopping malls also publish their own magazines.

Maps

Aside from the simple maps in the ubiquitous free tourist literature, the O'ahu Visitors and Conventions Bureau and other organizations put out folding pocket maps of the island that are available free at the airport and tourist brochure racks around the island. Various Honolulu City and County street maps can be found at bookstores around the island. Perhaps the best and most detailed of the island maps is the University of Hawai'i Press reference map, *Map of O'ahu, The Gathering Place.* This map can also be found at gift and sundries shops around the island. Other useful and detailed maps of the island are the Rand McNally *O'ahu, Honolulu* map and the AAA *Honolulu Hawaii* map. If you are looking for detail, the best street map atlas of O'ahu is a spiral-bound publication by Phears Mapbooks called *The O'ahu Mapbook,* also available at bookshops around the island.

The **Waikiki Business Improvement District** (www.waikikibid.org) publishes a free detailed map of Waikiki with an entertainment calendar, important phone numbers, and a TheBus quick reference guide to major attractions. You can pick up a map at the police substation at Kuhio Beach Park or from one of the friendly aloha ambassadors that walk Waikiki's main drags solely to help visitors. They wear fluorescent yellow shirts, blue hats, and blue shorts.

MONEY AND FINANCES

Currency

Hawai'i uses U.S. currency. U.S. coinage in use is $0.01 (penny), $0.05 (nickel), $0.10 (dime), $0.25 (quarter), $0.50 (half dollar), and $1 (uncommon); paper currency is $1, $2 (uncommon), $5, $10, $20, $50, and $100. Bills larger than $100 are not in general circulation. Since 1996, new designs have been issued for the $100, $50, $20, $10, and $5 bills. Both the old and new bills are accepted as valid currency.

Banks

Full-service bank hours are generally Monday through Thursday 8:30am-4pm and Friday 8:30am-6pm. A few banks offer limited Saturday service, and weekday hours will be a bit longer at counters in grocery stores and other outlets. All main towns on O'ahu have one or more banks. Virtually all branch banks have automated teller machines (ATMs) for 24-hour service, and these can be found at some shopping centers and other venues around the island. ATMs work only when the Hawaiian bank you use is on an affiliate network with your home bank. Of most value to travelers, banks sell and cash traveler's checks, give cash advances on credit cards, and exchange and sell foreign currency (sometimes with a fee). Major banks on O'ahu are American Savings Bank, Bank of Hawaii, Central Pacific Bank, and First Hawaiian Bank; each has numerous branch offices throughout the island.

Traveler's Checks

Traveler's checks are accepted throughout Hawai'i at hotels, restaurants, rental car agencies, and in most stores and shops. However, to be readily acceptable they should be in U.S. currency. Some larger hotels that frequently have Japanese and Canadian guests will accept their currency. Banks accept foreign-currency traveler's checks, but it'll mean an extra trip and inconvenience. It's best to get most of your traveler's checks in $20 or $50 denominations; anything larger will be hard to cash in shops and boutiques, although not in hotels.

Credit Cards

More and more business is transacted in Hawai'i using credit cards. Almost every form of accommodation, shop, restaurant, and amusement accepts them. For renting a car, they're a must. With credit card insurance readily available, they're as safe as traveler's checks and even more convenient. Write down the numbers of your cards in case they're stolen, and keep the numbers separate from the wallet. Don't rely on credit cards completely because some establishments—some

bed-and-breakfasts and small local eateries, for example—only accept cash.

Taxes

Hawai'i does not have a state sales tax, but it does have a general excise tax of 4.712 percent, which will be added to sales transactions and services. In addition, there is an accommodations tax of 9.25 percent, so approximately 14 percent will be added to your hotel bill when you check out.

COMMUNICATION AND MEDIA
Post Offices

There are more than a dozen post offices in Honolulu (800/275-8777) and one in each of the major towns on the island. The normal business hours for window service at many of these are Monday through Friday 9am-4:30pm and Saturday 9am-2pm, although some branch offices have slightly different hours. The main post office in downtown Honolulu (335 Merchant St.), located next to the King Kamehameha statue, has window hours Monday through Friday 9am-4:30pm. The Waikiki branch (330 Saratoga Rd.) has window hours Monday through Friday 9am-4:30pm, Saturday 9am-1pm.

Telephone

The telephone system on O'ahu is modern and comparable to any system on the mainland. For land lines, any phone call to a number on O'ahu is a **local call**; it's **long distance** when dialing to another island (even though the area code for the entire state of Hawai'i is 808) or beyond the state. With standard long distance service, long-distance rates go down at 5pm and again at 11pm until 8am the next morning. Rates are cheapest from Friday at 5pm until Monday at 8am. Many long-distance companies have moved to a flat rate per minute fee structure, however, so check with your accommodation. Local calls from public telephones cost $0.50. Emergency calls are always free. Public telephones are found at hotels, street booths, restaurants, most public buildings, and some beach parks. It is common to have a phone in most hotel rooms and condominiums, although a service charge is often collected, even on local calls. You can direct dial from Hawai'i to the mainland and more than 160 foreign countries. Undersea cables and satellite communications ensure top-quality phone service. Toll-free calls are preceded by 800, 888, 877, or 866; there is no charge to the calling party. Many are listed in this guide.

Cell phone reception is generally very good throughout the state of Hawai'i. However, as anywhere, you will find pockets where reception is poor or nonexistent.

For directory assistance, dial: 411 (local), 1-555-1212 (interisland), or 1-800/555-1212 (toll-free).

Newspapers

Besides special-interest Chinese, Japanese, Korean, Filipino, and military newspapers, O'ahu has one major daily, the *Honolulu Star Advertiser* (www.staradvertiser.com). It's $0.75 daily or $2 on Sunday. The alternative free press *Honolulu Weekly* (www.honoluluweekly. com) adds a different perspective to the mix. Aside from feature articles on pertinent local issues, it has a thorough calendar of local arts and events. Other weekly or monthly free papers that you might encounter include *Midweek*, the *North Shore News*, and *Ka Leo O Hawai'i*, the University of Hawai'i at Manoa campus newspaper.

Libraries

There are 24 public libraries on O'ahu, and these include the **Hawaii State Library** (478 S. King St., 808/586-3500), located next to 'Iolani Palace in downtown Honolulu, and the **Library for the Blind and Physically Handicapped** (402 Kapahulu, 808/733-8444). Library cards are available for visitors and non-residents for $25 (valid for five years), and $10 for up to three months. The library system offers numerous services, including Internet access and reference information (808/586-3621) during library hours. Business hours for each library differ, so check with the one you want to

visit. Brochures listing hours and other general information are available at all libraries and online. For additional information, see the Hawaii State Public Library System website: www.librarieshawaii.org.

Radio

O'ahu's radio stations are a true reflection of the culture, whether you're listening to news and talk radio, or local music. Here are a few stations to tune in when you're driving or in your hotel room:

- **KHPR 88.1 FM:** National Public Radio 1
- **KIPO 89.3 FM:** National Public Radio 2
- **KTUH 90.3 FM:** University of Hawai'i at Manoa student radio
- **KHCM 97.5:** Country music
- **KDNN 98.5 FM:** Island music (also available on iHeartRadio)
- **KCNN 100.3 FM:** Island music
- **KUCD 101.9 FM:** Modern rock
- **KINE 105.1 FM:** Hawaiian music
- **KPOI 105.9 FM:** Classic rock

LOCAL RESOURCES
Emergencies

For **police, fire, or ambulance** anywhere on O'ahu, dial **911**. For **nonemergency police** assistance and information, call 808/529-3111. In case of a natural disaster such as hurricanes or tsunamis on O'ahu, call the **Civil Defense** at 808/523-4121 or 808/733-4300. The **Coast Guard Search and Rescue** can be reached at 800/552-6458. The **Sex Abuse Treatment Center Hotline** is available at 808/524-7273 for cases involving sexual assault or rape crisis.

Weather, Marine Report, and Time of Day

For recorded information on local island weather, call 808/973-4381; for marine conditions phone 808/973-4382; and for the surf report, call 808/973-4383. For surf information on the Internet, check www.surfnewsnetwork. com or call 808/596-SURF. For time of day, call 808/643-8463.

Consumer Protection and Tourist Complaints

If you encounter problems with accommodations, bad service, or downright rip-offs, try the following: **The Chamber of Commerce of Hawaii** (808/545-4300), **Office of Consumer Protection** (808/587-3222, www.hawaii.gov/dcca/ocp), or the **Better Business Bureau** (808/536-6956).

Auto Service

AAA (1130 Nimitz Hwy., Ste. A170, 808/736-2886, www.hawaii.aaa.com, 9am-5pm Mon.-Wed. and Fri., 9am-7pm Thurs., 9am-2pm Sat.) has an O'ahu office in the Nimitz Center, just west of Hilo Hattie. Stop here for maps, Triptik maps, the Hawaii Tourbook, and other AAA information and travel agency services. If you're an AAA member, call 800/222-4357 for 24-hour roadside assistance.

Camping Permits

Camping permits for City and County of Honolulu managed campgrounds can be obtained through the Department of Parks and Recreation. Walk-in permits are available at the Frank Fasi Municipal Building (650 S. King St.) DPR Permits Office, or online at https://camping.honolulu.gov. For state-run campgrounds, reservations and permits are best obtained at through the website, www.hawaiistateparks.org.

WEIGHTS AND MEASURES

Hawai'i, like all of the United States, employs the "English method" of measuring weights and distances. Basically, dry weights are in ounces and pounds; liquid measures are in ounces, quarts, and gallons; and distances are measured in inches, feet, yards, and miles. The metric system is known but is not in general use.

Electricity

The same electrical current is in use in Hawai'i as on the U.S. mainland and is uniform throughout the islands. The system functions on 110 volts, 60 cycles of alternating current (AC); type A (two-pin) and type B (three-pin) plugs are used. Appliances from Japan will work, but there is some danger of burnout, whereas those requiring the normal European current of 220 volts, as well as those using other types of plugs, will not work.

Time Zones

There is no daylight saving time in Hawai'i. When daylight saving time is not observed on the mainland, Hawai'i is two hours behind the West Coast, four hours behind the Midwest, five hours behind the East Coast, and 11 hours behind Germany; add one hour to these times during daylight saving time months. Hawai'i, being just east of the International Date Line, is almost a full day behind most Asian and Oceanian cities. Hours behind these countries and cities are: Japan, 19 hours; Singapore, 18 hours; Sydney, 20 hours; New Zealand, 22 hours; Fiji, 22 hours.

RESOURCES

Glossary

The following list provides a basic vocabulary of Hawaiian words in common usage that you are likely to see or hear. Becoming familiar with them is not a strict necessity, but knowing what they mean will definitely enhance your experience and make speaking with local people more congenial. Many islanders spice their speech with certain words. Feel free to use them when you feel comfortable. You might even discover some Hawaiian words that are so perfectly expressive they'll become regular parts of your vocabulary. Many Hawaiian words have been absorbed into the English language and are found in English dictionaries. The definitions given are not exhaustive, but are generally considered the most common.

'a'a: sharp, rough lava
'ae: yes
ahupua'a: pie-shaped land divisions running from mountain to sea
aikane: friend, buddy
'aina: land
akamai: smart, clever, wise
akua: a god, divine
akua lapu: ghost stories
akua li'i: literally, "little spirits"
alahe'e: native Hawaiian shrub
ali'i: a Hawaiian chief or noble
aloha: common greeting or word of parting meaning hello, good-bye, love, and welcome
'amakihi: yellow Hawaiian honeycreeper (type of bird)
ana: cave
anuenue: rainbow
ao: daylight

'a'ole: no
'apapane: native Hawaiian forest bird
'aumakua: a personal or family god, often an ancestral spirit
auwe: alas
'awa: plant found throughout Polynesia; a calming, mildly intoxicating drink is made from the root (also known as kava)
'elepaio: native Hawaiian forest bird
haku: crown lei
hala: leaf
halakahiki: pineapple
halau: longhouse, when used with hula it means school
hale: house or building
hale koa: military hotel in Waikiki
hana: work
hanai: literally means to feed; commonly used as a term for adopted parents or children (not in a formal or legal sense); a close relationship
haole: literally means no breath; used to describe foreigners or Caucasians
hapa: of mixed ethnicity
hapai: pregnant
hapu'u: native Hawaiian fern
he'e nalu: surfing
heiau: a sacred rock structure used as a temple to worship the gods
hili: to braid
holomu'u: an ankle-length dress that is much more fitted than a mu'umu'u, and often worn on formal occasions
hono: bay
honu: sea turtle
ho'oilo: traditional Hawaiian winter that began

in November

ho'olaule'a: a celebration, usually a party or gathering

ho'omalimali: sweet talk, flattery

huhu: angry, irritated

hui: a group of people or a meeting

hukilau: a shoreline fishing gathering where everyone helps to pull (*huki*) fish to shore in a huge net

hula: a native Hawaiian sacred dance

huli: to turn over; chicken on a rotisserie barbecue is called *huli huli* chicken

humuhumunukunukuapua'a: Hawaiian reef triggerfish

i'a: fish

'ie'ie: pandanus (plant) endemic to the Pacific Islands

'i'iwi: a red Hawaiian honeycreeper (type of bird)

'iliahi: native Hawaiian sandalwood tree

'ilima: shrub with yellow and orange blossoms

imu: an earthen oven

'inamona: condiment made from roasted kukui nut

ipo: sweetheart

ipu: gourd

kahako: a macron used to differentiate between short and long vowels in the Hawaiian language

kahili: a tall pole topped with feathers used by an *ali'i* to announce his or her presence

kahuna: priest, sorcerer, or doctor

kahuna 'ana'ana: black magic

kahuna lapa'au: ancient Hawaiian healer

kai: the sea

kala: the sun

kalo lo'i: taro growing in small ponds

kalua: roasted underground in an *imu*

kama 'aina: a child of the land; a longtime island resident of any ethnic background

kanaka: man or commoner; used to distinguish a Hawaiian from other races

kane: man

kapu: forbidden, taboo; keep out, do not touch

kau kau: slang for eating or food

kauwa: war

keiki: child or children

kiawe: algaroba tree from South America covered in long, sharp thorns commonly found in Hawai'i along the shoreline

koa: endemic Hawaiian tree

kokua: help

kolohe: rascal

kona: leeward side of any Hawaiian Island; a wind blowing from the south or west

konane: a traditional Hawaiian game similar to checkers

ko'olau: windward side of the island

ku'auhau: genealogy, lineage

kui: to string

kukui: candlenut tree; the Hawai'i state tree

kuleana: homesite; a person's right

Kumulipo: ancient Hawaiian genealogical chant that records the pantheon of gods, creation, and the beginning of humankind

kupua: demigods in Hawaiian mythology

kupuna: a grandparent or ancestor

lama: small- to medium-sized Hawaiian tree

lanai: veranda or porch

lani: sky or heavens

lau hala: the leaf (*lau*) of the pandanus (**hala**) tree; used often in mat and sail weaving

lei: a necklace or garland made of flowers, plants, shells, or nuts

limu: seaweed

lolo: crazy

lomi lomi: traditional Hawaiian massage

lua: the bathroom

luakini heiau: native Hawaiian place of worship where human and animal blood sacrifices were made

lu'au: a celebratory party thrown for birthdays, graduations, or other reasons to feast and enjoy music and dance

mahalo: thank you

mahele: division; the Great Mahele of 1848 broke up traditional common lands and enabled private ownership of property

mahina: moon

mahu: traditionally a third gender similar to a transvestite; today it refers to a gay man

maile: a fragrant vine used in lei making

maka'ainana: native Hawaiians that lived off the land

makai: toward the ocean

make: dead, deceased

malo: a traditional native Hawaiian loincloth

mamo: endemic Hawaiian bird that is now extinct

mana: supernatural or divine power, energy

manini: small, or frugal

manuahi: free, extra

mauka: toward the mountains

mauna: mountain

mele: a song or chant

Menehune: the legendary "little people" of Hawai'i said to possess magical powers

moa: chicken, fowl

moana: the ocean

moe: sleep

mo'o ali'i: genealogy of the chiefs; chiefly line of succession

mo'o kahuna: genealogy of succession of priests

mo'olelo: story, tale, myth

mua: man's eating house

mu'umu'u: an ankle-length dress with a high neckline made from aloha print fabric

nani: beautiful

naupaka: native Hawaiian shrub found at the beach and in the mountains

nui: big, large

'ohana: a family

'ohi'a: endemic Hawaiian tree with bottlebrush flowers

'ohi'a 'ahihi: tree with clusters of delicate red flowers

'okina: a unicameral consonant letter used to mark a glottal stop in the Hawaiian language

'okolehau: traditional fermented beverage made from *ti* root

oli: chant

olona: cord

'ono: delicious

'o'o: small Kauaian forest bird

'opihi: a limpet that clings to rocks and traditionally gathered as food

'opu: belly, stomach

pahoa: dagger

pahoehoe: smooth, ropy lava

pakalolo: marijuana

pake: a Chinese person; cheap

pali: a cliff

paniolo: a Hawaiian cowboy

pau: finished, done

pau hana: happy hour

pilau: stinky, a bad smell

pilikia: trouble, bad news

po: night, darkness; obscurity; the realm of the gods

poi: a glutinous paste made from the pounded corm of taro

poke: local Hawaiian dish with cubes of raw fish

pono: peaceful, righteous

pua: flower

pueo: Hawaiian owl

puka: a hole of any size

pupu: appetizer

pu'u: hill

tapa: a traditional paper cloth made from beaten tree bark

ti: a broad-leafed plant with red, green, and variegated leaves used for wrapping food and religious offerings

tutu: grandmother

ukulele: a small, guitar-like instrument with four strings

ulana: woven mats

wahine: woman

wai: water

wana: black spiny sea urchin

wauke: small paper mulberry tree

wela: hot

wiki: fast, quickly

wili: to wind, twist, or screw

wiliwili: native Hawaiian tree

Suggested Reading

Oʻahu is the hub of a vibrant regional book publishing industry. Look for these top publishers: the **University of Hawaiʻi Press** (www.uhpress.hawaii.edu) has the best overall general list of titles on Hawaiʻi; the **Bishop Museum Press** (www.bishopmuseum.org/press) puts out many scholarly works on Hawaiiana, as does **Kamehameha Schools Press** (http://kspress.ksbe.edu); **Bess Press** (www.besspress.com), **Mutual Publishing** (www.mutualpublishing.com), **Island Heritage** (www.islandheritage.com), and **Watermark Publishing** (http://bookshawaii.net) all have general interest Hawaiiana books. In addition, a website specifically oriented toward books on Hawaiʻi, Hawaiian music, and other things Hawaiian is **Hawaii Books** (www.hawaiibooks.com).

ASTRONOMY

Rhoads, Samuel. *The Sky Tonight—A Guided Tour of the Stars over Hawaii.* Honolulu: Bishop Museum, 1993. This book has star charts for every month in Hawaiʻi.

COOKING

Beeman, Judy, and Martin Beeman. *Joys of Hawaiian Cooking.* Hilo, HI: Petroglyph Press, 1977. A collection of favorite recipes from Big Island chefs.

Choy, Sam. *Little Hawaiian Cookbook for Big Appetites.* Honolulu: Mutual Publishing, 2003. A collection of the famous chef's favorite recipes to execute in your kitchen.

Fukuda, Sachi. *Pupus, An Island Tradition.* Honolulu: Bess Press, 1995. A selection of tasty island appetizers.

Tuell, Bonnie. *Island Cooking.* Honolulu: Mutual Publishing, 1996. This cookbook has an array of island recipes including *pupu,* dinner, and desserts.

Wong, Allen. *New Wave Luau.* Berkeley: Ten Speed Press, 1999. Award-winning chef Alan Wong shares his wonderful Hawaiian food recipes.

CULTURE AND HISTORY

Barnes, Phil. *A Concise History of the Hawaiian Islands.* Hilo, HI: Petroglyph Press, 1999. An easy-to-read examination of the main currents of Hawaiian history and its major players, focusing on the important factors in shaping the social, economic, and political trends of the islands.

Buck, Peter. *Arts and Crafts of Hawaii.* Honolulu: Bishop Museum Press, 1957. The most definitive work on traditional Hawaiian crafts from household use to religious significance.

Cordy, Ross. *Exalted Sits the Chief.* Honolulu: Mutual Publishing, 2000. Cordy, a University of Hawaiʻi professor, offers wonderful insight into the formation of the Hawaiian culture and society up until the pre-contact period.

Daws, Gavan. *Shoal of Time, A History of the Hawaiian Islands.* Honolulu: University of Hawaiʻi Press, 1974. A highly readable history of Hawaiʻi dating from its discovery by the Western world to its acceptance as the 50th state.

Fuchs, Lawrence. *Hawaii Pono.* Honolulu: Bess Press, 1961. A detailed, scholarly work presenting an overview of Hawaiʻi's history based upon ethnic and sociological interpretations. Encompasses most socioethnological groups from native Hawaiians to modern entrepreneurs.

Handy, E. S., and Elizabeth Handy. *Native Planters in Old Hawaii.* Honolulu: Bishop

Museum Press, 1972. A superbly written, easily understood scholarly work on the intimate relationship of pre-contact Hawaiians and the land.

Ii, John Papa. *Fragments of Hawaiian History.* Honolulu: Bishop Museum, 1959. Hawai'i's history under Kamehameha I as told by a Hawaiian who actually experienced it.

Kamehameha Schools Press. *Life in Early Hawai'i: The Ahupua'a.* 3rd ed. Honolulu: Kamehameha Schools Press, 1994. Written for schoolchildren to give them a better understand the basic organization of old Hawaiian land use and its function, this slim volume is a good primer for people of any age who wish to understand this fundamental societal fixture.

Kirch, Patrick V. *Feathered Gods and Fishhooks: An Introduction to Hawaiian Archaeology and Prehistory.* Honolulu: University of Hawai'i Press, 1997. This scholarly, lavishly illustrated, yet very readable book gives new insight into the development of pre-contact Hawaiian civilization. It focuses on the sites and major settlements of old Hawai'i and chronicles the main cultural developments while weaving in the social climate that contributed to change.

Lili'uokalani. *Hawaii's Story by Hawaii's Queen,* reprint. Honolulu: Mutual Publishing, 1990. Originally written in 1898, this moving personal account explains Hawai'i's inevitable move from monarchy to U.S. Territory as witnessed by its last queen, Lili'uokalani.

McBride, L. R. *Practical Folk Medicine of Hawaii.* Hilo, HI: Petroglyph Press, 1975. An illustrated guide to Hawai'i's medicinal plants as used by the *kahuna lapa'au* (medical healers). Includes a thorough section on ailments, diagnosis, and the proper folk remedies. Illustrated by the author, a renowned botanical

researcher and former ranger at Hawai'i Volcanoes National Park.

Tayman, John. *The Colony.* New York: Scribner, 2006. An in-depth look and true story of how the fear of leprosy swept across Hawai'i and exiled many to Moloka'i.

FAUNA

Fielding, Ann, and Ed Robinson. *An Underwater Guide to Hawai'i.* Honolulu: University of Hawai'i Press, 1987. The amazing array of marine life found throughout the archipelago is captured in glossy photos with accompanying informative text and reference guide.

Hawaiian Audubon Society. *Hawaii's Birds.* 5th ed. Honolulu: Hawaii Audubon Society, 1997. Excellent bird book giving description, range, voice, and habits of the more than 100 species. Slim volume; good for carrying while hiking.

Hobson, Edmund, and E. H. Chave. *Hawaiian Reef Animals.* Honolulu: University of Hawai'i Press, 1987. Colorful photos and descriptions of the fish, invertebrates, turtles, and seals that call Hawaiian reefs their home.

Kay, Alison, and Olive Schoenberg-Dole. *Shells of Hawai'i.* Honolulu: University of Hawai'i Press, 1991. Color photos and tips on where to look.

Mahaney, Casey. *Hawaiian Reef Fish, The Identification Book.* Planet Ocean Publishing, 1993. A spiral-bound reference work featuring many color photos and descriptions of common reef fish found in Hawaiian waters.

Pratt, Douglas. *A Field Guide to the Birds of Hawaii and the Tropical Pacific.* Princeton, NJ: Princeton University Press, 1987. Useful field guide for novice and expert bird-watchers covering Hawai'i as well as other Pacific Island groups.

Pratt, Douglas. *A Pocket Guide to Hawaii's Birds*. Honolulu: Mutual Publishing, 1996. A condensed version of Pratt's larger work with a focus on bird's of the state.

Tomich, P. Quentin. *Mammals in Hawai'i*. Honolulu: Bishop Museum Press, 1986. Quintessential scholarly text on all mammal species in Hawai'i with description of distribution and historical references; lengthy bibliography.

FLORA

Kepler, Angela. *Hawaiian Heritage Plants*. Honolulu: University of Hawai'i Press, 1998. A treatise on 32 utilitarian plants used by the early Hawaiians.

Miyano, Leland. *A Pocket Guide to Hawai'i's Flowers*. Honolulu: Mutual Publishing, 2001. A small guide to flowers readily seen in the state. Good for the backpack or back pocket.

Pratt, Douglas H. *A Pocket Guide to Hawai'i's Trees and Shrubs*. Honolulu: Mutual Publishing, 1998. A great trailside companion for identifying native and common trees and shrubs.

Sohmer, S. H., and R. Gustafson. *Plants and Flowers of Hawai'i*. Honolulu: University of Hawai'i Press, 1987. The authors cover the vegetation zones of Hawai'i, from mountains to coast, introducing the wide and varied floral biology of the islands with a history of the evolution of Hawaiian plantlife.

Wagner, Warren L., Derral R. Herbst, and H. S. Sohner. *Manual of the Flowering Plants of Hawai'i*, revised edition, vol. 2. Honolulu: University of Hawai'i Press in association with Bishop Museum Press, 1999. Considered the bible of Hawai'i's botanical world.

Whitton, Kevin. *A Pocket Guide to Hawai'i's Botanical Gardens*. Honolulu: Mutual Publishing, 2009. A colorful and informative guide to 35 botanical gardens across the state.

Valier, Kathy. *Ferns of Hawaii*. Honolulu: University of Hawai'i Press, 1995. One of the few books to treat the state's ferns as a single subject.

LANGUAGE

Pukui, Mary Kawena, and Samuel Elbert. *Hawaiian Dictionary*. Honolulu: University of Hawai'i Press, 1986. The best dictionary available on the Hawaiian language. The *Pocket Hawaiian Dictionary* is a less expensive, condensed version of this dictionary and adequate for most travelers with a general interest in the language.

Pukui, Mary Kawena, Samuel Elbert, and Esther T. Mookini. *Place Names of Hawaii*. Honolulu: University of Hawai'i Press, 1974. The most current and comprehensive listing of Hawaiian and foreign place-names in the state, giving pronunciation, spelling, meaning, and location.

Schutz, Albert J. *All About Hawaiian*. Honolulu: University of Hawai'i Press, 1995. A brief primer on Hawaiian pronunciation, grammar, and vocabulary.

MYTHOLOGY, LEGEND, AND LITERATURE

Beckwith, Martha. *Hawaiian Mythology*. reprint. Honolulu: University of Hawai'i Press, 1976. Over 60 years after its original printing in 1940, this work remains the definitive text on Hawaiian mythology. If you are only going to read one book on Hawaii's folklore, this should be it.

Beckwith, Martha. *The Kumulipo*. reprint. Honolulu: University of Hawai'i Press, 1972. Translation of the Hawaiian creation chant, originally published in 1951.

Kalakaua, His Hawaiian Majesty, King David. *The Legends and Myths of Hawaii*. Edited by R. M. Daggett, with a foreword by Glen Grant. Honolulu: Mutual Publishing, 1990. Originally published in 1888, in this volume

Hawai'i's own King Kalakaua draws upon his scholarly and formidable knowledge of the classic oral tradition to bring alive ancient tales from pre-contact Hawai'i.

Melville, Leinanai. *Children of the Rainbow.* Wheaton, IL: Theosophical Publishing, 1969. A book on higher spiritual consciousness attuned to nature, which was the basic belief of pre-Christian Hawai'i. The appendix contains illustrations of mystical symbols used by the *kahuna.*

Pukui, Mary Kawena, and Caroline Curtis. *Hawaii Island Legends.* Honolulu: The Kamehameha Schools Press, 1996. Hawaiian tales and legends for preteens.

Pukui, Mary Kawena, and Caroline Curtis. *Tales of the Menehune.* Honolulu: The Kamehameha Schools Press, 1960. Compilation of legends relating to Hawai'i's "little people."

NATURAL SCIENCES AND GEOGRAPHY

Clark, John. *Beaches of O'ahu.* Honolulu: University of Hawai'i Press, 1997. Definitive guide to beaches, including many off the beaten path with maps and black-and-white photos.

Hubbard, Douglass, and Gordon Macdonald. *Volcanoes of the National Parks of Hawaii.* reprint. Volcanoes, HI: Hawaii Natural History Association, 1989. Details the volcanology of Hawai'i by documenting the major lava flows and their geological effect on the state.

Macdonald, Gorden, Agatin Abbott, and Frank Peterson. *Volcanoes in the Sea, The Geology of Hawaii.* Honolulu: University of Hawai'i Press, 1983. The best reference to Hawaiian geology. Well explained for easy understanding; illustrated.

Ziegler, Alan C., *Hawaiian Natural History, Ecology, and Evolution.* Honolulu: University of Hawai'i Press, 2002. An overview of Hawaiian natural history with a treatment of ecology and evolution in that process.

SPORTS AND RECREATION

Alford, John, D. *Mountain Biking the Hawaiian Islands.* Ohana Publishing, 1997. A good off-road biking guide to the main Hawaiian islands.

Ambrose, Greg. *Surfer's Guide to Hawai'i.* Honolulu: Bess Press, 1991. Island-by-island guide to surfing spots.

Ball, Stuart. *The Hiker's Guide to O'ahu.* Honolulu: University of Hawai'i Press, 2000. This excellent guide includes hikes across O'ahu with topo maps and detailed directions.

Finney, Ben, and James D. Houston. *Surfing, A History of the Ancient Hawaiian Sport.* Los Angeles: Pomegranate, 1996. Features many early etchings and old photos of Hawaiian surfers practicing their native sport.

McMahon, Richard. *Camping Hawai'i: A Complete Guide.* Honolulu: University of Hawai'i Press, 1997. This book has all you need to know about camping in Hawai'i, with descriptions of different campsites.

Morey, Kathy. *Oahu Trails.* Berkeley, CA: Wilderness Press, 2003. Morey's book is complete with useful maps, historical references, official procedures, and plants and animals encountered along the way.

Sutherland, Audrey. *Paddling Hawai'i,* revised edition. Honolulu: University of Hawai'i Press, 1998. All you need to know about sea kayaking in Hawaiian waters.

Internet Resources

GOVERNMENT

City and County of Honolulu
www.honolulu.gov
The official website of the City and County of Honolulu. Includes information on city government, county data access, visitor information, and information on business and economic development.

Department of Park & Recreation
www1.honolulu.gov/parks
Resource for city and county camping information, obtaining permits, park and trail closures, beach access, and park rules and regulations.

Honolulu International Airport
http://hawaii.gov/hnl
The official website has all the information you need to successfully navigate the Honolulu International Airport.

State of Hawai'i
www.hawaii.gov
The official website for the state with comprehensive information covering government organizations, health, business, and many other services.

TOURISM

Alternative Hawaii
www.alternative-hawaii.com
A source for the path less traveled, ecofriendly general information, and links to specific businesses, with some cultural, historical, and events information.

Best Places Hawaii
www.bestplaceshawaii.com
This site has general and specific information about all major Hawaiian islands, a vacation planner, and suggestions for things to do and places to see, eat, and stay.

Hawaii Ecotourism Association
www.hawaiiecotourism.org
Official Hawaii Ecotourism Association website with information on traveling in Hawai'i, activities, and links to member organizations and related ecotourism groups.

Hawai'i State Foundation on Culture and the Arts
www.state.hi.us/sfca
This site features a calendar of arts and cultural events, activities, and programs held throughout the state.

Hawaii Visitor and Convention Bureau
www.gohawaii.com
The official site of the Hawaii Visitors and Convention Bureau, the state-run tourism organization, has information about all the major Hawaiian islands: transportation, accommodations, eating, activities, shopping, Hawaiian products, an events calendar, a travel planner, and a resource guide for a host of topics, as well as information about conventions.

Hawaiian Music Island
www.mele.com
This is one of the largest music websites to focus on Hawaiian music, books, and videos. It features Hawaiian music culture, concert schedules, Hawaiian music awards, and links to music companies and musicians.

Index

List of Maps

Acknowledgments

The first edition of *Moon O'ahu* was published in 1990. Its original author was J.D. Bisignani (1947-1997), whose *Japan Handbook* (1983) was one of Moon's founding publications. The next five editions of *Moon O'ahu* were revised by Joe and by Robert Nilsen (also the author of *Moon South Korea*), who took over as sole author after Joe's death in 1997. Joe and Bob brought the same spirit of adventure to their Hawai'i coverage as they did to Moon's pioneering coverage of Asia. We wish them both aloha.

www.moon.com

DESTINATIONS | ACTIVITIES | BLOGS | MAPS | BOOKS

MOON.COM is ready to help plan your next trip! Filled with fresh trip ideas and strategies, author interviews, informative travel blogs, a detailed map library, and descriptions of all the Moon guidebooks, Moon.com is all you need to get out and explore the world—or even places in your own backyard. While at Moon.com, sign up for our monthly e-newsletter for updates on new releases, travel tips, and expert advice from our on-the-go Moon authors. As always, when you travel with Moon, expect an experience that is uncommon and truly unique.

KEEP UP WITH MOON ON FACEBOOK AND TWITTER
JOIN THE MOON PHOTO GROUP ON FLICKR

MAP SYMBOLS

Expressway	Highlight	Airfield	Golf Course
Primary Road	City/Town	Airport	Parking Area
Secondary Road	State Capital	Mountain	Archaeological Site
Unpaved Road	National Capital	Unique Natural Feature	Church
Trail	Point of Interest		Gas Station
Ferry	Accommodation	Waterfall	Glacier
Railroad	Restaurant/Bar	Park	Mangrove
Pedestrian Walkway	Other Location	Trailhead	Reef
Stairs	Campground	Skiing Area	Swamp

CONVERSION TABLES

$°C = (°F - 32) / 1.8$
$°F = (°C \times 1.8) + 32$
1 inch = 2.54 centimeters (cm)
1 foot = 0.304 meters (m)
1 yard = 0.914 meters
1 mile = 1.6093 kilometers (km)
1 km = 0.6214 miles
1 fathom = 1.8288 m
1 chain = 20.1168 m
1 furlong = 201.168 m
1 acre = 0.4047 hectares
1 sq km = 100 hectares
1 sq mile = 2.59 square km
1 ounce = 28.35 grams
1 pound = 0.4536 kilograms
1 short ton = 0.90718 metric ton
1 short ton = 2,000 pounds
1 long ton = 1.016 metric tons
1 long ton = 2,240 pounds
1 metric ton = 1,000 kilograms
1 quart = 0.94635 liters
1 US gallon = 3.7854 liters
1 Imperial gallon = 4.5459 liters
1 nautical mile = 1.852 km

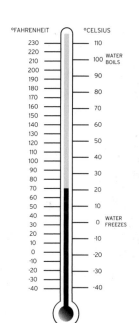

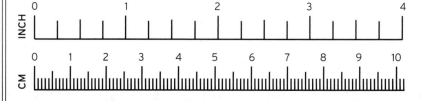

MOON O'AHU

Avalon Travel
a member of the Perseus Books Group
1700 Fourth Street
Berkeley, CA 94710, USA
www.moon.com

Editor: Leah Gordon
Series Manager: Kathryn Ettinger
Copy Editor: Ashley Benning
Graphics Coordinator: Darren Alessi
Production Coordinator: Darren Alessi
Cover Designer: Darren Alessi
Map Editor: Mike Morgenfeld
Cartographers: Chris Henrick, Mike Morgenfeld
Indexer: Rachel Kuhn

ISBN-13: 978-1-61238-111-4
ISSN: 1534-0511

Printing History
1st Edition – 1990
7th Edition – November 2013
5 4 3 2 1

Text © 2013 by Kevin Whitton and Avalon Travel.
Maps © 2013 by Avalon Travel.
All rights reserved.

Some photos and illustrations are used by permission
and are the property of the original copyright
owners.

Front cover photo: Waikiki, Diamond Head © age
fotostock / SuperStock
Title page photo: © Kevin Whitton
Color interior photos: All © Kevin Whitton except
page 21 (bottom right) and page 27 (top left) ©
Turtle Bay Resort; page 27 (bottom left) © The
Kahala Hotel & Resort

Printed in Canada by Friesens

Moon Handbooks and the Moon logo are the property
of Avalon Travel. All other marks and logos depicted
are the property of the original owners. All rights
reserved. No part of this book may be translated or
reproduced in any form, except brief extracts by a
reviewer for the purpose of a review, without written
permission of the copyright owner.

All recommendations, including those for sights,
activities, hotels, restaurants, and shops, are based
on each author's individual judgment. We do not
accept payment for inclusion in our travel guides,
and our authors don't accept free goods or services
in exchange for positive coverage.

Although every effort was made to ensure that
the information was correct at the time of going
to press, the author and publisher do not assume
and hereby disclaim any liability to any party for any
loss or damage caused by errors, omissions, or any
potential travel disruption due to labor or financial
difficulty, whether such errors or omissions result
from negligence, accident, or any other cause.

KEEPING CURRENT

If you have a favorite gem you'd like to see included in the next edition, or see anything
that needs updating, clarification, or correction, please drop us a line. Send your com-
ments via email to feedback@moon.com, or use the address above.